Cisco Meraki Fundamentals

Cloud-Managed Operations

Arun Paul

Mike Woolley

Medi Jaafari

Jeffry Handal

Cisco Press

Cisco Meraki Fundamentals

Cloud-Managed Operations

Arun Paul, Mike Woolley, Medi Jaafari, Jeffry Handal

Published by:
Cisco Press
Hoboken, New Jersey

1 2024

Library of Congress Control Number: 2024931249

ISBN-13: 978-0-13-816757-8

ISBN-10: 0-13-816757-5

Warning and Disclaimer

This book is designed to provide information about the Cisco Meraki cloud-managed networking platform and solutions. Every effort has been made to make this book as complete and as accurate as possible, but no warranty or fitness is implied.

The information is provided on an "as is" basis. The authors, Cisco Press, and Cisco Systems, Inc. shall have neither liability nor responsibility to any person or entity with respect to any loss or damages arising from the information contained in this book or from the use of the discs or programs that may accompany it.

The opinions expressed in this book belong to the author and are not necessarily those of Cisco Systems, Inc.

Please contact us with concerns about any potential bias at https://www.pearson.com/report-bias.html.

Trademark Acknowledgments

All terms mentioned in this book that are known to be trademarks or service marks have been appropriately capitalized. Cisco Press or Cisco Systems, Inc., cannot attest to the accuracy of this information. Use of a term in this book should not be regarded as affecting the validity of any trademark or service mark.

Special Sales

For information about buying this title in bulk quantities, or for special sales opportunities (which may include electronic versions; custom cover designs; and content particular to your business, training goals, marketing focus, or branding interests), please contact our corporate sales department at corpsales@pearsoned.com or (800) 382-3419.

For government sales inquiries, please contact governmentsales@pearsoned.com.

For questions about sales outside the U.S., please contact intlcs@pearson.com.

Feedback Information

At Cisco Press, our goal is to create in-depth technical books of the highest quality and value. Each book is crafted with care and precision, undergoing rigorous development that involves the unique expertise of members from the professional technical community.

Readers' feedback is a natural continuation of this process. If you have any comments regarding how we could improve the quality of this book, or otherwise alter it to better suit your needs, you can contact us through email at feedback@ciscopress.com. Please make sure to include the book title and ISBN in your message.

We greatly appreciate your assistance.

GM K12, Early Career and Professional Learning: Soo Kang

Alliances Manager, Cisco Press: Caroline Antonio

Director, ITP Product Management: Brett Bartow

Managing Editor: Sandra Schroeder

Development Editor: Ellie C. Bru

Senior Project Editor: Tonya Simpson

Copy Editor: Bill McManus

Technical Editors: Dave Kounas
Ryan Miles
Kyle Murdock

Editorial Assistant: Cindy Teeters

Cover Designer: Chuti Prasertsith

Composition: codeMantra

Indexer: Timothy Wright

Proofreader: Barbara Mack

CISCO.

Americas Headquarters	Asia Pacific Headquarters	Europe Headquarters
Cisco Systems, Inc.	Cisco Systems (USA) Pte. Ltd.	Cisco Systems International BV Amsterdam,
San Jose, CA	Singapore	The Netherlands

Cisco has more than 200 offices worldwide. Addresses, phone numbers, and fax numbers are listed on the Cisco Website at www.cisco.com/go/offices.

About the Authors

Arun Paul serves as a technical solutions architect at Cisco Meraki, focusing on supporting public sector – SLED customers in the Midwest states. With more than a decade of experience in the technology industry, Arun has held diverse roles ranging from engineering to technical sales.

Arun's tech journey began as a software engineer at the Cisco Catalyst 6500 BU, where he played a pivotal role as a point of contact for Catalyst design recommendations and escalations. Arun showcased his innovative spirit by proposing Cisco innovation ideas and process improvements.

Beyond corporate roles, Arun co-founded a security consulting and training business, gaining valuable entrepreneurial experience. This venture provided insights into customer challenges in the modern technology landscape. Arun holds an MS in Information Security from George Mason University, graduating with a Distinguished Achievement Award.

Arun has consistently demonstrated dedication to excellence, innovation, and customer success throughout his career, earning accolades and awards for his noteworthy contributions to the field.

Mike Woolley is a support product specialist at Cisco Meraki with more than eight years of experience dedicated to supporting Meraki products and solutions. Starting in 2016 after receiving a BT in Network Administration from Alfred State College, Mike began as an intern within Meraki Support in San Francisco and rose through to the highest tiers of the technical support structure. Through this experience Mike has worked directly with customers and deployments of all types and sizes. From independent small businesses to massive international corporations, Mike has developed a tried-and-true approach to working with Cisco Meraki solutions based on these experiences. During this time Mike has also written and contributed to core pieces of Meraki documentation and has since become a leading source of knowledge within his specialization of Meraki's cellular-enabled product lines.

Mike currently lives in western New York with his wife Sara and their dog Noki and enjoys occasional outdoor activities like dirt biking and snowmobiling when not helping on the family farm or playing tabletop games.

Medi Jaafari has more than two decades of industry experience in roles ranging from advanced engineering architectures to director of engineering for a startup ISP colocation specializing in LAN/WAN transport, IoT, SDWAN, SASE, ZTNA, XDR, and observability for multinational, multitenant environments. Medi was an early participant in SDN networking developments working with key tier-one U.S.-based universities while at Cisco and is currently a technical solutions architect for the Cisco Meraki business unit, with more than five years of experience working closely on product design with a focus on SW features, UI, and AI design.

Jeffry Handal is a principal solutions engineer at Cisco. He completed his bachelor's and master's degrees in electrical engineering at Louisiana State University (LSU) and has more than 18 years of experience in the area of information communication technology, with special interest in IPv6, cybersecurity, big data, and experimental networks. Before joining Cisco, Jeffry was a very active customer, always pushing the envelope designing and maintaining networks with new technologies, testing new protocols, and providing Cisco and others a large-scale testbed for new products, features, and functionality. Currently, he plays an active role in several Cisco groups (e.g., TACops, IPv6 Ambassadors, Security Technical Advisory Group, Meraki).

Outside of work, Jeffry is an active volunteer in organizations ranging from search and rescue operations with the Air Force to humanitarian technology groups such as NetHope. He sits on several boards within IEEE, actively promotes IPv6 adoption via different task forces, volunteers to teach networking classes in third-world countries, and promotes STEM for women and minorities. In addition, Jeffry serves the public through his participation in conferences and standards bodies (IETF, IEEE); speaking at local and international events (Internet2, CANS, IPv6 Summits, AI/ML Symposiums, IEEE events, WALC, Cisco Live); contributing to and reviewing publications; and appearing as a guest in podcasts like IPv6 Buzz and Meraki Unboxed. He is a big promoter of technological change for the betterment of humanity.

About the Technical Reviewers

Dave Kounas has more than 26 years of experience in IT, including more than 17 years of networking experience designing and supporting enterprise networks. Dave worked in biotech, Wall Street finance, and manufacturing before joining Cisco in 2016. He joined the Meraki team in 2019 as a technical solutions architect, working closely with public sector and commercial customers to design reliable, high-performance networks.

Ryan Miles has more than 28 years of experience in the networking industry working for the U.S. Air Force, as an IT technical instructor, at a large healthcare provider, and for networking companies Cisco, Brocade, and Mist.

Over the past 15 years at Cisco, Ryan has worked as an enterprise networking consulting systems engineer focused on Cisco's wireless, switching, and security platforms. In 2016 Ryan joined the Meraki team as a senior technical solutions architect. Ryan has designed some of Meraki's largest and most complex global customer deployments. He is also a field advisor for the Meraki IoT product line of cameras and sensors, the Cloud Dashboard Platform, and for Cisco's broader Networking Experiences portfolio.

Kyle Murdock, CCIE R&S No. 2455, is a technical solutions architect for Meraki. During his 27 years at Cisco he has held many roles, including TAC engineer and team lead, service provider advanced services engineer, service provider and commercial systems engineer, and now Meraki technical solutions architect. Kyle is passionate about cloud-managed networking and especially switching. Outside of work, he builds and launches high-power rockets and holds a TRA Level 2 certification.

Dedications

We would like to remember the late Gordon Hughes, a good friend who helped us unlearn and relearn STP in the new world; we miss you.

I want to express my deepest gratitude to those who played a crucial role in bringing this book to life. First and foremost, a heartfelt thank you to my family for their unwavering support throughout the entire two-year writing process. Your encouragement has been my inspiration, and I am grateful for the steadfast belief you've shown in this endeavor.

A special appreciation goes to Mike Woolley and his family, who believed in this project. Thank you for the wonderful partnership and your commitment to deadlines; you have been the harshest critic of our writing standards and have been crucial in keeping us grounded and ensuring the timely delivery of this project.

I extend my thanks to Medi for your invaluable contribution in elevating the quality of the content. Your dedication has truly made a difference.

To Jeffry, your wisdom has played a vital role in defining the overall framework of this book. Thank you for sharing your insights and contributing to the depth of this work.

To all those who have otherwise supported and contributed to this book, thank you. Your belief, partnership, and wisdom have shaped this project, and I am genuinely grateful for each one of you.

—*Arun Paul*

I would like to dedicate this book to all my friends and family who supported us and put up with everything while writing this book.

To my wife Sara, thank you for putting up with the moments of stress and late nights as we navigated the not-as-simple-as-it-seems process of taking an idea and actually making a book out of it while also moving halfway across the country. Your loving support and understanding made immeasurable contributions to our success.

To the rest of my family and friends, I promise I will have more free time now. Thank you all for your support and curiosity about the project; your interest and support helped to fuel the fire and keep driving us to completion.

And to my fellow authors:

Arun, thank you for coming up with the initial idea and inviting me to partner with you early on. You never lost faith in the project and what it could be, even when it felt like it was all falling apart. Your vision accompanied by unending faith and optimism made all the difference.

Medi, thank you for your solutions expertise and wealth of knowledge you allowed us to tap into. Your contributions helped solidify the scope of this book and enable more approachable solutions while saving us a lot of additional research.

Jeffry, your perspective and input provided valuable insight into different approaches and solutions, as well as helping to define the content layout and flow that would evolve into our working template for multiple chapters of content. This book would look very different if it weren't for your input early on.

—*Mike Woolley*

First, I want to recognize our families for putting up with us for being so many times in front of a computer. This is time we will never get back, but their unwavering love and support allowed us to cope. Second, I thank our friends, managers, and leaders for encouraging us to experiment, try something new, and cheering us on.

Next, I want to thank those before us who created the industry of the Internet that has forever transformed the way we live, work, and create. They inspired the generation that we are part of. Now, it is up to us to inspire the next generation by making technology easier to tinker with and use for good.

I am thankful for my fellow co-authors for driving our mission and making it come to reality. Any one of us alone would be able to do it; however, collectively, the ingredients for completing something useful in a timely manner was possible only as a team. Arun was our passion, Woolley our coach, and Medi our vision. I am especially thankful for Arun and Woolley taking our technical depth and putting it into practical words, thereby fulfilling our hopes and dreams to democratize technology for all.

Finally, it is not every day that four people from different walks of life with diverse careers, experiences, and personal backgrounds come together to attempt something outside their comfort zone, i.e., writing. Contributing to writing a book is no easy feat. However, I would not trade the hours spent for anything because of the weekly camaraderie it created among us. Sometimes it served to destress us from our daily routine; other times it forced us to keep the creative muscle active; on many occasions, we solved technical problems we were facing in our day jobs; and other times, it simply allowed for laughs. At the end of the day, it is not about the technology but the human connections it creates. Thank you, Arun, Woolley, and Medi for this journey.

—*Jeffry Handal*

Acknowledgments

Many people helped contribute to this book in one way or another, and our sincere thanks goes out to each and every one of you no matter how large your contribution. Particularly, we acknowledge all of our colleagues at Meraki and Cisco, without whom we wouldn't have had much to write about.

A special thanks to the following people, without whom this book would not have been written:

- **Brett Bartow** and **Ellie Bru:** Your guidance and patience as we navigated the writing process was invaluable, and without you, we certainly never would have made our way to the end.

- **Denise Donohue:** A guiding mentor and the driving force behind the realization of this book. Thank you for pushing us to pursue the idea in the first place and helping wrap our heads around the process that would eventually lead to the completion of the project.

- **Kyle Murdock** and **Benton Heles** (MS Ninjas), **Dave Kounas** (MR Ninja), **Chad Yates** (MX Ninja), **Larry Woods**, and **Ryan Miles** (IoT Ninjas): Your domain expertise and valuable feedback on our writing styles significantly contributed to elevating the quality of our work.

- A special shout-out to **Craig Stork**, Cisco SA, for his guidance and assistance with ISE integration.

- And our official, unofficial consultant, **Varughese Cherian**, who jumped in and wholeheartedly assisted us in our time of need.

Contents at a Glance

Contents

Icons Used in This Book

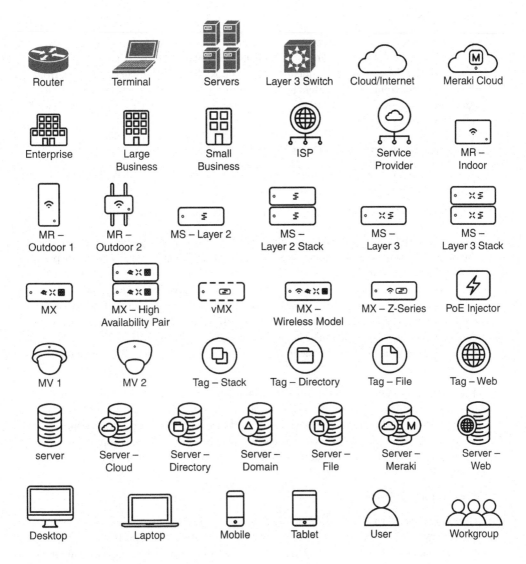

Router	Terminal	Servers	Layer 3 Switch	Cloud/Internet	Meraki Cloud
Enterprise	Large Business	Small Business	ISP	Service Provider	MR – Indoor
MR – Outdoor 1	MR – Outdoor 2	MS – Layer 2	MS – Layer 2 Stack	MS – Layer 3	MS – Layer 3 Stack
MX	MX – High Availability Pair	vMX	MX – Wireless Model	MX – Z-Series	PoE Injector
MV 1	MV 2	Tag – Stack	Tag – Directory	Tag – File	Tag – Web
server	Server – Cloud	Server – Directory	Server – Domain	Server – File	Server – Meraki	Server – Web
Desktop	Laptop	Mobile	Tablet	User	Workgroup

Reader Services

Register your copy at www.ciscopress.com/title/9780138167578 for convenient access to downloads, updates, and corrections as they become available. To start the registration process, go to www.ciscopress.com/register and log in or create an account*. Enter the product ISBN 9780138167578 and click Submit. When the process is complete, you will find any available bonus content under Registered Products.

*Be sure to check the box that you would like to hear from us to receive exclusive discounts on future editions of this product.

Foreword

The State of Work

Work is no longer a physical place you go to. While the concept is not new, we knew we would eventually get there in the distant future. However, through a series of world events and accelerated by the pandemic of the 2020s, the adoption curve[1] of work from anywhere went from early adopters to late majority in a span of a few weeks. With the pandemic being over, we have skipped back to the early majority. Despite that "setback," a few things are clear:

- New ways of defining work have emerged.

- Depending on the platforms leveraged, data from these new models of operating has created a baseline.

- The IT world has undergone a transformation in front of our very eyes.

Let's unpack the above observations a little more. What is work? Work, as defined by the physics world, means the transfer of energy from applying a force to create displacement.[2] Putting that in the digital context, work is the means (force) by which we advance business objectives (energy measure) to obtain outcomes (displacement). How we get to those outcomes is not defined by a place. This is only possible because of pervasive, fast connectivity. Despite having a large swath of Earth's population not enjoying this kind of connectivity, the world economies are keeping an eye on this to bridge the gap with the expectation of pushing forward the next economic revolution that will increase human productivity.

The unstated unknown in all this is the central role the information communications technology industry and professionals will play in this transformation. Central to this theme is the digital adaptation to the analog world we had been used to operating. With digital comes data. With data comes new insights, informed decision-making, and expanded visibility into what we can do. How do we manage it all? Do we need a platform?

The Platform Solution

IT engineers are turning into data managers without even knowing it. We would even dare to say this has been the case forever. When we troubleshoot a problem, we are creating data or, viewed differently, gathering data from where it exists, processing it, and then making decisions to get to a resolution in a very manual way. The downsides of the process are that investments have to be made in the tooling required to be effective, and the experience of the person consuming the data matters. At the end of the day, this all translates into a time equation. Fast is not fast enough. Therefore, we need to evolve our approach into a platform-driven methodology for data management.

---

1   https://en.wikipedia.org/wiki/Technology_adoption_life_cycle
2   https://www.britannica.com/science/work-physics

You are about to read a book that will challenge the ways you have done things in networking. Realize you are leaving your comfort zone and pursuing new horizons to improve your "time equation" problem. You seek the utopia we have always wanted, which is end-to-end control, management, and visibility of operations. For that, a platform-thinking mindset must emerge. The difference between today's platforms and those of the not-too-distant future will be more data being gathered with automated processing to make a decision to resolve a problem or enable an outcome. The question is, does the platform you use have the ability to evolve with you into this future?

In this book, the authors plan to show that what Cisco has built with the Meraki platform is an effective tool to "manage" data and get to outcomes quicker—without the complexity. In other words, it is a platform for automation that is growing to include more than just traditional core networking. The Meraki platform is expanding to include physical security and IoT, and that is only the beginning. As we add an IP to more things, it just means it is another data source we can use to enrich our decision-making.

As you peruse these pages, think of the possibilities, the what-ifs you would solve within the confines of your operation. Having a platform challenges you to tackle a problem, build a solution within the constraints of the system to produce a desired outcome. Embrace the design, build, optimize approach that is deeply rooted in the data-rich foundation of the Meraki platform. Embrace the change. That is the Meraki way.

—Jeffry Handal

Introduction

A founding concept of Meraki was the idea of making networking simple. That goal is something Meraki still strives to achieve throughout all its products to this day. This book was conceived with that concept in mind and has been organized into chapters of related sections that begin with explaining the overarching organization and operation of the Cisco Meraki cloud-managed platform and gradually move toward more general design philosophy and use cases for the Meraki cloud platform.

The goal of this book is to help provide a better understanding of cloud-based management with Meraki devices and highlight the operational and administrative differences between a cloud-managed Meraki network and a more traditional network.

Topics covered by this book include the general organization and operation of the Meraki cloud, the basics of administering a network within the Meraki Dashboard, how Meraki can be integrated and automated with non-Meraki tools and services, as well as some Meraki-specific best practices. We will also provide an overview of what a day in the life of an administrator of a Meraki-based platform might look like, including monitoring an existing deployment and how the cloud platform assists in identifying and troubleshooting potential issues more easily.

Whenever referring to a page in the Dashboard, we use a standard convention to indicate the appropriate navigation menu options in the Dashboard to reach the indicated page. For example, if the navigation path is presented as **Security & SD-WAN > SD-WAN & Traffic Shaping > Uplink Selection**, that indicates to hover over the Security & SD-WAN navigation tab on the left, then select the link for **SD-WAN & Traffic Shaping** on the pop-out menu (see Figure 0-1), then scroll to the Uplink Selection section of the SD-WAN & Traffic Shaping page.

If the navigation path is presented as Organization > Change Log, that indicates to hover over the **Organization** tab on the left, then select the link for **Change Log** on the pop-out menu (see Figure 0-2).

All topics covered in this book are explored in more detail and depth in the Meraki official documentation, which you can access by visiting https://documentation.meraki.com. You can also find additional resources by visiting https://meraki.cisco.com or reaching out to one of Meraki's friendly sales representatives.

The Meraki Dashboard is a constantly evolving and changing entity, with new features and updates coming frequently. The information presented in this book is as accurate as possible at the time of writing. Given the required timelines and limitations involved in writing and publishing a book, there will inevitably be changes or updates that are unable to be included in the final copy. We have strived to cover the topics in this book in a way that allows the information presented to be applicable through future developments and evolutions of the Meraki platform as best as possible.

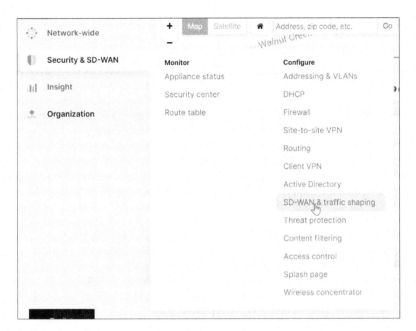

Figure 0-1 *Navigating to the Security & SD-WAN > SD-WAN & Traffic Shaping Page in a Dashboard Network*

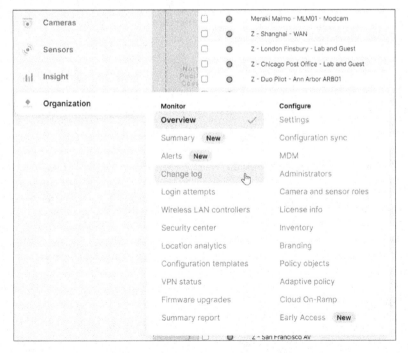

Figure 0-2 *Navigating to the Organization > Change Log Page in a Dashboard Organization*

Why Meraki?

When considering networking solutions, there are a myriad of available options from numerous different companies. In this sea of options, why should Meraki be the solution of choice?

After being acquired by Cisco in 2012, Meraki was quickly acknowledged as one of the fastest growing and most successful business entities within Cisco. It is now leading the way with Cisco's push for cloud-managed solutions through the design of Meraki's full stack of cloud-managed products, designed from the ground up for cloud management. By utilizing the power of the cloud for management, Meraki has been able to build a simple, scalable solution that allows for easy management through a single pane of glass: the Meraki Dashboard.

By utilizing the capabilities of the Dashboard, Meraki has enabled administrators to simplify their "day 1" operational deployments to near zero-touch, where a device can be configured on the cloud long before installation; then, once deployed, automatically come online and apply the configuration by just providing the device with an active Internet connection.

The Dashboard also plays a pivotal role to simplify "day 2" (daily operations) like maintenance and optimization of existing deployments. Capabilities such as cloud-based firmware management for all Meraki devices significantly reduce the amount of time and effort required to keep critical devices up to date with the latest firmware and security patches across platforms. An additional advantage of the cloud-based management design of the Dashboard is the ability to use APIs and web integrations to easily automate almost every feature of network, device, and even client management across the entire organization.

With these options and the focus on cloud management, the Meraki Dashboard also allows for a reduction in OPEX for customers, as the single pane of glass allows a single administrator to more easily monitor, manage, and troubleshoot multiple sites when compared to a more traditional deployment.

Supporting a Different Experience

Included with all Cisco Meraki licensing is access to Meraki's highly rated 24/7 support team. With multiple offices around the globe, Meraki Support is always ready and available to assist any Meraki customer at any time. Meraki Support strives to provide actual solutions to customer problems instead of focusing on ticket closure or call length metrics. In other words, Meraki Support engineers are dedicated to helping you solve your problem no matter how big or small.

A significant advantage of the cloud-based solutions offered by Meraki through the Dashboard is the ability for a Support engineer to work with the same views and data that are displayed to customers, reducing the back-and -forth exchanges traditionally needed to provide data and logging to Support for analysis. In many instances, Meraki Support directly gathers the necessary data directly from the Dashboard. This helps to significantly reduce troubleshooting time and mean time to resolution (MTR) for customer issues.

Meraki Support is also able to quickly diagnose and provide RMAs (return material authorizations) for covered devices, with the advantage of cloud monitoring to allow for early detection of certain issues before a device fails completely. This allows Meraki to alert customers of certain issues, such as a potential hardware failure, and begin the proactive replacement process before the device fails completely and causes a more significant impact.

An example of this ability in action is the clock component failures seen across the industry around 2017. This issue resulted from a faulty clock component commonly installed in devices across the industry that was discovered to fail prematurely after a period of operation, resulting in an inoperable device. Several Meraki hardware products were identified as containing the problematic component and, through the use of the Dashboard, Meraki was able to reach out and initiate a proactive replacement program for all customers using an affected device. This allowed the devices to be identified and proactively replaced before encountering significant issues resulting from the faulty clock component.

All Cisco Meraki RMAs are proactive, meaning that once the RMA is approved, a new device is immediately in the process of being express shipped to the destination to replace the failing or failed device before requiring the failed device to be shipped back. All replacement devices also include a free return shipping label to allow the failed device to be returned to Meraki at no cost.

Meraki devices are strategically placed in Cisco resource depots around the world to allow for advanced 4 hour or less RMAs through the purchase of additional advanced RMA coverage for mission-critical devices. When combined with Meraki's included limited lifetime warranty for most devices, Meraki provides excellent replacement ability to ensure that your networks stay up and running for as long as possible.

For the curious customer looking to get their hands on Meraki equipment to see if the Cisco Meraki platform is the right fit for their deployments, Meraki offers the ability to See/Try/Buy Meraki equipment through its Sales Trial programs. Sales Trials allow customers to work with a Cisco Meraki representative to determine what Meraki products would best fit the requirements of the deployment and allow them to trial real Meraki hardware in their own environment at no cost with the option to purchase the trial hardware or return the hardware back to Meraki at the end of the trial. Trials also include full access to Meraki Support resources to assist in troubleshooting any issues that may arise during the trial. This allows for trials to be leveraged in a more effective way within an actual environment as opposed to reviewing datasheets or observing performance in a controlled lab scenario. Thus, customers can make more informed purchasing decisions and feel confident in how the hardware will perform in their unique environment.

Meraki offers some clear advantages when compared to other, more traditional deployment solutions. If you are curious to learn more about how the topics previously mentioned are accomplished and what it looks like to work with the Meraki Dashboard and manage a Meraki network, read on to Chapter 1, which begins discussing the Meraki cloud architecture, how Meraki handles device-to-cloud communications, and how Meraki safely handles data in the cloud and between sites.

Who Should Read This Book?

This book is intended to provide an overview and general understanding of the experiences, products, and capabilities offered by the Cisco Meraki cloud platform at any scale. This book introduces each of Meraki's multiple cloud-managed solutions—MX appliances, MS switches, MR access points, MV cameras, and more—and provides helpful advice for planning or working with Meraki deployments, including more advanced tips and considerations for administrators who are planning for or working with very large or complex deployments.

While the primary audience for this book is IT professionals who are unfamiliar with Meraki and are looking to either learn more about how a Meraki solution might work in their environment or learn how to better work with an existing Meraki solution recently acquired, the content has been written with the intent of providing new and useful information to both those familiar and unfamiliar with the Meraki platform.

Special care has been taken to highlight numerous "Pro Tips" throughout the text, which are typically lesser known pieces of information or recommendations you won't find in any other documentation. These have been chosen and highlighted specifically based on the experiences of the authors while troubleshooting customer deployments and are intended to provide helpful assistance like pointing out commonly overlooked configuration steps, or alternate approaches or solutions that may not be immediately obvious. With information gathered from multiple decades' worth of combined experience, even the most seasoned network operator will likely find new information or approaches in this book for working with the Cisco Meraki platform.

Book Structure

The book is organized into five parts.

Part I: Knowledge Is Power: Understanding the Cloud Architecture

- **Chapter 1: Cisco Meraki Cloud Architecture Basics:** This chapter provides an introduction and overview of the Meraki cloud architecture, including the core hosting services around the world and how the Meraki organization structure works to enable powerful and secure cloud-managed solutions at any scale.

- **Chapter 2: Building the Dashboard:** This chapter goes into detail on the Meraki cloud organization structure, including covering the basic setup and configuration process of a new organization, such as defining administrators, creating networks, and claiming licenses and devices. It also shows how the Dashboard simplifies the workload of several common administrative tasks, such as creating and reviewing alerts or reports from within the Dashboard.

Part II: Building a Scalable Foundation with Dashboard

- **Chapter 3: The Meraki Admin Experience:** This chapter depicts a day in the life of a Meraki administrator. It explores using the Dashboard to check the overall health of the organization's network and make sure that all Meraki products are working securely. It also describes how to find and use the latest features in Meraki to keep your technology up to date. The chapter also explores ways to connect events from different products and network services to find problems more quickly. It is intended as a practical introductory guide for administrators to manage their network effectively using Meraki solutions.

- **Chapter 4: Automating the Dashboard:** This chapter is focused on using automation both within and outside the Meraki Dashboard to further reduce the management workload for a deployment. Topics range from using built-in Dashboard tools to generate reports and manage configuration at scale, to incorporating external solutions using Meraki's robust API support that enables automated deployment, configuration, and reporting abilities.

Part III: The MX—The Cloud-Managed Swiss Army Knife

- **Chapter 5: MX and MG Best Practices:** This chapter introduces the primary functions of Meraki's security/WAN appliance series of devices and covers the basic and advanced security and routing features offered by these devices, including Meraki AutoVPN, AMP, content filtering, and basic traffic shaping. The chapter also touches on the MG line of cellular WAN uplinks offered by Meraki and provides recommendations for their practical deployment and operation.

- **Chapter 6: MX SD-WAN Best Practices:** This chapter is dedicated specifically to Meraki's advanced SD-WAN (software-defined wide area network) solution offered by the MX series of devices. Built over the AutoVPN solution discussed in Chapter 5, this chapter introduces Meraki's SD-WAN solution and guides customers in choosing between a basic policy and more advanced options, including application-specific metrics, to better fine-tune the traffic in their SD-WAN deployments.

Part IV: The Ultimate Cloud-Managed Access Layer

- **Chapter 7: Meraki Switching Design and Recommendations:** This chapter covers Meraki's switching product line and design best practices, including the new cloud-managed Catalyst switches. The chapter explains how the modern hybrid world of on-premises and cloud-managed switches benefits from the best of both worlds, while still achieving interoperability and cross-platform micro-segmentation capabilities. The chapter also covers how the Meraki Dashboard brings visibility into network-wide topology and operational visibility for both cloud-based and monitored Catalyst product lines.

- **Chapter 8: Meraki Wireless Best Practices and Design:** This chapter dives into the key aspects of designing, building, and optimizing with Meraki wireless access points, with a particular focus on converged hardware. It highlights the Wireless

Health features of Meraki, offering insights into how these features assist in identifying the root cause of issues. The chapter also explores the impact of AI-powered automation features in maintaining the wireless infrastructure at peak performance levels. It also covers the design principles behind achieving enterprise-grade roaming using Meraki wireless technology. This chapter provides a concise yet comprehensive guide to implementing best practices for a robust and efficient Meraki wireless network.

Part V: The Environment: The Next Frontier

- **Chapter 9: MV Security and MT (IoT) Design:** This chapter looks at Meraki's IoT technology and its unique architecture, which simplifies camera and IoT integration and operation. It discusses the various modes of access and ease of searching and retrieving footage from Meraki cameras on the Meraki platform as well as how Meraki's MT line of IoT devices can be deployed alongside MV cameras to provide additional monitoring and insights.

Appendix A: Meraki Licensing: This appendix is intended to provide a brief overview of the available Meraki licensing models, including their operation and how the differences between licensing models may impact your planning and operations, to help you ensure you choose the most appropriate licensing model for each deployment.

Figure Credits

Figure 9-10: Google LLC

Chapter 1

Cisco Meraki Cloud Architecture Basics

This chapter provides an introduction to the Meraki Cloud architecture, including an overview of Meraki's distributed hosting services around the world that enable the Dashboard and cloud management to function securely and reliably. We also take a look at how the Dashboard organization structure works to enable powerful and secure cloud-managed solutions at any scale. Many of the following topics and concepts will be revisited in greater detail throughout this book.

Dashboard Architecture

The first step in working with a Meraki-based cloud management platform is to understand the basic hierarchical structure of the Meraki Dashboard with regard to Dashboard administrators, organizations, networks, and templates. The basic hierarchical structure of the Meraki Dashboard is demonstrated in Figure 1-1.

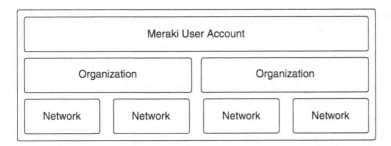

Figure 1-1 *Basic Hierarchical Structure of the Meraki Dashboard*

The *organization* is the largest organizational structure in the Meraki Dashboard. Dashboard organizations can consist of one or many individual *networks*, which can either exist as standalone networks or be attached to templates as template children.

In addition, the organization contains all devices and licenses that have been added to the inventory for use in networks within the organization. At a basic level, each customer and their devices are likely contained within one or several networks within a single organization. However, with larger or more advanced deployments, there are several reasons for splitting networks and devices across multiple organizations. We will discuss those situations in more detail later in the book when examining more complex deployments and configurations.

Every Meraki Dashboard user accesses the Meraki Dashboard by first visiting https://dashboard.meraki.com and logging in with a Dashboard Administrator account. This, in turn, permits access to any Dashboard organization(s) for which that account currently has privileges. Dashboard Administrator accounts can have different access levels within each organization for which they have privileges, as these permissions are defined on a per-account, per-organization basis. For example, the same Dashboard Administrator account may have full administrator rights in one organization but may be limited to read-only rights for specific networks in another organization. We will cover the different administrator types and privileges in Chapter 2, "Building the Dashboard."

Dashboard networks that exist within a given organization can contain one or more devices, depending on the network type. The network level is where the majority of device configuration is stored in the Dashboard. When an administrator adds a new device, such as an access point, to a Dashboard network, the device automatically inherits the current network-level configuration for that device type. From there, if necessary, the administrator can apply specific device-level configurations to that device to override or further build on the existing network-level configuration. This simplifies the configuration of new devices because they automatically inherit the same default/network-level configurations as other devices already in the network as soon as they are added.

Templates are similar to networks in that they define the initial default configurations for devices across multiple Dashboard networks. However, devices are not added directly to a template. Instead, they are added to a network that is itself bound to a template. In this case, the template defines the default network settings that the devices within that network inherit. If the network is moved to a different template, the device configurations in that network are automatically updated to reflect the new template settings. We will discuss templates in more detail later in this book.

Configuration options at the per-device level vary slightly based on the specific device type and deployment but are generally available for device-specific settings such as the management IP/VLAN and other port- or interface-specific settings required for network connectivity. Fortunately, with the use of device tagging and configuration profiles available within each network, it's easy to make device-specific configurations for many Dashboard settings if required. We'll discuss utilizing device tagging to scope features and configurations in detail in Chapter 2.

Cloud/Back-end Architecture

All Meraki customer management data is hosted in data centers spread around the world across five geographic regions. Each region contains a pair of geographically separated, independent data centers that replicate customer management data, as well as Meraki service data such as the Dashboard and any API-related services, between them in real time. This design allows for rapid failover between data centers within any region in the event of a catastrophic failure of a data center. Figure 1-2 visualizes the hierarchy of the Meraki cloud back end from the data center to each hosted organization.

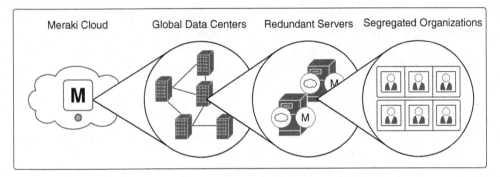

Figure 1-2 *The Hierarchy of the Meraki Cloud Back End*

The following are the five Meraki regions and their respective redundant data center locations:

- Americas: USA/USA

- Canada: Canada/Canada

- EMEA: Germany/Germany

- Asia/Pacific: Australia/Singapore

- China: China/China

Management data consists of the following buckets of data and does not include user data such as traffic passing over the network to the Internet:

- **User records:** Includes the user account email and company name as well as any other optionally provided information such as the username or address associated with a user account

- **Configuration data:** Includes network settings and device configurations created in the Dashboard

- **Analytics data:** Includes network client traffic analytics and location data, which helps to provide insights into traffic patterns across deployments

- **Any customer assets uploaded directly to the Dashboard:** Includes assets such as custom floor plans and logos

Customer user data, which includes actual user traffic such as web browsing, VoIP calls, internal application traffic, and so forth, does not flow through the Meraki cloud. It instead flows directly to the original destination either on the local network, encrypted over a VPN, or directly out across the WAN, as needed.

This type of distributed back-end architecture enables Meraki to provide highly available data directly from within each region to support the reliable communication required for cloud management of devices across the world. All Meraki data centers have a 99.99% uptime service level agreement (SLA), provide 24/7 automated failure detection, maintain real-time data replication between data centers, and undergo daily penetration testing by an independent third party.

Additionally, customer management data is backed up and stored nightly with regional third-party cloud-based storage services to ensure customer management data is always available in the event of a catastrophic failure and to ensure compliance with all regional data storage regulations.

Because customer management data is backed up and stored regionally (and for other reasons discussed later in this chapter), Cisco Meraki recommends that customers who intend to deploy devices across multiple regions create a unique Dashboard organization to host the devices deployed within each region.

Pro Tip   Regional hosting details for a given organization are available in the footer of any Dashboard page within that organization.

In the event that connectivity between devices and the Meraki Cloud Controller is completely severed, Meraki devices utilize an out-of-band architecture. This architecture allows devices to continue to function while running their last known configuration to preserve network functionality even when Meraki hosted services are unreachable. This is discussed further in the next section.

You can find more details on the customer data collected by Meraki and on Meraki's data centers, including additional specifics of how data is stored and replicated within data centers and the underlying architectures involved, by searching the official Meraki documentation at https://documentation.meraki.com or by visiting https://meraki.cisco.com/trust.

Device to Cloud Communication

Cloud management of Meraki devices involves bidirectional communication between the Meraki device and the Meraki Cloud Controller over a secure, AES256-encrypted HTTPS tunnel, as shown in Figure 1-3. All Meraki devices contain hardware cryptography chips and utilize X.509 certificate authentication when building their management tunnels to ensure that all communications between the device and cloud are encrypted and secure.

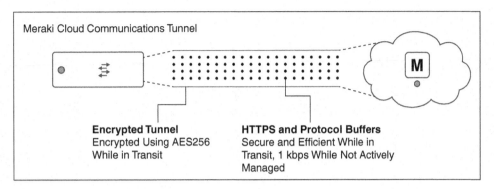

Figure 1-3 *The Encrypted Cloud Communication Tunnel*

When bringing a device online for the first time, it must establish communication with the Cloud Controller over an active Internet connection to download, store, and apply the current Dashboard configurations (if any exist) and any pending firmware upgrades. If the device is unable to establish communication, it will simply continue to run the default out-of-box configuration and factory firmware until that communication is established.

After a device has established communication with the cloud controller and successfully downloaded its configuration, it will regularly upload device and network usage information back to the Meraki cloud. This data is used to generate the Dashboard analytics data displayed to users for a given device or network when working in the Dashboard UI.

If the device and cloud controller lose communication, any historical analytics data will be temporarily stored locally on the device for as long as possible or until communication between the device and cloud controller is restored, at which point all available historical data will be uploaded. Due to the efficient and secure management tunnel in use between devices and the Meraki cloud, this management traffic is limited to just 1 kbps per device while the device is not being actively managed, to ensure minimal additional data usage in customer networks.

When a configuration change is made from the Dashboard or via an API call, the cloud controller notifies the device that a new configuration is available, at which time the device initiates a connection back to the controller to download and apply the new configuration, typically within just a few seconds of the changes being saved to the cloud controller. Figure 1-4 demonstrates this configuration update process.

If the device is for any reason unreachable from the controller, the new configuration is generated and stored. It will be pushed down to the device as soon as it reestablishes communication with the cloud controller. In the meantime, the device will continue to run the locally stored, last known configuration until it receives an updated configuration from the cloud controller once communication is restored. This design ensures that devices are always running the most up-to-date configurations available to them whenever possible.

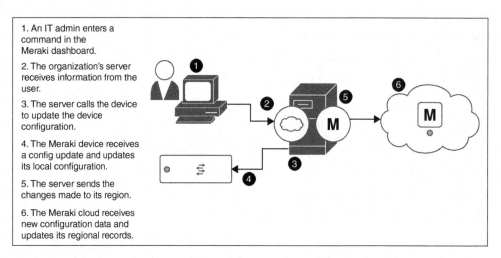

1. An IT admin enters a command in the Meraki dashboard.

2. The organization's server receives information from the user.

3. The server calls the device to update the device configuration.

4. The Meraki device receives a config update and updates its local configuration.

5. The server sends the changes made to its region.

6. The Meraki cloud receives new configuration data and updates its regional records.

Figure 1-4   *The Device Configuration Update Process*

Data Security and Retention

Meraki's data storage and retention policies are designed to provide secure storage for data uploaded to and used by the Meraki Dashboard across all regions of the world.

As discussed in the previous section, all data transferred between Meraki devices and the Meraki cloud is exchanged via a secure and proprietary encrypted communications tunnel between the Meraki cloud and each Meraki device. Any customer-uploaded data, such as custom floor plans or logos, is stored and made available only to authorized Dashboard users within the appropriate organization or network for which that data exists. This ensures that only authenticated users with the correct permissions are able to access any uploaded assets. Once uploaded to the cloud controller, all further data backups are restricted and fully encrypted using AES256 to ensure high levels of security for any data stored by Meraki.

Customer management and analytics data uploaded to the Dashboard is stored locally in the region where that Dashboard organization is hosted. For example, data for organizations hosted in the EMEA region is stored in Meraki data centers located within the EMEA region.

The specific retention policies for customer management and analytics data vary based on the age, type, amount, and geographic location of the data. For example, data such as client usage data, organization changelog data, and historical event log data will expire after reaching a maximum number of stored entries or passing a predefined age of the stored data, whichever happens first.

The Meraki maximum time limits for storing data are as follows:

■ For data stored within the European Union (EU), Meraki retains that data for a maximum total of 14 months: 12 months of general availability plus 2 months of additional retention via secure data backups. After 14 months, the data will expire regardless of the number of stored entries, to remain in compliance with local regulations.

■ For data stored anywhere in the rest of the world (i.e., outside of the EU), Meraki retains that data for a maximum of 26 months: 24 months of general availability plus 2 months of retention via secure data backups before expiring.

As previously indicated, some types of data might expire before reaching the preceding maximum data lifetime due to the large amount of data generated. For example, the organization changelog and device event log data for some organizations may reach the maximum number of stored entries long before the maximum data retention period. To ensure that this data does not expire too quickly to be usable for large organizations, Meraki also implements a minimum data retention policy for certain types of data such as the previous examples, which will ensure that data remains accessible for a minimum of 30 days before being expired, regardless of the amount of data contained within that time frame.

For additional and more specific information on the types of data stored by Meraki, the specific data retention lifetimes, and other policies applicable to each data type and region, visit https://documentation.meraki.com and view the article "Cloud Data Retention Policies" and other related articles.

Note   The "Additional Reading" section at the end of this chapter provides the full URL for every article that is cross-referenced in this chapter. Alternatively, you can search for the article title at https://documentation.meraki.com to locate it.

Firmware Management and Lifecycle

Meraki strives to provide simple management of firmware for all devices across every product line. As a part of this effort, firmware upgrades to the latest Stable or Stable Release Candidate firmware may be automatically scheduled by Meraki for customer networks to ensure that devices are always running a current, fully supported firmware. These automatic upgrades are scheduled according to the day of the week and time of day that the customer has designated in the Network-wide > General configuration menu, and Meraki sends appropriate notifications 7 to 14 days before the upgrade takes place to allow customers the opportunity to cancel or reschedule the upgrade if required. If after upgrading firmware a customer would like to revert to the previous version for any reason, they can manually schedule firmware rollbacks for any recently upgraded networks.

Every firmware release goes through an extensive testing process, including stability, performance, and regression testing, to ensure that each stable release meets the requirements to be labeled as such. The public firmware rollout process follows three stages that every firmware is required to pass through to receive the stable release designation: Beta, Stable Release Candidate, and Stable. Figure 1-5 shows the Dashboard view for the current Stable firmware versions across products.

Figure 1-5   *Latest Stable Firmware Versions as Viewed in the Dashboard*

Beta firmware is made available for customers who wish to take advantage of new features or bugfixes as soon as they are available. All beta firmware has already gone through internal stability, performance, and regression testing to help limit unforeseen negative impacts for customers who choose to run this new release on any production networks. The current beta firmware is always fully supported by the Meraki support and engineering teams and can be considered analogous to "early deployment" firmware of other industry products.

Using beta firmware versions requires customers to opt in to participate in the beta program before upgrading, after which they may see additional automatic upgrades scheduled by Meraki, as described previously, to keep their networks up to date with the most recent beta releases.

After a successful formal review of an existing beta firmware version by the Meraki software and product teams, the new firmware may be promoted to a Stable Release Candidate (RC). Once a firmware has been designated as a Stable RC, Meraki will begin scheduling a limited set of customer networks to upgrade to the new Stable RC firmware. As noted previously, these automatic upgrades can be rescheduled, canceled, or reverted via the Dashboard any time after being automatically scheduled.

Once a Stable RC firmware version hits a threshold of deployment across all deployed nodes around the world, it triggers another formal review by the Meraki software and product teams. If the Stable RC version receives a favorable review and meets the full set of requirements for a given product line, it will then be promoted to a full Stable release. After receiving the Stable designation, the firmware will continue to be automatically scheduled for customer networks running now outdated firmware and will also become the default firmware version for all newly created networks of a given device type.

The actual firmware upgrade process is identical across all product lines. Once a firmware upgrade has been scheduled, the cloud controller begins the upgrade process at the scheduled time by pushing to the relevant device(s) a configuration update that includes the new firmware information. The device(s) will then initiate a connection back to the Meraki cloud to download the new firmware from the controller before rebooting to apply the upgrade.

Because of the way Meraki has implemented firmware upgrades, devices continue to serve clients and function normally while downloading and preparing the new firmware. As a result, the only interruption to normal operation is the reboot of the device to reload into the new version. If for any reason the new firmware fails to load or the device is unable to regain connectivity to the cloud controller after the upgrade, the device will simply reboot and revert to the previous running firmware and configuration, which remains stored on the device until the upgrade is marked as successful. We will cover in depth the steps involved in checking firmware statuses and scheduling upgrades in Chapter 3, "The Meraki Admin Experience."

Meraki MS series switches and MR series access points also offer some additional features when configuring firmware upgrades to help reduce the impact of multiple devices downloading and applying a firmware upgrade at once. When scheduling firmware upgrades for MR access points, the option is available to stagger the upgrade across devices in the network in an effort to reduce the interruption to network clients, or to minimize the upgrade time by pushing the upgrade to all devices at once.

For MS switches, the option to configure "staged upgrades" is available. This option enables a customer to group switches in a network into upgrade groups, which allows the switches to be upgraded in a defined sequence based on their grouping and order. Scheduling staged upgrades for MS switches is discussed in further detail in Chapter 7, "MS Switching Design and Recommendations."

For more information on the specifics of the firmware release cycle and upgrade process, visit https://documentation.meraki.com and view "Meraki Firmware Release Process" and other related firmware documentation.

Summary

From the distributed back-end architecture to the encrypted management tunnels, this chapter covered how the Dashboard is able to provide simple, secure, and reliable cloud-based solutions across the globe. Whether you're deploying a single network or 1,000 networks, the Dashboard is designed from the bottom up around the concept of cloud management to provide an easy-to-use yet powerful interface that can manage equipment in nearly any location through a single pane of glass.

Next, Chapter 2 discusses the initial Dashboard creation and setup process, including some of the organization-wide configuration options, such as how administrator roles and privileges are defined on the Dashboard, how tags in the Dashboard can be used to manage device configurations and administrator permissions, and how the Dashboard is able to use the power of cloud configuration to assist in troubleshooting potential issues in your networks.

Additional Reading

Meraki Cloud Architecture: https://documentation.meraki.com/Architectures_and_Best_Practices/Cisco_Meraki_Best_Practice_Design/Meraki_Cloud_Architecture

Data Stored on the Meraki Primary Controller: https://documentation.meraki.com/General_Administration/Organizations_and_Networks/Data_Stored_on_the_Meraki_Primary_Controller

Cloud Data Retention Policies: https://documentation.meraki.com/General_Administration/Privacy_and_Security/Cloud_Data_Retention_Policies

Meraki Firmware Release Process: https://documentation.meraki.com/General_Administration/Firmware_Upgrades/Meraki_Firmware_Release_Process

Chapter 2

Building the Dashboard

Unlike traditional equipment that requires physical access or dedicated management access to be configured, all Cisco Meraki devices get their configurations directly over the Internet from the Meraki cloud. Once a device has been added to a Dashboard network within an organization, the only true prerequisite for getting the device up and running is an active Internet connection that allows the device to communicate with the Meraki cloud. However, before a device can fetch a configuration, all the surrounding Dashboard objects must first exist.

This chapter provides a brief overview of some of the initial setup steps and general configuration of the Dashboard that apply to any Dashboard organization and covers some of the base configurations that are touched less frequently in day-to-day operations, sometimes only during the initial setup of a new deployment. The first half of the chapter covers the processes of creating a new Dashboard account and organization, creating networks within the organization, adding devices to those networks, and scoping administrative permissions on new Dashboard administrator accounts within the organization. The latter half of the chapter discusses the use of tags to scope device configurations and administrator privileges and introduces Dashboard alerts and Meraki's powerful, cloud-enabled alert hub feature. Whenever relevant, we provide additional references to online Meraki documentation that goes into more detail about the specific related feature or process.

You can find multiple detailed articles that cover the first-time setup process with Meraki by visiting https://documentation.meraki.com and accessing the "Getting Started with Meraki" section on the main page.

Pro Tip All the creation and configuration steps discussed in this chapter (along with most processes and configurations on the Dashboard) can be automated through the use of the Meraki Dashboard API, which is discussed further in Chapter 4, "Automating the Dashboard."

Creating an Organization

Before you can create any networks or configurations, you first need to create a
Dashboard organization. Go to the Meraki Dashboard home page, https://
dashboard.meraki.com, and click **Create an Account**. Then, select a Dashboard
hosting region, which will affect the data storage and privacy settings for the Dashboard
organization that you create—refer to Chapter 1, "Cisco Meraki Cloud Architecture
Basics," for more details. Figure 2-1 shows the new account creation page.

Figure 2-1   *The New Account Creation Page on https://dashboard.meraki.com*

To create your account, you must provide contact information, such as an email address
and organization name, and create a password. Next, complete the CAPTCHA test and
then click **Create Account**. As a reminder, after creation, regional hosting information for
any Dashboard organization is available in the footer of any page within that organization, an example of which is shown in Figure 2-2.

When creating a new organization with an existing Dashboard Administrator account,
the process is the same. However, after entering an email associated with an existing
account, the Dashboard automatically detects the existing account and updates to reflect
the use of an existing account, as shown in Figure 2-3.

Last login
6 days ago from 67.248.████████ NY

Current session started
7 minutes ago

Data for BGP Test Org 2 (organization ID: 58546█████████21) is hosted in **North America**

Figure 2-2   *The Regional Hosting Information for an Example Lab Organization*

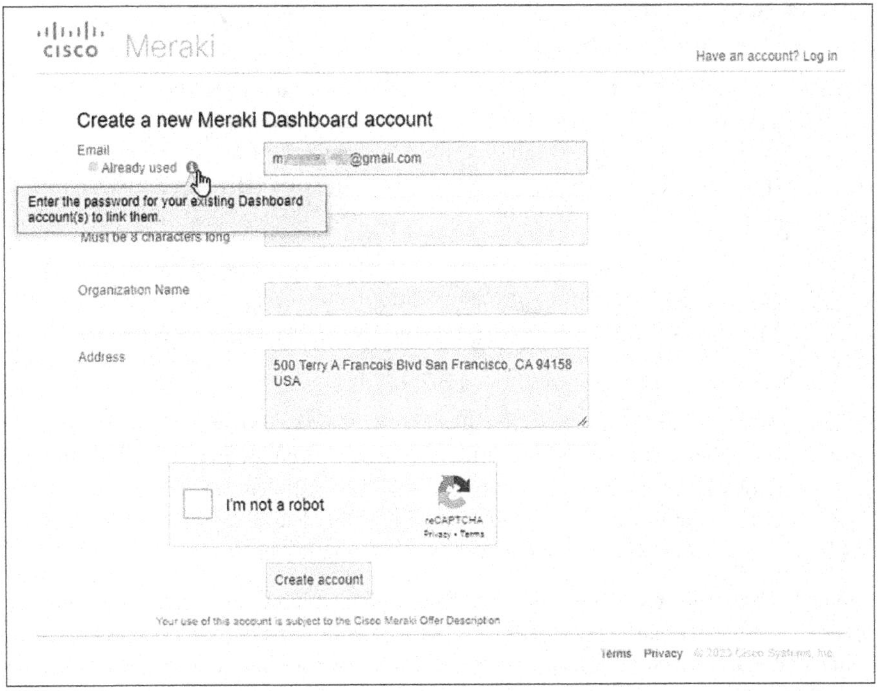

Figure 2-3   *The New Organization Creation Page for an Existing Dashboard Account*

For more information on the specifics of creating a Dashboard account or organization, visit https://documentation.meraki.com and view the "Creating a Dashboard Account and Organization" article and other related documentation.

Note   The "Additional Reading" section at the end of this chapter provides the full URL for every article that is cross-referenced in this chapter. Alternatively, you can search for the article title at https://documentation.meraki.com to locate it.

Creating a Network

Immediately after you create an organization, you are presented with the option to either create a network in the new organization or to add devices to the organization inventory. For purposes of this discussion, choose to create a network. That way, you'll have a network available to add your devices to after they are claimed to the inventory.

When creating a new network, two types of Dashboard networks are available:

- **Combined hardware network:** Allows multiple device types to be added in a single network, such as an MX security appliance alongside an MS switch and several MR access points. (Hereafter referred to as a *combined network*.)

- **Standalone hardware network:** Created per device type and only allows devices of a single type to be added. For example, if creating a standalone Camera network, only MV video cameras can be added to the network in the Dashboard; trying to add an MR access point to the network will return an error. (Hereafter referred to as a *standalone network*.)

Pro Tip   Standalone networks are often useful when working in a multi-vendor mixed environment to help avoid potential client tracking issues on the Dashboard.

Combined networks offer some significant advantages compared to standalone networks. For example, combined networks offer unified monitoring and reporting for all devices in the network, improved client tracking and traffic visibility, and centralized management in the Dashboard. Because of these advantages and more, the default selected network type is a combined network when creating a new network in the Dashboard.

A combined network is an excellent option when the same physical location or physical address is shared across platforms. In addition, using a combined network is recommended whenever it makes sense to logically group devices together into a single management group; leverage this to your advantage.

One of the most impactful differences between a combined network and a standalone network is the capability of a combined network to provide a wealth of additional insight through the use of advanced client tracking methods across different devices in the same network; this makes it easy to compare data from across devices to help identify potential problems. We will explore the impact and power of client tracking in a combined network in more depth in later chapters.

Figure 2-4 shows a part of the client details view of a wireless client in a combined network with an MX alongside several MS switches and MR access points.

Pro Tip   Adapt the network construct as your needs evolve. Combined networks can always be split out into their constituent standalone networks, and multiple standalone networks can be merged into a single combined network in most situations.

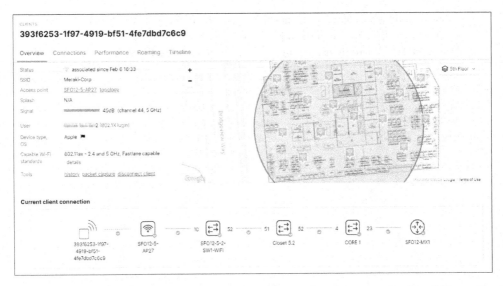

Figure 2-4 *A Partial View of the Client Details Page of a Client in a Combined Network at a Cisco Meraki Campus*

For more detailed information on the differences between combined and standalone networks in the Dashboard, visit https://documentation.meraki.com and view the "Combined Dashboard Networks" article.

After you decide to create either a combined network or standalone network, you have the option to create the new network with a default configuration, bind the new network immediately to an existing configuration template, or clone the configuration of another existing network of the same type. This makes it quick and easy to create new networks later when expanding your organization, especially for organizations that might have multiple sites with similar or nearly identical configurations.

In your new example organization, create a basic combined network with just the default configuration. Because this is a combined network, it will also allow you to take advantage of the additional client tracking and troubleshooting capabilities of the Dashboard that are present only in combined networks.

Pro Tip   Trial networks and test labs can be used as starting points when creating configuration templates in the future to save time and effort down the road.

Claiming and Adding Devices

After creating a network, you can begin adding devices or jump to directly configuring many of the available network-level settings for the new network. For now, you will start by adding devices to the new network before doing any configuration.

Before you add any devices to the new network, you first need to make sure that the devices are available to use in the organization inventory, shown in Figure 2-5, and reachable on the Dashboard by navigating to **Organization > Inventory**.

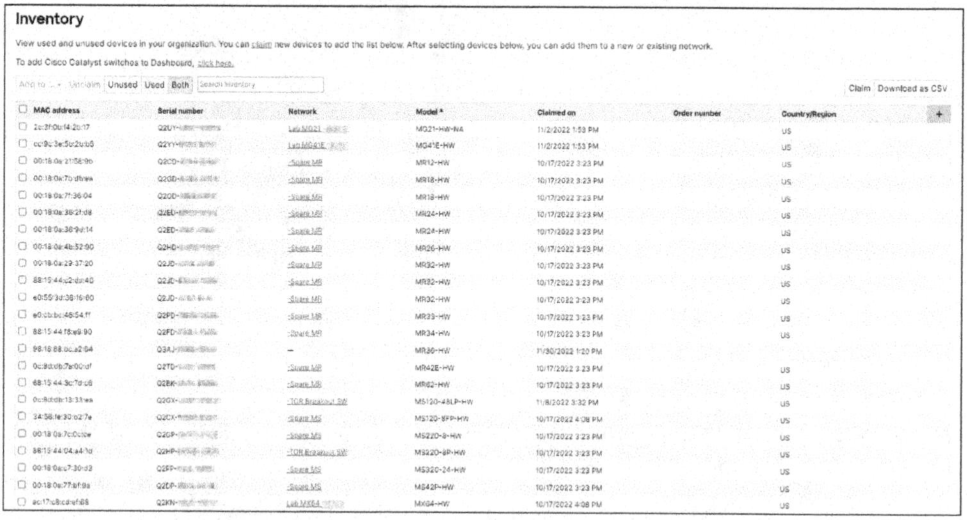

Figure 2-5 *The Inventory Page of a Lab Organization Full of Devices*

The organization inventory acts like a repository for all Meraki devices available to be used in a given organization. It maintains a searchable list of all devices in the organization and provides details such as a device's model, MAC address, serial number, most recent claim date, and current network name. The inventory is an excellent resource to keep a record of what you own, and you can easily export it to help you prepare for the dreaded yearly asset or inventory audit.

To be deployed in a network, a device must be claimed to the inventory of the organization in which it is to be deployed. Simply click the **Claim** button on the Inventory page of the organization and follow the prompts. You can claim devices either on a per-device basis with a list of individual serial numbers or as a group by claiming the order number. For illustration purposes, this chapter assumes that you have an order number for a brand-new site containing one MX security appliance, one MS switch, two MR access points, and one MV camera.

Pro Tip Get into the habit of claiming by order number whenever possible. When using the order number to claim devices, all devices and the associated license keys on the order are added to the Dashboard in one click. It will save you time and effort, especially when large quantities or devices are involved.

It's important to note that the view and workflow of the organization inventory has been updated for organizations using Meraki's Per-Device Licensing (PDL) model. However, the purpose and general functionality of the inventory remains the same. Therefore, we will refer to the default co-termination view for this chapter. The PDL model and associated changes brought to the Dashboard with it are discussed further in Appendix A, "Meraki Licensing."

Now that your organization has devices available in the inventory, it's time to add them to the new network and begin configuring them. For convenience, after selecting any unused device(s) in the inventory and clicking the **Add To** drop-down button (see Figure 2-5), you are given the option to select any existing available network or to create a new network, with the same options available as when creating a network from the Organization > Create Network page. Since a combined network already exists in your example organization, you can directly add all the newly claimed devices to that network and begin any additional configuration.

Defining Administrators and Privileges

For organizations with multiple administrators that require access to the Dashboard, Meraki has designed the Dashboard such that an organization can designate various administrative roles with different permission levels (from the Organization > Administrators page). This allows administrative rights to be scoped on a per-account basis to allow for full organization read/write access, a mix of read-only and write access at either the organization level or per-network level, or special permission roles such as Camera-only or Monitor-only administrators. These special permission roles have uniquely restricted access to Dashboard networks, which will be briefly discussed in comparison to standard administrators later in this section.

Pro Tip   All organizations should maintain control of at least two full organization administrator accounts to prevent accidental loss of access to the organization in the event of an account lockout.

At the organization level, accounts can be assigned one of the following levels of organization privilege:

- *Full* organization-level access, which allows full read/write access to the entire organization.

- *Read-only* access, which provides full visibility to every page and configuration in the Dashboard but restricts the ability to make or save any changes within the organization.

- *None*, which both hides all pages located under the Organization tab and the Navigation tab itself and restricts the account to only the network-level permissions explicitly specified.

In addition to, or in place of, the organization-level permissions, administrator accounts can also have per-network permissions applied to them. This allows for accounts to be restricted to view or modify only a specific subset of networks within the organization based on the permissions assigned to that administrator for each network. Per-network permissions allow for Full access, Read-only access, or Monitor-only access to be configured for each network or network group specified.

Any networks that are not included in the permissions assigned to an administrator account are not shown in the Dashboard for that user. This allows for very granular permissions assignments within each organization in the Dashboard, helping to provide maximum security and control while ensuring that each account has the necessary visibility and access to complete their responsibilities.

Pro Tip   Full organization read/write access supersedes any network-level access configured for the same account. Accounts configured with Read-only organization-level access can still be given write access to individual networks within the organization. Remember to follow the least privilege philosophy when designating roles.

Special Access Roles

Guest Ambassador, Camera-only, and Monitor-only administrator roles are unique types of network-level permissions focused on use cases that can be granted to provide only limited access to networks within an organization. These are useful for larger organizations that may wish to provide accounts with access to various monitoring capabilities of the Dashboard without exposing the detailed configurations for the related networks.

Guest Ambassadors are accounts that are able to view or modify only the list of Meraki authenticated users in networks. This covers accounts used by Client VPN when configured for Meraki Authentication as well as accounts used for wireless Sign-on splash pages when configured for Meraki Authentication. Guest Ambassador accounts are only able to add, update, and authorize or deauthorize user accounts for specific SSIDs or Client VPN connections. They are presented with a special view of the Dashboard, referred to as the User Management portal, instead of the standard Dashboard view. Persons intended to take advantage of this role include but are not limited to executive admins for a site, frontline helpdesk members, or front desk staff.

Camera-only organization administrators are created by assigning only the "all cameras in this organization" permissions target to an administrator account. This role allows an account to view only networks within the organization that contain MV cameras and interact only with cameras while in those networks. Any other devices also included in those networks will not be visible to a Camera-only admin.

This role provides the following three unique levels of access to select between for cameras in the organization:

- **View and export all footage:** Provides the most access and allows viewing of live camera feeds, viewing of recorded historical video, and exporting of historical video footage for download or external storage. This access level could be useful for higher-level administrative staff who may require access to review and export historical footage as the result of an incident investigation.

- **View all footage:** Allows for viewing of live camera feeds and recorded historical video but does not allow creation of video exports. This access level could be used for staff who may be required to review recent footage in the event of a potential incident, but who should not be allowed to export or create copies of any captured video.

- **View live footage:** The most restrictive level, allows only viewing of live camera feeds. Recorded historical data is not accessible at all. This access level could be used for an account that requires only live streaming, such as a monitoring display.

For more granular control, Dashboard Administrator accounts can have network-level camera permissions configured for them within each network. This allows for the same levels of access control as the Camera-only organization administrator but on a more granular level, with the option to select between all cameras in the network, individual cameras, or groups of cameras based on configured device tags. This type of granular permissions control is also available for MT sensor data.

Pro Tip   Network-level Camera-only administrator settings can be configured for combined networks from the Network-wide > Administration > Camera-only Admins section of the Dashboard, and from the Cameras > General > Camera Admins section for Camera-only networks.

Administrators with the Monitor-only role for a given network are similar to Read-only administrators but also have their Dashboard access in that network restricted to a limited selection of pages available under the Monitor column in the popout menu for the selected platform. Figure 2-6 shows a comparison between the view of a Read-only admin (left) and the view of a Monitor-only admin (right) for a security appliance network.

Figure 2-6   *A Comparison of the Pages Available to a Read-Only Admin (Left) and a Monitor-Only Admin (Right)*

SAML Roles

To more easily manage administrative access to the Dashboard, Meraki has also implemented both IdP-Initiated and SP-Initiated SAML 2.0 support for Dashboard administrators. This allows for simple and easy management of administrative permissions for large numbers of Dashboard users by leveraging an existing identity provider (IdP) such as ADFS, OneLogin, or Azure AD to quickly scope permissions across an entire organization's worth of administrators through the use of SAML roles in the Dashboard.

To enable SAML for an organization, navigate to the **Organization > Settings** page and enter the SHA1 fingerprint of the X.509 certificate from the identity provider. Next, to configure SAML administrator roles, go to the **Organization > Administrators** page and configure them in the SAML Administrator Roles section. SAML administrator roles have the same available permissions options and operate in very much the same way as a standard Dashboard Administrator account, but they rely on the "role" attribute, included in the SAML assertion sent during logon, to match a defined SAML administrative role in the Dashboard, which determines the permissions assigned to the newly logged-in SAML administrator. This allows different SAML administrators to be automatically assigned different permissions based on the SAML role matched during SSO logon. These SAML roles can be created and defined on a custom, per-organization basis and do not require matching any sort of predefined roles in the Dashboard.

In addition to defining the roles on the Organization > Administrators page, you can create special Camera-only roles for use with SAML authentication to allow for the same granular functionality as the network-level Camera-only admins discussed previously. To configure these special Camera-only roles, navigate to the **Organization > Camera Roles** page and configure them similarly to both the SAML administrator roles and the network-level Camera-only administrator permissions.

After you define the role name, which is matched against during the logon process, you can define network access for users with this role to either all networks containing cameras or select groups of networks based on applied network tags. Camera roles share the same three permission levels as the non-SAML camera admins and can also have access to either all cameras in each network or restricted access to select groups of cameras within the allowed networks based on device tags. This allows for equal parity of administration capabilities between SAML and non-SAML administrator accounts on the Dashboard to ensure an appropriate level of access control regardless of account type.

SAML integrations like this significantly speed up the process (and reduce the effort) to create new organizations and scope administrative access for large companies, allowing for faster deployments and a greater focus on network and device configuration instead of copying and re-creating existing administrator accounts and permissions for a new deployment.

Pro Tip   SAML can be configured to provide access across multiple organizations for a single account by using matching X.509 fingerprints and identical "role" attributes across organizations.

Similar to SAML administrator integration, Meraki also offers integration with Cisco XDR (Formerly known as SecureX) Sign-On for authentication on the Dashboard. Similar to other SAML solutions, this allows a user to authenticate with the Dashboard directly through the XDR Sign-On page. However, unlike traditional SAML administrator accounts, XDR accounts do not use SAML roles to define administrator privileges. Instead, XDR administrator accounts are created like a regular Dashboard Administrator account, except that after enabling XDR integration from the Organization > Settings page, a new toggle option is shown when creating the new administrator account that allows the authentication method to be specified as either Email or Cisco XDR Sign-On.

This feature allows for any existing Cisco Security customers to easily integrate the Meraki Dashboard with their existing Cisco Security authentication process and add access to the Meraki Dashboard directly to an existing Cisco Security deployment, thereby making it easier to conduct forensic analysis or enrich threat intelligence data with the Meraki platform too.

Maintaining Control of the Dashboard

Now that you have created a new organization and claimed devices and licenses to it, it's imperative to take a moment to reflect on some best practices for maintaining access to and control of your Meraki platform:

- Keep at least two non-SAML organization administrator accounts with full access.

- Have at least one administrator account use an email domain under your control.

- Require multi-factor authentication (MFA) for all administrator accounts.

- Maintain full organization permissions for owners of Meraki hardware and licenses.

- Revoke or resign privileges when there is an administrative change.

Maintaining access and control of the Meraki Dashboard is extremely important. Meraki Support cannot create, remove, or modify any administrator privileges in a customer organization for any reason. If you as an administrator lose access to your Dashboard account, recovery options are available. However, if you are unable to recover access to your account and are unable to utilize another account with full organization-level access, you run the risk of losing access to control your platform entirely. Because of this, it's imperative that you take appropriate measures to maintain access to each organization and appropriately delegate permissions to other administrator accounts.

Pro Tip   Read-only administrator accounts can be useful when using the Meraki Dashboard API for gathering data to prevent accidental changes. By having separate API-enabled accounts with different permission levels, you can reduce the risk of automation-related accidents.

For more details about Dashboard administrators and permissions, check out the "Managing Dashboard Administrators and Permissions" and "Configuring SAML Single Sign-on for Dashboard" documents (and other related articles) at https://documentation. meraki.com.

Tagging to Scope

This section covers the basics of using tagging for both networks and devices in the Dashboard to assist in day-to-day management and reporting across the organization. Using tags allows for the easy implementation and scaling of configurations as well as the creation of more detailed reports than those available by default on the Dashboard. This section introduces only a few of the most common and most powerful use cases for tags in Dashboard.

Intro to Tags

Tags in the Dashboard are very powerful in the right hands and can be used to do many different things, such as the following:

- Help organize objects on the Dashboard, like devices or networks, into easily searchable groups for speedy filtering or navigation.

- Easily define the scope of and later modify the specific networks an administrator or group of administrators has access to.

- Modify device-specific configurations such as VPN participation or enabling/ disabling the broadcasting of an SSID.

- Help manage and secure client devices that have been enrolled in Meraki Systems Manager, Meraki's mobile device management (MDM) and enterprise mobility management (EMM) system.

Tags can be created and applied to both Dashboard networks (via the Organization > Overview page) and individual devices in those networks (from the device details page). These are referred to as network tags and devices tags, respectively, and they function similarly but distinctly.

Pro Tip   To create network tags, navigate to the **Organization > Monitor > Overview** page, check the box next to the appropriate network(s), select the **Tag** drop-down menu at the top of the page followed by **Add**, type the name of the tag, and then click the **Add** button.

Tagging for Administrative Privileges

Network tagging can be used to easily help scope administrative permissions (discussed in the previous section) within the Dashboard across networks. Through the use of network tags, you can easily group networks and then use those groupings to assign administrative permissions to multiple administrators without requiring each individual network be specified for each administrator.

By tagging multiple networks with the same network tag, the option to assign administrative permission targets based on the network tag becomes available, as shown in Figure 2-7. This provides a quick method to easily assign permissions across multiple administrator accounts to groups of networks and allow those groups to be updated and modified as needed by simply adding or removing the appropriate network tag.

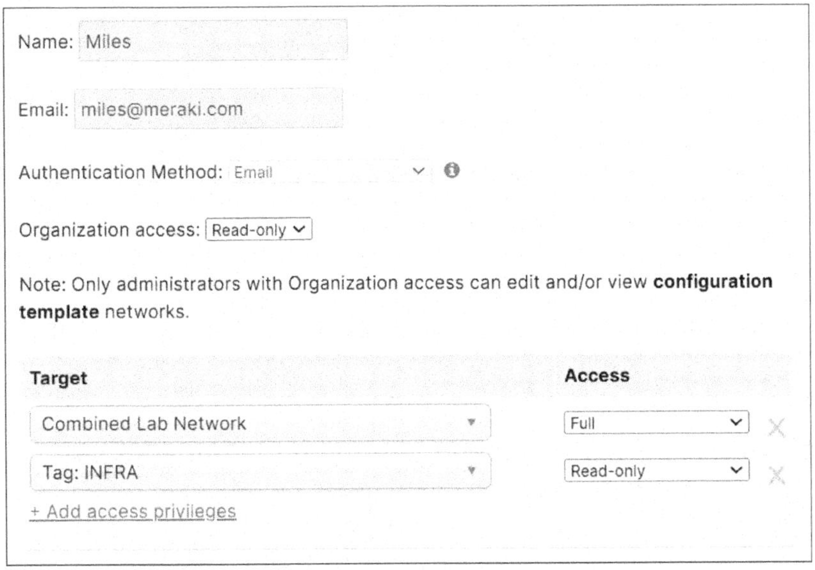

Name: Miles

Email: miles@meraki.com

Authentication Method: Email

Organization access: [Read-only ∨]

Note: Only administrators with Organization access can edit and/or view **configuration template** networks.

Target		Access	
Combined Lab Network	▼	Full ∨	✕
Tag: INFRA	▼	Read-only ∨	✕
+ Add access privileges			

Figure 2-7 *An Administrator Account Configured with Different Permissions for Different Network Groups Based on the Applied Network Tag*

Network and Device Configurations

Similar to tagging for administrative purposes, you can manage certain Dashboard configurations through the use of device and network tags. Two of the most prominent uses of tagging for configuration management in the Dashboard are configuring SSID availability on MR access points and configuring non-Meraki VPN peer availability for MX and Z series devices.

Configuring SSID Availability on MR Access Points

By default, all access points (APs) in the same Dashboard network broadcast all enabled SSIDs. However, you can change the default behavior by configuring availability on the **Wireless > SSID Availability** page, shown in Figure 2-8. Enabling the Per-AP Availability option on a given SSID allows you to select from a list of currently applied device tags on access points within that network to selectively enable the chosen SSID to be broadcast from only access points that have the selected tag applied. Once configured, this provides an easy way to scope SSID availability for multiple SSIDs across multiple access points by simply adding or removing the matching tag for an SSID to/from any access point.

Figure 2-8   *An SSID Configured to Broadcast Only from APs That Have the LAB Tag Applied in the Dashboard*

Pro Tip   Leverage a tag-based strategy to reduce the number of SSIDs an AP has to advertise, thereby reducing potential noise and interference.

Configuring Non-Meraki VPN Peer Availability for MX and Z Series Devices

Another common implementation of network tags is to use them to scope non-Meraki VPN peer configurations across different networks in the Dashboard. To simplify the configuration of non-Meraki VPN peers across multiple Dashboard networks, the non-Meraki VPN peer configurations entered on the Dashboard are configured at an organization-wide level, meaning that, by default, when a non-Meraki peer is configured, that peering configuration is pushed to all MX and Z series devices with VPN enabled. This allows a non-Meraki peer to be configured one time on the Dashboard and have that configuration available to any Meraki device that needs to build a tunnel to that peer.

But what if not all Meraki devices should be attempting to build a VPN tunnel to that peer? In that case, you can use network tags to scope the availability of non-Meraki VPN peer configurations similarly to how you can use device tags to scope SSID availability. When configuring non-Meraki VPN peers on the **Security Appliance > Site-to-Site VPN** page, an Availability field is presented for each non-Meraki peer that enables you to select from any currently defined network tags from either Security Appliance or Combined networks. In this case, network tags are used because they are not dependent on a specific device and will allow the VPN configuration scope to remain unchanged when swapping or replacing security appliances. This also has the added advantage of only requiring a single tag application for high availability (HA) pairs.

Pro Tip Non-Meraki VPN peer configurations can also be explicitly scoped to No Networks to retain but disable the current configuration in the Dashboard.

Meraki Systems Manager

When working with Meraki Systems Manager, Meraki's MDM/EMM solution, tags become a critical aspect of managing devices and configuration payloads. There are currently four types of tags used in System Manager networks: device tags, policy tags, user tags, and schedule tags.

The various types of tags in a Systems Manager network can be used to group and organize enrolled client devices as well as scope app and profile deployment for easy management of large numbers of devices in a network. Tags in Systems Manager can even be updated dynamically based on current device attributes such as location or security policy compliance. This allows the Dashboard to automatically adjust the configuration of a device so that only compliant devices remain in scope of a given app or profile. For example, access to a specific application or wireless profile might be granted only to devices that remain within a specific geographic area near an office, or only to devices that currently have a lock screen and PIN enabled.

Given the wide variety of unique configurations and potential complexity of the use of tags within a Systems Manager network, details about specific implementations and configurations are beyond the scope of this book. For more information about Meraki Systems Manager and the use of tags for device management within it, you can find articles covering every aspect of Systems Manager in the "SM – Endpoint Management" section on the home page of https://documentation.meraki.com.

Dashboard Alerting and Reporting

Now that you are familiar with the basics of creating an organization, including the networks and administrators that make up the organization, and understand some of the ways you can simplify the management of the Dashboard through the use of network and device tags to scope permissions and configurations, this section shows you some of the options that are available for configuring the most common general alerts and monitoring features. This information will enable you to leverage the platform to help reduce mean time to resolution (MTTR) through the inherent automation offered by Meraki.

Alerts are configured and generated on a per-network basis (or, sometimes, per-device basis), meaning that each network in the Dashboard can be uniquely configured to alert appropriately based on the network and alert type. As we strive to help you find the needle in the haystack, we have elevated the visibility of alerts to the organization-level alert hub, shown in Figure 2-9 and discussed further at the end of this section.

Figure 2-9   *The Organization-Level Alert Hub for the Cisco Meraki Organization*

Email alerts, Webhooks, syslog messaging, and SNMP monitoring all allow for easy integration of Dashboard alerts with nearly any existing or custom monitoring and reporting solution. While similar, each of these reporting methods has a different approach to alerting and reporting that we will briefly discuss, starting with email alerts.

Dashboard Email Alerts

All Dashboard networks can be configured to generate email alerts for a variety of event types. These range from more generic, network-wide alerts, such as a configuration change or network usage/utilization alert, to more specific alerts, such as when a gateway access point becomes a repeater due to a loss in wired connectivity or whenever specific network clients connect or disconnect from the LAN. Alerting options are available for every Dashboard network from the Network-wide > Alerts page.

Each network type offers both generic, network-wide alerts and a set of alerts specific to network type. Each alert setting in each network can be set to use the default recipient list defined for that network or can be configured with a custom list of additional recipient emails to allow for tailored alerting across networks and devices. Certain alerts also have customizable triggers (i.e., scratching the surface of a machine learning foundation) available, allowing even further tailoring of alerts for specific sites or events.

For example, MR access points have the ability to generate email alerts and send them to a custom list of recipients when clients connected to a specified SSID experience a degraded signal quality, based on the selected SNR threshold, for more than the chosen amount of time. This type of alerting integrates the ability of the Meraki Dashboard not only to actively track and monitor client states on the network over time and use that information to intelligently alert when clients are receiving an unintended experience, but also to avoid potentially false alerts that could be triggered by brief outlying conditions.

An example of a more granular alert for MX security appliances is to alert whenever specified clients either connect or disconnect from the LAN of that network. In this case, the clients are selected from the entries of the Dashboard client list for that network and are configured to generate an alert whenever they begin responding to ARP requests from the MX or stop responding for more than 35 seconds.

While email alerts offer easy and powerful alerting abilities for any Dashboard network, the options discussed in the following sections offer even greater abilities to customize alert thresholds as well as integrate Dashboard alerting with other monitoring solutions to help take advantage of the power of the Meraki cloud with many existing monitoring solutions.

Webhooks

Webhooks are a standard type of alert/trigger that use an HTTP request triggered by an event to log that event to a remote system and trigger some form of action based on the event. They allow for the same alert configurations and level of granularity as email alerts. They also provide a great method of configuring network or device alerts that can be easily integrated with an existing alerting or monitoring system or used to build a wide variety of custom solutions based on the webhook delivery system. Figure 2-10 shows a report from a custom solution built on Webhooks to track the networks with the most changes being reported in the changelog.

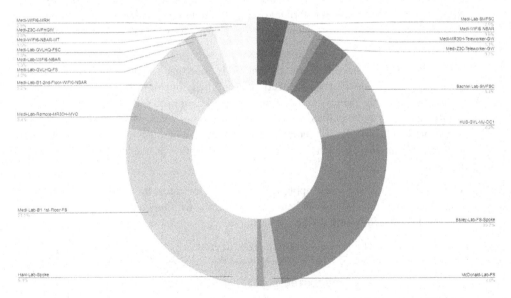

Figure 2-10 *A Report Built from a Custom Solution Utilizing Webhooks to Track Changelog Entries for Networks Across an Organization*

Webhooks are sent directly from the Meraki cloud and utilize a clearly formatted JSON message to report events and event details to a uniquely configurable URL that can point to nearly any cloud-accessible HTTPS webhook receiver or forwarder. This type of quick and easily configured alerting option allows for nearly endless integration options with existing monitoring platforms to log and report alerts from across multiple Dashboard networks, or the ability to create custom solutions that are even capable of automating tasks through the use of Webhook notifications and the Dashboard API to respond to network events as they happen. A few popular examples of platforms that come to mind are SecureX orchestration, Zapier builds, and Cisco Webex Teams.

For a detailed introduction to webhooks as well as several integration examples and other related documentation, check out https://developer.cisco.com/meraki/webhooks/.

Syslog

Syslog reporting is one of the most common types of monitoring and, next to email alerts, is one of the simplest types of monitoring to configure. Unlike email alerts and webhook notifications, syslog messages are sourced directly by the device instead of being sourced by the Meraki cloud. This allows for event reporting and monitoring even if communication to the Meraki cloud is unavailable.

Syslog event reporting is able to report and log multiple event types ranging from all Event Log–generating events, to all client URL requests based on observed HTTP GET requests, to real-time inbound and outbound flow creation, IDS alerts, and more. By exporting this information in real time to a local or remotely reachable syslog server, you can gather a detailed historical log of both general activity on the network and more specific alerts and events.

Configuring syslog reporting on the Dashboard is done on a per-network basis from the Network-wide > General > Logging section. From there, one or more syslog servers can be configured for the devices in the current network. For each server, a unique IP address or URL and port can be defined as well as a unique set of roles, which define the types of events that will be sent to that server. Each server can be uniquely configured within each network, allowing for as much granularity or customization as needed for each network and server.

While syslog seems like an old approach, thanks to new algorithms and more compute power being available, syslog can help to build a story with much more context. For example, take the following syslog message:

```
KIAH_MX67 security_event ids_alerted signature=1:43687:2 priority=3
timestamp=1675316156.777581 shost=00:EE:2E:EC:D1:E1 direction=egress
protocol=udp/ip src=10.11.11.7:37456 dst=10.67.0.22:53 decision=blocked
message: INDICATOR-COMPROMISE Suspicious .top dns query
```

Now apply a natural language machine learning algorithm and combine it with other log sources, and an old technology becomes a new approach to analysis and automation that can be executed on. Do not dismiss old technology; enhance it with new techniques.

You can find more information about syslog reporting with Meraki devices at https://documentation.meraki.com by searching for **syslog.**

SNMP and SNMP Traps

SNMP is also enabled from the Logging section of the Network-wide > General page. However, SNMP reporting is a bit unique compared to email alerts, webhooks, and syslog reporting. With SNMP, you have the option to either poll devices directly at their management interfaces to gather detailed device statistics such as interface counters and other device-level specifics, or to poll out to the Meraki Cloud Controller to gather information about the device and network status from the cloud perspective.

When being polled directly, devices such as the Meraki MX security appliance, MS switches, and MR access points all support endpoints from both the commonly used SNMPv2-MIB and IF-MIB. This is yet another feature that supports quick and easy integration with any new or existing monitoring systems.

When polling the Meraki Cloud Controller, the proprietary MERAKI-CLOUD-CONTROLLER-MIB must be used to support the custom endpoints available by polling the Cloud Controller directly. Fortunately, this MIB is easily available to download directly from the SNMP Configuration section of any Dashboard network and follows the standard MIB formatting to allow it to be easily imported to any SNMP polling system. Polling the Meraki Cloud Controller offers the option of scale and centralization. You have to configure it only once; even if your organization grows, the same configuration will accommodate this growth without having to make any repeat configuration updates, thereby saving time and effort in the long run.

Meraki also supports the use of SNMP traps for generating alerts in a more active fashion. When enabled and configured, SNMP traps are generated directly from the Meraki Cloud Controller and sent to the configured monitoring server over the Internet. Therefore, the receiving server must be publicly accessible by the Cloud Controller. SNMP traps specifically are configured from the Network-wide > Alerts page. When SNMP traps are enabled, you can configure a receiving server IP address and port in the SNMP Traps section.

The actual per-network alert configuration for SNMP traps is done in the same way as email alerts, except that you enter **snmp** instead of a destination email address when enabling an alert. This results in an SNMP trap being sent to the configured receiver server from the Meraki cloud when the related alert is triggered.

Pro Tip   Meraki supports the use of SNMP versions 1, 2c, and 3 for direct device polling and SNMP versions 2c and 3 for Cloud Controller polling and traps.

Automated Summary Reports

Another powerful reporting tool available in the Dashboard is the ability to generate summary reports for either individual networks or groups of networks (or devices), up to and including the entire organization (as shown in Figure 2-11). Unlike other reporting methods, summary reports can be generated either on demand (from the Organization > Summary Report page) or on a defined schedule and emailed to a list of recipients (as configured on the same page).

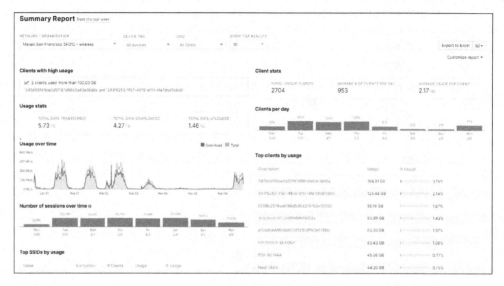

Figure 2-11   *An Example Summary Report from the Meraki Organization*

Summary reports show data over time for the selected device(s) or network(s) and time-frame. This includes, when available, more generic network details such as general usage over time, top SSIDs by usage, or unique client counts and average client usage. Summary reports also provide some more client-specific details such as top client devices by usage and top applications by usage.

> **Pro Tip**   When setting different time periods, data will be smoothed at different rates. Therefore, select appropriate time period granularity for the intended use case.

When generating a summary report, you can filter the networks and devices included in the report based on a combination of an individual Dashboard network or organization, device tag, and SSID (or all SSIDs). The subsequent results are also filtered to display for only the chosen timeframe and to include only the fields selected when creating the report. This all can be configured for either manually generated summary reports or auto-matically generated summary reports.

Like email alerts, when creating an automated report, you can define the list of recipients uniquely per report, with the additional ability to define the report frequency uniquely for each destination. By doing so, the same report can be generated and sent to different destinations based on the need of each destination. For example, one destination may get a newly generated report each day, while another may get that same report but only once per week. Or, separate reports could be generated, with an automatic daily report going out each day and an automatic weekly report covering the preceding week going out at the end of each week.

Meraki Insight Alerts

An additional option offered by Meraki, known as Meraki Insight, is capable of more advanced monitoring and alerting than the methods previously discussed. Meraki Insight is designed specifically to provide advanced monitoring capabilities for both general connectivity and uplink health as well as application-specific monitoring to allow for much more granular reporting and monitoring of a site's performance for those with an MX appliance installed. More detailed information relating to Meraki Insight is provided in Chapter 5, "MX and MG Best Practices," as well as at https://documentation.meraki.com/MI.

When enabled, the default Insight monitoring configuration is able to provide a wealth of information about the general uplink health of a device, such as the total uplink usage, average throughput, average latency, loss, and even jitter of each uplink. From the Insight > WAN Health page on the Dashboard, shown in Figure 2-12, these detailed statistics are easily viewable for every Insight-enabled network in the organization.

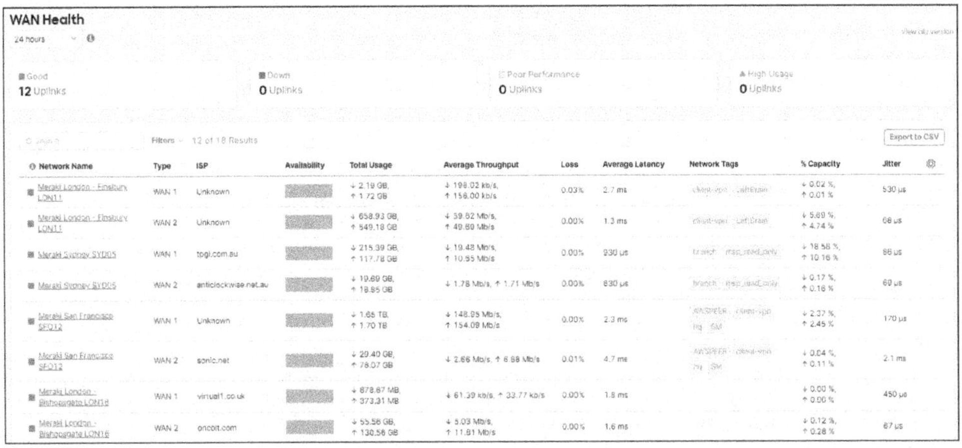

Figure 2-12 *An Example WAN Health Page Showing Health Statistics for Multiple Insight-Enabled Networks*

Additionally, the Insight VoIP Health feature offers the ability to configure VoIP monitoring to specifically monitor performance to any configured VoIP servers, and the Insight Web App Health feature offers the ability to configure custom per-application monitoring. These features and their options will be discussed in detail in later chapters. The focus of this is the alerting options available through Insight.

The majority of Insight-related alerts are configured on the Insight > Alerts page on the Dashboard. From there, you can configure alerts related to either WAN health or VoIP health. You can configure each alert type either uniquely for each network or for multiple

Insight-enabled networks at once. This enables you to quickly configure general alerts, such as >50% packet loss on an uplink for more than 5 minutes within a 10-minute period, across multiple networks. You can also easily configure more specific alerts, such as WAN2 experiencing utilization higher than 50 Mbps for 2 minutes or more within a 5-minute window, only for the networks that require that additional level of detailed monitoring.

Tables 2-1 and 2-2 detail the currently available WAN and VoIP Insight alert types and their customizable triggers for each network.

Table 2-1 *Overview of Configurable Insight WAN Alerts*

WAN Alert	Example Customizable Trigger
Uplink Status	Uplink X status changes.
Uplink Packet Loss	Uplink X packet loss is greater than 5% for 5 minutes or more, within a 15-minute window.
Uplink Utilization	Uplink X usage is greater than 1500 Kbps for 20 minutes or more, within a 60-minute window.
Uplink Latency	Uplink X latency is greater than 60 ms for 5 minutes or more, within a 15-minute window.

Table 2-2 *Overview of Configurable Insight VoIP Alerts*

VoIP Alert	Example Customizable Trigger
Packet Loss	Packet loss to the selected VoIP endpoint is greater than 3% on Uplink X for 5 minutes or more, within a 15-minute window.
Latency	Latency to the selected VoIP endpoint is greater than 60 ms on Uplink X for 5 minutes or more, within a 15-minute window.
MOS	MOS to the selected VoIP endpoint drops below 3.5 MOS on Uplink X for 10 minutes or more, within a 30-minute window.

Almost all Insight-related alerts are configured from the Insight > Alerts page on the Dashboard, except when configuring for monitored web applications. To configure monitored web applications and their related alerts, you have to navigate directly to **Insight > Web App Health**. From there, you can select from numerous web applications to actively monitor their performance. For each selected application, details like HTTP response time, general latency, application throughput, total network usage, and more are monitored to provide an extremely detailed set of application performance metrics based on the observed traffic in each network. These details are aggregated and analyzed to report on the LAN, WAN, and server performance of a specific application to help monitor and diagnose application performance issues.

In addition to the predefined or manually defined performance thresholds for each application, you can also configure thresholds with the use of Smart Thresholds. This allows you to determine application performance thresholds based on the actual, observed performance of a given application in each network to fine-tune the monitoring and alerting for each application in the unique network being monitored.

To configure alerts, specifically for monitored web applications, you first need to configure the application monitoring. Then, once that is completed, you can enable alerts on a per-application basis by simply selecting **Manage Alerts** from the **Web App Health** page.

Pro Tip   Meraki Insight alerts can also be configured to trigger Webhooks, just like standard email alerts. Leverage them for more advanced automations.

Smart Thresholds and web application monitoring with Meraki Insight are discussed in further detail in Chapter 5. You can also find more information via the "MI – Meraki Insight" section on the home page of the official Meraki documentation site at https://documentation.meraki.com.

Alert Hubs

When working in a large organization with the potential for multiple simultaneous alerts, it can be helpful to have a single location to view only the most important information. This is where the alert hub and organization alert hub mentioned at the start of this section come into play.

The standard, network-level alert hub is viewable by clicking the bell icon in the top-right corner of any Dashboard network page and provides a quick and easily accessible summary of any active alerts across all devices in the current network.

The organization alert hub provides a similar alert-focused overview but at the organization level, displaying alerts, alert priority, and device details from across all devices across all networks in the organization. By simply navigating to **Organization > Alerts**, you can quickly view and filter for the most important alerts relating to configuration issues, such as automatically detected VLAN mismatches, stack misconfigurations, and more. Additionally, you can view alerts for device connectivity issues, such as unreachable devices or 802.1X failures, device health issues, such as fan or PSU failures, and even Insight-related alerts for selected LAN or WAN services.

These alert hubs help to greatly simplify the effort required to monitor device and network statuses in detail across multiple networks within an organization, allowing administrators to more quickly identify issues and resolve them with less effort. This benefit also extends to those working across multiple organizations, as the organization alert hub provides a quick and easy way to get an accurate and detailed overview of the current potential issues present across networks within each organization without requiring a direct touch to any individual network.

Global Overview

One additional Meraki Dashboard feature to be aware of regarding the creation and monitoring of multiple Dashboard organizations is the new Global Overview page (formerly referred to as MSP view), shown in Figure 2-13. This special overview is available to administrator accounts that have permissions assigned across multiple Dashboard organizations by simply selecting Global Overview from the Organization drop-down menu when logged in to any organization.

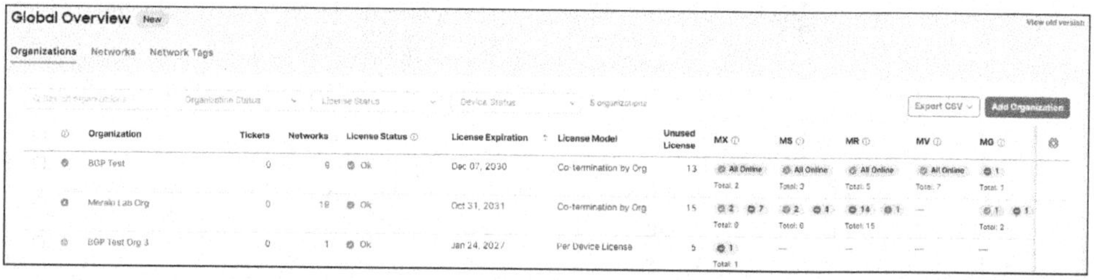

Figure 2-13 *An Example Global Overview Page Showing the Statuses of Several Organizations*

Despite the old name, the Global Overview page is not restricted to managed service provider (MSP)-related services. Organizations such as franchises and conglomerates are able to take advantage of it too. While originally designed with MSPs in mind, the Global Overview page is a helpful resource that provides an organization-level overview of multiple organizations in a single location. With the Global Overview page, you can easily view detailed information about the overall network and device states within each organization as well as the current licensing state of each organization. From this view, you can also click the **Add Organization** button to create new organizations without having to navigate through the login page.

Pro Tip   You can filter networks across organizations based on configured network tags, thereby allowing for easy filtering of networks across multiple organizations from the Global Overview page.

The Global Overview page helps to present a unified view of the entire business organization even when that is spread across multiple Dashboard organizations. This helps to further enable strategic segmentation of assets and deployments across different locations, business units, and even entirely separate managed entities while maintaining a simple and easy-to-use interface across the entire experience. More information can be found by reviewing the "Global Overview" document at https://documentation.meraki.com.

Summary

This chapter first covered the simple steps to create a new organization from scratch and a new deployment within that organization, highlighting just how little effort is required to set up a brand-new deployment. It also discussed how the granular administrative privileges offered through the Dashboard can be used to best manage Dashboard access and easily create special access roles for unique accounts to fit the needs of nearly any business, including the use of SAML authentication.

Additionally, this chapter touched on several ways to use device and network tags in the Dashboard to further scope device configurations and administrative privileges, allowing for even further customization and granularity to best fit the needs of each unique user.

Finally, you received a brief overview of the multiple alerting options available through the Dashboard, including email alerts, webhooks, SNMP, and more. These options offer the opportunity to easily integrate Dashboard monitoring and reporting with many other solutions, such as SolarWinds or Zabbix.

Now that you have an understanding of how the Dashboard is built, the basics of interacting with the Dashboard, and general monitoring of existing deployments, it is time to get an idea of what this all actually looks like when working with the Meraki Dashboard on a day-to-day basis.

Chapter 3 provides a look at what a random day for an administrator of a Meraki organization might be like, from the basics like checking the status of the organization to more advanced tasks such as troubleshooting any potential problems or complaints related to the network. Chapter 3 also highlights the Dashboard features that make many of those day-to-day tasks simpler and easier than ever before.

Additional Reading

Getting Started with Meraki: https://documentation.meraki.com/Getting_Started_with_Meraki

Creating a Dashboard Account and Organization: https://documentation.meraki.com/General_Administration/Organizations_and_Networks/Creating_a_Dashboard_Account_and_Organization

Combined Dashboard Networks: https://documentation.meraki.com/General_Administration/Organizations_and_Networks/Combined_Dashboard_Networks

Managing Dashboard Administrators and Permissions: https://documentation.meraki.com/General_Administration/Managing_Dashboard_Access/Managing_Dashboard_Administrators_and_Permissions

Configuring SAML Single Sign-on for Dashboard: https://documentation.meraki.com/General_Administration/Managing_Dashboard_Access/Configuring_SAML_Single_Sign-on_for_Dashboard

SM – Endpoint Management: https://documentation.meraki.com/SM

Alerts and Notifications: https://documentation.meraki.com/General_Administration/ Cross-Platform_Content/Alerts_and_Notifications

Meraki Webhooks: https://developer.cisco.com/meraki/webhooks/

MI – Meraki Insight: https://documentation.meraki.com/MI

Alerts Management in Meraki Insight: https://documentation.meraki.com/MI/ Alert_Management_in_Meraki_Insight

Global Overview: https://documentation.meraki.com/General_Administration/ Cross-Platform_Content/Global_Overview

Chapter 3

The Meraki Admin Experience

Over the years, the Meraki platform has expanded beyond just traditional networking and is getting closer to the utopia we all seek—a platform that can be used to manage all digital operations in one, single integration. This chapter explores the design intent and layout of the Meraki Dashboard to help you visualize your cloud-managed operations. This chapter also provides some insight into the ways that Meraki is working to enhance the administrative experience across the board. As you'll see, the Dashboard utilizes the power of Meraki's cloud-enabled platform to provide detailed summary and overview information to help administrators monitor and proactively address potential issues in their day-to-day workflow before those issues begin to cause larger impacts across the organization.

Note Refer to Chapter 2, "Building the Dashboard," for more information on how to set up your Meraki account, create a Dashboard organization, and perform initial setup actions such as creating administrators, assigning privileges, or claiming licenses and hardware.

The Organization Overview page, shown in Figure 3-1, is the first page displayed after logging in or selecting an organization to work within. You also can navigate to it directly from the navigation pane on the left by selecting **Organization > Overview.**

Once you are logged in to your Dashboard organization, you can verify the region where your current organization is hosted. View current session information by checking the footer of any page in the Dashboard, as shown in Figure 3-2.

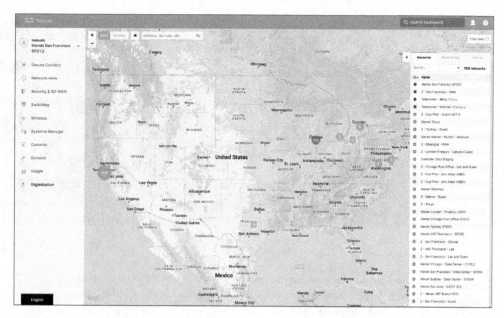

Figure 3-1   *The Organization Overview Page for the Cisco Meraki Organization Showing the Map Alongside the Network List in Collapsed Form*

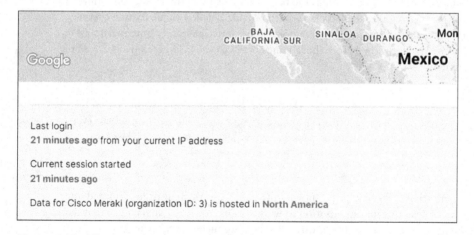

Figure 3-2   *The Current Session and Organization Hosting Details for an Example Organization*

Org-wide Health

The Organization Overview page in your Meraki Dashboard provides a high-level overview of each of the networks contained within the current organization. Its purpose is to elevate data to help you find the "needle in the haystack." You can expand the network list view by selecting the left-facing arrow at the top left of the network list on the right of the page, and add additional columns to get more overview information, such as Firmware Status or Network Health, for each of the listed networks by clicking the **+** button in the top-right corner of the table and selecting the column or columns to add, as shown in Figure 3-3.

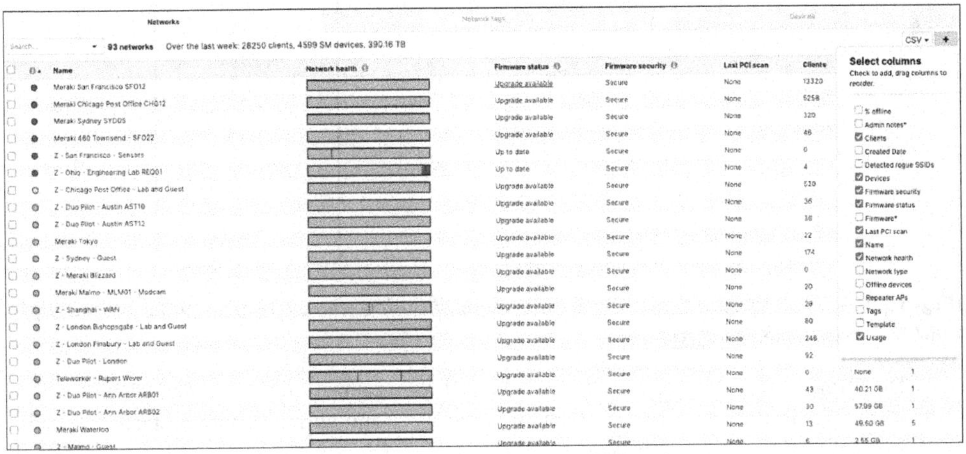

Figure 3-3   *The Organization Overview Page Showing the Expanded Network List for the Cisco Meraki Organization*

For example, to view firmware-related statuses for each network in the organization, click the **+** sign and select the **Firmware Security** and **Firmware Status** options to add the corresponding columns to the table.

Pro Tip   Most tables in the Meraki Dashboard can display additional columns of related information.

Firmware Status

Meraki manages device firmware statuses on a per-network basis and will notify administrators when an optional firmware upgrade is available for a given network with the Upgrade Available status in the Firmware Status column, as shown in Figure 3-4. A status of Upgrade Scheduled indicates a firmware upgrade has actively been scheduled for the specified network.

The Firmware Security column reports whether any critical security patches are missing for specific devices in a given network outside the general firmware availability. If a status of Custom is displayed in the Firmware Status column, that indicates that a specific firmware has been statically configured to run on one or more devices in the network by Meraki Support, in which case you will need to engage Meraki Support to remove the static mapping before any additional changes can be made to the firmware for that network.

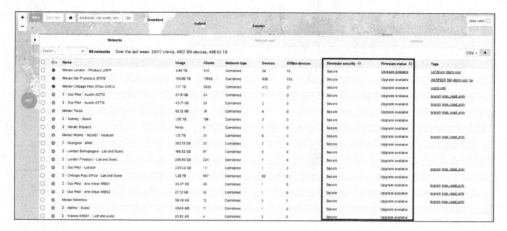

Figure 3-4   *The Organization Overview Page Showing the Current Firmware Security and Status of Each Network*

The Organization Overview page provides quick, organization-wide visibility and easily accessible notifications related to firmware security and current upgrade status for each network within the organization.

For more information on firmware updates and best practices, see the "Cisco Meraki Firmware FAQ" article at https://documentation.meraki.com.

Note   The "Additional Reading" section at the end of this chapter provides the full URL for every article that is cross-referenced in this chapter. Alternatively, you can search for the article title at https://documentation.meraki.com to locate it.

Detailed Firmware Status and Security

You can find more detailed visibility regarding firmware security and status across the organization by navigating to **Organization > Firmware Upgrades** and clicking the **All Networks** tab, shown in Figure 3-5. This page provides a detailed overview of every network within the organization and its current firmware-related statuses.

All networks

Network	Device type ▼		Status	Availability
TELEWORKER - London	Wireless Template	Any status	● Good ⊕	Upgrade available
TELEWORKER - San Francisco	Wireless Template	● Critical	● Good ⊕	Upgrade available
Teleworker - GSD Spencer_Gage	Wireless (bound to template)	● Warning	● Good ⊕	Upgrade available
Teleworker - Manabu Sakurai	Wireless (bound to template)	● Good	● Good ⊕	Upgrade available
Teleworker - Kash Saeed	Wireless (bound to template)	MR 28.6.1	● Good ⊕	Upgrade available
Teleworker - Rupert Wever	Wireless (bound to template)	MR 28.6.1	● Good ⊕	Upgrade available
Meraki 460 Townsend - SFO22	Wireless	MR 28.6.1	● Good ⊕	Upgrade available

Figure 3-5   *The All Networks View of the Firmware Upgrades Page for the Cisco Meraki Organization*

As shown in Figure 3-5, you can open the **Status** drop-down menu to quickly highlight networks with their current firmware in Critical or Warning states, like in Figures 3-6 and 3-7, respectively. Networks have a Warning status when their currently running firmware has an end-of-support date set within the next 6 months, and networks have a Critical status when the running firmware is past the end-of-support date. This option is one way to quickly see what sites are potentially in a time-sensitive situation that needs quick attention.

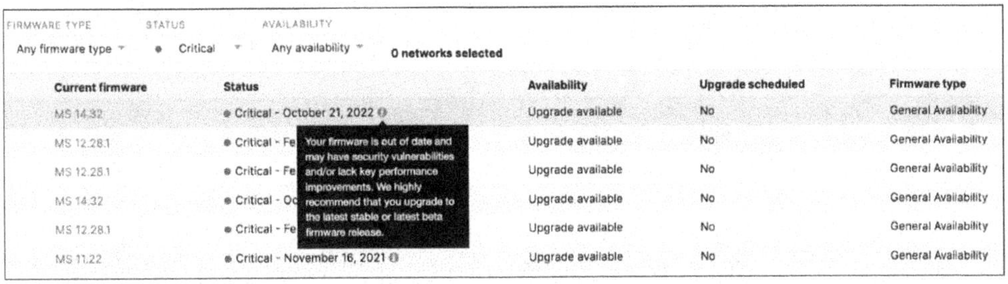

Figure 3-6 *Networks in the Cisco Meraki Organization That Have Critical-Level Firmware Alerts*

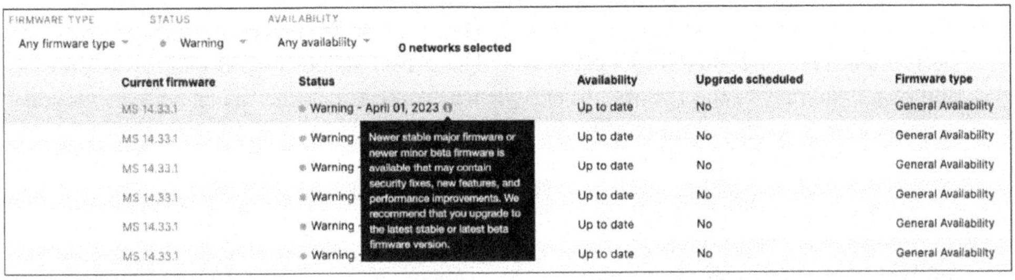

Figure 3-7 *Networks in the Cisco Meraki Organization That Have Warning-Level Firmware Alerts*

Getting to know the current status of all your networks and prioritizing sites that require security patches helps to ensure that your networks are up to date on security posture, compliance, and availability.

Proactive Replacements

Because Cisco Meraki strives for the highest-quality hardware and user experience possible, much of the Meraki hardware comes with a lifetime replacement warranty. However, no mass-manufacturing process is perfect, and sometimes a problematic component might not be discovered until long after the equipment has been manufactured and sold. In the unlikely event there is an unforeseen product defect that Meraki is unable to address before distributing the equipment to customers, the Meraki platform is capable of handling the complex task of tracking known hardware or product defects and proactively alerting administrators who manage potentially affected devices so that they can replace those devices before they fail or cause a significant impact to operations. An excellent example of a defect that produced an industry-wide impact is the Intel clock component failures that occurred around 2018.

While Meraki will actively alert any customer who may be operating an affected device in which a defect is discovered, organization administrators can always check at any time to see if any devices in their organization are eligible for a proactive replacement program. To do so, open the **Help** menu at the top of any Dashboard page and click the **Hardware Replacements** link.

Pro Tip   The proactive replacement program is different from the proactive RMA process available for devices that have failed outside of a known mass defect.

For more information regarding Meraki Return Materials Authorization (RMA) and end-of-life (EOL) policies, refer to the "Returns (RMAs), Warranties and End-of-Life Information" article at https://documentation.meraki.com.

Dashboard Early Access Program

Meraki is continuously working to enhance the design of the Dashboard to improve performance and usability for its customers. This effort includes developing new features and pages to improve the Dashboard experience. You can explore the latest features and pages opting in to the Dashboard Early Access program.

Pro Tip   You can find detailed, up-to-date information about new features and firmware support for all Meraki products on Meraki's "Firmware Features" documentation page at https://documentation.meraki.com/Firmware_Features.

To opt in to specific Early Access Dashboard features, go to the **Organization > Early Access Program** page, shown in Figure 3-8, and use the toggle switches to enable or disable new features in the Dashboard, such as new pages, UI designs, or new features, before they are pushed to the wider Dashboard audience. To give you an idea of what types of enhancements are available through the Early Access Program, the following subsections briefly introduce a few of the currently available options (marked 1 through 4 in Figure 3-8) that are particularly relevant to the day-to-day administrator experience. Keep in mind that new features are always being developed, so this is just a snapshot of the future of the Meraki Dashboard at the time of writing.

Magnetic Design System

Use this toggle to enable the newest iteration of the Dashboard UI, known as Magnetic, which not only overhauls the visual appearance of the Dashboard while maintaining a familiar layout but also enables the options for many more related features and pages within the new UI. This new design also acts as a building block of the new, next-generation unified Cisco UI design coming to modern Cisco dashboards.

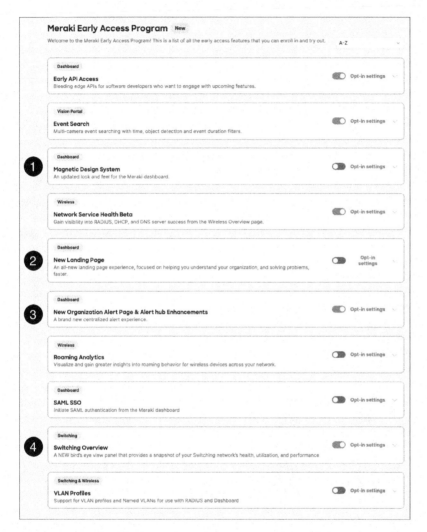

Figure 3-8 *The Meraki Early Access Program Page, Allowing You to Opt In or Out of New Dashboard Features*

New Landing Page

Use this toggle to enable the Organization Summary page, shown in Figures 3-9 and 3-10, which provides an updated and clearer high-level overview of the health of devices across all the networks in your organization. You can view this page after enabling the feature by navigating to **Organization > Summary.**

Figure 3-9 *The Health Section of the New Organization Summary Page Available in the New Landing Page*

	Name	Usage	Clients	Tags	MX	MS	MR	MV	MG
○	Z - Meraki Blizzard	39.5 MB	3		🔅 1				
○	Z - Ohio - Engineering Lab REQ01	113 KB	1		🔅 1				
○	Meraki Chicago Post Office CHG12	7.95 TB	5920	client-vpn					
○	Meraki San Francisco SFO12	115.23 TB	15288	AWSPEER client-vpn hq SM			🔅 14		
○	Z - Wireless Concentrator - Engineering SF	94.7 MB	3		🔅 1				
○	Z - Chicago Post Office - Lab and Guest	2.68 TB	581			⚠ 1			
○	Z - Shanghai - WAN	1.62 TB	25						
○	Meraki Tokyo	100.38 GB	24	branch msp_read_only					
○	Meraki San Jose - SJC01	165.61 GB	37						
○	Meraki Chicago - Data Center - CHGL5	1.90 TB	21						

Rows per page 10 ▾ ‹ [1] 2 3 … 10 ›

Figure 3-10 *The Networks Section of the New Organization Summary Page for Networks Within the Cisco Meraki Organization*

The Networks section of this page reports a more detailed device health summary for each network, allowing you to quickly assess the status and health of each network across the organization more easily than ever before.

New Organization Alert Page & Alert Hub Enhancement

Use this toggle to enable the Organization Alerts page, shown in Figure 3-11, as well as the network-level Alert Hub. The Organization Alerts page provides a consolidated view of alerts for all platforms deployed across the organization. To access this page, navigate to **Organization > Alerts** from any Dashboard page.

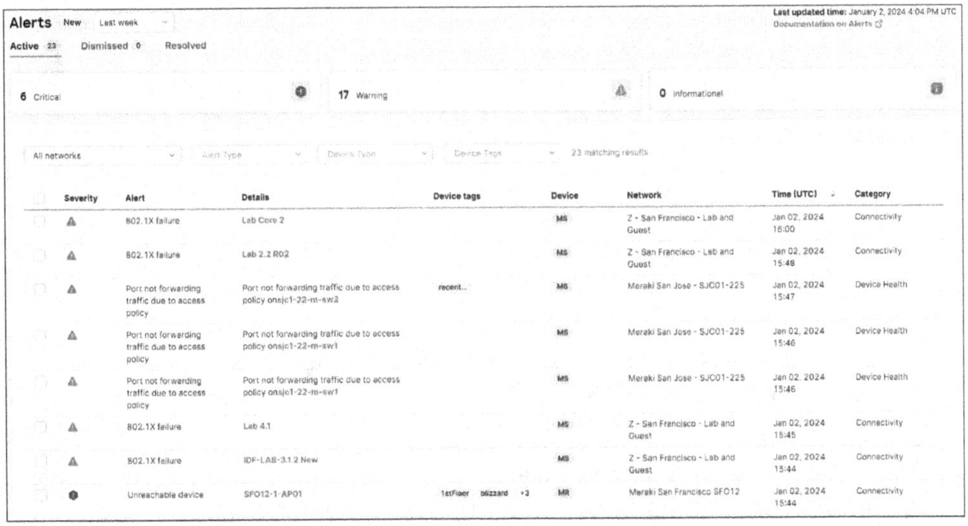

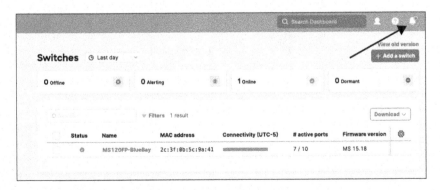

Alerts New Last week
Last updated time: January 2, 2024 4:04 PM UTC
Documentation on Alerts
Active 23 Dismissed 0 Resolved
6 Critical
17 Warning
0 Informational
All networks
Alert Type
Device Type
Device Tags
23 matching results
Severity Alert Details Device tags Device Network Time (UTC) Category
802.1X failure Lab Core 2 MS Z - San Francisco - Lab and Guest Jan 02, 2024 16:00 Connectivity
802.1X failure Lab 2.2 R02 MS Z - San Francisco - Lab and Guest Jan 02, 2024 15:48 Connectivity
Port not forwarding traffic due to access policy Port not forwarding traffic due to access policy onsjc1-22-m-sw2 recent... MS Meraki San Jose - SJC01-225 Jan 02, 2024 15:47 Device Health
Port not forwarding traffic due to access policy Port not forwarding traffic due to access policy onsjc1-22-m-sw1 MS Meraki San Jose - SJC01-225 Jan 02, 2024 15:46 Device Health
Port not forwarding traffic due to access policy Port not forwarding traffic due to access policy onsjc1-22-m-sw1 MS Meraki San Jose - SJC01-225 Jan 02, 2024 15:46 Device Health
802.1X failure Lab 4.1 MS Z - San Francisco - Lab and Guest Jan 02, 2024 15:45 Connectivity
802.1X failure IDF-LAB-3.1.2 New MS Z - San Francisco - Lab and Guest Jan 02, 2024 15:44 Connectivity
Unreachable device SFO12-1-AP01 1stFloor blizzard +3 MR Meraki San Francisco SFO12 Jan 02, 2024 15:44 Connectivity

Figure 3-11 *The New Organization Alerts Page*

The Organization Alerts view provides an easy to check report of device statuses across all networks in an organization and can be filtered to narrow the displayed results based on severity, alert type, network, or device type. This provides an excellent top-down view of any alerts present across an organization regardless of organization size or deployment distribution, which results in a shorter time to identify issues, leading to a quicker time to resolution.

When working on any page within an individual network, the network-level Alert Hub notification icon appears in the upper-right corner of the window, as shown in Figure 3-12. This feature provides an easy to access view that consolidates all alerts for the current network into a single panel, as shown in Figure 3-13. These are the same alerts that you can view from the Organization Alerts page but filtered to show only alerts for the currently selected network. From this panel, you can quickly navigate to a problematic device or easily triage a series of alerts for a given network to make addressing the inevitable issue a less stress-inducing task.

Search Dashboard
View old version
Switches Last day
+ Add a switch
0 Offline
0 Alerting
1 Online
0 Dormant
Filters 1 result
Download
Status Name MAC address Connectivity (UTC-5) # active ports Firmware version
MS120FP-BlueBay 2c:3f:0b:5c:9a:41 7 / 10 MS 15.18

Figure 3-12 *The Alert Hub Notification Icon*

For more information on the new Organization Alerts page and Alert Hub, visit https://documentation.meraki.com and view the "Alerts" article.

Switching Overview

Use this toggle to access the new Switching Overview feature, which consolidates key performance indicators and provides crucial planning information related to switches in a given network. Details like port utilization, PoE budget, and more help Dashboard users to have clearer visibility when reviewing device provisioning and statuses, thereby assisting in planning for future network needs.

You can access the Switching Overview panel after enabling the feature by going to the **Network-wide > Clients** page of any network and selecting the **Switches** modal of the Health section, as demonstrated in Figure 3-14.

More information on the new Switching Overview feature is available at documentation. meraki.com in the "Switching Overview – MS Health" document.

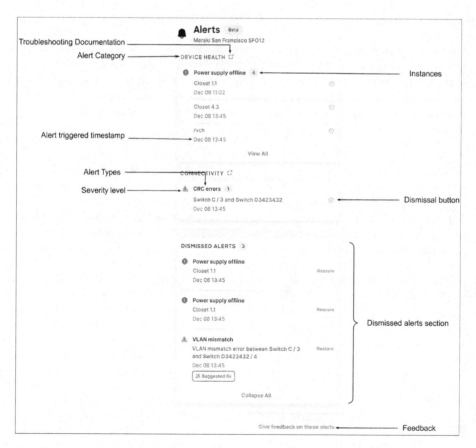

Figure 3-13   *The Alert Hub Notification Panel for the Cisco Meraki San Francisco Campus Network*

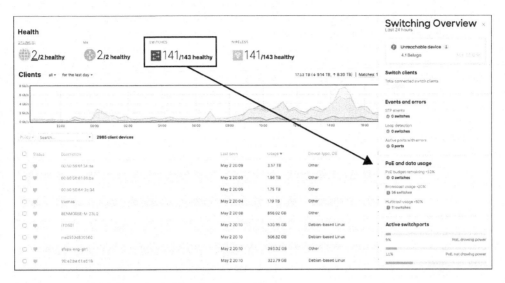

Figure 3-14 *The New Switching Overview Feature*

Global Overview

For administrators who need to manage multiple organizations within the Meraki Dashboard, the Global Overview page, shown in Figure 3-15, provides a summarized overview of the health of all networks and devices an administrator has access to across all organizations. This page also introduces a few additional key features to help manage multiple organizations, like visibility into Meraki support tickets across each organization, license statuses (including unused licenses and expiry dates), and quick reference of device health within each organization.

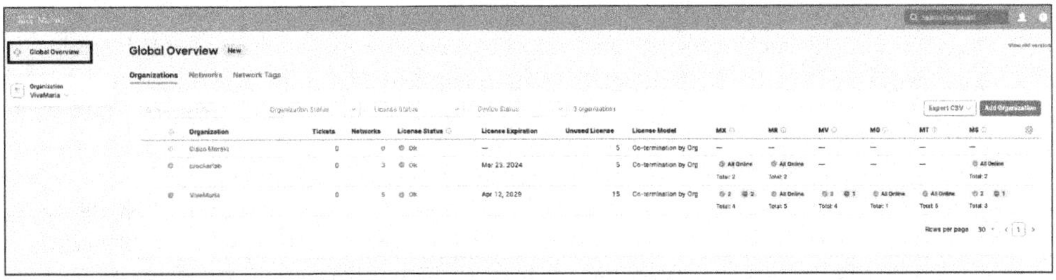

Figure 3-15 *The Global Overview Page Showing Three Different Organizations*

The Global Overview page is designed to simplify the interaction across organizations for administrators who need to maintain and monitor multiple Dashboard organizations by providing the most useful information for each organization in an easily accessible summary.

You can find more information on the Global Overview feature at https://documentation.meraki.com in the "Global Overview" document.

Network-wide Health Views

After reviewing the high-level summaries at the organization level, it's time to drill down into some of the network-specific pages and views to get a more detailed picture of the health and overall status of a network and its clients.

Network-wide and Uplink Health

To get to the detailed reports and data for a given network in an organization, click the network name from the Organization Summary or Organization Overview page, or select the network from the Networks panel on the left.

After navigating to a specific network, you are presented with the Network-wide > Clients page. The Health section, shown in Figure 3-16, provides a quick reference report for the uplink status (if available) and the device statuses of any Meraki hardware currently added to the network. From this section of the page, you can click each icon to view the product details page for each hardware platform available.

Figure 3-16   *The Network Health Summary on the Network-wide > Clients Page*

Below the Health section is the Clients section, which includes a list of all recently seen clients on the network, a summary of traffic and client usage, and a more detailed traffic analysis of client traffic, which you can view by selecting the **Show** link under the Applications pie chart to the right of the usage summary. An example of the fully expanded Application Details view is shown in Figure 3-17.

The Application Details section is powered by Cisco Network-Based Application Recognition (NBAR), which provides visibility into more than 1500 of the most popular applications. NBAR-enabled platforms are able to better analyze and identify client traffic to enforce more granular Layer 7 firewall rules and policies, configurable from the Security & SD-WAN > Firewall page (see Figure 3-18) or within a Network-wide > Group Policy (see Figure 3-19), allowing for tighter policing of user traffic with less effort than ever before.

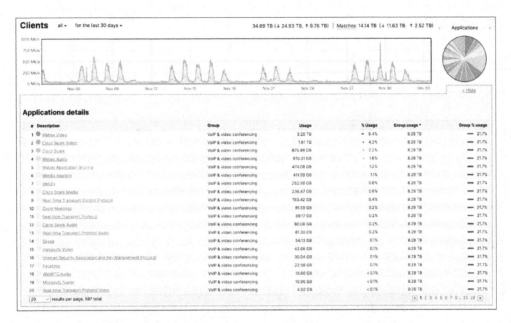

Figure 3-17 *Application Visibility on the Network-wide > Clients Page*

Pro Tip Application Visibility and Control (AVC) details are available on the Clients page, with quick sort options and additional details regarding client usage for each application by selecting the application from the list.

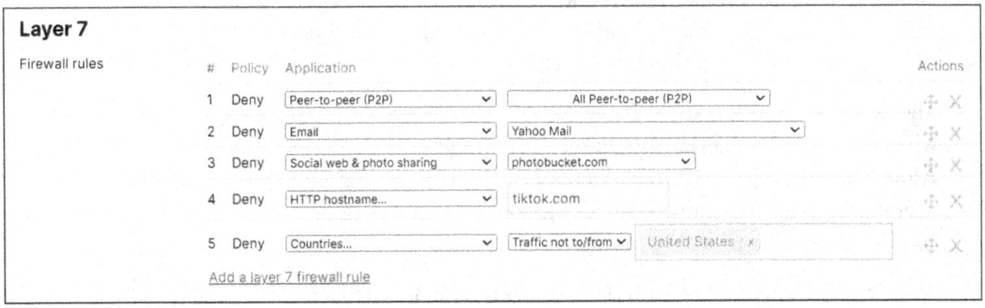

Figure 3-18 *An Example Set of Layer 7 Firewall Rules Utilizing Several NBAR-Based Application Rulesets*

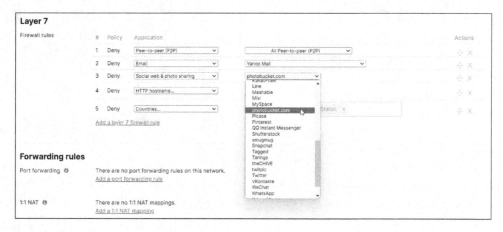

Figure 3-19   *An Example of the Detailed Application-Level Granularity Available for Devices Using NBAR*

To confirm the minimum supported firmware versions for Meraki MX, MS, and MR platforms to allow enabling of NBAR functionality, visit https://documentation.meraki.com and view the article 'Next-gen Traffic Analytics – Network-Based Application Recognition (NBAR) Integration.' You can find more information about NBAR classifications in the same article and by viewing Cisco's NBAR-related documentation at www.cisco.com (search for the keyword **NBAR**).

Wireless Network Health

Wireless networks sometimes are prone to issues, whether they be deployment related, client related, or even just environmental. Fortunately, the Meraki platform has again embraced the power of the cloud to actively monitor and report on the health and performance of any Meraki wireless networks.

The Wireless Health feature of the Meraki Dashboard offers some significant advantages when trying to troubleshoot issues such as client connectivity or authentication failures. As an example, Figure 3-20 shows the health overview for a wireless network on a Cisco Meraki campus. From this page, it's clear that the network and its clients are functioning smoothly overall and without issue.

Now if you compare that with the view in Figure 3-21 from a different network, the value of the Wireless Health feature and its ability to clearly demonstrate client-impacting issues becomes immediately obvious, as you can quickly and easily see at a glance that there is an authentication-related issue for several devices, unlike the previous network shown in Figure 3-20.

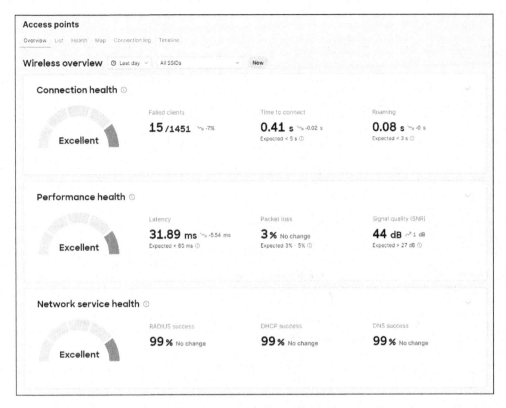

Figure 3-20   *The Wireless Overview for a Cisco Meraki Campus, Showing a Well-Functioning Wireless Network with No Notable Issues*

From this point, you can review the rest of the report to get more details about where the issue may lie. The rest of the Wireless Health page reports several other helpful perspectives, such as issues by SSID, AP, individual client, and even by device type, to help scope and further narrow down potentially impacting issues. This makes it easy to determine if a specific SSID is improperly configured, if a specific AP is connected to an incorrect port, or if a specific client or client type is having issues that are otherwise not present for other clients or client types.

As Figure 3-22 shows for a simple home network, the Wireless Health feature can provide extremely valuable information when you're trying to determine the potential scope and impact of a reported behavior.

As just demonstrated, Meraki's Wireless Health feature helps to take the guesswork out of attempting to triage a wireless issue by providing important details that help to determine the scope and impact of a behavior from a quickly accessible and easy to interpret report. This helps to save time and refocus troubleshooting efforts in appropriate directions, leading to a faster time to resolution for many issues than a more traditional troubleshooting approach.

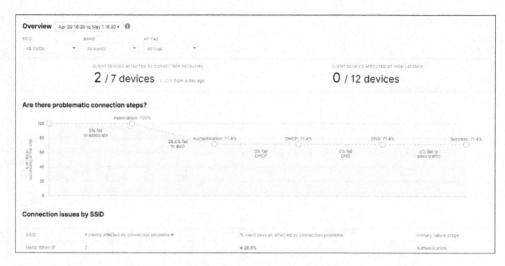

Figure 3-21   *The Wireless Health Report for an Example Network, Showing Failures Relating to Authentication for Two Clients*

The Wireless Health feature is discussed in much further detail in Chapter 8, "Introduction to Meraki MR Access Points."

Connection issues by SSID

SSID	# clients affected by connection problems ▾	% client devices affected by connection problems	Primary failure stage
Hertz When IP	2	● 28.6%	Authentication

5 ∨ results per page   ‹ 1 ›

Connection issues by client

Client device	% failed connections	# failed connections ▾	Primary failure stage
large-6cdea9000517	● 85.2%	23 / 27	Authentication
8c:de:a9:00:04:97	● 83.3%	5 / 6	Authentication
floor-cam-345@faa309a2	● 33.3%	1 / 3	Authentication
Mike's S21plus	● 0%	0 / 1	Association
Sara's S21	● 0%	0 / 1	Association

5 ∨ results per page   ‹ 1 2 ›

Connection issues by AP

AP	# clients affected by connection problems ▾	% client devices affected by connection problems	Primary failure stage	# failed connections
Living Room MR36H	2	● 28.6%	Authentication	29 failed connections

5 ∨ results per page   ‹ 1 ›

Figure 3-22   *Additional Details of the Wireless Health Report for the Network Showing Client Authentication Issues*

Automated Topology Views

Stepping down from the organization views into a specific network, Meraki's integrated topology views can provide full-stack visibility for any Dashboard network containing MS switches. Using Cisco Discovery Protocol (CDP) and Link Layer Discovery Protocol (LLDP) data reported by the devices in the network, the Meraki Dashboard is able to intelligently construct multiple types of topology maps to allow for a quick and up-to-date reference of the current deployment topology.

This feature is another location where the combined networks discussed in Chapter 2 bring some significant advantages when compared to a standalone network consisting of only a single device type. When working in a combined network, each Meraki device is able to report data back to the Dashboard regarding any network connections between devices, allowing for a more comprehensive view of the topology of the network.

As previously mentioned, the Dashboard is able to build multiple types of topology reports based on the information available for each network, including Layer 2, Layer 3, and multicast routing topologies. You can view all topologies by navigating to the **Network-wide > Topology** page from the related network.

Network-wide Layer 2 Topology

The Layer 2 topology diagram, an example of which is shown in Figure 3-23, is based on advertised LLDP and CDP data that has been learned and reported back to the Dashboard by Meraki devices. Through the use of this information, the Dashboard is able to present an automatically generated, dynamic, and interactive Layer 2 topology map of a network.

Pro Tip   Hovering over a device icon or link between devices provides more detailed information about the object and provides a direct link to that client, device, or related port.

This type of automatic and dynamic topology diagram can be immensely useful when attempting to track down a client or device, or when trying to determine the traffic flow/path of a given client. When looking at the Network-wide > Client Details page for any current client on the network, the most recent edge device closest to the client is listed as well as a link to the Layer 2 topology for the network, as shown in Figure 3-24. Clicking that link will automatically highlight the path through the network to the client in question, like the example shown in Figure 3-25.

Corp AV 7.1
IDF7.2-Corp Stack1
IDF7.2-Corp Stack2
IDF7.3-Corp Stack1
IDF7.3-Corp Stack2
IDF7.3-Corp WiFi1
IDF7.4-Corp WiFi1
CHG12-MX1
MDF7.1-Corp CORE

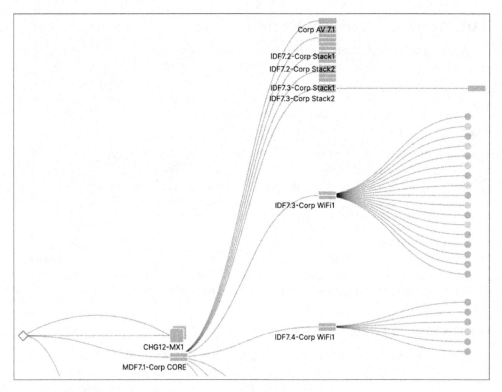

Figure 3-23 *A Partial View of the Layer 2 Topology Diagram for the Meraki Corp Network*

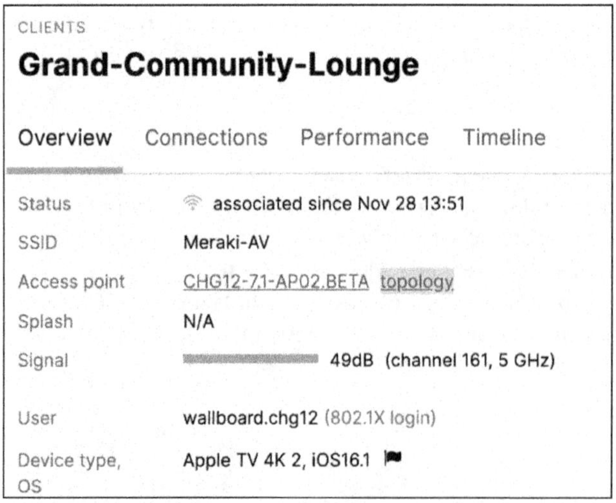

CLIENTS
Grand-Community-Lounge
Overview
Connections
Performance
Timeline
Status
associated since Nov 28 13:51
SSID
Meraki-AV
Access point
CHG12-7.1-AP02.BETA topology
Splash
N/A
Signal
49dB (channel 161, 5 GHz)
User
wallboard.chg12 (802.1X login)
Device type, OS
Apple TV 4K 2, iOS16.1

Figure 3-24 *The Topology Link for a Client on the Client Details Page*

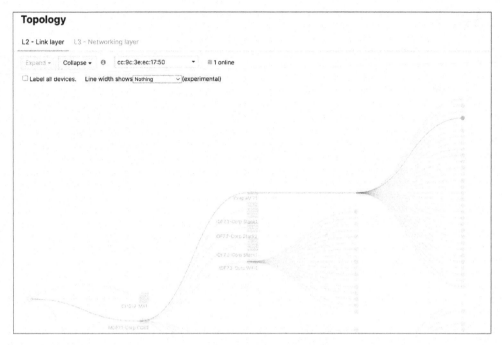

Figure 3-25   *The L2 Topology Page, with the Path to the Previously Selected Client Highlighted*

Network-wide Layer 3 Topology

The Topology page also includes the option to view the Layer 3 topology for the network, as shown in Figure 3-26, by selecting the L3 – Networking Layer tab. This view displays a dynamic layout of the Layer 3 topology of the network based on the current Dashboard configuration for MX and MS devices.

Network-wide Multicast Topology

For networks that have multicast routing enabled, you can configure the Layer 3 Topology page to show the current multicast topology as an overlay on top of the existing Layer 3 topology by checking the **Show Multicast Topology** check box, as shown in Figure 3-27. This provides a highlighted view of the multicast topology specifically.

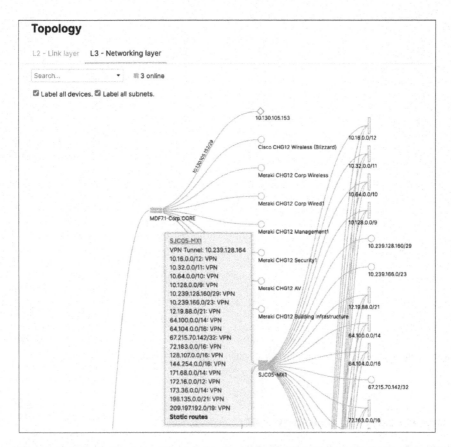

Figure 3-26   *A Portion of the L3 Topology Page for a Cisco Meraki Campus Network*

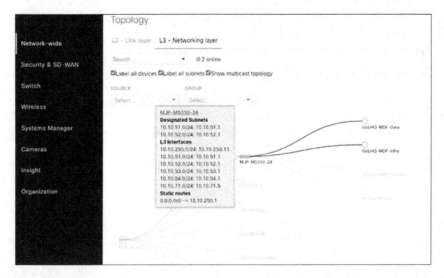

Figure 3-27   *An Example Multicast Topology Highlighted on Top of the Layer 3 Topology of a Network*

Summary

As you've seen in this chapter, the Meraki platform utilizes the cloud to help present the Dashboard as a unified interface that is easy to navigate and embraces the power of cloud communication and management. This allows Meraki to offer features like the ability to easily view and manage firmware for an entire organization from a single page or provide detailed topology maps and troubleshooting information based on observed trends and behaviors in a network. These types of enhancements are only possible by aggregating client and device data in ways that were previously not feasible without the cloud. Meraki uses all of this and more to help drive a better administrator experience no matter what task you're trying to accomplish.

Next, Chapter 4 introduces how you can further enhance the power of the Meraki platform through the use of automation, both inside and outside the Dashboard.

Additional Reading

Best Practices for Meraki Firmware: https://documentation.meraki.com/Architectures_and_Best_Practices/Cisco_Meraki_Best_Practice_Design/Best_Practices_for_Meraki_Firmware

Cisco Meraki Firmware FAQ: https://documentation.meraki.com/General_Administration/Firmware_Upgrades/Cisco_Meraki_Firmware_FAQ

Firmware Features: https://documentation.meraki.com/Firmware_Features

Returns (RMAs), Warranties and End-of-Life Information: https://documentation.meraki.com/General_Administration/Other_Topics/Returns_(RMAs)%2C_Warranties_and_End-of-Life_Information

Alerts: https://documentation.meraki.com/General_Administration/Cross-Platform_Content/Global_Alerts_Widget

Switching Overview – MS_Health: https://documentation.meraki.com/MS/Meraki_MS_Beta/Switching_Overview_-_MS_Health

Global Overview: https://documentation.meraki.com/General_Administration/Cross-Platform_Content/Global_Overview

Next-gen Traffic Analytics – Network-Based Application Recognition (NBAR) Integration: https://documentation.meraki.com/General_Administration/Cross-Platform_Content/Next-gen_Traffic_Analytics_-_Network-Based_Application_Recognition_(NBAR)_Integration

Network Topology: https://documentation.meraki.com/MS/Monitoring_and_Reporting/Network_Topology

Chapter 4

Automating the Dashboard

Now that you are familiar with the most common interactions with the Dashboard and the Meraki platform, it's time to discuss a major advantage of the Meraki platform: ease of automation. When you're working with the Meraki platform, you can automate numerous tasks and actions, many in a variety of ways. Nearly any task that you can perform in the Dashboard via the web UI can also be automated through one or more of the methods that are covered in this chapter.

Configuration Templates

The simplest form of automation available on the Dashboard is the implementation of configuration templates. Configuration templates can be used to automatically configure networks for deployment, and to automatically update the configuration of multiple networks from one location. This allows for a single configuration point for nearly any option within the Dashboard UI that can then be replicated across multiple sites through just a few clicks. Templates can be used to configure any device type within the Meraki platform, making them potentially one of the most powerful Dashboard tools available.

How Do Templates Work?

It's important to understand how templates operate in the Dashboard to be able to take full advantage of their capabilities and avoid some of the more common pitfalls. Creating a template is similar to creating a regular network in that it can be created as a combined template or as a standalone type such as security appliance only or switch only; see Figure 4-1 for an example.

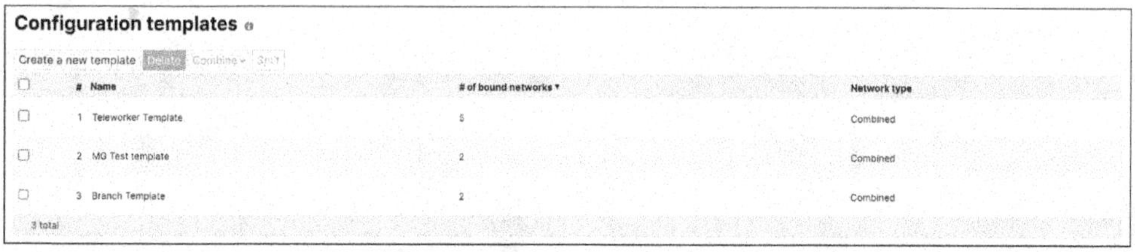

Figure 4-1   *Short Example List of Configuration Templates as Viewed from Organization > Configuration Templates in the Dashboard*

Unlike regular Dashboard networks, however, configuration templates only hold configurations and do not contain any individual devices. Instead, networks are attached to templates as child networks, which allows them to inherit the template-level configurations that apply to any devices in those networks.

This enables you to create and configure a template and then push that configuration to any network that is attached to the template as a child network without requiring additional manual configuration. Because most configurations can be set at the template level through the combination of network-level settings and device profiles, for many deployments, a single template can be configured and used to deploy hundreds of sites with minimal to no network-specific configurations required.

Using a configuration template can greatly simplify the configuration and deployment process when creating a new network, whether that be something as simple as a basic teleworker endpoint or something more complex like an entire store or branch network. As an example of the options available in configuration templates, this section demonstrates using a template for the MX subnetting and VLAN configurations, which can be defined at the template level in either of two different ways: same subnetting or unique subnetting. Keep in mind as you read through this introductory section on templates that while the focus is on MX use cases, you can use templates for devices other than MX security appliances, with several unique features offered for different device types, such as MR and MS devices using templates. For now, focusing on a single product will enable you to concentrate on how you can use templates in the Dashboard.

When configuring VLANs at the template level, you choose a subnetting method for each VLAN from the Subnetting drop-down list, as shown in Figure 4-2. The options are Unique or Same. If you select Same for a given VLAN, every security appliance attached to the template will be configured with an identical subnet and interface IP address for that VLAN. This option is great for consistency among sites that require only local and Internet access, but it would cause routing issues, due to the duplicate subnets for sites, where multiple locations may need to communicate over VPN back to a central hub location. For that reason, VLANs created using the Same subnetting option cannot be enabled for AutoVPN.

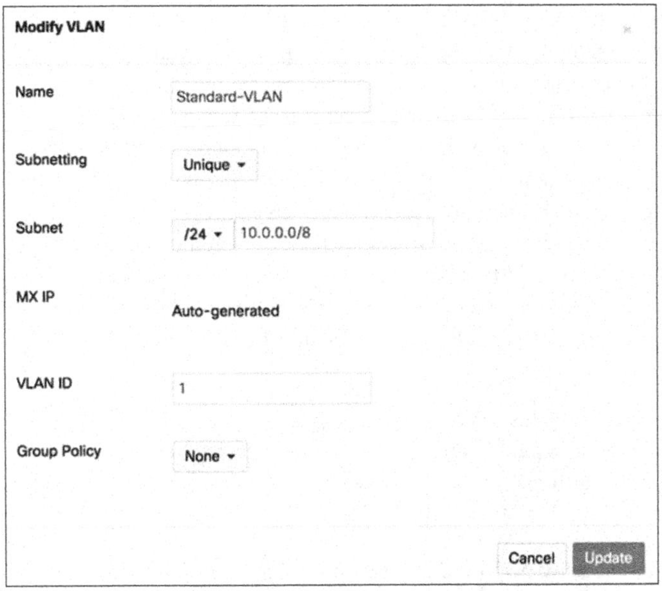

Modify VLAN   ✕

Name   Standard-VLAN

Subnetting   Unique ▾

Subnet   /24 ▾   10.0.0.0/8

MX IP
                  Auto-generated

VLAN ID   1

Group Policy   None ▾

                                        Cancel   Update

Figure 4-2 *Demonstrating a Unique Subnet Configuration for a VLAN in a Template*

In a situation like that, you can choose the **Unique** subnetting option for one or more VLANs on the template, as in Figure 4-2. This requires that you define a subnet pool on the template for the VLAN in question as well as a child subnet size to determine the number of addresses that should be allocated from the available subnet pool for that VLAN to each child network. For example, if your subnet pool for the VPN-enabled VLAN on a template is configured as 10.0.0.0/8, then you can choose to uniquely allocate an appropriate number of addresses for that VLAN to each child network, automatically ensuring that no overlapping subnets exist for each template child. For example, you could set the allocation size down to a /29 or /30 if very few unique addresses are required at each site or set it all the way up to a /10 if required, or anywhere in between to best match the needs of the deployment.

The MX subnetting options are just one of many examples of how configurations can be created and customized at the template level based on the needs of the child networks. Each device type has a multitude of options when creating related template configurations, allowing for nearly endless customization of each template and the associated child network and device configurations.

Local Overrides

Being able to quickly and easily deploy new networks from a predefined configuration is a massive boost when you are trying to deploy a number of similar sites, but what if not every site should share an identical configuration, or if you want to further tweak a specific site's configuration after deployment without modifying the entire template configuration? This is where template local overrides come into play.

Local overrides enable you to manually override certain configurations of template child networks from the template-assigned values. Many, but not all, settings can have a local override configured if the template-assigned value is undesirable for any reason. As an example, this can be extremely useful for deployments configured for unique subnetting that are using a very strict subnetting scheme across sites, as by default the subnets for a given child network are taken at random from the pool of available subnets defined at the template level. For example, a network may be assigned two /25 subnets from a template pool of 10.0.0.0/8, but there is no guarantee that the chosen subnets will be contiguous from the previous site that was deployed from the same template, or even between themselves at the same site. As a result, it may be necessary to manually adjust the assigned subnets to remain in line with a predefined addressing scheme across different sites.

Pro Tip   Subnets allocated from templates to child networks will never overlap with an existing configured subnet within the organization unless this ability is explicitly enabled by Meraki Support for your organization.

Local overrides like this can be easily performed by simply navigating directly to the child network in question and modifying the configuration in that network, very similar to a network that is not bound to a configuration template. While not every setting can be configured with a local override, many of the most common configurations across devices can be, to still allow for further customization as needed even when attached to a configuration template.

Template Caveats and Limitations

When working with templates, there are some important considerations that you should take into account. One of the most common issues relating to the usage of templates is a result of how the unique subnetting is assigned to template children and how some deployments that employ summary routes can interact.

As part of the validation to ensure that the unique subnets handed out to template child networks are unique and to help keep the process as generally simple and straightforward as possible, the Dashboard automatically checks the current configuration of all related networks in the organization to ensure that no existing subnets or static routes overlap with the newly assigned unique subnet range. This ensures that in a large, AutoVPN-enabled topology, there are no unexpected overlapping routes. As a result, deployments that advertise large summary routes like 10.0.0.0/8 or 172.16.0.0/16 from a VPN hub will experience validation issues when trying to deploy new templated networks with unique subnets if the unique subnet range is contained within the advertised summary route. While this is an entirely valid design and helps to reduce the number of routes advertised to each spoke site, the related validation failure when deploying new sites once this topology is established is clearly an unwanted effect.

Fortunately, for customers who are looking to operate with this design, this strict validation can be modified by Meraki Support to apply only to other networks under the same template, allowing that validation to be partially bypassed and for new template child sites to be successfully deployed with unique subnet ranges inside the advertised summary routes.

In this case, however, it is imperative that you manually monitor and maintain a list of active and VPN-enabled subnets across the organization, as it is possible to see overlapping subnets automatically assigned between networks attached to different templates within the same organization. If an overlapping subnet is assigned and needs to be resolved in this situation, a local override can always be configured for the related network to manually configure a nonoverlapping subnet range for the child network.

One caveat that is specific to MX security appliance hardware and templates is how templates handle logical versus physical port numbering for MX appliances. Over the years, Meraki has developed and released a number of different MX models, each designed with a specific purpose and niche to fill within the market. As time has gone on, these purposes and niches have grown and evolved, and so has the MX product line to match. As a part of this growth and evolution, the physical port numbering scheme for different MX models has also evolved. Because of this, not every MX is consistent when referencing a physical port from the Dashboard configuration. For example, some models of MX use the physical port 1 as the primary uplink, making physical port 2 the first LAN port. Other models have a dedicated and labeled Internet port for the primary uplink, with the labeled port 1 acting as the first LAN port.

Obviously, this can cause some confusion when making a template-level configuration for the MX LAN ports. The important aspect to remember in this situation is that the Dashboard configuration at the template level is always referencing the logical function of a port, not necessarily the physical label. So when configuring port 3 of an MX on a template, that configuration will apply to the logical LAN port 3, whether that be the port physically labeled as port 3 on the device or not.

Pro Tip   You can find a matrix of Dashboard port mappings and their physical port counterparts for every model of MX in the "MX Cold Swap" document at https://documentation.meraki.com. Scroll down to the "Port Mapping for Different MX Models" section.

Another minor caveat to be aware of applies when you are using MV cameras with templates. Currently, Dashboard networks containing MV cameras can be attached to templates as template children and function as expected, with the exception of making template-level configurations for MV cameras. Due to the nature of how MV camera configurations are handled and the uniqueness of each camera and associated configuration within a deployment, all device configurations for the related MV cameras must still be done from within the child network.

The final potential caveat to be aware of applies when unbinding or removing a network from a template. Doing so presents two options for the configuration of the network after being removed from the template: Unbind and Retain Configurations or Unbind and

Clear Configurations. Shown in Figure 4-3, these options allow administrators to unbind a network from a given template and either retain the current template-derived configuration or revert the network configuration to the state prior to binding the network to the template.

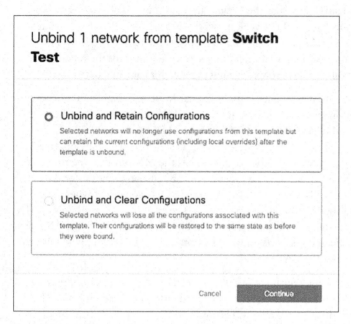

Figure 4-3   *The Configuration Selection View Shown when Unbinding a Child Network from a Template*

Pro Tip   Binding a network to a template always overwrites the current configurations with a new configuration based on the new template.

Template Best Practice Considerations

When working with templates, there are some general best practices to keep in mind. One of the most important general best practices is to remember that templates are designed to facilitate the quick and easy deployment of multiple networks that are intended to have nearly identical configurations. While the option of configuring local overrides does exist, for sites that have noticeable differences in configuration, it's recommended to create separate templates for each type of deployment. This applies not only to large differences, such as completely different site types or sizes, but also to smaller differences, such as minor requirements between groups of locations. Consider the differences between a teleworker deployment and a series of satellite offices. While both are excellent candidates for the use of templates, they most likely should not be contained under the same template.

As an example of a smaller yet no less important difference, in a deployment of satellite offices, the number of VLANs required may differ depending on the need for guest wireless at each location. In this example, the satellite sites could be split across two different templates, with one template configured with an additional VLAN and appropriate firewall rules and filtering for the guest wireless for sites that specifically require it. This allows for simpler management of the deployment, as it reduces the number of local overrides that might need to be configured for child networks and it helps to further centralize the configurations for each site.

Another best practice to keep in mind for large deployments is that, because network-level configurations like the running firmware versions for child networks are also configured at the template level, it may be helpful to split a deployment up across more than one identical template to allow for more granular control over future firmware upgrades. With this approach, you can begin by rolling out a new firmware upgrade to only a subset of sites across the entire deployment to reduce the unintentional impact of a potential issue related to the firmware upgrade or other configuration change.

Additionally, splitting large deployments across multiple templates like this allows for more granular control over the AutoVPN topology for each template and the deployment as a whole. For example, a deployment spanning across the US sites could be split into two templates, one for sites located in the eastern half of the country and one for the western half. From there, the "Eastern" template could have the east hub configured as the primary VPN hub and the west hub configured as a backup VPN hub in case of a failure of the primary, while the "Western" template could be configured to use the same VPN hubs but in opposite priority. This would help ensure that VPN traffic is split more evenly between the two hubs to both reduce average latency for traffic passing through the hubs and reduce the day-to-day load placed on each hub, outside of a situation where one of the hubs becomes unavailable—in that case the sites will automatically fail over to their configured secondary VPN hub until their primary hub becomes available again.

For more information regarding templates, their operation, and other best practice recommendations, visit https://documentation.meraki.com and search using the keyword **template**.

Using Webhooks, Syslog, and SNMP to Trigger Outside Automation

Now that you've been introduced to the use of templates within the Dashboard to help automate network configuration, it's time to start thinking outside the Dashboard. With the help of tools such as webhooks, syslog, and SNMP, you can build custom solutions to trigger automation outside of the Dashboard based on activities and events happening within the Dashboard.

The potential possibilities for automation based on webhooks, syslog, and SNMP are nearly endless due to the widespread adoption of these technologies and their ability to allow easy communication and integration across different platforms. Because of the impossibly wide variety of custom solutions that could be created and used, this book provides only a few brief examples of different ways you can use each technology to trigger some form of outside automation. The specifics of the outside automation and its implementation are left as an exercise for the reader.

Webhooks

Webhooks are possibly the simplest way to implement external automation from the Dashboard. All that is required is a publicly accessible webhook receiver that is able to receive and process webhook messages from the Meraki cloud. As the example in Figure 4-4 shows, automated webhooks contain JSON messages that are both human- and machine-readable and are sent for any alerts that have been configured to generate a webhook on a per-network basis from the Network-wide > Alerts page. Because of the flexibility offered by using JSON messages, there is a huge variety in the way webhook receivers can be implemented. From dedicated monitoring and management systems like SolarWinds, Zendesk, and PagerDuty to more customized solutions like spreadsheets and chatbots, the potential options and possibilities when discussing webhook receivers are nearly as endless as the ways this information can be used after it is received.

```json
{
    "version": "0.1",
    "sharedSecret": "secret",
    "sentAt": "2022-09-07T14:14:14.620233Z",
    "organizationId": "2930410",
    "organizationName": "My organization",
    "organizationUrl": "https://dashboard.meraki.com/o/VjjsAd/manage/organization/overview",
    "networkId": "N_24329156",
    "networkName": "Main Office",
    "networkUrl": "https://n1.meraki.com//n//manage/nodes/list",
    "networkTags": [],
    "deviceSerial": "Q234-ABCD-5678",
    "deviceMac": "00:11:22:33:44:55",
    "deviceName": "My access point",
    "deviceUrl": "https://n1.meraki.com//n//manage/nodes/new_list/000000000000",
    "deviceTags": [
        "tag1",
        "tag2"
    ],
    "deviceModel": "MR",
    "alertId": "0000000000000000",
    "alertType": "APs came up",
    "alertTypeId": "started_reporting",
    "alertLevel": "informational",
    "occurredAt": "2018-02-11T00:00:00.123450Z",
    "alertData": {},
    "enrollmentString": "my-enrollment-string",
    "notes": "Additional description of the network",
    "productTypes": [
        "appliance",
        "switch",
        "wireless"
    ]
}
```

Figure 4-4 *An Example of Webhook JSON Data Alerting That an AP Came Up*

You can use webhooks purely for external logging of alerts or you can use them for automation by configuring the webhook receiver to take additional actions after processing webhooks that meet a defined criterion. Webhooks can be particularly useful for defining more specific alert criteria than what's available on the Dashboard directly. For example, you could configure a webhook receiver to automatically begin sending alert messages to on-call staff only if multiple sites report a given event within a specified timeframe, such as multiple devices offline across sites or multiple VPN tunnel drops within a few minutes. Or, you could configure a webhook receiver to help enhance change management control by monitoring all configuration changes across all networks but only sending additional alerts through Webex Teams when configuration settings are changed for specific, potentially sensitive networks.

You can find more detailed information regarding webhooks both at https://developer.cisco.com/meraki/webhooks/ and in the article "Webhooks" at https://documentation.meraki.com.

Note The "Additional Reading" section at the end of this chapter provides the full URL for every article that is cross-referenced in this chapter. Alternatively, you can search for the article title at https://documentation.meraki.com to locate it.

Syslog

Similar to using webhooks, you can use syslog messages to trigger outside automation based on network events and alerts. The primary differences between using webhooks and syslog for automation are the types of alerts that are sent and the source of the messages.

Unlike webhooks, which are sent by the Meraki cloud over the Internet to a publicly accessible receiver, syslog messages are generated directly from the device and can be sent to either a publicly reachable syslog server or to an entirely internal or local logging location, depending on your needs and deployment.

While webhooks can be individually configured for each alert type, syslog messages are grouped into roles of message types that can be configured per network. Typically, these roles are focused on reporting Event Log–generating events. For example, some of the common syslog groups are Security Events, which will generate a syslog message when an IDS/IPS- or AMP-related event is triggered, and Air Marshall Events, which will generate a syslog message whenever an MR access point has an Air Marshall event logged, such as a channel change due to a DFS event.

Other, more generic, event-based syslog roles can also be configured, such as Security Appliance Event Log, which will simply report every Event Log–generating event for MX security appliances in the chosen network, and Wireless Event Log, which performs the same function but for all MR access points in the network.

The following is an example syslog message reporting a new DHCP lease, including timestamp, client identifiers, and additional details about the lease in question:

```
Sep 12 16:05:15 192.168.10.1 1 1599865515.687171503 MX84 events dhcp
lease of ip 192.168.10.68 from server mac E0:CB:BC:0F:XX:XX for client
mac 8C:16:45:XX:XX:XX from router 192.168.10.1 on subnet 255.255.255.0
with dns 8.8.8.8, 8.8.4.4
```

One option available through syslog messages that is not available via webhooks is the ability to configure roles for either Flows or URLs, which provide significantly more visibility into the operation of a network and the activities of its clients, but at the expense of a large amount of data being generated in real time. For example, both the Flow and URL roles will actively report every new IP session or HTTP GET, respectively, that is observed by an MX security appliance for any client on the network. While this clearly provides a wealth of insight and information into the activities and traffic patterns present on the network, it can also generate a very large amount of data for even a relatively quiet network.

The following is an example syslog message demonstrating a new Flow being reported:

```
1374543986.038687615 MX84 flows src=192.168.1.186 dst=8.8.8.8
mac=58:1F:AA:CE:61:F2 protocol=udp sport=55719 dport=53 pattern:
allow all
```

Here is an example syslog message demonstrating a new HTTP GET request being reported:

```
1374543213.342705328 MX84 urls src=192.168.1.186:63735
dst=69.58.188.40:80 mac=58:1F:AA:CE:61:F2 request: GET https://www...
```

With the use of these roles, you can create powerful automation based on simple triggers such as when a client attempts more than a specific number of blocked requests within a period of time, or multiple requests to certain destinations.

For more information about the specifics of Meraki's syslog implementation, including configuration guides and full examples of each syslog message, visit https://documentation.meraki.com and search using the keyword **syslog**, or visit https://documentation.meraki.com/General_Administration/Monitoring_and_Reporting/Meraki_Device_Reporting_-_Syslog%2C_SNMP%2C_and_API.

SNMP

SNMP is also a potential option that can be employed for automation with any Meraki platform. One notable difference between SNMP and webhooks or syslog is that when using SNMP, you have the choice to poll directly to a local interface on a device or to poll out to the Meraki Cloud Controller, depending on your use case and the specific information you're looking to acquire.

When polling out to the Meraki Cloud Controller, you need to use the proprietary Meraki Cloud Controller MIB, which you can download from any network after enabling SNMP for that network. This requires the network management system (NMS) to be able to reach out to the Meraki cloud over the public Internet, but it also provides access to much of the device-reported data from just a single polled entity, such as (but not limited to) the following:

- Device serial/MAC
- Device status (online/offline/alerting)
- Device last contacted at time
- Device public IP address
- Device connected client count
- Device interface list
- Device interface stats (SentPkts/RecvPkts/SentBytes/RecvBytes)
- Configured VLAN details
- Configured SSID details

When polling directly to a device, you can obtain additional, more detailed data from the device level through the support of the industry-standard IF-MIB and SNMPv2-MIBs. This requires polling to multiple different entities because, unlike polling out to the Meraki Cloud Controller, polling directly to a device requires each related device be polled directly. This method, however, offers some additional advantages, such as the ability to perform all polling through locally controlled network paths and the additional data points provided through the use of the industry-standard IF-MIB and SNMPv2-MIBs.

SNMP is excellent for providing additional visibility and monitoring for a network or deployment with the use of an NMS, but where SNMP really comes into play in regard to automation is through the use of SNMP traps. Unlike traditional SNMP polling, which is relatively passive and requires the NMS to reach out to an endpoint to get updated information, SNMP traps allow for active notification and alerting of events through the use of SNMP. When configured to do so, the Meraki Cloud Controller will generate an SNMP trap to be sent to the configured NMS over the Internet, allowing for real-time alerting of events such as (but not limited to) the following:

- Uplink status change
- Device becomes reachable/unreachable from the Meraki cloud
- Port connected/disconnected
- Port speed change
- Port UDLD errors
- Configuration settings changed
- Radius server unreachable

- Warm spare failover

- Client IP conflict

By integrating SNMP traps, you can use SNMP in conjunction with a publicly accessible NMS to provide more active alerting regarding device-level events as they happen and trigger additional alerting or actions based on received traps without worrying about polling intervals or other caveats that could arise when using SNMP without traps configured.

For more detailed information about using and configuring SNMP and SNMP traps with the Meraki platform, visit https://documentation.meraki.com and search using the keyword **SNMP**.

Dashboard API

All the forms of automation discussed thus far rely heavily on an outside framework to process information generated by either a device or the Meraki cloud and trigger some form of external action. With the Dashboard API, you can take this concept and expand it beyond just monitoring and alerting to start actively reacting and responding based on the information received, or to automate tasks that would otherwise require manual interaction with the Dashboard UI, such as creating new deployments or modifying existing configurations.

In addition to the widely used Dashboard API, several other popular, platform-specific APIs are available through the Meraki platform, such as the Scanning API, which provides Wi-Fi and Bluetooth Low Energy (BLE) location analytics data gathered from Meraki access points, and the MV Sense API, which is used to aggregate people and vehicle detection data from MV cameras. These APIs all operate in the same way as the general Dashboard API, but they are able to perform more specialized interactions with the Meraki platform to take advantage of additional, product- and platform-specific features that are outside the scope of the standard Dashboard API.

Pro Tip   The Meraki Developer Hub (https://developer.cisco.com/meraki/) offers multiple beginner-level and in-depth tutorials for the Dashboard API as well as other APIs available with the Meraki platform.

What Is the Dashboard API and How Is It Used?

The Dashboard API is likely the most powerful form of automation available for the Meraki platform due to its availability of options and ease of integration with external solutions.

As a result of how the Dashboard has been designed, nearly every action in the Dashboard can be performed through the use of the Dashboard API. In fact, many of the actions performed within the Dashboard UI utilize the same Dashboard API endpoints on the back end to perform the change. This design supports a nearly limitless range of interactions with the Dashboard through any custom solution that is able to use REST API to interact with the Meraki cloud platform.

With the use of the Dashboard API, the potential for automation of nearly any task with your solution of choice is only a few clicks away once API access to an organization has been configured. With the ability to either pull information down from the Dashboard or push changes back up, the Dashboard API can be used for basic data gathering and monitoring, similar to SNMP, where API requests are made out to the Meraki Cloud Controller to return either device or network statistics or current device or network configurations. However, the Dashboard API can also be used to enable powerful automation that can actively respond to changing conditions and push changes to the Dashboard in response to those conditions. The coming sections demonstrate just a few ways the Dashboard API can be used, covering several simple examples of automation that can be accomplished through the use of the API.

Pro Tip   API calls are rate limited to ten calls per second, per organization. Using Action Batches allows for combining of multiple API calls into a single call, helping to avoid rate-limiting issues.

Before the Dashboard API can be used, it must be enabled on a per-organization basis, then each account within each organization must generate its own unique API key for that organization. For accounts that have access to multiple organizations, API access must be individually enabled and configured for each organization, then the API keys must be generated for that account within each organization.

API Tips and Tricks

When you use the Dashboard API, there are several important things that you should keep in mind. Primarily, any account that has API access enabled has the same level of access within a given organization through the API as when navigating the Dashboard UI directly. This means that the API key associated with that account is just as valuable as the username/password for that same account (if not more valuable), because once configured, API access does not require additional forms of authentication (like 2FA) before changes can be made. As a result, a compromised account with API access or a compromised API key can be used to wreak havoc on a much larger scale, and in a shorter timeframe, than can an account without access to the API or other automation tools.

Additionally, due to the nature of the API and related automation flows, the potential to make an unintended change as a result of a wrong network or device ID is greater, which can then be magnified to a much larger scope through the use of automation than if the accidental change were made to just a single network or device from within the UI. For this reason, it's common for heavy API users to create separate accounts specifically for the use of the API. By creating accounts that are used only for API access, you can reduce the chance of a personal account being compromised and leaking access to the API, or potentially reduce the impact of a compromised API key through the use of administrative restrictions and scoping on the API account.

For example, if there are ten personal Organization Administrator accounts for use within the UI and two dedicated API accounts, one configured with read-only access and the other configured for full read/write access to the entire organization, the risk of a compromised API key is reduced in the event an administrator's personal account is compromised in any way. Additionally, should the need to terminate one of the personal administrator accounts arise for any reason, this allows any existing API workflows to remain unaltered, as they can continue to use the dedicated API account and associated API keys without having to update an existing API key to reflect the new account.

By separating the API access into different accounts/keys, one for read-only access and one for read/write access, you can again reduce the scope of potential impact if the read-only API key is compromised. This can be useful for large companies in which multiple accounts or processes may require read access to obtain information about an organization, network, or device via the API, but only select users or processes should have the ability to push changes. By restricting the more commonly used read-only API key, you further reduce the chance of a major outage caused by unexpected or unauthorized changes via the API.

More details about the operation of the Dashboard API, as well as sample projects and tutorials to gain experience working with the API, are available at https://developer.cisco.com/meraki/api-latest/.

Dashboard API Examples

This section presents two Dashboard API examples:

- Automated API-based organization status
- Automated MR naming based on upstream switch

Each of these examples assumes that the necessary initial API setup and access for the relevant organization has been completed. You can find details on enabling API access for an organization at https://documentation.meraki.com by searching using the keyword **API**.

The following examples are designed to demonstrate the power of the Dashboard API through just a few simple steps and can be applied with any API solution, from simple, handmade scripts to popular platforms such as Postman or any other REST API–capable solution.

Note that when running these API calls, you need to replace the relevant details such as API keys, organization IDs, device IDs, and so forth with your own data for your account and devices. The following sections use example details that have been sanitized for the purpose of explanation.

Automated API-based Organization Status

To start, you need to determine the organization IDs for the organization you want to monitor. You can do so by sending a GET request to the endpoint, as shown in Example 4-1, which will return a list of organization details for all organizations the related API key has access to, as shown in Example 4-2.

Example 4-1   *Curl Request to Get a List of Organizations This User Has Access To*

```
curl -L --request GET \
--url https://api.meraki.com/api/v1/organizations \
--header 'Content-Type: application/json' \
--header 'Accept: application/json' \
--header 'X-Cisco-Meraki-API-Key: 75dd5334befXXXXXXXXXXXXX163c0a3fa0b5ca6'
```

Example 4-2   *Curl Request Response Containing Organization Details for Each Organization This User Has Access To*

```
{
        "id": "{ORG_ID_HERE}",
        "name": "Meraki Sandbox Org",
        "url": "https://n1001.meraki.com/o/7XXXXXrb/manage/organization/overview",
        "api": {
            "enabled": true
        },
        "licensing": {
            "model": "co-term"
        },
        "cloud": {
            "region": {
                "name": "North America"
            }
        },
        "management": {
            "details": []
        }
    }
```

Once you have determined the organization ID that you want to use, you can make another GET request (see Example 4-3) to return the current device statuses and details of every device in that organization (see Example 4-4).

Example 4-3 *Curl Request to Get Device Statuses for All Devices in the Chosen Organization*

```
curl -L --request GET \
--url https://api.meraki.com/api/v1/organizations/{ORG_ID_HERE}/devices/statuses \
--header 'Content-Type: application/json' \
--header 'Accept: application/json' \
--header 'X-Cisco-Meraki-API-Key: 75dd5334befXXXXXXXXXXXXXX163c0a3fa0b5ca6'
```

Example 4-4 *Curl Request Response Containing Device Details for Every Device in the Chosen Organization*

```
[
    {
        "name": "Bridge Gateway",
        "serial": "Q2BK-XXXX-ABCD",
        "mac": "88:15:44:55:66:77",
        "publicIp": "74.84.202.49",
        "networkId": "N_6558XXXXX850059",
        "status": "online",
        "lastReportedAt": "2023-05-12T15:43:19.453000Z",
        "productType": "wireless",
        "model": "MR32",
        "tags": [
            "Bridge",
            "Gateway"
        ],
        "lanIp": "192.168.1.5",
        "gateway": "192.168.1.1",
        "ipType": "dhcp",
        "primaryDns": "192.168.1.1",
        "secondaryDns": null
    },
    {
        "name": "Attic Camera",
        "serial": "Q2BV-YYYY-ABCD",
        "mac": "e0:cb:aa:bb:cc:dd",
        "publicIp": "74.84.202.49",
        "networkId": "L_65583XXXXX5845837",
        "status": "online",
        "lastReportedAt": "2023-05-12T15:43:32.448000Z",
        "productType": "camera",
        "model": "MV21",
        "tags": [],
```

```
        "lanIp": "172.16.1.5",
        "gateway": "172.16.1.1",
        "ipType": "dhcp",
        "primaryDns": "8.8.8.8",
        "secondaryDns": "8.8.4.4"
    }
]
```

From there, you simply need to parse the responses and record the status of each device listed. You can do this in many different ways, but for purposes of demonstration, Example 4-5 shows what the parsed response output may look like using Regex, a popular method of parsing JSON responses.

Example 4-5 *Parsed Responses to Show Only Relevant Details for the Current Device Status*

```
"name": "Bridge Gateway"
"serial": "Q2BK-XXXX-ABCD"
"status": "online"
"lastReportedAt": "2023-05-12T15:43:19"

"name": "Attic Camera"
"serial": "Q2BV-YYYY-ABCD"
"status": "online"
"lastReportedAt": "2023-05-12T15:43:32"
```

Once complete, the remaining portion of the automation would require configuring or scripting this series of commands and actions to take place at an automated interval that best fits the current deployment and monitoring needs. This would allow for a detailed historical record of every device status in the organization that is stored and accessible outside of the Dashboard UI.

Automated MR Naming Based on Upstream Switch

This example demonstrates how easy it can be to automatically update a device name to reflect the location of that device in the network. Similar to the previous example that required a known organization ID to be used to get the status of devices within the organization, in this example you first need to determine the serial number of the device or devices in question. You can accomplish this either through an API call to list the devices within a given network or by loading a predefined list of serial numbers that should be modified.

Once you have confirmed the serial number that should be updated, you can make your first call to the device in question to return the LLDP/CDP information for a connected port. Examples 4-6 and 4-7 demonstrate using a basic MR access point, so only a single LAN port is returned.

Example 4-6 *Curl Request to Get the Recorded LLDP and CDP Neighbor Information for Ports from a Specific Device*

```
curl -L --request GET \
--url https://api.meraki.com/api/v1/devices/Q2BK-XXXX-ABCD/lldpCdp \
--header 'Content-Type: application/json' \
--header 'Accept: application/json' \
--header 'X-Cisco-Meraki-API-Key: 75dd5334befXXXXXXXXXXXXXX163c0a3fa0b5ca6'
```

Example 4-7 *Curl Request Response Containing the CDP and LLDP Neighbor Details for Each Port of the Device*

```
{
"sourceMac": "00:11:22:33:44:55",
    "ports": {
        "1": {
            "cdp": {
            "deviceId": "e0553dabcdef",
            "portId": "Port 11",
            "address": "00:11:22:33:44:55",
            "sourcePort": "1"
            },
            "lldp": {
            "systemName": "MS350-24X-1",
            "portId": "11",
            "managementAddress": "00:11:22:33:44:55",
            "sourcePort": "1"
            }
        }
    }
}
```

Now that you have obtained the LLDP/CDP details for the LAN port of the AP, you can parse that response to extract the upstream device name and connected port number, as shown in Example 4-8. In this instance, the LLDP data provides a more human-friendly device name, so use that.

Example 4-8 *Extracted Output Showing the Upstream Device Name and Connected Port*

```
"systemName": "MS350-24X-1"
"portId": "11"
```

This gives a new device name for the AP of "Bridge Gateway - MS350-24X-1 / 11."; From here, you can perform a GET request for the remaining device attributes to ensure that all the related details are up to date. Examples 4-9 and 4-10 show the related API call and response to retrieve the device details for your access point, ensuring you are working with your intended device.

Example 4-9 *Curl Request to Return and Confirm the Details of the Selected Access Point*

```
curl -L --request GET \
--url https://api.meraki.com/api/v1/devices/Q2BK-XXXX-ABCD \
--header 'Content-Type: application/json' \
--header 'Accept: application/json' \
--header 'X-Cisco-Meraki-API-Key: 75dd5334befXXXXXXXXXXXXX163c0a3fa0b5ca6'
```

Example 4-10 *Curl Request Response Showing the AP Details*

```
{
    "lat": 43.468725028745396,
    "lng": -72.17831212980673,
    "address": "",
    "serial": "Q2BK-XXXX-ABCD",
    "mac": "88:15:44:55:66:77",
    "lanIp": "192.168.1.5",
    "notes": "",
    "tags": [
        "Bridge",
        "Gateway"
    ],
    "url": "https://n1001.meraki.com/Meraki-Wireless/n/Itjxxxxx/manage/nodes/new_
list/14XXXXX5784",
    "networkId": "N_6558XXXXXX50059",
    "name": "Bridge Gateway",
    "model": "MR32",
    "firmware": "wireless-26-8-3",
    "floorPlanId": null
}
```

Example 4-11 shows the API request sent to configure the new device name for the access point based on the current network location and upstream device.

Example 4-11   *Curl Request to Update the Device Attributes and Rename the Access Point*

```
curl -L --request PUT \
--url https://api.meraki.com/api/v1/devices/Q2BK-XXXX-ABCD \
--header 'Content-Type: application/json' \
--header 'Accept: application/json' \
--header 'X-Cisco-Meraki-API-Key: 75dd5334befXXXXXXXXXXXXX163c0a3fa0b5ca6' \
--data '{
    "name": "Bridge Gateway - MS350-24X-1 / 11",
    "lat": 43.468725028745396,
    "lng": -72.17831212980673,
    "serial": "Q2BK-XXXX-ABCD",
    "mac": "88:15:44:55:66:77",
    "tags": [ "Bridge","Gateway" ],
    "address": "",
    "moveMapMarker": false
}'
```

While this example only refers to a single device, you can easily extend it to multiple devices by providing a list of serial numbers and iterating through this process for each serial number.

Taking this one step further, you could easily configure an additional level of automation that would retrieve the serial number and current device name of all APs, for example, then go through the same steps used in the previous two API examples to compare the current device name with the current LLDP/CDP data from the device and, if necessary, update the device name to reflect the new LLDP/CDP data and location. You could configure this to run automatically once per week or at a similar limited interval, with a manual list of devices being run on a new deployment or when replacing a failed device as needed.

MT Automation

The Meraki MT line of devices is a family of cloud-managed, IoT environmental sensors that are capable of monitoring and alerting through the Meraki Dashboard, allowing further visibility into the physical state of a deployment through the use of the Meraki cloud platform. The MT series of sensors is capable of monitoring various environmental statuses such as temperature, humidity, air quality, door open/close, and more. Through these sensors, you can utilize Dashboard alerts to trigger outside automation, as discussed previously, or you can utilize a device like the MT30 Smart Automation Button to trigger specialized automation from directly within the Dashboard.

Dashboard-Based Automation

When using the MT30 Smart Automation Button, you can configure unique automation actions from the Dashboard based on a simple button press. Actions that can be triggered by a single button push include generating custom SMS or email notifications, recording a snapshot from a specified MV camera, toggling configurations like SSIDs or switchport access, or generating custom webhook alerts.

This configuration is accomplished by defining automation rules from within the Dashboard for each MT30 automation button. You can configure a trigger to be as simple as any press of the button or to be more precise, such as requiring a long press (1+ seconds) to trigger the action, which helps to reduce accidental triggers. Figure 4-5 shows an example of the Dashboard trigger selection options.

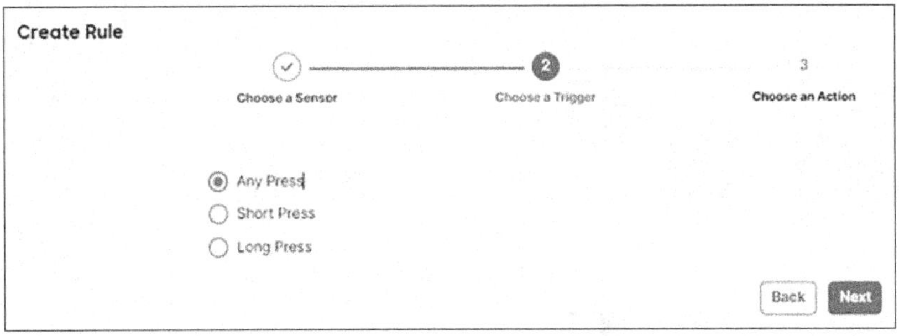

Figure 4-5   *The Choose a Trigger Options in the Automation Rule Creation Modal in the Dashboard*

After you define a trigger, you need to define the automation action for the trigger. This is easily configurable from a list provided when navigating through the rule creation module in the Dashboard, as shown in Figure 4-6.

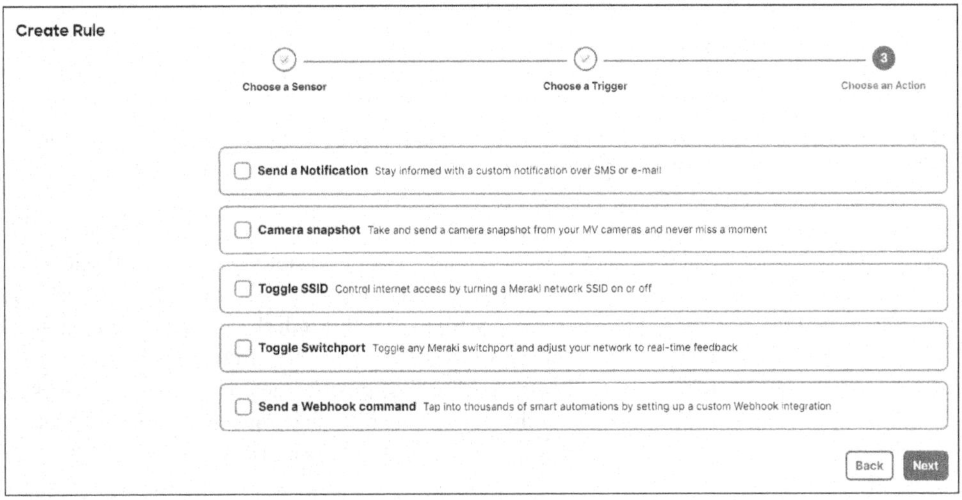

Figure 4-6   *The Choose an Action Options in the Automation Rule Creation Modal in the Dashboard*

For example, if you're configuring a rule to trigger a snapshot from an MV camera on a long press, first choose the **Long Press** trigger and then choose the **Camera Snapshot** action. As you can see in Figure 4-7, you can select up to five cameras to record a snapshot when triggered and you can then configure a custom list of recipients for those snapshots.

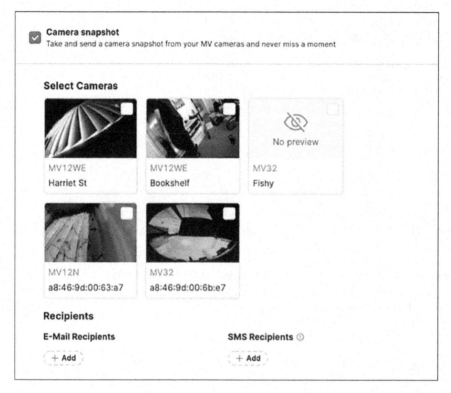

Figure 4-7   *The Camera Selection and Recipient Configuration View in the Automation Rule Creation Modal in the Dashboard*

Alternatively, you could configure the rule to trigger a custom webhook notification, in which case you can create a custom webhook message to suit your needs and select which webhook receivers should receive the alert, as shown in Figure 4-8. This option enables you to create essentially entirely custom alerts through the Meraki cloud platform, as the contents of the webhook alert could contain nearly anything and can be sent to nearly any webhook receiver, allowing for limitless possibilities. This allows for quick and easy integration with popular third-party automation platforms like IFTTT (If This Then That) or any other platform capable of receiving and parsing custom webhook notifications.

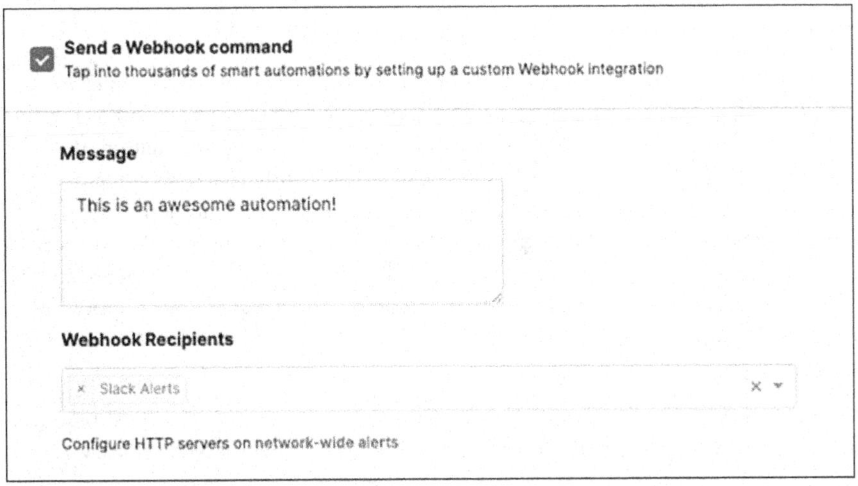

Figure 4-8 *The Custom Webhook Command View in the Automation Rule Creation Modal in the Dashboard*

Once you have defined the automation rule, the last step is to assign devices to an automation rule. As demonstrated in Figure 4-9, this is where you determine which devices will trigger specific rules when activated. This allows you to create custom automation rules quickly and easily from within the Dashboard and assign and reconfigure them as needed to best suit your current requirements.

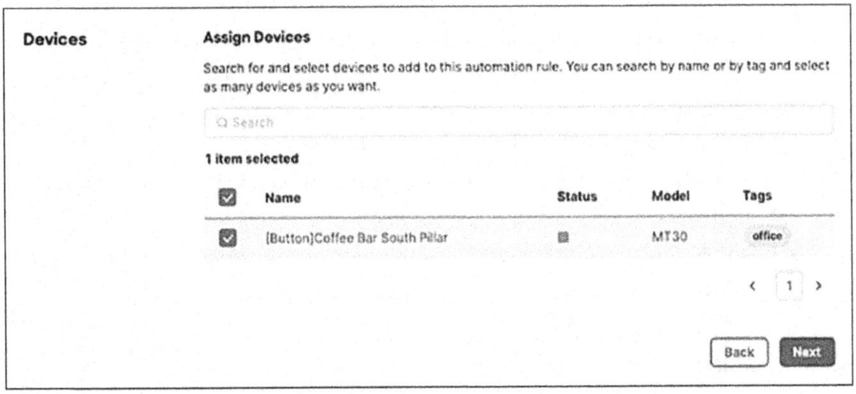

Figure 4-9 *The Device Assignment View in the Automation Rule Creation Modal in the Dashboard*

The MT series of sensors is discussed in more detail in Chapter 9, "IoT Design." You can find additional information regarding using MT sensors for automation at https://documentation.meraki.com by accessing the "MT – Sensors" section on the main page.

Summary

As you can see, the Meraki platform offers some powerful options when it comes to automation, both inside and outside of the Dashboard UI. From templates and MT automation rules to syslog, SNMP, and webhooks for triggering external automation, the potential possibilities are endless. While this chapter only lightly touched on the potential possibilities these types of automation can provide, the implementation of these automation capabilities can be as unique and varied as the number of Meraki platform deployments, enabling Meraki customers to tailor the operation of the Dashboard to best match their workflows and to spend time working on the tasks that are most important instead of dedicating resources to performing simple, repetitive tasks related to maintaining or deploying a site.

In the next chapter, you will encounter some of the more platform-specific best practices to keep in mind when planning the configuration and deployment of MX security appliances.

Additional Reading

Managing Multiple Networks with Configuration Templates: https://documentation.meraki.com/General_Administration/Templates_and_Config_Sync/Managing_Multiple_Networks_with_Configuration_Templates

Meraki Device Reporting – Syslog, SNMP, and API: https://documentation.meraki.com/General_Administration/Monitoring_and_Reporting/Meraki_Device_Reporting_-_Syslog%2C_SNMP%2C_and_API

Webhooks: https://documentation.meraki.com/General_Administration/Other_Topics/Webhooks

Cisco Meraki Dashboard API: https://documentation.meraki.com/General_Administration/Other_Topics/Cisco_Meraki_Dashboard_API

MT Automation Builder: https://documentation.meraki.com/MT/MT_General_Articles/MT_Automation_Builder

Meraki Dashboard API: https://developer.cisco.com/meraki/api-latest/

Meraki Webhooks: https://developer.cisco.com/meraki/webhooks/

Meraki Alert Webhooks: https://developer.cisco.com/learning/labs/dne-meraki-webhooks/introduction/

Meraki Location Scanning API: https://developer.cisco.com/learning/labs/dne-meraki-location-scanning-python/launch-the-location-scanning-api-receiver/

Meraki Captive Portal: https://developer.cisco.com/learning/labs/dne-meraki-captive-portal/introduction-to-the-meraki-captive-portal-lab/

Meraki Vision (MV) Sense: https://developer.cisco.com/learning/labs/dne-meraki-mvsense/introduction/

Chapter 5

MX and MG Best Practices

The previous chapters focused on how Cisco Meraki utilizes the power of the cloud through the Meraki Dashboard to provide a powerful and flexible interface that enables administrators to more easily deploy, monitor, and operate their networks. In this chapter and the next several chapters, the focus shifts to the major product lines available from Meraki, providing an overview of the product lines themselves, their most important and overlooked features, and some product-specific best practices to keep in mind when deploying various Meraki products.

This chapter and Chapter 6, "MX SD-WAN Best Practices," start at the edge, focusing on the Meraki MX security appliance (aka WAN appliance) and Meraki MG cellular gateway lines. Working our way down the stack, Chapter 7, "Meraki Switching Design and Recommendations," covers the Meraki MS line of switches, Chapter 8, "Introduction to Meraki MR Access Points," focuses on Meraki MR access points, and Chapter 9, "IoT Design," presents Meraki MV cameras and the Meraki MT line of IoT sensors.

This chapter describes the basic operation of MX security appliances, including routing, security integrations, and general Auto VPN deployment and operation, and then briefly covers the MG line of cellular gateways. Chapter 6 is a continuation of the MX focus, specifically on the more advanced SD-WAN feature set that operates on top of the basic Auto VPN fabric.

Note The features and designs discussed in this chapter refer to MX security appliances. However, note that many features discussed in this chapter are also available in the Meraki Z-series teleworker gateway.

The MX security appliance line is Meraki's second-oldest product line and is commonly classified as a next-generation stateful firewall. The MX line of devices is capable of both basic stateful Layer 3 access control for clients and more advanced filtering, including HTTP content filtering and intrusion detection and prevention system (IDS/IPS) services.

Additionally, MX devices are able to act as VPN hubs as part of Meraki's Auto VPN solution to provide connectivity, as well as more advanced services, to clients across sites and locations.

MX Scaling

When designing a deployment and determining the appropriate model of edge device to choose, there are multiple aspects to take into consideration regarding not only the current requirements of a site but also the potential future requirements.

Aspects that directly impact which specific model of hardware to choose include the number of local and remote users that are expected, the number of VPN tunnels that may be needed to access remote resources, the expected traffic mix, the required throughput, and any necessary security features or other advanced features.

For example, a small satellite office with fewer than ten users that requires only a single VPN tunnel back to the HQ hub and only to access internal resources would likely be able to be supported by a base model MX. However, if that same office required strict traffic filtering and security policies alongside additional VPN tunnels to access other remotely hosted resources across different locations that involve frequent large file transfers (such as in the medical field or similar), they may need to consider installing a larger model of MX that will be better suited to running the additional load caused by more advanced security features like Advanced Malware Protection (AMP) and IPS in conjunction with the higher VPN-related traffic load.

Luckily, Meraki offers a wide variety of security appliance models to adequately take on nearly any use case, from the Z-series teleworker gateways, designed for remote workers with limited requirements, to the fully featured top-end models of MX security appliances, designed for high-capacity workloads.

You can find specifics on individual MX/Z-series models and their capabilities by reviewing the document "MX Sizing Principles" (available at https://meraki.cisco.com/product-collateral/mx-sizing-guide/) or by contacting a Meraki sales representative.

Deployment Modes

When deploying an MX security appliance, two modes of operation are available: Routed mode and Passthrough or VPN Concentrator mode. To configure the mode of operation, navigate to the **Security & SD-WAN > Addressing & VLANs** page (where you can also choose the client tracking method).

Routed Mode

When configured in Routed mode, the MX acts as a typical L3 edge firewall, routing traffic directly between locally defined or VPN-accessible subnets and performing network address translation (NAT) on all Internet-bound traffic to the WAN IP of the device. This is the default mode of operation and provides access to the full suite of available features on the platform.

Passthrough or VPN Concentrator Mode

Passthrough or VPN Concentrator mode allows the MX to either be used as a one-armed VPN concentrator or placed inline as a transparent L2 bridge between the WAN and LAN ports. When configured for this mode, the MX will not route Layer 3 traffic or perform any sort of NAT for traffic passing through the MX.

When configured in Passthrough or VPN Concentrator mode, the following features (and more) are still able to be implemented and will affect client traffic passing through the MX:

- Layer 3 and Layer 7 firewall rules
- Traffic shaping rules
- Traffic analysis
- Intrusion detection
- Security and content filtering
- Client VPN
- Site-to-site VPN (including both Meraki Auto VPN and non-Meraki VPN)

For more information about deployment modes for MX, visit https://documentation.meraki.com and search using the keyword **MX Deployment**.

Note The "Additional Reading" section at the end of this chapter provides the full URL for every article that is cross-referenced in this chapter. Alternatively, you can search for the article title at https://documentation.meraki.com to locate it.

Security

There are a number of potential security features and integrations that can be configured for MX devices. Some of these are available for all customers, like HTTP content filtering, while others such as Advanced Malware Protection (AMP) require an additional Advanced Security license to be applied to the network in the Dashboard. You can find more information about different licensing tiers and Meraki licensing in general in Appendix A, "Cisco Meraki Licensing," or by going to https://documentation.meraki.com and searching using the keyword **license**.

Through proper planning and configuration, you can use these security features to create a layered approach to security, ensuring coverage from multiple potential attack vectors and creating a "security onion" that is significantly more effective at protecting users and data than any single feature.

L3/L7 Firewall

As previously mentioned, the MX line of security appliances is capable of L3 stateful access control in addition to more advanced inspection and filtering. Alongside the standard Layer 3 IP-based access control lists, which support both IP- and FQDN-based rules as well as policy object groups, MX security appliances also offer industry-leading application-based firewall services for more advanced control and filtering of network traffic.

The Meraki platform leverages its capability to directly integrate with established Cisco technologies to include the powerful Cisco Network Based Application Recognition (NBAR) technology in Meraki devices. This allows for the creation of powerful Layer 7 firewall rules (see Figure 5-1) that can be tied to more than 1,500 different web applications to allow for more granular and enhanced application-based filtering than ever before.

Figure 5-1   *Example Layer 7 Firewall Configuration*

In addition to the NBAR-powered application-based Layer 7 firewall rules, the Dashboard also offers the ability to configure geolocation-based Layer 7 rules to deny traffic to/from (or NOT to/from) specified countries based on geolocated IPs. This ability provides a simple and easy-to-configure method of tightly restricting traffic to or from unwanted destinations without requiring a large manual ruleset or other outside integration.

Additionally, as with nearly all edge firewalls, MX devices are able to be configured with inbound forwarding rules for port forwarding, 1:1, or 1-Many NAT.

HTTP Content Filtering (TALOS)

Alongside the L3/L7-based filtering, MX security appliances offer the ability to implement HTTP content filtering that utilizes Cisco TALOS Intelligence for URL classification. By utilizing Cisco Talos Intelligence, Meraki helps to ensure that URL classifications are as up to date as possible while offering a wide variety of content categories to choose from, allowing your filtering configuration to be tailored to the specific needs of any deployment. Figure 5-2 shows the Dashboard view of the Content Filtering page, which you can access via **Security & SD-WAN > Content Filtering**. This feature also allows for a more consistent configuration across Cisco platforms, simplifying your deployment planning.

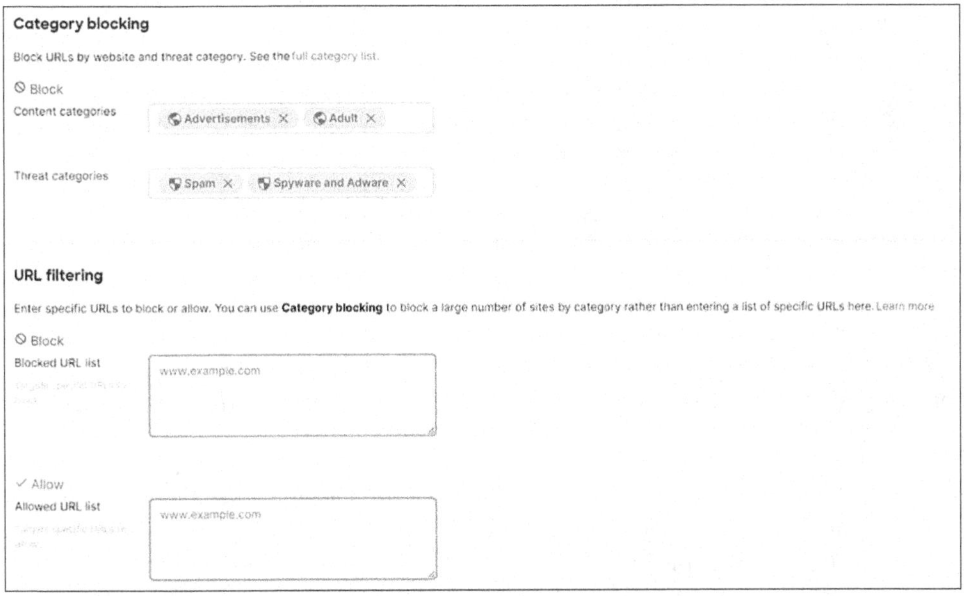

Figure 5-2   *Content Filtering Configuration Page on the Dashboard*

The Content Filtering page is designed to make URL lookups and blocking easily and quickly configurable. By integrating URL lookups with Cisco TALOS directly into the Content Filtering page, the Dashboard makes it easy to look up individual URLs and determine the TALOS threat rating as well as the categorization of that URL.

Cisco AMP

The Meraki Advanced Malware Protection feature, accessible from the Security & SD-WAN > Threat Protection page (see Figure 5-3) utilizes the Cisco AMP cloud and actively monitors and scans HTTP file downloads to help identify and stop malware or other malicious software from being downloaded to clients within the network. With the ability to provide both real-time and retroactive alerts for potentially malicious file downloads, the Meraki AMP feature can provide valuable edge security to help protect clients and prevent malware from being introduced to your network.

Pro Tip   Although most modern applications have moved to using HTTPS, there are still many functions on the Internet and applications running HTTP only. Do not let your guard down—cover your bases with AMP.

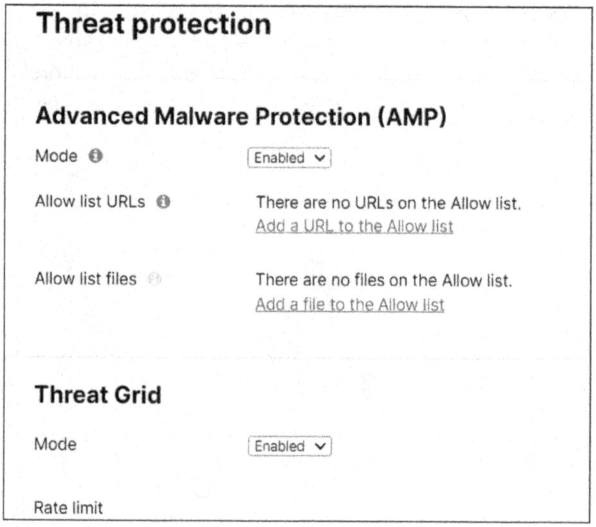

Threat protection

Advanced Malware Protection (AMP)

Mode ⓘ   [Enabled ⌄]

Allow list URLs ⓘ   There are no URLs on the Allow list.
                             Add a URL to the Allow list

Allow list files   There are no files on the Allow list.
                             Add a file to the Allow list

Threat Grid

Mode   [Enabled ⌄]

Rate limit

Figure 5-3   *Cisco AMP Configuration Section of the Threat Protection Page in the Dashboard*

AMP functions by identifying a downloaded file and comparing that with known file dispositions received from the AMP cloud. If a file received a Malicious disposition in the AMP cloud, then the MX will block that file download. If the disposition returns Clean or Unknown, then the download will be allowed. In the event that an Unknown file is downloaded and then later is determined to be malicious, a retroactive alert is issued by the Dashboard, including any related client details, and any future downloads of that file will be blocked.

In addition to the basic AMP functionality, if a Cisco Threat Grid license is available, then Cisco Threat Grid integration can be configured. This allows an MX to upload qualified Unknown disposition files to Threat Grid for analysis, where a report is generated based on the submitted files, including a threat score for the file in question. This allows for even greater visibility into file downloads and file dispositions, potentially allowing for an even quicker response in the event of a previously unknown threat.

IDS/IPS

Alongside Cisco AMP, you can configure the IDS/IPS feature set for even further security monitoring. When enabled, the IDS/IPS feature set inspects all routed traffic passing through the MX while looking for potentially malicious traffic patterns. These traffic patterns are referred to as *signatures* and are grouped into specific rulesets based on a determined severity score for each signature. When configuring IDS/IPS (see Figure 5-4), you can choose from three rulesets, composed of different signatures based on threat level, depending on your deployment and security needs: Connectivity, Balanced, and Security. Each of these rulesets provides increasingly more strict or potentially impactful signatures, allowing you to tailor your IDS/IPS functionality based on the specific needs of each site.

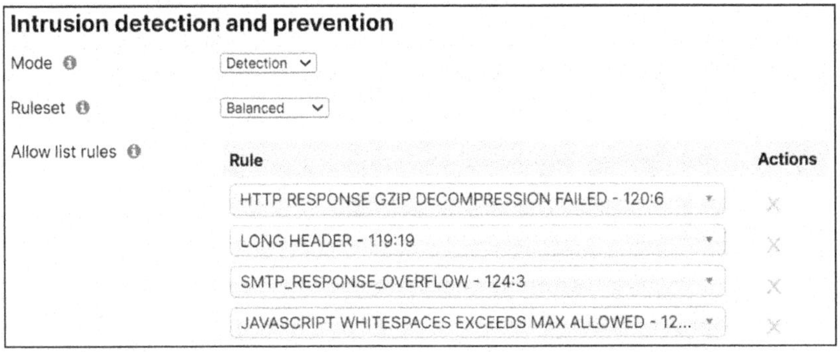

Intrusion detection and prevention

Mode ⓘ	Detection ∨
Ruleset ⓘ	Balanced ∨

Allow list rules ⓘ

Rule	Actions
HTTP RESPONSE GZIP DECOMPRESSION FAILED - 120:6 ▾	✕
LONG HEADER - 119:19 ▾	✕
SMTP_RESPONSE_OVERFLOW - 124:3 ▾	✕
JAVASCRIPT WHITESPACES EXCEEDS MAX ALLOWED - 12... ▾	✕

Figure 5-4 *IDS/IPS Configuration Section of the Threat Protection Page in the Dashboard*

The IDS and IPS systems function identically other than the specific action each takes when a malicious signature is detected. When configured in IDS (Detection) mode, an alert is generated in the Security & SD-WAN > Security Center page and event details are logged, but the traffic is not actually blocked by the MX and is allowed to flow.

When configured for IPS (Prevention) mode, when a malicious signature is detected, the MX will actively block the remaining traffic related to that flow in an attempt to disrupt the malicious activity, in addition to generating an alert in the Security Center on the Dashboard.

Pro Tip With the introduction of subscription licensing, security functions like AMP and IDS/IPS become foundational for all license tiers.

Cisco Umbrella

Through the use of the Meraki Dashboard, MX devices can also be integrated with Cisco Umbrella to utilize predefined Umbrella content filtering and security policies. Utilizing a simple API-based integration, this feature creates a secure IPsec tunnel between the MX and Umbrella Secure Internet Gateway (SIG) endpoint to allow all Internet-bound traffic from network clients to be forwarded through the Umbrella SIG gateway for inspection and filtering before reaching the final destination. This allows multiple branch sites to be quickly and easily configured to utilize Umbrella security policies within the Meraki Auto VPN/SD-WAN fabric, reducing the need for per-site security configurations within the Dashboard and allowing for more seamless integration with an existing Umbrella security solution.

For more information about Cisco Umbrella integration, including specific configuration steps, detailed operation, and licensing requirements, visit https://documentation.meraki.com and view the article "Automatically Integrating Cisco Umbrella with Meraki Networks."

Pro Tip   It is best to stop "bad" traffic closest to the source. Cisco Umbrella integration also exists for MR APs to help mitigate risk closer to the clients, saving processing power along the path.

Dashboard Group Policy

While each of the security features mentioned previously can be configured on a network-wide basis, there are times when certain clients should have more specific policies applied than the network-wide defaults. While it certainly is possible to use static or dedicated IPs to create unique rules to bypass or enforce additional Layer 3 firewall rules, this creates additional overhead and doesn't bypass features such as content filtering, Layer 7 firewall rules, and Cisco AMP.

For situations like this, where specific clients or users require a different set of rules or policies than the network-wide configuration, you configure group policies and assign them to either enhance or override network-wide configurations for specific clients, users, or even entire subnets. Figure 5-5 shows several group policies, each configured to allow special network access for group members, while Figure 5-6 shows the detailed configuration for an example group policy.

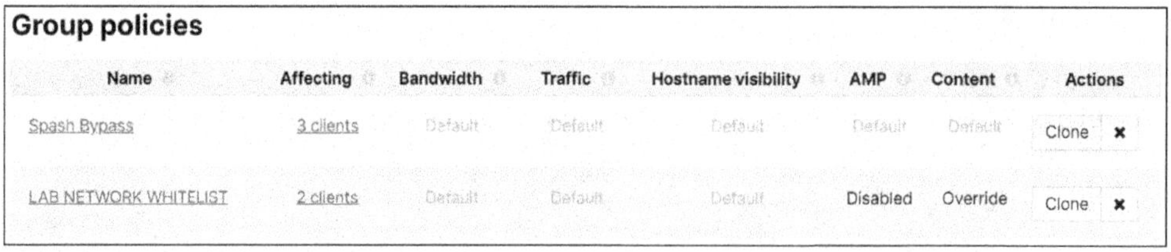

Group policies							
Name	Affecting	Bandwidth	Traffic	Hostname visibility	AMP	Content	Actions
Spash Bypass	3 clients	Default	Default	Default	Default	Default	Clone ✖
LAB NETWORK WHITELIST	2 clients	Default	Default	Default	Disabled	Override	Clone ✖

Figure 5-5   *Example Group Policies List in the Dashboard*

To create group policies, navigate to the **Network-wide > Group Policy** page on the Dashboard. If you want to assign group polices manually to a specific client device, go to the **Network-wide > Clients** page, select the client, and use the **Policy** drop-down list to apply a new policy to the client. You also can choose to automatically assign group policies to specific users through the use of either Active Directory or RADIUS integration by passing specific attributes, such as Filter-ID in the case of RADIUS, matching an associated group policy configured on the Dashboard during the logon process.

Figure 5-6 *Example Configuration for a Specific Group Policy*

Using an integration like Active Directory or RADIUS allows administrative users, for example, to automatically be provided with increased network access based on their needs without having to manually reassign device policies or create manual exceptions. This can greatly reduce the overhead required for troubleshooting and daily administration, as users will automatically be assigned an appropriate access policy based on the information passed during user logon, regardless of the device currently in use.

To find more detailed information on group policies, their application, and integrations with Active Directory or RADIUS, visit https://documentation.meraki.com and search using the keywords **group policy**.

Adaptive Policy (SGT)

Meraki has also implemented support for the Cisco TrustSec architecture with a feature called Adaptive Policy. Designed to offer improved management and scalability over more traditional access control methods, Adaptive Policy utilizes Security Group Tags (SGTs) to provide IP-agnostic policy and identity propagation throughout the network without reliance on traditional access control lists. By utilizing inline traffic tagging similar to 802.1Q trunking, Adaptive Policy allows for centrally defined security policies to be enforced across the network based on the SGTs applied to traffic instead of a source/destination IP, port, or other application-based policy.

While supported by most MX devices, Adaptive Policy, along with its functionality and configuration, is discussed in more detail in Chapter 7, "MS Switching Design and Recommendations."

VPN

As briefly mentioned previously, MX security appliances are capable of several different VPN implementations, allowing flexibility in your deployment to connect with VPN peers around the world. This section provides a brief overview of those implementations, which are discussed in more detail later in this chapter. You can access all of the following configurations by navigating to the **Security & SD-WAN > Site-to-Site VPN** page on the Dashboard.

Meraki Auto VPN

Meraki Auto VPN simplifies traditional VPN configuration to just a few clicks from in the Dashboard to create a fully functional and secure VPN topology across your entire organization.

Auto VPN utilizes the power of the Meraki cloud to quickly and easily create VPN peering configurations for multiple sites within a Dashboard organization. Through the use of multiple redundant cloud-hosted VPN registry endpoints, each device in an Auto VPN topology is able to provide local device details such as public IP and selected UDP ports to the registry. From there, that registry information is then exchanged across all relevant members of the Auto VPN topology to automatically bring up VPN tunnels directly between the local device and any configured peers, without requiring any unique configurations for each site. Figure 5-7 shows a network configured as an Auto VPN hub with the Management subnet enabled for VPN access and advertisement.

With the ability to configure either a traditional hub-and-spoke topology, a full mesh topology, or something in between, Auto VPN enables you to configure and deploy an entire Auto VPN topology from within the Dashboard with just a few clicks. It also greatly simplifies both the configuration and maintenance of your VPN topology. The VPN registry is consistently updated by each device to account for potentially changing uplink IPs over time, potentially eliminating the need for a dedicated static IP at each location.

Site-to-site VPN

Type ❶   ○ Off
                    Do not participate in site-to-site VPN.

                ◉ Hub (Mesh)
                    Establish VPN tunnels with all hubs and dependent spokes.

                ○ Spoke
                    Establish VPN tunnels with selected hubs.

Exit hubs ❶   Add a hub

VPN settings

IPv4 VPN subnet
translation ❶ | Enabled | Disabled |

Local networks

Name	VPN mode	Subnet	Uplink
GUEST	Disabled ▾	④ 192.168.23.0/24	Any
		⑥ 2601████████7e::/64	WAN 2
NAT64	Disabled ▾	④ 192.168.64.0/24	Any
		⑥ 2601████████7d::/64	WAN 2
MANAGEMENT	Enabled ▾	④ 192.168.95.0/24	Any
		⑥ 2601████████7f::/64	WAN 2
MOONBASEv4	Disabled ▾	④ 10.10.0.0/16	

Figure 5-7   *Network Configured as an Auto VPN Hub with Several Subnets Enabled for VPN Access and Advertisement*

Client VPN

In addition to the revolutionary Auto VPN solution, Meraki MX security appliances also offer the option for a direct L2TP/IPsec VPN connection for remote clients, referred to as Client VPN. This provides direct access to local resources hosted behind the MX to clients connecting remotely through the use of the built-in L2TP/IPsec functionality of the client by creating an encrypted tunnel directly between the client and the MX WAN. Client VPN allows the use of several different types of authentication, including Meraki cloud-hosted authentication, Active Directory, and RADIUS, to allow secure and easy integration with nearly any existing deployment.

> **Pro Tip**   Google was the first to omit an L2TP VPN client (in the Android OS), and other companies are signaling that they intend do the same.

Cisco AnyConnect

In addition to Client VPN, Meraki security appliances also support the use of Cisco AnyConnect for remote client connectivity. This further simplifies the required configuration for remote clients through the use of the AnyConnect client to create an SSL-based VPN, removing the need to configure an L2TP/IPsec VPN directly on the end device. Additionally, this allows for the use of AnyConnect profiles, which can be a powerful tool for providing more advanced configurations to client devices such as backup server lists, authentication timeouts, ISE posturing, and more.

> **Pro Tip**   The AnyConnect client option offers a richer feature set that is more robust than Client VPN from a security perspective. Consider this when deciding which VPN client method to support.

Non-Meraki VPN

When connecting to devices that are unable to utilize Meraki's Auto VPN technology, such as to Meraki devices outside of the current organization or to non-Meraki devices via VPN, a more traditional approach is required to bring up the VPN connection.

> **Pro Tip**   Think of this section as "Non-Auto VPN Configuration" because it pertains to manually configured traditional IPsec tunnels. This includes tunnels to other Meraki devices outside the Auto VPN domain of the organization.

Located at the bottom of the Security & SD-WAN > Site-to-Site VPN page is the Organization-wide Settings section, in which you can configure two primary features: the site-to-site VPN outbound firewall and connections to any non-Meraki VPN peers.

The Non-Meraki VPN Peers section, shown in Figure 5-8, is where you can create more traditional IPsec VPN peer configurations. You can also scope each peer to have its peering configuration apply only to specific MX devices in one or more Dashboard networks in the organization through the use of network tags, as discussed in Chapter 2, "Building the Dashboard."

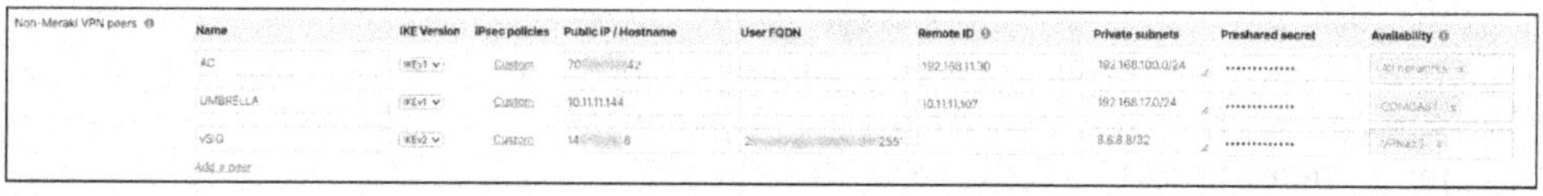

Figure 5-8   *Example Non-Meraki VPN Peer Configuration*

Routing

In addition to the previously discussed security features offered by the MX series, MX devices are also capable of performing L3 routing through a number of different configurations, including basic static routing for IPv4 and IPv6, dynamic VPN routing, BGP for IPv4 and IPv6, and OSPFv2 and OSPFv3.

This section briefly covers some of the more impactful aspects to keep in mind when routing with a Meraki security appliance, as well as some additional recommendations. For more detailed information about the implementation and functionality of routing for Meraki security appliances, visit https://documentation.meraki.com and view the article "MX Routing Behavior."

Route Priority

When planning your routing configuration for a deployment, it's important to keep in mind how the different route types are prioritized compared to each other. From the perspective of the MX, there are seven different types of routes, each with its own priority relative to the others.

The types of routes and their priority are listed here, with the highest priority listed first and lowest priority listed last:

1. Directly connected/local subnets

2. Client VPN

3. Static routes

4. Auto VPN routes

5. Non-Meraki VPN peers

6. BGP learned routes

7. Default uplink/NAT

For any given traffic destination, the traffic will be routed based on the highest-priority matching route. If there are no more-specific routes that match the destination, then the traffic will be forwarded out the default uplink over the currently active Internet interface. By properly planning and taking advantage of route priorities, you can employ multiple routes to quickly and easily create robust failover mechanisms. When combined with the Meraki SD-WAN solution, discussed in Chapter 6, this can create a powerful failover solution to help ensure minimal downtime for critical applications.

Static Routes

You can configure static routes on a per-device basis directly on the **Security & SD-WAN > Addressing & VLANs** page under the Static Routes header within the Routing section of the page.

When working with manually configured static routes, there are a few considerations and best practices to keep in mind. Primarily, it's critical to have a complete picture of the entire routing topology and to configure appropriate return routes for any traffic that would be routed over a static route.

Configuring appropriate return routes is specifically important to prevent an asymmetric routing situation in which traffic is routed from one site via a static route to an internal or MPLS link but return traffic is routed back to that site via a different path, such as over an Auto VPN connection between sites, because the opposing site is missing the appropriate static route for the return traffic.

Additionally, when working with static routes, it's important to ensure that the appropriate route-tracking mechanism is configured for each route. For each static route configured, there is an Active setting to configure a condition that must be satisfied for the static route to be marked as active or available; the choices are Always, While Next Hop Responds to Ping, and While Host Responds to Ping.

A condition such as the next hop responding to ICMP, or a specific endpoint reachable across the static route responding to ICMP, can be configured for each route to ensure that only static routes that are able to provide appropriate connectivity are marked as active. When combined with the route priorities mentioned previously, this can be used to create a robust failover mechanism that allows a configured static route to be the preferred route for a given destination, such as over an internal or local MPLS link on the LAN, while allowing for failover to either an Auto VPN or non-Meraki VPN peer route in the event connectivity via the static route is lost.

OSPF

When working with an existing environment that utilizes OSPF for routing, it's important to be aware that Meraki's MX security appliances, at the time of writing, only support a limited OSPF implementation. Specifically, MX devices only support OSPF in the following configurations:

- Routed mode with only a single LAN

- Passthrough or Concentrator mode

Additionally, it's important to be aware that an MX is not able to learn routes advertised by any OSPF neighbors; it is only able to advertise available Auto VPN routes to OSPF neighbors. Because of this, when deployed in a topology that utilizes OSPF and Auto VPN, any MX utilizing OSPF on the LAN will require matching static routes be configured for any locally advertised OSPF subnets to allow those routes to be advertised into the Auto VPN topology.

For more detail about Meraki's OSPF implementation for MX devices, visit https:// documentation.meraki.com and search using the keyword **OSPF**.

BGP

Unlike OSPF, Meraki offers a robust BGP implementation with the MX and Z-series of devices and is able to both learn and advertise routes through BGP. For example, all MX and Z-series devices utilize iBGP to exchange routes over the Auto VPN topology. All devices configured in Passthrough or Concentrator mode (or Routed mode devices running compatible firmware) are also able to advertise and learn routes via configured eBGP neighbors.

To configure BGP, navigate to the **Security & SD-WAN > Routing** page on the Dashboard. An MX will learn or advertise routes to eBGP or iBGP peers under the following conditions:

- A VPN spoke will learn routes advertised to it by other Auto VPN peers via iBGP.

- An MX in Passthrough or Concentrator mode will learn routes advertised to it by other Auto VPN peers and re-advertise these iBGP-learned routes to available eBGP peers.

- An MX in Passthrough or Concentrator mode will learn routes advertised to it by its eBGP peers and re-advertise these eBGP-learned routes to other Auto VPN peers via iBGP.

- An MX in Passthrough or Concentrator mode will advertise local networks that are not directly connected and are configured on the Site-to-Site VPN page via iBGP, but it will not advertise via eBGP to external peers.

Outside these Meraki-specific route advertisement behaviors, Meraki's BGP implementation is fairly standard and is intended to integrate seamlessly with nearly any existing deployment utilizing BGP.

Deploying Meraki Auto VPN

As briefly discussed earlier in this chapter, Meraki Auto VPN is a proprietary Meraki technology that automates VPN tunnel creation and management by utilizing the power of the Meraki Dashboard and cloud management to allow quick and easy configuration of VPN tunnels to any other Meraki MX or Z-series device within the same Dashboard organization.

Meraki has significantly simplified the VPN setup and WAN failover mechanisms by leveraging the Dashboard, which is aware of the full configuration of every organization, including the status of all other Auto VPN participants in each network within the organization. This makes the Meraki Auto VPN setup a simple and easy to implement solution that automates IPsec Phase I and Phase II configurations to create VPN connections between devices across networks.

When using Meraki Auto VPN, it's important to understand the distinction between the VPN management traffic that traverses between the devices and the Meraki cloud and the actual VPN tunneled traffic that carries user data between sites, as visualized in Figure 5-9.

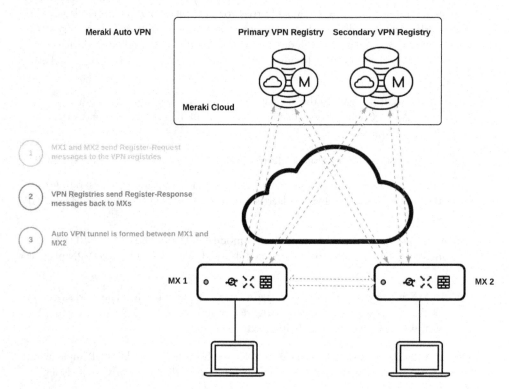

Figure 5-9   *Meraki Auto VPN Traffic Architecture*

Auto VPN management traffic is exchanged between devices and the Meraki cloud and is used to exchange connectivity details like peer IPs and ports to enable the negotiation of VPN tunnels between peers. The actual VPN tunnel that carries user data between sites is established directly between devices like a traditional VPN tunnel and does not traverse the Meraki cloud in any way. Figure 5-9 demonstrates the difference between paths taken by Meraki management data and paths taken by user data traversing between sites.

You can find more information on the segregation of user data and management data by visiting https://meraki.cisco.com/trust/#data.

Configuring Auto VPN

Figure 5-10 shows the Security & SD-WAN > Site-to-Site VPN page of a network configured as an Auto VPN spoke pointing back to two different hub devices, with the primary hub configured as a default route (full tunnel). For many sites, this is nearly all the configuration required to establish the Auto VPN topology across the organization.

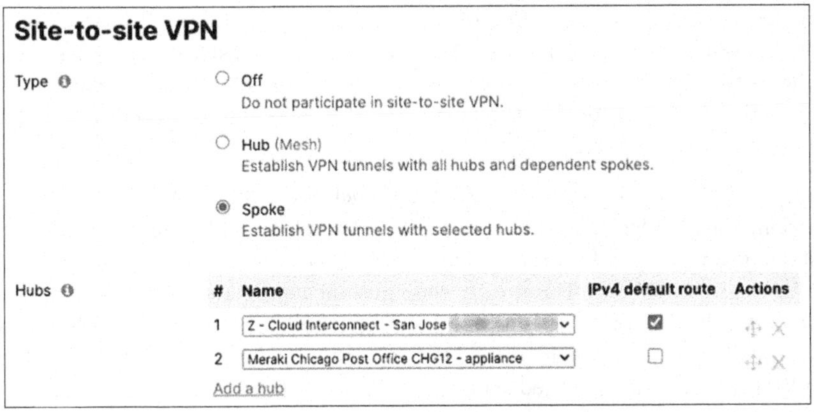

Site-to-site VPN

Type ⓘ
- ○ Off
  Do not participate in site-to-site VPN.

- ○ Hub (Mesh)
  Establish VPN tunnels with all hubs and dependent spokes.

- ◉ Spoke
  Establish VPN tunnels with selected hubs.

Hubs ⓘ

#	Name	IPv4 default route	Actions
1	Z - Cloud Interconnect - San Jose ▾	☑	⊹ ✕
2	Meraki Chicago Post Office CHG12 - appliance ▾	☐	⊹ ✕

Add a hub

Figure 5-10 *Example Auto VPN Configuration Showing a Spoke Site Configured for Two Hubs, One of Which Is Configured with a Default Route/Full Tunnel Configuration*

When you're configuring Auto VPN from the Dashboard UI, the VPN Settings section of the Site-to-Site VPN page makes it easy to select the local subnets that are allowed to participate in the VPN topology by simply selecting either **Enabled** or **Disabled** from the VPN Mode drop-down list for each subnet at each site, as shown in Figure 5-11, where only one of the four local subnets is configured for VPN access.

Pro Tip   You can also define VPN access for each subnet by editing the subnet on the **Security & SD-WAN > Addressing & VLANs** page.

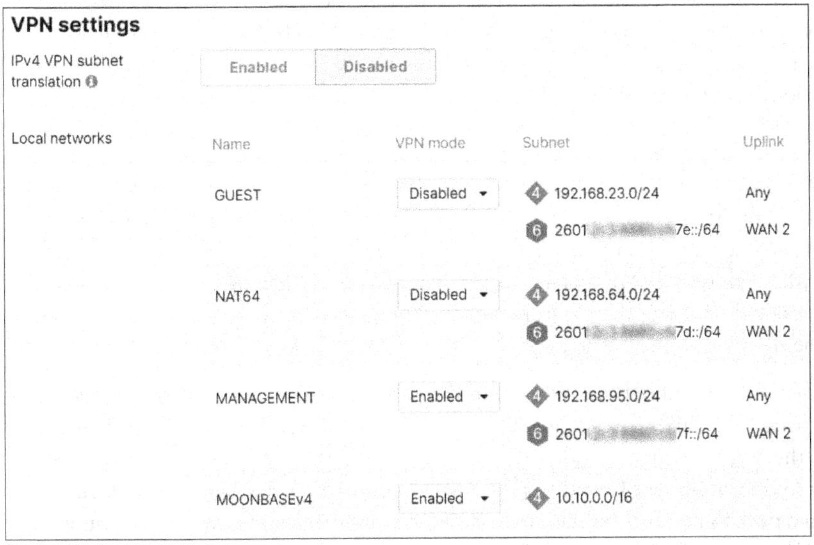

VPN settings

IPv4 VPN subnet translation ⓘ   [Enabled] [Disabled]

Local networks

Name	VPN mode	Subnet	Uplink
GUEST	Disabled ▾	④ 192.168.23.0/24	Any
		⑥ 2601...7e::/64	WAN 2
NAT64	Disabled ▾	④ 192.168.64.0/24	Any
		⑥ 2601...7d::/64	WAN 2
MANAGEMENT	Enabled ▾	④ 192.168.95.0/24	Any
		⑥ 2601...7f::/64	WAN 2
MOONBASEv4	Enabled ▾	④ 10.10.0.0/16	

Figure 5-11 *VLAN/Subnet Availability Configuration for an Auto VPN–Enabled Peer*

This configuration option helps to reduce the number of unique subnets required across sites, as VLANs/subnets that do not require VPN access can be reused across locations and only the VPN-enabled subnets require a unique address space within the organization. This is especially useful for templated networks, which are discussed further in Chapter 4, "Automating the Dashboard."

Additionally, Meraki makes it easy to create a full tunnel Auto VPN configuration. By simply checking the IPv4 Default Route box for the related Auto VPN hub, all client traffic will automatically be routed across the Auto VPN connection to the selected hub to be forwarded to the destination. This greatly simplifies the configuration by removing the need to explicitly advertise a default route from each hub, as required in a more traditional deployment. If the IPv4 Default Route box is not checked, only traffic destined for advertised VPN subnets will be routed across the VPN.

Pro Tip   More advanced deployments like those utilizing DC-DC failover may still require manual route advertisement configuration to allow for proper route tracking and failover.

Hub Versus Spoke

Meraki's hub and spoke model very closely resembles a traditional hub and spoke model, where any device configured as a hub will attempt to establish a direct VPN tunnel and learn/advertise any available routes between itself and all other hubs and any assigned spokes. Likewise, a site configured as a spoke will only form tunnels and learn/advertise routes to the configured hub(s).

This model allows for a great amount of flexibility, because each site can be configured as either a hub or spoke in the topology depending on the need. Whether configuring your VPN topology as a full mesh by configuring all sites as hubs, as a traditional hub and spoke model, or as something in between, the Meraki Auto VPN solution makes configuration and deployment simple and easy.

NAT Traversal

When you're configuring an Auto VPN topology, it's important for each site to have the proper NAT traversal configuration. By default, all Meraki sites use automatic NAT traversal, which employs UDP hole punching in addition to the automatic negotiation of connection details through the cloud-hosted VPN registry to allow sites to quickly and easily bring up a VPN connection.

For sites that are located behind an unfriendly upstream NAT, such as Carrier-Grade NAT (CGNAT) used by cellular carriers, or that otherwise require a specific port be manually specified, the VPN Settings section of the Site-to-Site VPN page has a NAT Traversal option that you can set to **Manual** (see Figure 5-12), which enables you to configure a static public port to be used for all VPN-related communication for the MX contained in that network.

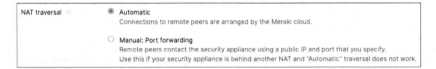

Figure 5-12 *NAT Traversal Configuration on the Site-to-Site VPN Page in the Dashboard*

For more detailed information on how to set up and operate Meraki Auto VPN, visit https://documentation.meraki.com and view the article "Automatic NAT Traversal for Auto VPN Tunneling Between Cisco Meraki Peers."

Hub and Spoke Recommendations

There are many recommendations and best practices covering VPN deployments that may be applicable based on your specific deployment needs. However, due to the varied needs of different deployments, including scale and hardware selection, this section covers only some basic recommendations to help point you in the right direction during your deployment.

You can find more detailed information on best practices for specific use cases at https://documentation.meraki.com or by reaching out to the Meraki sales organization or your existing Meraki account team.

Sizing It Right

When planning and deploying your Auto VPN topology, there are several best practices to keep in mind to ensure optimal performance. The first and most important practice is to ensure that the model of MX deployed at each location is capable of handling the required load. As discussed in the "MX Scaling" section earlier in this chapter, different models of MX hardware have different maximum capabilities, so it's crucial that the chosen model of device is capable of supporting the expected load not only from the number of connected tunnels and peers, but also for any additional security features that will be configured.

Properly sizing your model selection is imperative to designing a deployment that will be able to provide consistent and stable performance not only on initial deployment but also for the foreseeable future and accommodate any expected growth. For example, a deployment that currently consists of only five satellite sites with a single main hub may be able to operate the hub using a mid-tier model of hardware for the initial deployment, but if the number of satellite offices is expected to expand rapidly over the next two years, the original hub MX device may not be able to fully support the future number of required tunnels and security features without a noticeable performance impact. This, of course, depends heavily on many factors specific to the deployment, such as how many tunnels are needed, the amount of traffic passing through those tunnels, and the number and types of additional security features configured. However, proper sizing is a very important aspect to keep in mind during the initial planning phases of the deployment.

Pro Tip   Voice (VoIP) and other small packet traffic is notorious for a high performance impact compared to other types of traffic for all firewalls, not just Meraki devices. This may impact your sizing decisions depending on the types of traffic that are expected to pass over Auto VPN. Therefore, it's important to analyze and understand the types of traffic that are passing through your networks.

To ensure proper sizing when planning your deployment, we recommend engaging the Meraki sales organization or your local VAR, who can assist in proper review of your deployment and make additional sizing recommendations based on projected future use.

Hub Prioritization

Meraki has worked to ensure that deploying Auto VPN is as simple as possible while still ensuring that you are able to perform more advanced configuration to fine-tune the deployment to best suit your needs. For larger deployments that may employ multiple Auto VPN hubs for failover or load balancing, the ability to configure specific hub priorities for each spoke becomes paramount to ensure proper traffic flows.

By allowing each spoke configuration to have multiple hubs defined with a priority for each, Meraki enables you to easily balance traffic loads from different spokes across multiple hubs while still ensuring alternate paths are available if a hub becomes unreachable for any reason. This is particularly useful for large deployments that may be implementing more advanced configurations involving multiple redundant hubs, such as DC-DC failover.

Full Tunnel Versus Split Tunnel

In addition to using hub prioritization to balance traffic loads, you can choose between full tunnel and split tunnel configurations for each spoke site to limit the amount of traffic passing over Auto VPN, which reduces the load requirements on hub devices. As mentioned previously, the IPv4 Default Route check box for each hub can be configured to enforce a full tunnel configuration, requiring all Internet-bound traffic to pass over Auto VPN and traverse out the selected hub. Figure 5-13 shows a spoke site that has two hubs configured, one of which has been configured as a default route/full tunnel.

This type of configuration may be required for compliance reasons, but for sites that do not require this configuration, we typically recommend employing a split tunnel configuration. By leaving the IPv4 Default Route check box for a hub unchecked, you can ensure that only traffic specifically destined for an advertised route from the hub will be sent over Auto VPN. This can significantly reduce the traffic load on both the hub and spoke MX for sites that do not require a full tunnel configuration.

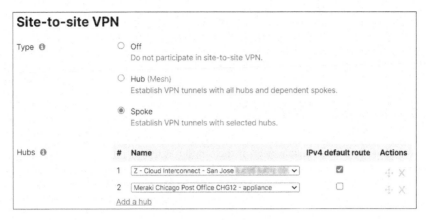

Figure 5-13 *Example Auto VPN Configuration Showing a Spoke Site Configured for Two Hubs, with the Primary Hub Configured to Provide an IPv4 Default Route to the Spoke*

Advanced Configurations

For some large deployments, additional advanced routing configurations are available that can be configured based on specific needs. Most customers and deployments do not need these configurations, as they are designed for extremely large customers that exceed the typical deployment scale. As a result, these advanced configurations are not directly available on the Dashboard to standard administrators, but Meraki Support can enable them if the deployment in question meets the required criteria.

An example of an advanced routing configuration is the ability to modify how routes are advertised between spokes and hubs within a deployment. By default, all configured hubs automatically form tunnels and exchange routes with all other hubs in the organization, and each hub also advertises all spoke routes it receives from connected spokes to other spokes. Certain very large deployments may require limiting these behaviors due to the scale of their deployment and route table limitations across multiple hubs and spokes.

An example is a large organization with spoke sites spread across the country, where each spoke needs to communicate only with its associated hub and no other spokes. It's possible for the number of spoke routes from other spoke sites connected to the same hub to cause an unwanted and unnecessary performance impact for the smaller devices at each spoke site. In this case, Meraki Support can enable a configuration for the organization that prevents the hub from advertising other connected spoke routes back to each spoke, limiting the routes each spoke receives to just those directly connected to the selected hub.

This type of advanced configuration allows for the hardware requirements of each spoke site to be based on the usage of that specific spoke site, instead of having to also accommodate the potential additional load caused by large numbers of unnecessary routes from other spike sites within the same Auto VPN topology.

As noted previously, most customers and deployments do not need these advance configurations. However, if you think your deployment may benefit from a more advanced configuration like this, we recommend reaching out to the Meraki sales organization or your Meraki account team to review the deployment.

Monitoring Your Deployment

As demonstrated in Chapter 3, "The Meraki Admin Experience," the Dashboard is able to provide valuable monitoring insights across the board through the use of cloud monitoring. In addition to the organization- and network-wide monitoring options shown in Chapter 3, Meraki has many device-specific monitoring tools available. This section takes a brief look at some of the monitoring tools and reports available for MX and Z-series devices.

Meraki Insight

Meraki Insight (MI) is a powerful solution designed to monitor the performance of Internet uplinks and the web-based applications using those uplinks. With the proliferation of web-based and cloud-hosted applications, Meraki Insight is designed to help provide insightful end-to-end visibility to customers for their most important web applications and traffic. Figure 5-14 illustrates how an MX device combines passive data analysis, active endpoint probing, and the power available through cloud-based data review and reporting to present data in MI that can help to significantly reduce troubleshooting efforts and incident resolution times by assisting to pinpoint potential causes of poor performance.

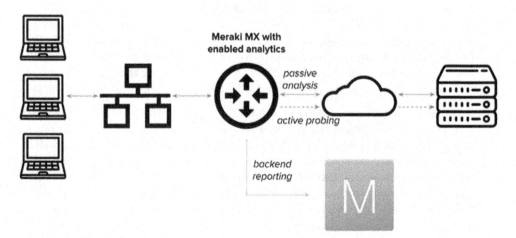

Figure 5-14   *Meraki Insight Data Gathering Flow*

Pro Tip   Meraki Insight analytics require an additional Dashboard license applied to participating networks.

The Meraki Insight solution is divided into three areas of data monitoring: Web Application Health, WAN Health, and VoIP health. This section provides some general insight into the operation and functionality of Meraki Insight and how it can be used to simplify monitoring the performance of your deployments. All areas of Meraki Insight allow for configuring multiple alerts based on configurable alert conditions, which are briefly covered in the "Insight Alerts" section later in the chapter.

For more detailed information on the operation and configuration of individual MI features, refer to https://documentation.meraki.com and search using the keyword **Insight**.

Web Application Health

Accessible by navigating to the Insight > Web Application Health page on the Dashboard, Web Application Health is designed to monitor the performance of defined web-based applications or traffic. This traffic is passively monitored on a per-flow basis, with the related traffic metadata securely uploaded and analyzed in the Meraki cloud to determine if any detected performance issues are introduced within the local network, WAN, or even at the application level. This monitoring process is designed around the use of deep packet inspection, similar to Meraki's AMP and IDS/IPS solutions, to gather information at both the application and network layer to provide valuable performance insights.

Figure 5-15 shows several tracked web applications and their current status overviews. For each tracked web application, the Dashboard is able to provide a report regarding recent application performance as well as generate alerts based on defined performance thresholds. These performance thresholds can use Meraki's default values for any pre-defined applications, manually configured for each application, or configured to use Smart Thresholds. Smart Thresholds allow for enhanced monitoring by observing typical traffic patterns and tailoring each application performance threshold based on real-world observed performance. This allows for performance thresholds to be fine-tuned based on the real-world performance of each application within each deployment, providing more accurate alerts by automatically determining typical performance thresholds and generating alerts only when true anomalous behavior is observed for that application at a given location.

By selecting a given application and network, you can view a detailed report of recent application traffic including an overall performance score, total network usage, latency, loss, HTTP response time, and more. To give you an example of the depth of detail provided for each tracked web application, Figures 5-16 through 5-19 display several of these reports.

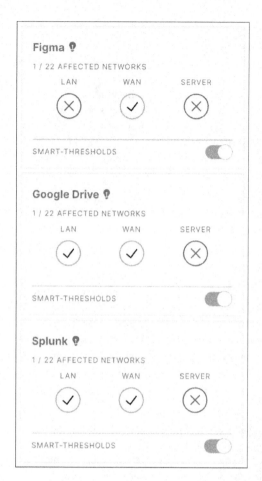

Figure 5-15 *Example of Several Tracked Web Applications in Meraki Insight and Their Statuses*

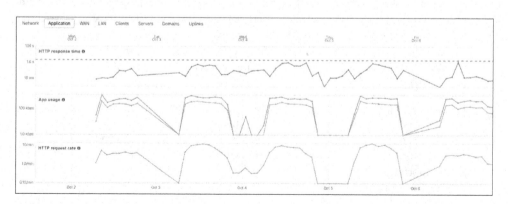

Figure 5-16 *Historical Application Data for a Tracked Web Application as Part of Meraki Insight Monitoring*

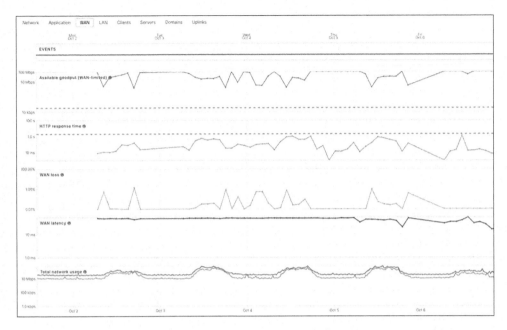

Figure 5-17   *Historical WAN Data for a Tracked Web Application as Part of Meraki Insight Monitoring*

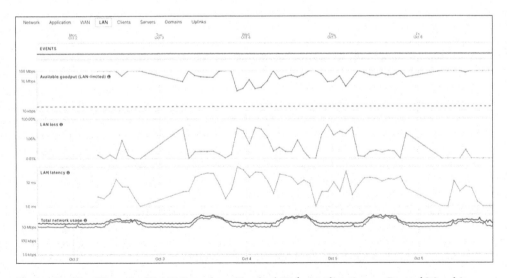

Figure 5-18   *Historical LAN Data for a Tracked Web Application as Part of Meraki Insight Monitoring*

| Network | Application | WAN | LAN | Clients | **Servers** | Domains | Uplinks |

Servers	Score	Requests ▼	Available goodput	Response time
172▨▨▨10	66	6772	3.3 Mbps	610 ms
142▨▨▨46	72	2977	3.5 Mbps	470 ms
142▨▨▨206	99	2837	4.3 Mbps	18 ms
172▨▨▨6	99	2590	100 Mbps	12 ms
142▨▨▨78	69	2245	4.9 Mbps	530 ms
142▨▨▨38	99	2041	5.3 Mbps	10 ms
142▨▨▨74	78	1909	4.4 Mbps	350 ms
142▨▨▨14	76	920	9.4 Mbps	390 ms
142▨▨▨174	91	743	6.6 Mbps	140 ms
142▨▨▨38	65	559	1.8 Mbps	610 ms

Figure 5-19 *Historical Server Data for a Tracked Web Application as Part of Meraki Insight Monitoring*

With the ability to select from a large number of predefined, common web applications, or manually define your own custom traffic selection to monitor, the data offered by Meraki Insights Web Application Health solution can provide valuable insights into unexpected application behavior and help to quickly scope troubleshooting efforts to reduce incident resolution times and improve overall performance and uptime.

WAN Health

Similar to Web Application Health, WAN Health is designed to monitor the performance of WAN uplinks across multiple sites and provide additional insights into detected performance issues for general WAN connectivity. By selecting one of multiple, custom configurable, publicly accessible endpoints on the WAN, information such as total usage, loss, average latency, jitter, and more is directly available for every WAN uplink across all participating sites (see Figure 5-20). This provides a great starting point when you're looking into reported connectivity issues for different sites and enables you to easily pinpoint when the cause of unexpected connectivity behavior is due to a remote or upstream issue.

VoIP Health

VoIP Health is similar to WAN Health in that it is configured to monitor specific, custom endpoints and provide reporting related to the quality of connections to each endpoint. However, unlike WAN Health, which is intended to monitor generic, publicly accessible endpoints to report on general uplink connectivity and health, VoIP Health is intended to monitor connections to specific VoIP endpoints, either public or private, to provide more detailed data specific to the paths used by critical VoIP traffic.

As a result, the data provided by VoIP Health (see Figure 5-21) is specifically tailored to VoIP applications and troubleshooting. Information such as the path MOS, loss, latency, and jitter is at the forefront of reported data to directly assist in monitoring and troubleshooting VoIP-related behaviors.

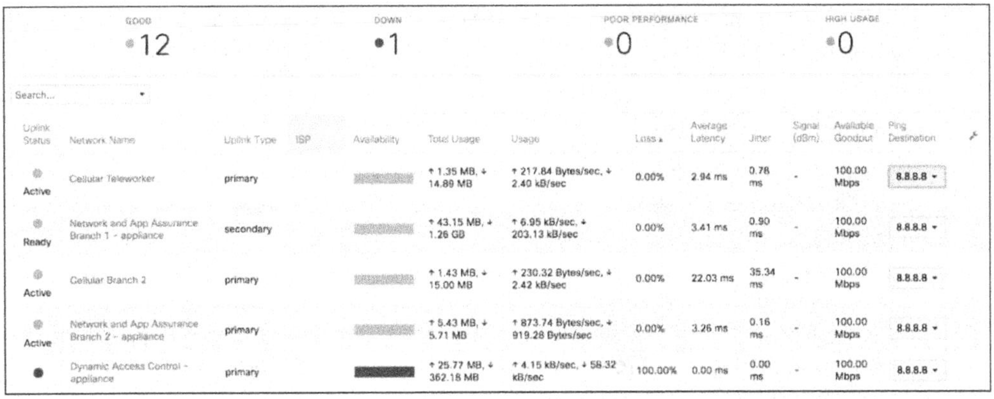

Uplink Status	Network Name	Uplink Type	ISP	Availability	Total Usage	Usage	Loss ▲	Average Latency	Jitter	Signal (dBm)	Available Goodput	Ping Destination
Active	Cellular Teleworker	primary			↑ 1.35 MB, ↓ 14.89 MB	↑ 217.84 Bytes/sec, ↓ 2.40 kB/sec	0.00%	2.94 ms	0.78 ms	-	100.00 Mbps	8.8.8.8 ▾
Ready	Network and App Assurance Branch 1 - appliance	secondary			↑ 43.15 MB, ↓ 1.26 GB	↑ 6.95 kB/sec, ↓ 203.13 kB/sec	0.00%	3.41 ms	0.90 ms	-	100.00 Mbps	8.8.8.8 ▾
Active	Cellular Branch 2	primary			↑ 1.43 MB, ↓ 15.00 MB	↑ 230.32 Bytes/sec, ↓ 2.42 kB/sec	0.00%	22.03 ms	35.34 ms	-	100.00 Mbps	8.8.8.8 ▾
Active	Network and App Assurance Branch 2 - appliance	primary			↑ 5.43 MB, ↓ 5.71 MB	↑ 873.74 Bytes/sec, ↓ 919.28 Bytes/sec	0.00%	3.26 ms	0.16 ms	-	100.00 Mbps	8.8.8.8 ▾
●	Dynamic Access Control - appliance	primary			↑ 25.77 MB, ↓ 362.18 MB	↑ 4.15 kB/sec, ↓ 58.32 kB/sec	100.00%	0.00 ms	0.00 ms	-	100.00 Mbps	8.8.8.8 ▾

Figure 5-20   *WAN Health Data for Several Sites, Including One Site Currently Experiencing an Outage*

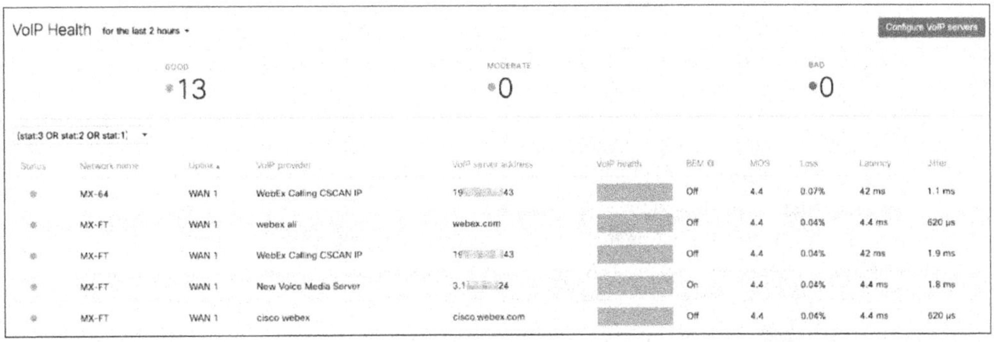

Status	Network name	Uplink ▲	VoIP provider	VoIP server address	VoIP health	BFM GI	MOS	Loss	Latency	Jitter
●	MX-64	WAN 1	WebEx Calling CSCAN IP	19░░░░43		Off	4.4	0.07%	42 ms	1.1 ms
●	MX-FT	WAN 1	webex ali	webex.com		Off	4.4	0.04%	4.4 ms	620 µs
●	MX-FT	WAN 1	WebEx Calling CSCAN IP	16░░░░43		Off	4.4	0.04%	42 ms	1.9 ms
●	MX-FT	WAN 1	New Voice Media Server	3.1░░░24		On	4.4	0.04%	4.4 ms	1.8 ms
●	MX-FT	WAN 1	cisco webex	cisco.webex.com		Off	4.4	0.04%	4.4 ms	620 µs

Figure 5-21   *VoIP Health Data for Several Endpoints on the VoIP Health Page in the Dashboard*

Insight Alerts

As part of the monitoring solution for Meraki Insight, you can configure specific alerts such as those based on application performance thresholds, WAN utilization, uplink status changes, packet loss, latency, MOS, and more. For alerts based on application performance thresholds, you configure per-application alert settings by navigating to the **Insight > Web App Health > Manage Alerts** page on the Dashboard.

For other alerts such as WAN Health or VoIP Health alerts, go to the **Insight > Insight Alerts** page. Insight Alerts are discussed in more detail in Chapter 2 as well as in the documentation online at https://documentation.meraki.com.

Configuring these alerts and their respective alert thresholds appropriately can serve to provide critical information as soon as unexpected behavior begins to appear. This helps to initiate the troubleshooting process faster and more efficiently by providing important details about the nature of the behavior and potential causes alongside the initial report, making resolution times shorter and improving the efficiency of your IT teams.

ThousandEyes Integration

In addition to the power offered through Meraki Insight alone, Cisco Meraki has also introduced support for ThousandEyes integration with Meraki Insight. This enables you to expand the monitoring functionality offered by Meraki Insight further by incorporating the power of ThousandEyes monitoring. ThousandEyes uses active monitoring (e.g., active probes) to measure performance. Through a simple and straightforward Dashboard integration process, you can quickly and easily incorporate ThousandEyes application endpoint monitoring with Meraki Insight reporting, providing a powerful application monitoring solution and enriching your data.

Monitoring VPN

Many deployments rely on VPN connectivity to remote resources to ensure secure communication between sites. This is one reason why Meraki has placed so much effort into designing the Auto VPN solution to help ensure maximum uptime with minimal configuration.

In addition to easy configuration, Meraki has made it a goal to provide simple and easy to understand monitoring for VPN connectivity across your organization. The VPN Status page is designed to provide detailed information about all VPN tunnels within your Meraki organization. This page provides real-time status updates between your Meraki Auto VPN peers as well as non-Meraki VPN peers. You can access the VPN Status page in either of two ways: by navigating to the **Organization > VPN Status** page, to view the status of all MX security appliances within your organization, or by navigating to the **Network-wide > VPN Status** page, to view monitoring data specifically for connectivity related to the chosen network.

These pages each display detailed information relating to the current tunnel status for each device and peer, as well as information about the per-device/peer usage, and latency. Figure 5-22 shows the organization-wide VPN Status page, while Figure 5-23 shows the VPN Status page for one specific network within that organization.

On the organization-level VPN Status page, you can hover over a specific network to highlight that network's data usage within the previous summary graphs, and you can select that network to open the network-wide VPN Status page for that network.

The network-wide VPN Status page includes both a peers table and an Uplink Decisions table. The Uplink Decisions table at the bottom of the page can be useful for monitoring active flows across the VPN tunnel and ensuring expected traffic is flowing between peers over the VPN as intended. Figure 5-24 shows an example of the Uplink Decisions table.

VPN Status for the last day
View old version
Usage
Latency
50% 90%
Networks
Download as
Status
Description
Usage
Latency (50%)
Latency (90%)
Peers
Subnets
Connectivity

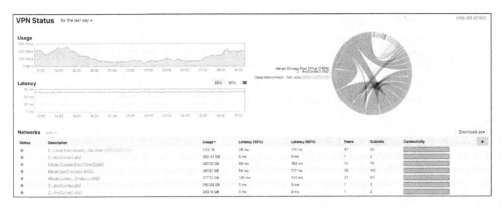

Figure 5-22 *Organization-wide VPN Status Page Showing the VPN Status Summary for Several Networks*

VPN Status › Meraki San Francisco SFO12 - appliance for the last day
View old version
Connectivity
Usage
Latency
50% 90%
30 site-to-site peers
110 exported subnets
0 Non-Meraki peers
Status
Description
Usage
Latency (avg)
Connectivity
VPN Registry: Connected. This WAN appliance is able to connect to multiple VPN registries using UDP port 9351.
NAT type: None (Public IP). This WAN appliance has a publicly accessible IP address and is using 50 39 as a contact point.
Encrypted. Using IPsec and AES encryption.

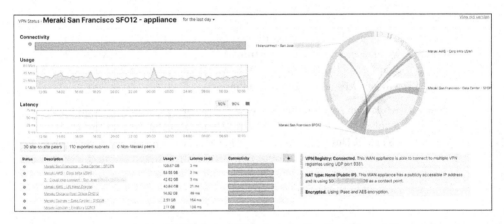

Figure 5-23 *Network-level VPN Status Showing the Per-Peer Tunnel Data and Connection Details for the Device in This Network*

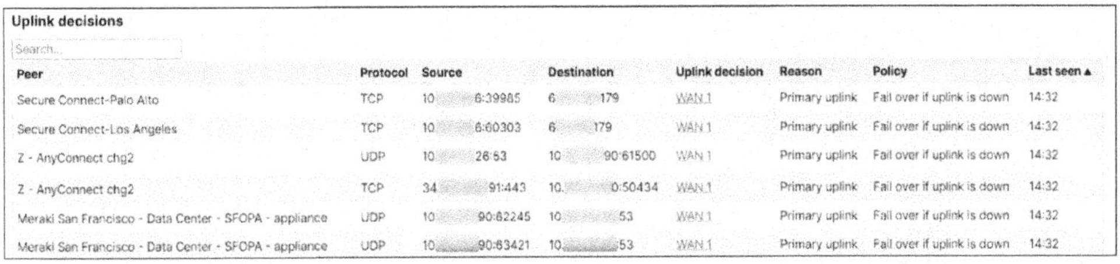

Uplink decisions
Search...
Peer
Protocol
Source
Destination
Uplink decision
Reason
Policy
Last seen
Secure Connect-Palo Alto TCP 10 6:39985 6 179 WAN 1 Primary uplink Fail over if uplink is down 14:32
Secure Connect-Los Angeles TCP 10 6:60303 6 179 WAN 1 Primary uplink Fail over if uplink is down 14:32
Z - AnyConnect chg2 UDP 10 26:53 10 90:61500 WAN 1 Primary uplink Fail over if uplink is down 14:32
Z - AnyConnect chg2 TCP 34 91:443 10. 0:50434 WAN 1 Primary uplink Fail over if uplink is down 14:32
Meraki San Francisco - Data Center - SFOPA - appliance UDP 10 90:62245 10 53 WAN 1 Primary uplink Fail over if uplink is down 14:32
Meraki San Francisco - Data Center - SFOPA - appliance UDP 10 90:63421 10 53 WAN 1 Primary uplink Fail over if uplink is down 14:32

Figure 5-24 *Uplink Decisions Table for a Network in the Network-level VPN Status Page*

From within the Peers table, you can hover over a specific peer to highlight that peer's data usage within the previous summary graphs, and you can select that peer to open the detailed VPN Uplink Monitoring page. This page shows historical monitoring results for encapsulated data within the tunnels across each uplink from the selected site to the selected peer, as well as any custom performance classes or VPN flow preferences that may be configured. This type of per-uplink tunnel monitoring data becomes particularly useful when employing any of Meraki's SD-WAN solutions, which are discussed in Chapter 6. Figure 5-25 shows an example of this uplink monitoring data for two Meraki campus sites, each with dual uplinks.

Reviewing Dashboard Alerts

As mentioned in Chapter 2, additional monitoring for Meraki devices beyond the email and Webhook alerts configured on the Network-wide > Alerts page is available through both the Alert Hub and Organization > Alerts page on the Dashboard. Each of these locations displays current alerts from across all available Meraki products, providing a quick and easy reference to review any active alerts within the network.

Alert Hub

The Alert Hub is available whenever you're working on a network-level page in the Dashboard and displays any active alerts from devices in the current network. These include MX security appliances and any other Meraki devices added to the network, such as MS switches, MR access points, and more.

From any network-level page on the Dashboard, you can open the Alert Hub for that network by clicking the bell icon at the top-right corner of the page, as shown in Figure 5-26. The Alert Hub alert categories, such as Device Health and Connectivity, enable you to quickly review and prioritize any active alerts based on their severity and potential impact. By selecting the **See Alerts for All Networks** link in the Alert Hub, you can quickly navigate to the **Organization > Alerts** page for a wider scope of review.

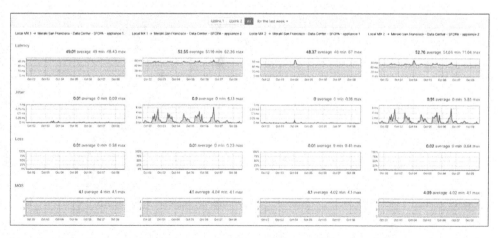

Figure 5-25 *Per-Uplink VPN Monitoring Data Showing Historical Results for the Tunnels Between Each Uplink of Two Peers*

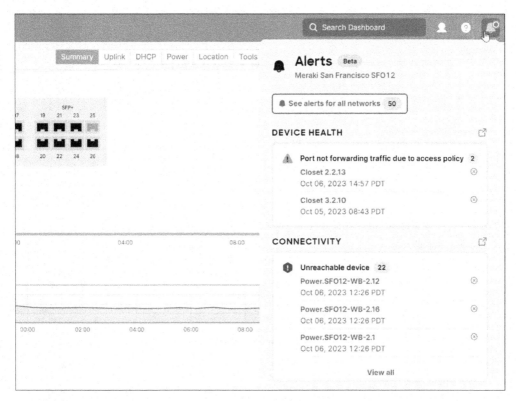

Figure 5-26 *Network Alert Hub Showing Several Alerts for Devices in the Current Network*

Organization Alerts

The Organization > Alerts page (see Figure 5-27) is similar to the network-level Alert Hub but operates at the organization level instead of the network level and provides a summary of all active alerts for all devices across networks within the organization. This page provides a single location to easily review all active or dismissed alerts for any device within the organization, making it ideal for general review of a deployment and providing easy access to immediately begin troubleshooting any alert, no matter what device or network is involved.

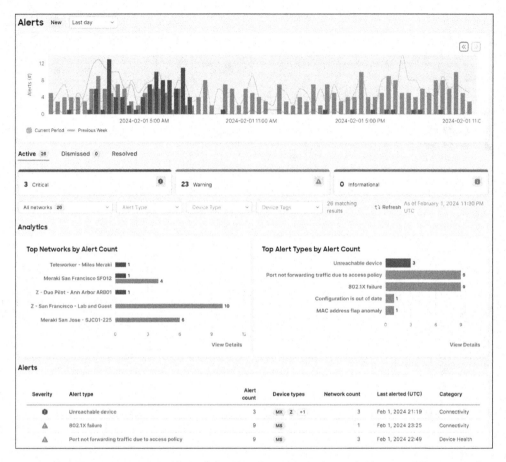

Figure 5-27 *Organization Alerts Page Showing Recent Critical Alerts and Warnings for Device Across Networks in the Organization*

Threat Assessment on Meraki Dashboard

After you configure any necessary security features like AMP or IDS, it's important to regularly review any potential threats detected by those features both to ensure their functionality and to address any potential issues stemming from within the network. In addition to the standard email alerts for threat detection, the Dashboard also provides the Security Center, a reporting page for all recent threat detection events. You can access this page via **Security & SD-WAN > Security Center** for the network-level Security Center and via **Organization > Security Center** for the organization-level Security Center.

This section provides a brief overview of the content available in the Security Center. For more details, visit https://documentation.meraki.com and search using the keywords **Security Center** or **threat protection**.

Security Center

The primary difference between the organization-level Security Center and the network-level Security Center is the level of reporting available, similar to the difference between the Alert Hub and the Organization Alerts page discussed previously. Both pages display details about detected security events, such as threat details, affected clients, and more, whether that be at the per-network level or organization/cross-network level, respectively. Figure 5-28 shows an example view of the organization-level Security Center page, identified as such by the presence of the Most Affected Networks section, which lists the total event counts for each network in the organization and is only present on the organization-level Security Center report.

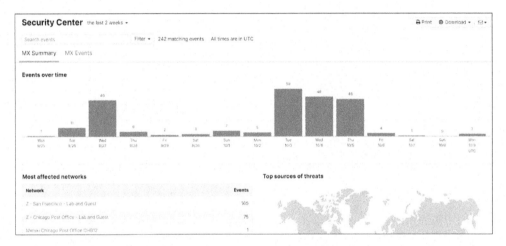

Figure 5-28 *Overview of the Organization > Security Center Page Showing Summary of All Security Events for All Networks over Last Two Weeks*

By default, the Security Center only displays malicious threat detection events, but you can use the Filter drop-down menu to also view clean events and unknown disposition events. This is particularly useful for confirming the operation of AMP or IDS/IPS, or for reviewing events that may have had their disposition retroactively updated after initially being reported as malicious.

Most Prevalent Threats

Threat detection is based on Cisco TALOS signature categories and will report based on the security level configured for IDS/IPS on the Security & SD-WAN > Threat Detection page for a given network. Whether configured for detection or prevention, detected threats will be reported (see Figure 5-29) as long as the detected threat is in the selected TALOS ruleset.

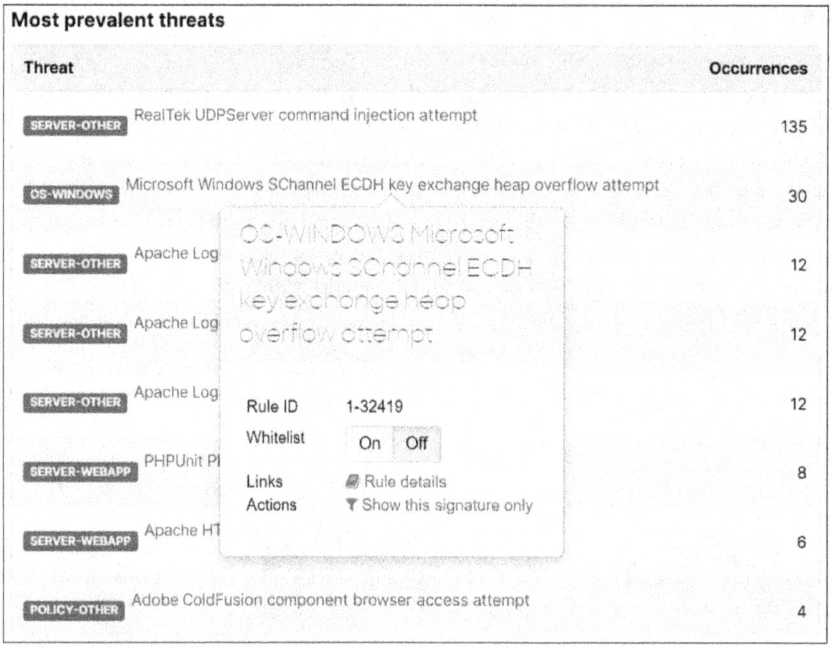

Most prevalent threats

Threat		Occurrences
SERVER-OTHER	RealTek UDPServer command injection attempt	135
OS-WINDOWS	Microsoft Windows SChannel ECDH key exchange heap overflow attempt	30
SERVER-OTHER	Apache Log	12
SERVER-OTHER	Apache Log	12
SERVER-OTHER	Apache Log	12
SERVER-WEBAPP	PHPUnit PI	8
SERVER-WEBAPP	Apache HT	6
POLICY-OTHER	Adobe ColdFusion component browser access attempt	4

OS-WINDOWS Microsoft Windows SChannel ECDH key exchange heap overflow attempt

Rule ID   1-32419
Whitelist   On   Off
Links   🔖 Rule details
Actions   ▼ Show this signature only

Figure 5-29   *Summary Report Showing the Most Prevalent Threats Across Devices in a Network*

Most Affected Clients

The Most Affected Clients view displays specific clients that have been most often flagged as involved in security events for the selected report timeframe. Figure 5-30 shows the most affected clients from the Organization > Security Center page, as evidenced by the client entries spanning multiple networks.

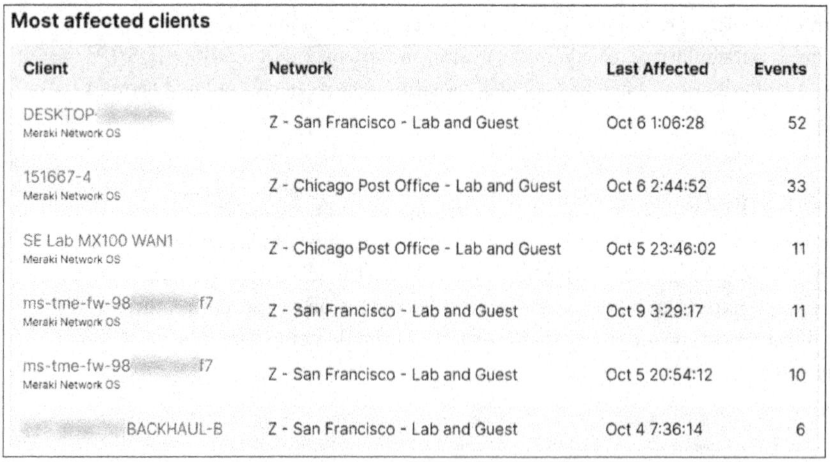

Most affected clients

Client	Network	Last Affected	Events
DESKTOP- Meraki Network OS	Z - San Francisco - Lab and Guest	Oct 6 1:06:28	52
151667-4 Meraki Network OS	Z - Chicago Post Office - Lab and Guest	Oct 6 2:44:52	33
SE Lab MX100 WAN1 Meraki Network OS	Z - Chicago Post Office - Lab and Guest	Oct 5 23:46:02	11
ms-tme-fw-98____f7 Meraki Network OS	Z - San Francisco - Lab and Guest	Oct 9 3:29:17	11
ms-tme-fw-98____f7 Meraki Network OS	Z - San Francisco - Lab and Guest	Oct 5 20:54:12	10
____BACKHAUL-B	Z - San Francisco - Lab and Guest	Oct 4 7:36:14	6

Figure 5-30   *Most Affected Clients in a Chosen Network, Shown in the Network-wide Security Center for That Network*

From here, each client can be directly pulled up in detail to view more information about either the specific client or the specific threat signatures involved.

Introduction to MG Cellular

In addition to the MX line of security appliances, Meraki offers an additional line of edge devices that provide a dedicated cellular gateway, known as the MG series. This line of devices is designed to provide a dedicated cellular uplink, or fixed wireless access (FWA), to any device capable of connecting to a wired Ethernet connection. The MG series can be deployed nearly anywhere in the world thanks to Meraki's never-ending efforts to obtain carrier certification from many of the largest cellular carriers all across the globe.

It is important to be aware that the MG series of devices, while designed to act as an edge uplink, are not designed to provide the same level of advanced features and functionality as the MX series of security appliances. The functionality of the MG series is more limited to provide a clearer focus on connectivity. For example, MG devices are not capable of security filtering, such as content filtering or IDS, or acting as a VPN endpoint for either Auto VPN or non-Meraki VPN connections.

For customers who want both fully featured security and cellular connectivity in a single device, Meraki does offer a Cellular series of MX devices (MX-C) that includes an integrated cellular modem. This allows a single device to function as both a cellular uplink and a fully featured security appliance. A notable caveat to this deployment compared to a separate security appliance and dedicated MG is that the MX must be placed in a location that provides adequate cellular signal for the cellular uplink, which may require some notable compromises in either performance or device location. This is discussed further in the "MG Deployment Considerations" section a bit later in the chapter.

Using an MG cellular uplink appropriately and achieving the best performance from it requires a basic understanding of cellular communication in general. Because cellular is a wireless technology, modern cellular standards share some similarities with modern Wi-Fi standards, especially when considering aspects of deployment such as signal strength and potential requirements for line of sight to provide a higher-performing connection.

Meraki currently offers several devices within the MG lineup that are capable of using different cellular standards, allowing you to choose the device that best fits your needs and available resources for each location.

4G LTE Versus 5G

4G LTE (Long Term Evolution) is a cellular standard that has become widespread around the world. It is capable of providing typical real-world speeds upward of >100 Mbps, although observed performance can and will vary based on multiple factors, including but not limited to signal strength and quality, radio congestion, and data rate limits imposed by the cellular carrier.

5G is the most recent standard to see widespread deployment and is designed to offer significantly increased throughput and lower latency as compared to 4G LTE, with potential throughput upward of 2 Gbps with the use of carrier aggregation. With this development in cellular technology, the use of a cellular uplink as a dedicated uplink has become more feasible than ever before.

5G connectivity comes in two types, 5G Non-Standalone (NSA) and 5G Standalone (SA), which are briefly explained further in the next section. At the time of writing, 5G deployment is still in relatively early stages, primarily available near large population centers where the smaller cell size and increased throughput offered by 5G are most impactful.

All Meraki MG devices currently support 4G LTE as the base standard for connectivity, with select models offering 5G connectivity.

5G NSA Versus 5G SA

There are currently two versions of 5G connectivity being deployed, 5G NSA and 5G SA. While both of these adhere to the new 5G standards, 5G SA is more capable of providing higher bandwidth and lower latency than 5G NSA, at the cost of significantly increased deployment and infrastructure costs for cellular providers.

Because of this increase in cost and complexity for deploying 5G SA, the 5G NSA standard was created. This intermediate standard is designed to provide 5G functionality while piggybacking the existing 4G LTE carrier networks. 5G NSA allows for the proliferation of 5G devices on carrier networks and an increase in performance compared to 4G LTE while reducing the initial deployment and upgrade costs associated with implementing a full 5G SA network.

Due to the current lack of availability of public 5G SA networks, MG devices that support 5G, such as the MG51, operate using either 4G LTE or 5G NSA, depending on availability and carrier configuration. Once 5G SA networks become more widely available, expect Cisco Meraki to release MG devices capable of utilizing full 5G SA connectivity.

Dashboard Monitoring for MG

The Dashboard UI is the primary method of monitoring your deployed MG devices. The Cellular Gateway > Cellular Gateways page provides a detailed overview of each device. By selecting a specific MG from the device list on that page, you can view the full device details page, such as the Security & SD-WAN > Appliance Status page for MX devices. In addition to viewing the standard connectivity information, including historical Dashboard connectivity and network data usage, you can view cellular-specific details by selecting the **Uplink** tab, as shown in Figure 5-31.

This tab shows all available cellular information for the current device, such as SIM details and radio status for both 4G and 5G radios, and shows network and data session details for the current connection. Additionally, if you require any custom SIM configurations and the device is online via a wired connection, you can apply custom APN configurations from this tab, and they will be pushed to the device on the next configuration fetch.

Figure 5-31   *Dashboard MG Uplink Tab Showing an MG51 with One SIM Currently Inserted and an Active 4G LTE Connection with Verizon*

MG Deployment Considerations

When reviewing your deployment and considering potential uplink options, it's important to take into consideration both the expected requirements of your cellular uplink and the physical and environmental restrictions that may impact the performance of a cellular uplink. Before you decide to use a cellular uplink, you should consider things like device location relative to your chosen cellular network and how the surrounding environment may impact signal transmission between your device and the nearest cellular tower. This will allow you to gain a better understanding of the potential maximum performance as well as any potential limitations you may face for each deployment.

Cellular—Primary or Backup?

Until relatively recently, cellular connectivity for business uplinks was typically over-looked or only used for backup connections of last resort or out of band connectivity. With the proliferation of 4G LTE and now the advent of 5G connectivity, the possibilities offered by a dedicated cellular uplink are growing to never-before-seen heights.

Many customers are now looking at a dedicated cellular uplink as a potential primary uplink for certain sites, such as locations where access to multiple ISPs for redundant circuits is impractical, or for temporary use while initially deploying a site while waiting for upstream ISP provisioning to complete before transitioning to a reliable backup connection that is mostly independent of traditional ISP infrastructure and service interruptions.

Determining whether to use a cellular uplink as a primary uplink will be heavily impacted by both the expected business needs for the uplink and the expected performance and cost of the cellular uplink as compared to a more traditional wired or satellite uplink. Each has potential trade-offs depending on the specific availability of connections in your area and the specific data costs associated with the cellular carriers available to choose from.

For example, many cellular plans have strict data caps, or limit throughput after crossing a certain data threshold for the month. While many carriers are also introducing business-grade plans, depending on your chosen provider and plans offered, this may strongly influence you to use the cellular uplink as a backup connection only to reduce unneeded data usage when a wired uplink is functional.

Alternatively, some locations may be limited in choice for wired uplinks but may have adequate 4G LTE coverage to allow for a cellular uplink to be used instead of a satellite uplink, providing potentially faster throughput and lower latency.

5G Line of Sight

5G cellular connections use higher frequencies and therefore have smaller service cell sizes and less signal penetration when compared to 4G LTE, resulting in more deploy-ment constraints for the location of cellular devices. Whereas a traditional router/firewall can be placed nearly anywhere within a building as long as it is relatively protected and has a wired connection to the rest of the network, placement of a cellular uplink requires more careful planning and consideration to ensure that it still provides an adequate cellular signal to maintain a functional connection.

Especially when working with 5G, for the reasons stated previously, the physical place-ment of your MG can have an immense impact on the performance of your cellular uplink. Although a 5G connection may still offer serviceable performance for a device located inside a building, to achieve maximum performance for a 5G connection, near or full line of sight (LoS) between the MG antenna and the cellular tower is necessary.

Pro Tip   Many online tools exist to show the placement of radio access networks (RANs) for different providers. This knowledge is very handy in determining carrier and device placement.

By design, Meraki MG are all outdoor rated, with certain models supporting additional external antennas, offering even greater placement options to ensure optimal signal conditions for your deployment. By separating the cellular uplink from the primary router/firewall, this allows an outdoor MG to be placed in the most optimal location, such as a roof mount, and allows an external antenna to be precisely positioned for maximum performance while still allowing for a reliable wired connection from the MG down to the rest of the network.

CGNAT and You

As previously mentioned, another caveat when working with cellular as a business uplink is that most cellular providers use Carrier Grade NAT (CGNAT), so it's important to understand at a basic level how CGNAT can affect your cellular deployment.

At the most basic level, CGNAT is very similar to standard NAT, altering traffic from multiple clients to share the same source IP address before egressing to the public Internet. However, CGNAT takes this to another level by operating at a much larger scale than traditional NAT, oftentimes implementing multiple levels of NAT within the carrier network before traffic egresses to the public Internet to allow potentially thousands of customers to share a single public IP. In effect, this can cause issues with many services that require the use of specific or consistent inbound ports for communication, such as VPN tunneling or port forwarding for inbound connections.

Many carriers that offer business-grade cellular plans also offer the option to either bypass CGNAT entirely or configure advanced forwarding to allow for greater compatibility with services like VPNs and port forwarding. However, this is highly carrier dependent and may not be available everywhere, so it's critical to explore all aspects of your proposed cellular solution to ensure that the carrier you choose can provide a level of service that works with your intended use case for your cellular uplink, whether that be as a primary uplink or a backup or out-of-band connection.

Pro Tip   Consider leveraging IPv6 to avoid the headaches of CGNAT.

Prestaging for Deployment

When deploying an MG cellular gateway, there are a few steps that you can take during prestaging of your gateway to help ensure a stable and smooth connection. Because of the nature of a cellular uplink, it's important to make sure the device is properly configured and up to date before mounting it on the roof and putting away the ladder.

To ensure maximum compatibility and device performance, we recommend first bringing the device online in an accessible location and allowing it to complete the initial Dashboard check-in and any pending firmware upgrades before fully deploying. By properly planning your deployment and prestaging the device, you can potentially save multiple service callouts to troubleshoot an unreachable device in difficult or inconvenient locations such as on a roof or other remote location.

The initial bring-up for MG devices has been designed to be as effortless as possible, with hundreds of the most common cellular carrier details preloaded on every MG, with the goal of providing immediate connectivity once a SIM is inserted. For many customers, prestaging the MG is as simple as inserting the SIM, powering on the MG, and waiting for it to check in to the Dashboard and complete any pending firmware upgrades before disconnecting the MG and taking it to the final install location.

For those using less common static or custom APNs, or who are otherwise unable to bring up cellular automatically with the default configurations available, MG devices are designed with several potential approaches to help assist in troubleshooting cellular connectivity.

Troubleshooting Meraki Devices

This section covers the primary tools available for troubleshooting Meraki devices directly, without access to the Meraki cloud. The details here apply to most Meraki products, such as MX security appliances, MS switches, MR access points, and MG gateways, but this section sticks with the MG focus for now, as the features discussed here are either product agnostic or apply only to MG/MX-C devices.

Although all Meraki devices are designed to provide as simple a deployment as possible, due to the wide variety of cellular carriers and configurations for each, Meraki cannot guarantee that the preloaded configurations on each MG will be able to provide connectivity directly out of the box. For this reason, MG cellular gateways utilize many of the same local troubleshooting methods as other Meraki devices, while also providing several ways of applying a custom cellular configuration or further troubleshooting connectivity issues specifically.

Local Status Page

Nearly all approaches to troubleshooting MG connectivity issues begin with accessing the Local Status page, a self-hosted configuration page provided with most Meraki devices (MX/MG/MS/MR) that is accessible only from the LAN of Meraki devices. From this page, you can gather basic connectivity information for troubleshooting, such as if the device is currently able to access various resources such as its local gateway, the Internet, and the Meraki cloud (see Figure 5-32). Importantly, after authenticating, you can also make configuration changes to the uplink configuration of the device in question.

For MG (and MX-C) devices, this means you can view details about the modem and any currently inserted SIM cards, as well as apply any custom configuration options, such as a static access point name (APN) or authentication details, needed to bring up the cellular connection (see Figure 5-33).

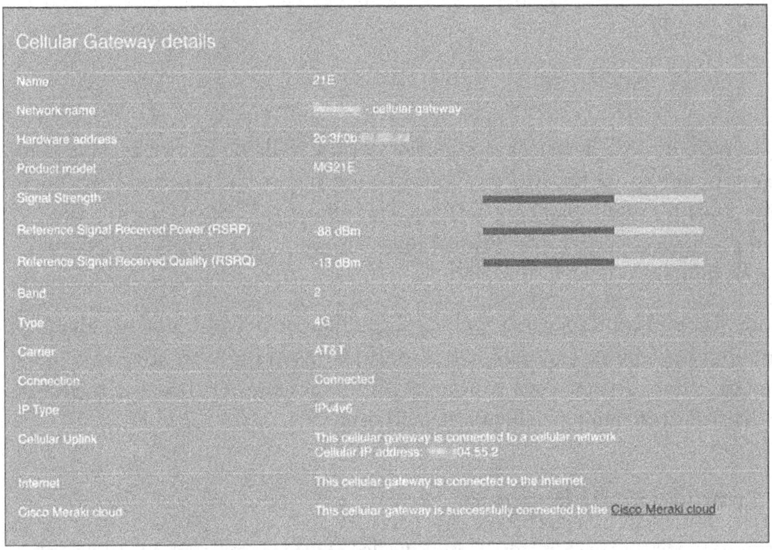

Figure 5-32   *Local Status Page of an MG Showing the Current Cellular Connection Details and Connectivity Test Results*

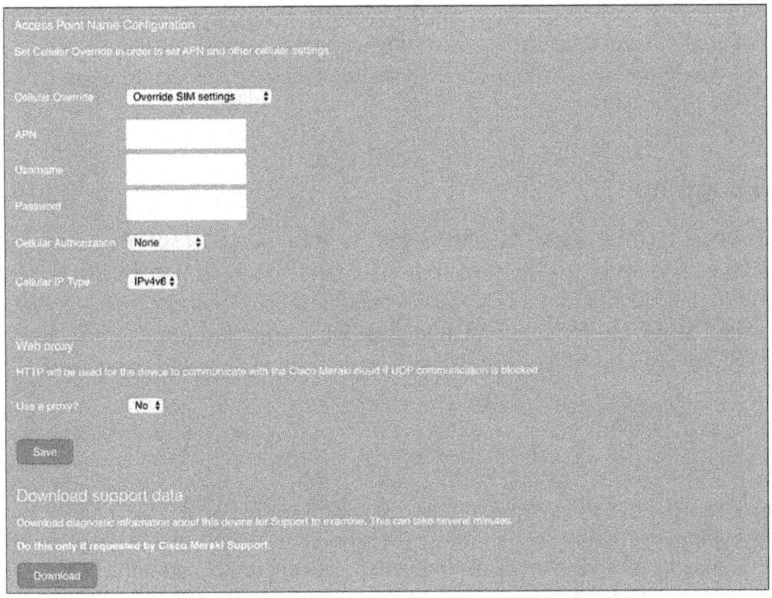

Figure 5-33   *Local Status Page of a Device with a Cellular Modem, Specifically Showing a Blank Custom Cellular APN Configuration*

Before you access the Local Status page, first ensure that you have a direct connection to a LAN port of the device and no other Internet or network connectivity. Then, access the Local Status page through a web browser either by URL (setup.meraki.com or my.meraki.com) or directly at the device IP. All Meraki devices support the use of the generic URL as well as device-specific URLs, such as switch.meraki.com and ap.meraki.com, respective to the device type in question.

Safe Mode

The Local Status page on MG devices has a special option available known as Safe Mode. This alters the configuration of the MG to allow it to use one of the physical LAN ports as a wired uplink port for additional connectivity. This allows the MG to be brought online via a wired connection over a traditional Internet uplink and complete the initial check-in to the Dashboard.

Using Safe Mode can prevent unnecessary data usage when devices are downloading initial firmware upgrades during prestaging. It also can be used for more advanced troubleshooting of cellular issues when working with Meraki Support because it allows direct device access despite failing cellular connectivity.

Support Data Bundle (SDB) Logging

Like the Local Status page itself, Support Data Bundle (SDB) Logging for Meraki Support is another feature that is widely available across the Meraki product line. Able to be generated and downloaded directly from the Local Status page after authenticating, SDB logs are used to provide an encrypted bundle of detailed logging information from a device to Meraki Support, allowing for a snapshot of the device state at nearly any given time. This typically is particularly useful when troubleshooting an unreachable or offline device, or for capturing logging for Meraki Support analysis immediately after an issue has presented.

Integrated DM Logging

Similar to SDB Logging, DM Logging is a method of recording logging specific to cellular communications to provide to Meraki Support for later analysis. Available for select MG devices, this tool again provides an encrypted bundle of cellular logging details that is specifically useful alongside associated SDB logging when troubleshooting a failing cellular connection without the ability to bring the device online via a wired connection.

Summary

This chapter covered the most notable features offered by Meraki MX security appliances, including support for Cisco AMP, TALOS-powered content filtering, Meraki Auto VPN, and Meraki Insight, as well as multiple important aspects to keep in mind both when planning your MX deployment and when operating and monitoring the deployment after the initial rollout.

In addition, this chapter briefly looked at how an MG cellular gateway can provide additional flexibility and connectivity for your deployments, such as providing a robust failover mechanism from a traditional ISP connection or by employing cellular as a primary uplink when a traditional ISP link is either unreliable or unable to provide the necessary level of connectivity.

Chapter 6 continues the focus on MX-related technology with a specific focus on Meraki's powerful SD-WAN solution that utilizes Meraki Auto VPN as an underlay to provide a solid foundation for an industry-leading SD-WAN overlay solution that is able to be built and configured directly from the Dashboard.

Additional Reading

Meraki Umbrella SDWAN Connector Deployment Guide: https://documentation.meraki.com/MX/Meraki_Umbrella_SDWAN_Connector/Deployment_Guide

Automatically Integrating Cisco Umbrella with Meraki Networks: https://documentation.meraki.com/MR/Other_Topics/Automatically_Integrating_Cisco_Umbrella_with_Meraki_Networks

Adaptive Policy Overview: https://documentation.meraki.com/General_Administration/Cross-Platform_Content/Adaptive_Policy/Adaptive_Policy_Overview

MX Routing Behavior: https://documentation.meraki.com/MX/Networks_and_Routing/MX_Routing_Behavior

Auto VPN Hub Deployment Recommendations: https://documentation.meraki.com/Architectures_and_Best_Practices/Auto_VPN_Hub_Deployment_Recommendations

Meraki Trust: https://meraki.cisco.com/trust/#data

Meraki SD-WAN: https://documentation.meraki.com/Architectures_and_Best_Practices/Cisco_Meraki_Best_Practice_Design/Best_Practice_Design_-_MX_Security_and_SD-WAN/Meraki_SD-WAN#Configuring_Auto_VPN_at_the_Branch

Port Forwarding and NAT Rules on the MX: https://documentation.meraki.com/MX/NAT_and_Port_Forwarding/Port_Forwarding_and_NAT_Rules_on_the_MX

Automatic NAT Traversal for Auto VPN Tunneling Between Cisco Meraki Peers: https://documentation.meraki.com/MX/Site-to-site_VPN/Automatic_NAT_Traversal_for_Auto_VPN_Tunneling_between_Cisco_Meraki_Peers

VPN Status Page: https://documentation.meraki.com/MX/Site-to-site_VPN/VPN_Status_Page

MX SD-WAN Best Practices

This chapter discusses the specifics of Meraki's SD-WAN over Auto-VPN implementation, including overviews and recommendations for configuring traffic policies and incorporating Meraki SD-WAN into your existing deployments. It also briefly touches on Meraki's powerful new SD-Internet feature set and highlights the new capabilities offered by this solution.

Introduction to Meraki SD-WAN

Software-defined WAN (SD-WAN) is a set of features that dynamically selects the optimal path to route traffic based on connection conditions (e.g., loss, latency, and traffic type). This helps ensure optimal performance for critical applications and real-time traffic such as VoIP. The availability of fast, reliable, and cost-effective broadband services has contributed to the ever-increasing adoption of SD-WAN solutions. With the increased adoption of SaaS applications and favorable market conditions driving price/Gbps down, traditional MPLS-based solutions have unwanted latency and bandwidth limitations, driving SD-WAN adoption rates.

The history of SD-WAN at Meraki goes back to 2015 with the Meraki IWAN project when the industry was awash with SDN offerings. This initial solution was based on Layer 3 and Layer 4 traffic data for making decisions, unlike the latest Layer 7–based solution. As of 2023, there are more than 35,000 global customers using Meraki SD-WAN solutions spanning multiple business verticals. Examples include but are not limited to healthcare clinics, 24/7 retail operations, banking operations, and entire school systems, to mention a few.

Pro Tip   Meraki refers to the underlying mechanism of its SD-WAN operation as *dynamic path selection (DPS)*, whereas most other SD-WAN solutions use the term *performance-based routing (PfR)*.

The Science of Transport Performance

Meraki MX security appliances use UDP probes approximately 100 bytes in size to continuously monitor performance across all available transport paths. These probes are unidirectional. Therefore, an MX high-availability pair with dual WAN links would have multiple probes passing via each available WAN uplink, including cellular uplinks. The default probe interval is 1 second. However, this is modified automatically to up to 10 seconds for very large deployments with thousands of Auto VPN nodes to avoid overloading devices with probe traffic and the associated monitoring overhead. Even though the Meraki support team may be engaged to manually change the probe interval, the Meraki way is to let the automation take care of the process. And take note, automation is a key parameter that has allowed Meraki SD-WAN to be simplified and scaled for any industry.

All Meraki devices synchronize their local Network Time Protocol (NTP) clock using the management plane back to the Meraki cloud. This synchronization is leveraged by MX security appliances to calculate the latency on each transport path using timestamp information contained in the data payload of the probes. The timestamps and other remaining data in the probe response packets are used to calculate the round-trip time (RTT), latency, jitter, and loss, which are all considered when calculating the Mean Operating Score (MOS) of a transport path. The MOS value is a commonly used general performance metric to quickly determine the average link quality for transport paths based on the metrics noted previously. The MOS is calculated to result in a value between 1 and 5, with the higher MOS value representing a better quality path.

Meraki will aggregate probe data over 30-second periods to use for monitoring and reporting of SD-WAN metrics, which in a typical network will provide 30 data points (one probe per second) to be used to determine link quality. For extremely large Auto VPN deployments where a 10-second probe interval is used, this still provides three probes per uplink path to be aggregated to calculate the network performance metrics. This probe logic is optimized to trigger failover between transport paths as quickly as possible, with the ability to reach sub-second failover times in some scenarios. This allows Meraki devices with proper SD-WAN implementations to provide high levels of reliability and connectivity for critical traffic across multiple transport circuits with minimal configuration.

Table 6-1 shows the various services and their expected failover and failback times for Meraki devices. The main parameter to note is the sub-second performance of DPS compared to other services. That is where the value of SD-WAN becomes realized.

Table 6-1   *Meraki Service Failover Times*

Service	Failover Time	Failback Time	SD-WAN
AutoVPN tunnels	30 to 40 seconds	30 to 40 seconds	No
DC-DC failover	20 to 30 seconds	20 to 30 seconds	No
Dynamic path selection	Sub-seconds to up to 30 seconds	Sub-seconds to up to 30 seconds	Yes

Service	Failover Time	Failback Time	SD-WAN
Warm spare	30 seconds or less	30 seconds or less	No
WAN connectivity	300 seconds or less	15-30 seconds	No

Note that the DPS time is the only SD-WAN–based failover time listed in Table 6-1 and that the true failover time will depend heavily on the policy type and configuration. In the vast majority of scenarios, failover will occur in 1 to 3 seconds, but with proper policy configurations, dynamic path failover can take less than 500 ms. In the instance of a complete circuit failure, the time to failover to a secondary path is near instantaneous and is less than 100 ms. Additionally, the 300-second time listed for general WAN connectivity failover is an absolute worst case scenario for a device experiencing intermittent WAN degradation. The 300-second WAN failover time in this case is not an SD-WAN implementation failover time despite often being touted as such by competitors.

Pro Tip   You can find details about the MOS and other performance metrics previously measured by navigating to the **Security & SD-WAN > VPN Status** page from the network of one peer, then selecting the entry for the related VPN peer in the Site-to-Site Peers table.

For additional details related to Auto VPN monitoring, uplink failover, and additional deployment best practices, visit https://documentation.meraki.com and read the article "Meraki Auto VPN General Best Practices" and other related articles.

Note   The "Additional Reading" section at the end of this chapter provides the full URL for every article that is cross-referenced in this chapter. Alternatively, you can search for the article title at https://documentation.meraki.com to locate it.

The Anatomy of SD-WAN Policies

Now that you are familiar with the basics of how Meraki MX devices monitor the performance of available transport paths, this section introduces the default SD-WAN policies used for uplink selection that are built in to the MX platform. You can find the SD-WAN policy settings in the Dashboard by navigating to the **Security & SD-WAN > Traffic Shaping** page and scrolling to the SD-WAN Policies section. SD-WAN policy settings are used to define the acceptable performance thresholds an uplink must meet to be marked as an available transport for routing traffic matching the configured condition.

The following subsections dissect each "attribute" that influences the target conditions being sought for the environment. Each attribute influences the outcome to help shift traffic as quickly and as correctly as possible thanks to all the data calculations the platform performs on the fly. By the end of this section, you will understand each aspect of the configuration shown in Figure 6-1.

SD-WAN policies

Internet traffic

Custom Expressions

Uplink Selection Policy	Traffic Filters	Actions
Prefer WAN 1. Fail over if poor performance.	10.240.10.0/24 to Any	✎ ✖
Add a preference		

Major Applications

Uplink Selection Policy	Traffic Filters	Actions
Load balance on uplinks that are suitable for performance class VoIP.	UDP from 10.11.11.0/24 to Office 365 Suite	✎ ✖
Add a preference		

VPN traffic

Uplink selection policy	Traffic filters	Actions
Prefer WAN 2. Fail over if poor performance for "WEBEX".	WebEx	✛ ✕
Prefer WAN 2. Fail over if poor performance for "MV CLOUD PROXY".	(TCP from Any to Any:30001)	✛ ✕
Prefer WAN 2. Fail over if poor performance for "UMBRELLA".	(ICMP from Any to 208.67.220.220)	✛ ✕
Prefer WAN 2. Fail over if poor performance for "VIDEO MUSIC".	YouTube	✛ ✕
Add a preference		

Custom performance classes

Name	Maximum latency (ms)	Maximum jitter (ms)	Maximum loss (%)	Actions
VIDEO MUSIC	(none)	(none)	5	✕
WEBEX	50	25	2	✕
UMBRELLA	55	(none)	3	✕
MV CLOUD PROXY	30	5	3	✕
Create a new custom performance class...				

Figure 6-1   *Example SD-WAN Configuration on the Dashboard*

SD-WAN Uplink Policies

The Dashboard provides several options for uplink selection policies when creating an SD-WAN policy, based on the following default policies shown in Figure 6-2 and discussed in the following paragraphs. These default policies are designed to assist in a quick and easy deployment for the most common use cases and provide excellent results without requiring manual thresholds to be defined on a per-network basis.

■ **Default policy** or **Connection Monitor Failover:** Shown as WAN1, WAN2, or Global Preference on the Dashboard. These policies require the recorded loss rate to be at least 60 percent loss before failing over from the chosen uplink to an alternate transport network. This policy type also ensures that failover would not happen if the alternate transport network also has >60 percent loss, to prevent failing over to another poor connection.

Pro Tip   When specifying either WAN1 or WAN2 (not Global Preference), the default failover criteria can be overridden by using a custom performance class, similar to when configuring Load Balancing.

■ **Load Balancing:** This policy is recommended to take full advantage of a Meraki SD-WAN solution and balances traffic flows across all available uplinks that satisfy the requirements of the selected performance class. By default, the Dashboard provides only a single performance class, VoIP, but additional custom performance classes can be created.

   ■ **VoIP:** This performance class requires the MOS of an uplink to be >3.5 to be considered an acceptable path. Flows will otherwise follow any other traffic routing policies to determine their transport path out an acceptable uplink. The 3.5 MOS value is set based on the cut-off for common CODECs used for VoIP and to help optimize the selected transport path for a higher quality experience. While this class is labeled VoIP, it is not specifically limited to VoIP traffic in any way and can be used with any traffic selection filter.

■ **Best for VoIP (Best MOS):** This policy results in choosing the best available transport path based on the highest MOS result. Related flows will immediately prefer the currently best-performing path across all available transport paths. This class is very sensitive to loss metrics. While this policy is labeled VoIP, it is not specifically limited to VoIP traffic in any way and can be used with any traffic selection filter.

Pro Tip   These predefined policies exist to give you a starting point; tuning the environment to known codecs used by the business or known application parameters (e.g., Citrix traffic sensitive to 150-ms latency but more resilient to loss) is highly recommended.

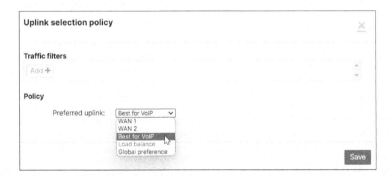

Figure 6-2   *Default SD-WAN Uplink Policies as They Appear in the Dashboard*

Custom SD-WAN Performance Classes

Meraki also provides the option to define any combination of latency, jitter, OR loss metric values to create custom SD-WAN performance classes.

> **Pro Tip** "OR" is capitalized here as a hint that calculations are based on a logical OR operator and not all parameters need be defined.

These custom performance classes are available to select for defining SD-WAN uplink decisions just like the default VoIP performance class under the Load Balancing policy discussed previously. One common use case for custom performance classes is to configure a class with application-specific metrics for sensitive web applications such as Office 365, an example of which is shown in Table 6-2.

Table 6-2 *Example Custom Performance Class for Office 365 Traffic*

SaaS	Max Latency (ms)	Max Jitter (ms)	Max Loss (%)
O365	200	50	5

> **Pro Tip** Meraki allows up to six custom performance classes to be defined per network.

Custom performance classes can also be used to route traffic based on custom SLA definitions or traffic service classes, as shown in the example in Table 6-3.

Table 6-3 *Series of Example Custom Performance Classes Based on Traffic SLA Class*

SLA	Max Latency (ms)	Max Jitter (ms)	Max Loss (%)
Platinum	150	20	1
Gold	250	40	3
Silver	500	50	10

The use of custom performance classes like these allows you to fine-tune a Meraki SD-WAN solution to provide the best performance for a wide variety of use cases in nearly any deployment.

For additional and more detailed information on the default and custom uplink performance classes available in the Dashboard, visit https://documentation.meraki.com and view the article "MX Load Balancing and Flow Preferences" and other related articles.

> **Pro Tip** You can use custom performance classes for traffic routing in both overlay SD-WAN and standard Internet-bound traffic (the latter is also known as SD-Internet).

Traffic Analysis and Identification

Meraki employs separate traffic identification methodologies for overlay SD-WAN and SD-Internet. Beginning with MX 16 firmware, Meraki devices now use an implementation of extended NBAR2 for overlay-based SD-WAN that can currently detect around 600 different types of application traffic. For Internet-based SD-WAN (i.e., SD-Internet), Meraki has implemented a custom solution that uses signature-based recognition to identify application traffic from many of the most commonly used applications. At some point, both these methodologies will merge and use only the full protocol packs of NBAR2. For more information on SD-Internet, visit https://documentation.meraki.com and access the article SD-WAN Internet Policies (SD-Internet).

The Dashboard comes with over 20 categories of predefined traffic entries that cover many of the most common traffic types, such as Office 365, SharePoint, and Webex, to allow for easy traffic identification when creating SD-WAN policies. This provides a quick and simple option to configure SD-WAN policies for many of the most commonly used applications without having to manually define individual application ports and IPs or domains.

In addition to the predefined traffic filters, the Meraki Dashboard also enables you to create custom traffic definitions to use for uplink selection, similar to custom performance classes. This allows for custom uplink selection policies that can be as generic as ANY source (within the scope of MX networks associated with Auto VPN), ANY destination, or any protocol. Alternatively, custom uplink selection policies can be configured for specific protocols, source IPs and subnets, destination IPs and subnets, domains, or any combination of these to allow for extremely granular traffic selection.

Pro Tip   "ANY" is capitalized here as a hint that the source or destination values can be configured with a logical ANY operator.

When destination domains are configured, the MX will snoop for the related DNS record and cache the results for the time to live (TTL) of the record to expedite future queries for the same domain.

Pro Tip   Make sure the DNS record for the domain configured returns an A record in the response. CNAME records will not yield proper identification of traffic.

You can configure custom traffic filters for uplink selection policies on the Dashboard by navigating to **Security & SD-WAN > SD-WAN & Traffic Shaping > SD-WAN Policies > Add Preference** and clicking the **Add** button (see Figure 6-3). Figure 6-4 shows an example of a custom traffic filter.

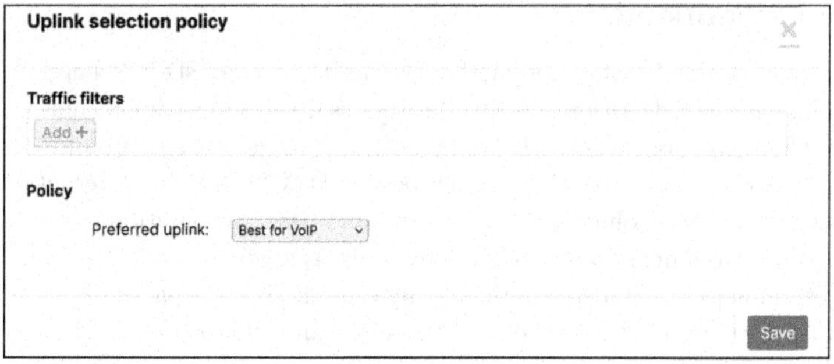

Figure 6-3   *Uplink Policy Module Before Creating Any Policies*

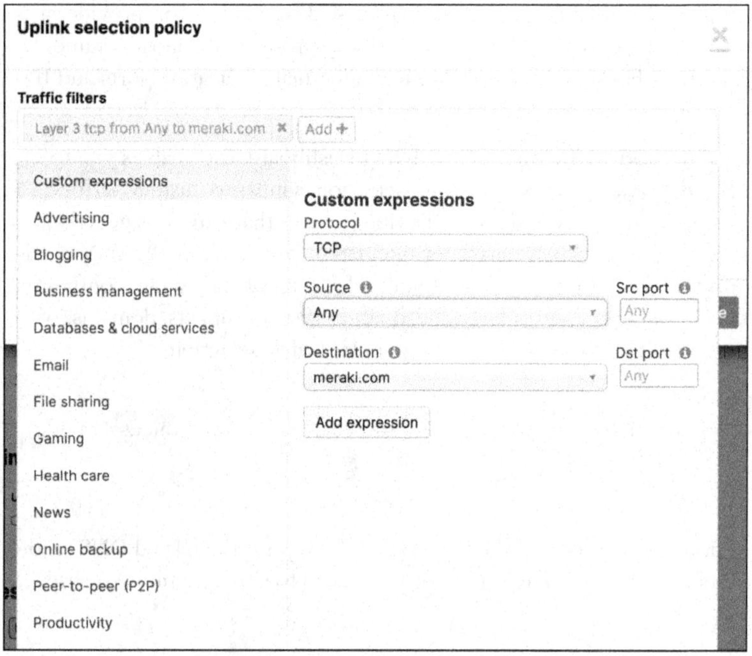

Figure 6-4   *Custom Expression Builder for Custom Uplink Policies*

Dynamic Path Selection Policies

Dynamic path selection (DPS) policies in the Dashboard can be configured as a simple mapping of an application to a specific uplink or configured with multiple conditional policies to ensure critical application traffic always takes the best available path. Even though the configuration is directed to an uplink interface, there are multiple virtual paths that may be taken through that interface. The exact virtual transport path chosen for the traffic will be dependent on the overall Auto VPN architecture (e.g., number of hubs).

Two of the primary configurations that influence these uplink decisions are the primary uplink preference and load balancing configuration, located in the Global Preferences section of the Security & SD-WAN > SD-WAN & Traffic Shaping page, as shown in Figure 6-5.

Pro Tip   It's important to note that if the Load Balancing option is set to Disabled in the Global Preferences section, none of the configured load balancing policies will take effect.

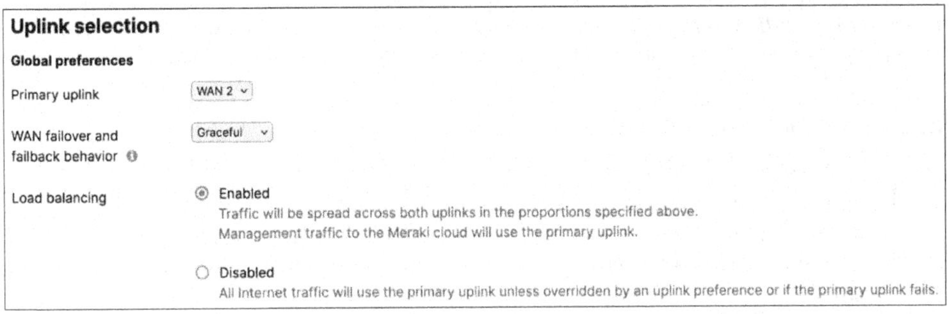

Uplink selection

Global preferences

Primary uplink   [WAN 2 ∨]

WAN failover and   [Graceful   ∨]
failback behavior ⓘ

Load balancing   ◉ Enabled
                        Traffic will be spread across both uplinks in the proportions specified above.
                        Management traffic to the Meraki cloud will use the primary uplink.

                      ○ Disabled
                        All Internet traffic will use the primary uplink unless overridden by an uplink preference or if the primary uplink fails.

Figure 6-5   *Global Preferences Section of the SD-WAN & Traffic Shaping Page*

Next you'll explore a few policy configuration examples for uplink selection based on commonly seen use cases. In the following examples, assume that the WAN1 uplink is a high-speed fiber network that you want to handle all your sensitive application traffic, and that the WAN2 uplink is a legacy DSL connection that you prefer to use as a backup connection or for noncritical application traffic.

Global Preference Policy

This section defines a basic example policy to act as a fallback policy. This policy will act as a catch-all, policy-based routing decision for traffic whose priority is somewhere between that of a business-critical application and an explicitly noncritical application—in this example, the traffic is labeled the "All Social web & photo sharing" category.

As a result, the policy shown in Figure 6-6 is configured to use the uplink preferences defined in the Global Preferences section of the SD-WAN & Traffic Shaping page (see Figure 6-5) with no other explicit requirements. In this case, because the Load Balancing option is set to Enabled in the Global Preferences section, you would see application traffic matching this policy load balanced across both uplinks.

Pro Tip   A policy such as this is not strictly necessary with most designs, as any traffic not matching an existing policy will by default follow the global routing preferences for primary uplink selection, load balancing, and failover.

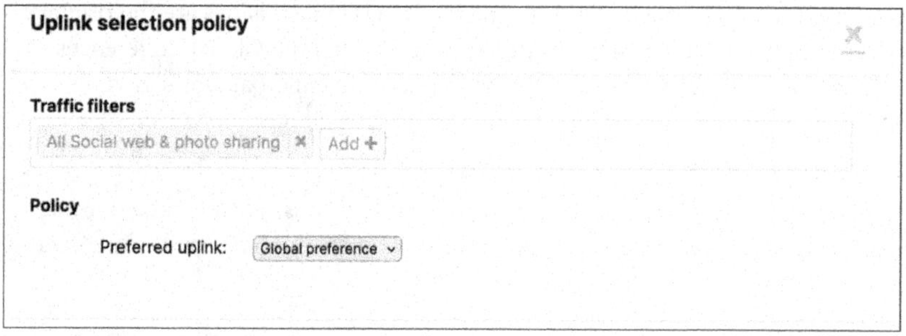

Figure 6-6   *Uplink Selection Policy to Send All Social Web & Photo Sharing Traffic Out Uplinks Based on the Global Routing Preference, Configured to Load Balance*

Basic Load Balancing Policy

When specifically configuring a load balancing policy, you need to first make sure the Load Balancing option is set to Enabled in the Global Preferences section of the SD-WAN & Traffic Shaping page, as previously shown in Figure 6-5. If you also set the Preferred Uplink option to Load Balance, the option to choose an uplink performance class is also shown.

In the example shown in Figure 6-7, the device will monitor all available transport paths and load balance matching traffic flows across paths matching the performance requirements of the selected performance class—in this case, a custom performance class called O365. This helps to ensure that all available bandwidth is provided to the application while also ensuring that all the participating transport networks are compliant with your custom performance criteria.

Load balancing policies also take into consideration the configured available bandwidth for all matching uplinks, which is used to perform weighted load balancing on a per-flow basis to help maintain equal relative utilization along each path. As an example, if the difference between the configured available bandwidth of the primary and secondary WAN uplinks is a 1:4 ratio, then the MX would load balance matching flows between those uplinks in a matching 1:4 ratio.

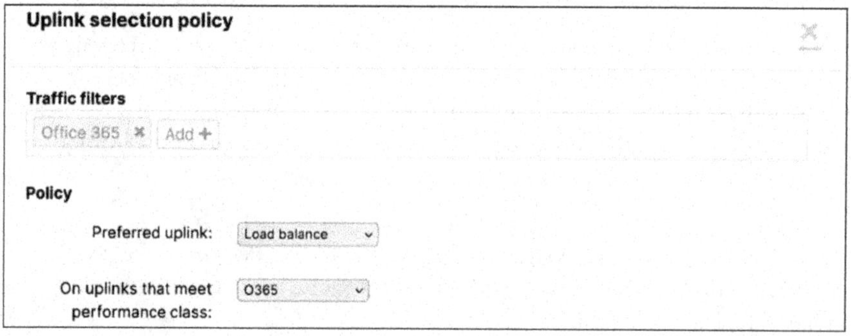

Figure 6-7   *Custom "Office 365" Uplink Policy*

Pro Tip   This load balancing behavior also applies to traffic that is load balanced via the Global Preferences configuration.

Basic Policy-Based Routing

Figure 6-8 is an example of configuring a non-business-critical application, Facebook, with a preferred uplink of WAN 2 and setting it to fail over only if that uplink is completely unavailable. In this configuration, Facebook traffic will continue to use WAN 2 irrespective of the performance score for that uplink as long as the uplink is available, since performance-based checks are not configured.

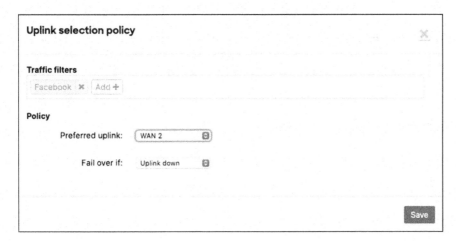

Figure 6-8   *Uplink Selection Policy to Route All Facebook Traffic over WAN 2 Unless Unavailable*

Performance-Based DPS

The configuration in Figure 6-9 shows one of our critical business applications, Office 365, selected as the traffic type with the default Best for VoIP uplink selection policy configured. The Best for VoIP policy will result in the device choosing only one path out of multiple available transport paths to route the application traffic based on the current highest MOS score across available transport paths.

With our example deployment, we would expect this policy to typically choose WAN 1. However, in the event the performance of WAN 1 drops below that of WAN 2, this policy would route Office 365 traffic over WAN 2 so long as that link has a higher MOS.

Figure 6-9 *Uplink Selection Policy Configured to Use the Uplink Marked Best for VoIP*

Policy Routing with Performance-Based DPS

This example takes the previous scenario one step further by adding a custom performance class. With this example configuration, shown in Figure 6-10, path selection will now only select between transport paths that satisfy the custom performance class o365. Office 365 application traffic is again selected as the traffic filter and will now flow over the preferred uplink of WAN 1 and fail over only if the link performance does not satisfy the custom performance class o365.

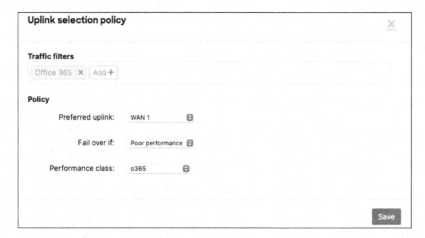

Figure 6-10 *Uplink Selection Policy Configured to Route Traffic over WAN1 Unless Failing to Meet the Performance Metrics of the Chosen Custom Performance Class*

SD-WAN over Cellular

Some Meraki security appliance models, such as the MX67C and MX68CW, have an embedded LTE modem to allow for cellular failover in the event of failure of the traditional wired uplinks. In addition to this traditional application as a backup connection for WAN failover, these models also have the capability to utilize both the wired and cellular connections concurrently. The option is located on the SD-WAN & Traffic Shaping page on the Dashboard. As shown in Figure 6-11, navigate to the Uplink Configuration section and set the Cellular Active Uplink option to **Enabled.**

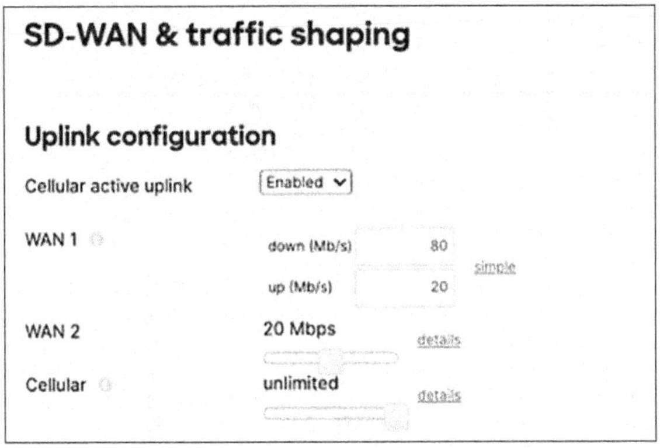

SD-WAN & traffic shaping

Uplink configuration

Cellular active uplink	Enabled ˅	
WAN 1	down (Mb/s) 80	simple
	up (Mb/s) 20	
WAN 2	20 Mbps	details
Cellular	unlimited	details

Figure 6-11 *Cellular Uplink Selected to Be an Always Active Part of the SD-WAN Decision Tree*

Pro Tip   The Cellular Active Uplink feature is only available for devices with integrated cellular modems. This logic does not work for USB modems.

When enabled, this feature configures the built-in cellular modem to take the place of the standard WAN 2 uplink, allowing for load balancing and active-active uplink SD-WAN deployments over the cellular uplink and a wired uplink, instead of requiring two wired uplinks. This enables additional flexibility in SD-WAN deployments, as it reduces the requirement from two local ISPs to a single ISP and a cellular service provider for each location. That provides more options when deploying a widespread SD-WAN implementation. In essence, the last-mile paths are different (i.e., one wired and one wireless), providing an additional layer of redundancy. In many cases, when using two terrestrial ISPs, they may be coming over the same conduit into a building, thus eliminating your Layer 1 path resiliency.

For more information about using SD-WAN over a cellular uplink, open the "Meraki SD-WAN" article on https://documentation.meraki.com and refer to the section "SD-WAN over Cellular Active Uplink."

Pro Tip   Enabling cellular SD-WAN disables the physical WAN 2 connection. Ensure that your cellular signal is good before you consider using this alternative SD-WAN path.

For administrators looking for the best cellular performance or to add a cellular uplink to an existing deployment, the Meraki MG series of devices are designed as dedicated cellular gateways with options for outdoor mounting for optimal placement and performance. The Meraki MG series is a multi-carrier solution that can provide high-speed, cellular-based, wireless WAN Ethernet connectivity not only to Meraki appliances but also to any L3 firewall or gateway router.

For more information on MG cellular gateways, visit https://meraki.cisco.com or https://documentation.meraki.com and search using the keyword **MG**.

SD-Internet

Meraki SD-WAN provides dynamic path selection and performance-based routing for overlay traffic. This is great for any traffic tunneled from one MX to another for applications hosted in private data centers or cloud applications. However, a local Internet breakout typically provides the best performance for SaaS applications like Office 365, Google services, or cloud-based VoIP services like Cisco Webex or Zoom. There are multiple reasons to consider steering SaaS traffic to direct Internet links. These include the increasing availability of reliable, faster, and cheaper Internet circuits and improved SD-WAN capabilities that can choose an optimal path based on the type of traffic without requiring a dedicated piece of hardware on the remote end.

To enable SD-Internet, also referred to as SD-WAN Internet Policies, on your MX, your Dashboard is required to have the SD-WAN tier of licensing applied and a supported firmware and device model deployed. For documentation on the supported MX models and other details regarding SD-Internet, read the "SD-WAN Internet Policies (SD-Internet)" article on https://documentation.meraki.com.

Once the prerequisites are met and the feature enabled, you will see the changes in the Internet Traffic section under SD-WAN Policies, as shown in Figure 6-12.

The SD-Internet configuration facilitates creating SaaS application-level policies, which excludes the traffic from traversing the VPN and any associated overhead and creates a more efficient local-breakout path. With this, you are still able to define custom performance classes for each application, similar to the other SD-WAN policies. SD-Internet policies are able to use the same custom performance classes that are available for VPN traffic.

Pro Tip It is advisable to add additional destination IP addresses for WAN uplink monitoring that are related to any SD-Internet applications. For example, add the IP of a SaaS/IaaS endpoint, or add the IP of the Cisco Umbrella DNS server (shown in Figure 6-13).

Pro Tip SD-Internet policies apply only to newly created flows and will not modify existing flows based on WAN performance changes.

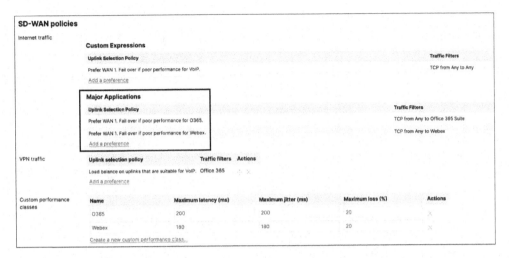

Figure 6-12 *SD-Internet Policy Section of the SD-WAN Policies Page on the Dashboard*

Figure 6-13 *Custom Uplink Monitoring Destinations Being Used to Help Monitor Link Quality to a Given Endpoint*

Integrating MPLS

In addition to a typical WAN connection, the Meraki SD-WAN solution also supports integrating a private MPLS connection to provide additional connectivity and deployment options.

MPLS on the LAN: Failover to Meraki Auto VPN

With Meraki, you can easily use an existing MPLS circuit to connect sites while adding an additional layer of failover redundancy by utilizing Meraki Auto VPN to provide a secure alternate route between sites in the event the MPLS link fails. In this scenario, failover from the MPLS link to the Auto VPN tunnel is achieved simply by configuring both sites with a local static route pointing over the MPLS link to the remote subnet(s), while on the remote side enabling Auto VPN participation for the same local subnet(s).

Pro Tip   A floating static default route is also an acceptable option to consider for your design.

The key to the operation and simplicity of this deployment is the ability to configure the local static route to be active only when a defined destination actively responds to ICMP ping requests. By configuring a known destination IP that is reachable through the same static route pointing across the MPLS link, the MX will now mark that route as active only if the MPLS link is up and the remote site is reachable. After configuring this on both sites, the internal routing priority of the route available over Auto VPN is less than that of the local static route pointing over the MPLS circuit, so traffic flows over the MPLS link in normal operation. However, if the MPLS connection fails and the sites lose the ability to ping across the MPLS link, the static route would be marked as Inactive and traffic would be routed over the Auto VPN route between sites, as shown in Figure 6-14. Once connectivity over the MPLS link is restored, new traffic flows will be routed back over the MPLS link until, gradually, all related traffic has moved back to traversing the MPLS link.

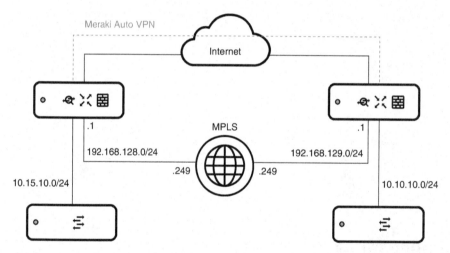

Figure 6-14   *Topology Diagram Showing Two Sites That Can Use Meraki Auto VPN as a Failover for an Existing MPLS Circuit*

This type of deployment allows for Meraki Auto VPN and SD-WAN to complement an existing MPLS deployment by providing a well-tuned, high-quality backup link for critical traffic in the event the traditional MPLS service becomes unusable. When combined with a more traditional MPLS deployment, Meraki's SD-WAN solution ensures that business-critical traffic is always able to traverse the most reliable path available, even when that path requires going out over the open Internet.

MPLS on the WAN: Meraki Auto VPN Overlay

There are many situations in which getting rid of MPLS altogether is not possible. For example, a company may have a long-term MPLS service contract that has an expensive exit clause, a site may have limited last mile options, or a site may have specific design requirements calling for MPLS. Whatever the case may be, MPLS connectivity can still be leveraged as a WAN transport for Meraki SD-WAN. Starting in MX13, when Auto VPN traffic traverses the MPLS network, the VPN packet headers have copies of the DSCP tags of the payload inside. Thereby, your MPLS carrier may still honor its service level agreements (SLAs) and commitment to your contract without having to decrypt or know what the traffic is inside the VPN tunnel.

When connecting an MPLS WAN, there are a few things to bear in mind:

- The WAN interface of the MX still needs to reach the cloud for communications such as updating the VPN registry for Auto VPN.

- You need to configure a static IP address on the WAN of the MX, just like you would do with a traditional router.

- The usual BGP exchange has now moved, and the routing will be more centralized with an MX hub.

Unpacking the previous observations, the Internet connectivity can be provided through an Internet breakout on the MPLS network itself, or it can happen via the MPLS network, through the data center, and out to the world via a firewall and border router. Traditional MPLS networks tend to assign a static address and use it for BGP exchange with the MPLS network. When the MX is added, you still configure the static address, so it has connectivity via the MPLS network. No BGP exchange takes place there, but at the hub MX instead. In other words, an Auto VPN overlay is created over the MPLS network, carrying the routes to the hub, where they get distributed into the network core. This centralizes and optimizes the routing because it happens in one place (assuming one hub for illustration purposes) instead of happening at every site. This simplifies deployments and reduces the time required to set up new sites.

The following are two additional advanced design features to consider:

- **VPN exclusions:** VPN exclusions are great for intelligently separating traffic to go straight to the Internet (e.g., SaaS traffic) for direct Internet access (DIA) links. However, you must consider what the behavior will be for this traffic when it gets put on the MPLS network. Is a default route advertised? Will the traffic be allowed to exit to the Internet? Where will it exit? While not a showstopper, you must consider the flow of traffic when this is put into play.

- **No-NAT:** No-NAT can be enabled by Meraki Support for the MPLS WAN link. However, be aware that no dynamic routing is available on the WAN interface (at the time of writing). Therefore, the MPLS provider needs to have a static route that points to prefixes behind the MX via the static address on the WAN.

As you can see, adding SD-WAN capabilities is viable with traditional MPLS as a WAN link. There are a few design considerations to be aware of, but it offers choice and flexibility in how and where to leverage it. MPLS is here to stay for a little while longer.

Summary

This chapter reviewed all the attributes that may be leveraged to support a branch leveraging SD-WAN on the Cisco Meraki MX. In addition, some of these attributes were brought to life with example use cases.

The section "The Science of Transport Performance" provided an idea of how an MX continuously monitors and calculates the performance of available WAN and cellular uplinks to match real time traffic requirements. The next several sections discussed how the MX platform provides the flexibility to configure a variety of uplink policies based on criteria ranging from simple uplink metrics to more advanced policies that involve application-level monitoring to create custom performance classes that best match a given application's requirements. Finally, this chapter covered how Meraki SD-WAN solutions can be leveraged across multiple types of uplinks to meet the needs of nearly any project or deployment.

Next, Chapter 7 sheds some light on many of the Meraki-specific features and capabilities available in the MS switching platform.

Additional Reading

Meraki Auto VPN General Best Practices: https://documentation.meraki.com/
Architectures_and_Best_Practices/Cisco_Meraki_Best_Practice_Design/Best_Practice_
Design_-_MX_Security_and_SD-WAN/Meraki_Auto_VPN_General_
Best_Practices

MX Load Balancing and Flow Preferences: https://documentation.meraki.com/MX/
Firewall_and_Traffic_Shaping/MX_Load_Balancing_and_Flow_Preferences

Best Practice Design – MX Security and SD-WAN: https://documentation.meraki.com/
Architectures_and_Best_Practices/Cisco_Meraki_Best_Practice_Design/
Best_Practice_Design_-_MX_Security_and_SD-WAN

SD-WAN Internet Policies (SD-Internet): https://documentation.meraki.com/
Architectures_and_Best_Practices/Cisco_Meraki_Best_Practice_Design/
Best_Practice_Design_-_MX_Security_and_SD-WAN/SD-WAN_Internet_Policies_
(SD-Internet)

IPv6 Support on MX Security & SD-WAN Platforms – LAN: https://
documentation.meraki.com/?title=MX/Networks_and_Routing/IPv6_Support_
on_MX_Security_%26_SD-WAN_Platforms_-_LAN

Meraki SD-WAN: https://documentation.meraki.com/Architectures_and_Best_Practices/
Cisco_Meraki_Best_Practice_Design/Best_Practice_Design_-_MX_Security_and_
SD-WAN/Meraki_SD-WAN

SD-WAN Monitoring: https://documentation.meraki.com/MX/Monitoring_and_
Reporting/SD-WAN_Monitoring

Meraki MX/Z Security and SD-WAN Licensing: https://documentation.meraki.com/
General_Administration/Licensing/Meraki_MX_Security_and_SD-WAN_Licensing

Chapter 7

Meraki Switching Design and Recommendations

Introduction to Meraki Switches

The Meraki MS line of switches has revolutionized how large, switched networks are built and managed, steering away from the cumbersome process of command line interface (CLI), box-by-box configurations or CLI script pushes that were prevalent historically. The Meraki platform approach to management of switching hardware enables organizations to harness the power of software-defined networking, enabling large-scale, intent-based configuration automation delivered entirely as a Software as a Service (SaaS) platform.

Through the adoption of software-defined, intent-based networking, Meraki switches offer many benefits, including eliminating complexity while deploying best practices at an elastic scale. They enable seamless execution of intent-based policy pushes, which include aspects like segmentation, Layer 2, Layer 3, multicast, and Quality of Service (QoS) configurations. Additionally, by utilizing the power of the Meraki Dashboard, Meraki switches can provide clear performance visibility, effective root cause analysis (RCA), and automated integration with other domains, such as security and observability, thereby drastically streamlining operations beyond the initial deployment phase.

Meraki Switching Design

The Cisco Meraki MS switching platform offers more than just connectivity and segmentation; it also provides advanced visualization and intelligence features that differentiate it from traditional switches. Here are some key points that further highlight the differentiation of Meraki switches in terms of network performance and security:

- **Cloud-based architecture:** Meraki's cloud-managed switches are controlled through the cloud-based Meraki Dashboard. This architecture offers the benefits of over-the-air management and visibility, providing simplified deployment, easy scalability, and remote management capabilities. For example, the ability to create templates and apply standard configurations across multiple switches or sites is a key feature of Meraki's network management system. This feature simplifies the task of managing large and distributed networks by ensuring consistency in configurations, thus reducing the likelihood of configuration errors that can lead to network issues.

- **Seamless integration:** Meraki MS switches support Cisco Security Group Tags (SGTs) as part of the Cisco TrustSec technology, enabling micro-segmentation implementation. SGTs provide a granular level of control over communication between different segments within a network. Meraki switches also integrate seamlessly with other Meraki devices, such as MR access points (SecurePort), MX security appliances, and endpoints using Systems Manager Enterprise Mobility Management, creating a unified network ecosystem. This integration allows for deeper visibility and coordination between network components, enhancing performance and security.

- **Centralized management:** The Meraki Dashboard provides a centralized management interface that allows administrators to monitor and configure multiple switches across different locations from a single pane of glass. It provides real-time telemetry and visibility into network performance and security events, making identifying and resolving issues easier.

The Dashboard provides the capability to select switch ports across multiple physical switches based on various criteria such as functionality, connected device, or tags with the Virtual Stacking feature, shown in Figure 7-1. This allows administrators to make bulk configuration changes to specific groups of switch ports, streamlining the management process and saving time.

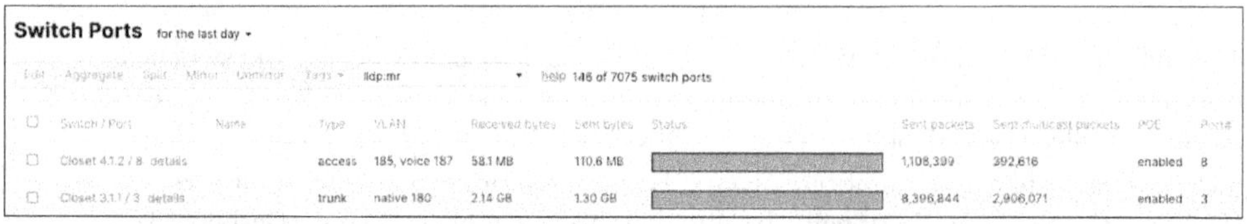

Figure 7-1   *Filtering Switch Ports to Just Those Reporting LLDP Data for Connected MR Access Points*

- **Network telemetry:** The Meraki platform collects a wide range of network telemetry data from the end-to-end network stack. It stores this information securely in a separate data lake for each tenant, ensuring the privacy and integrity of the data. The platform applies advanced data science techniques, including artificial intelligence (AI) and machine learning (ML), to analyze this telemetry data. These techniques can identify patterns and correlations that might be missed with traditional analysis methods. The outcome of this AI/ML analysis includes the generation of network alerts, which can proactively notify network administrators about potential issues before they impact network performance or user experience. This can drastically decrease downtime and improve overall network reliability.

Additionally, the AI/ML analysis also aids in identifying the root cause (RCA) across the platform. When a network issue arises, determining the exact cause can be a complex task due to the intricate interdependencies between various network components. By using AI/ML, the Meraki platform can accurately pinpoint the root cause of issues, making it easier for network administrators to resolve them quickly and efficiently. These outcomes can be used to automate tasks, optimize network performance, and enhance security. By analyzing the data, network administrators can identify patterns, detect anomalies, and make informed decisions to improve network operations.

■ **Topology View:** The Topology View in the Meraki Dashboard is a tool that provides a real-time, up-to-date visual representation of the network infrastructure. It includes all Meraki products, such as MS switches, MR access points, MX security appliances, MV cameras, MT sensors, and other Cisco devices. This real-time view allows administrators to quickly and easily understand network device connectivity, operational status, and relationships. As a result, it enables any IT team to manage an enterprise network more efficiently and effectively through automation, leading to better network performance and easier troubleshooting. Figures 7-2 and 7-3 show how the Topology View provides visibility into the end-to-end full stack Layer 2 network topology and Layer 3 network topology, respectively. Figure 7-4 shows how the Dashboard even provides insight into the status of unmanaged connected devices.

Note   When analyzing changes to connectivity, focus on working from right to left on topology page.

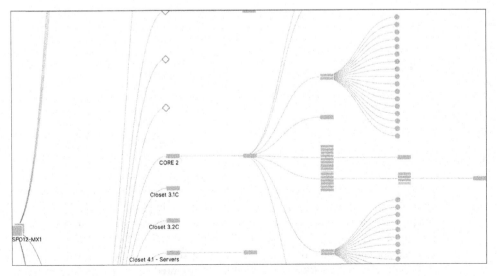

Figure 7-2   *Portion of the Full Stack Layer 2 Topology View*

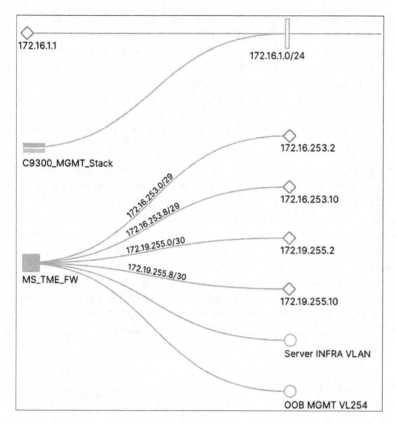

Figure 7-3   *Example of the Layer 3 Network Topology View*

Figure 7-4   *Showing Visibility into Non-Meraki Cisco Device on the Meraki Dashboard*

■ **Network access control:** Meraki switches support network access control (NAC), a security feature that allows network administrators to implement policies for managing network access based on a client device's compliance with defined criteria. Meraki MS switches offer the four most common 802.1X modes to accommodate most standard implementations. With NAC enabled on MS switches, a device must go through an authentication process before it is granted access to the network. This could involve validating credentials with a RADIUS server, checking the device's security posture, or both. If a device fails to meet the defined criteria, it can be denied access or placed in a restricted VLAN. NAC on Meraki MS switches also facilitates functions like guest VLANs for unauthenticated devices, voice VLANs for IP phones, and dynamic VLAN assignment for user-specific VLAN tagging. These features, when used collectively, enhance the network's security, flexibility, and manageability.

- **Firmware management with staged upgrades:** This feature provides an efficient way to manage and control the firmware versions running on your switches. Staged upgrades allow network administrators to roll out updates to a small portion of the network at a time, minimizing the risk of widespread issues and allowing for thorough testing before full deployment. This approach ensures minimal network disruption and provides a safety net, which make reverting to the previous firmware version easy if any problems arise during the upgrade, before the problems impact the entire network.

Designing a Wired Enterprise Network

In today's always-online world, designing a switching environment requires more careful consideration than ever. Various factors like Layer 2 design, Layer 3 scale and complexity, and high-availability features are designed to ensure optimal network performance, scalability, and security. Selecting the appropriate switching solution is critical for organizations seeking to optimize their network infrastructure. Cisco offers a diverse range of switches, including Catalyst, Meraki, and Nexus series. This section is intended to guide you through thoughtful consideration of your existing technology and dependencies to empower you in choosing the right Cisco switching product mix.

Cisco customers can opt for entirely cloud-managed solutions, like Meraki and the Catalyst platform on Meraki, because of their simplicity, scalability, and reduced overhead. Cloud-managed solutions allow for remote network management and provide automatic updates, reducing the need for dedicated IT staff and physical access to the hardware. Some customers choose a hybrid approach, leveraging the best of both on-premises and cloud-managed solutions. This can balance control and simplicity, allowing them to manage some aspects of their network in-house while taking advantage of the scalability and reduced complexity of cloud management for others.

Planning Your Deployment

The process of planning a switching deployment necessitates careful evaluation of various elements, including business priorities and the complexity of the deployment. For Layer 3 considerations, planning should encompass inter-VLAN routing, IP addressing, and the selection of routing protocols. At Layer 2, important considerations include the VLAN layouts, the selection and design of trunking protocols, and the design and implementation of Spanning Tree Protocol (STP). These components are integral to ensuring efficient traffic management and network stability.

Security planning is essential for successful switching deployments. This involves creating logical group policies for centralized policy definition and enforcement, allowing administrators to efficiently manage network access and usage based on user groups, thereby enhancing overall network security. Additionally, physical port security is crucial, aiming to prevent unauthorized connections by implementing measures such as 802.1X for network access control or using MAC address whitelisting to restrict device connections to specific ports.

Choosing a suitable network management approach requires a deep understanding of your network's specific requirements. These include the network's bandwidth and application needs. It's essential to assess the routing and MAC table size requirements to select a switch with the right capacity and performance. The number of devices and connections needed dictates the evaluation of port density and speed options. Power over Ethernet (PoE) considerations are key when choosing Meraki switches, requiring support for PoE standards and planning for future needs driven by newer Wi-Fi standards and ever-increasing IoT adoption. Switches offering multigigabit ports become crucial for newer Wi-Fi networks with high-performance devices that require multigigabit speeds. Therefore, careful consideration of these unique requirements ensures the optimal selection of switches tailored to your network's specific needs.

Meraki switches offer easy scalability due to their hot-swappable physical stacking feature. This means that the switches can be expanded or modified while the system is running, thus providing flexibility and reducing downtime. Scalability considerations ensure the network design accommodates future growth, and power requirements must be assessed for PoE devices. Features like redundant power supplies and modular fans for easy replacement enhance the network infrastructure's reliability and performance.

Selecting an appropriate hybrid management approach, which incorporates both on-premises and cloud-managed solutions, is crucial. This combines the control of onsite management with the flexibility and scalability of cloud services, providing a balanced and efficient system for managing your network infrastructure.

Selecting the Right Switch Product Mix

As mentioned, Cisco has multiple switching product lines, including Catalyst, Nexus, and Meraki, which are designed to solve specific use cases. It is essential to consider factors such as network size, deployment complexity, budget, available IT resources, and your unique network challenges when choosing the right combination of Catalyst, Nexus, and Meraki switches. Catalyst switches have become the de facto standard for complex deployments that need advanced Layer 2 and Layer 3 features. Cisco now offers flexibility in managing its Catalyst series switches. You can choose between on-premises management or cloud-based management using the Meraki platform.

Meraki switches are designed for automation and scalability, making them an excellent choice for rapid and efficient network deployments or refreshes. Meraki switches are a clear choice for deployment in a distributed environment such as remote sites or branch offices, where cloud management and simplified deployment are advantageous. Their cloud-managed nature allows for zero-touch provisioning: you can preconfigure switches in the Dashboard before they even arrive on site. Once they're plugged in, they automatically download their configurations from the cloud. This means that deploying or replacing Meraki switches can be done without needing highly technical staff on site, and without the time-consuming, manual configuration that traditional switches often require. Additionally, features like Virtual Stacking allow you to manage switch ports in bulk, even across multiple switches, further simplifying management and deployment. All these features make Meraki switches a great option for quickly refreshing old switches and scaling your network.

Using both Cisco Catalyst and Meraki switches in the same campus LAN can bring maximum value and benefits from each product line. For a brownfield project with complex requirements, such as multiple routing protocols and considerations like large TCAM tables, backplane capacity, CPU, and memory, a recommendation could be a combination of Cisco Catalyst and Nexus switches at the core, alongside Meraki switches handling Layer 2 traffic, as illustrated in Figure 7-5. Deploying Meraki switches at the access and distribution layers can offer greater visibility and insight into network performance and overall network health. Changes in network configuration, possible misconfigurations, and alerts often occur on switches closer to connected devices, access points, and users. The cloud-based Meraki platform provides intelligent monitoring, configuration management, and automation tools to address these challenges effectively.

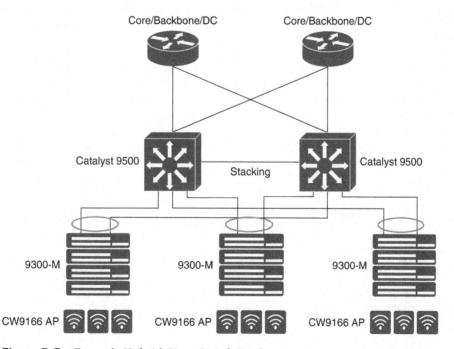

Figure 7-5 *Example Hybrid Cisco Switch Deployment*

The Dashboard also offers centralized management for Cisco Catalyst switches. This allows network administrators to view and manage all their Catalyst switches, like any other Meraki switches, from a single pane of glass, regardless of their geographical location, providing real-time monitoring capabilities and automate the process of security updates on Catalyst through the use of Meraki's cloud managed update process.

For visibility, Meraki features like network topology visualization, traffic analysis, and device health monitoring can provide valuable insights into the Catalyst network and aid in proactive management.

Consulting with a network expert or Cisco representative can help you determine the most suitable option for your unique network needs.

Planning Hybrid Campus LAN Architectures with Cloud Management

Designing a campus LAN is not a one-size-fits-all task. The scale can vary from a simple setup with a single switch and wireless access point at a small site, to a complex, multibuilding structure with high-density wired and wireless requirements. The deployment may demand high availability for network services with a low tolerance for risk, or it may allow for a fix-on-failure approach with acceptable service outages for a limited number of users. Factors like network capacity needs, device capabilities, compliance requirements, and organizational priorities typically drive the choice of platforms.

The Meraki document "Hybrid Campus LAN Design Guide (CVD)" at https://documentation.meraki.com provides a pre-validated design and deployment guide for a Hybrid Campus LAN, incorporating both Cisco and Meraki platforms. It covers various design guidelines, topologies, technologies, configurations, and considerations relevant to creating a highly available campus switching fabric. The guide also directs readers to general design best practices for Cisco Hybrid Campus LANs. Figure 7-6 illustrates a Hybrid Campus LAN architecture with Meraki and cloud managed Catalyst.

Note   The "Additional Reading" section at the end of this chapter provides the full URL for every article that is cross-referenced in this chapter. Alternatively, you can search for the article title at https://documentation.meraki.com to locate it.

Cisco offers various monitoring solutions, such as Cisco DNA Center and the Cisco Meraki Dashboard, that can provide comprehensive monitoring capabilities for Catalyst switches. These platforms collect data from the switches, analyze it, and present it in a centralized dashboard, enabling network administrators to monitor Catalyst switches remotely.

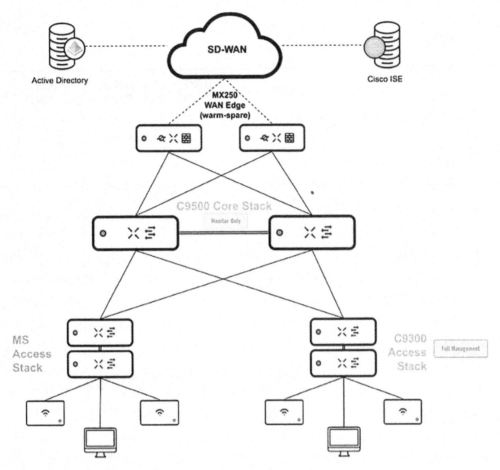

Figure 7-6 *Example Hybrid Campus LAN Architecture*

When using Catalyst switches with Meraki, there are two approaches to integration: cloud-monitored and cloud-managed. These differ slightly in their capabilities and operation, which we will talk about briefly here.

■ **Cloud-monitored Catalyst switches:** These switches are traditional on-premises switches that can now be monitored through the Meraki cloud, as depicted in Figure 7-7. Administrators can gain visibility into the switch's status, performance, and some level of configuration. However, the primary management and configuration of these switches is typically done through the on-premises Cisco DNA Center rather than the cloud.

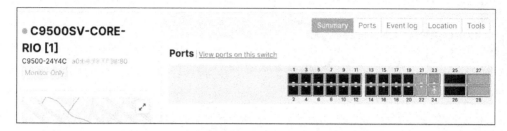

Figure 7-7   *Cloud Monitoring on Catalyst 9000 Series*

■ **Cloud-managed Catalyst switches:** These switches are either migrated from on-premises managed or preconfigured from the factory to be fully cloud-managed. As shown in the example in Figure 7-8, they are provisioned, configured, and monitored entirely through the cloud-based Meraki Dashboard. Administrators have complete control over the switch's configuration, policies, ability to deploy firmware updates, and full device monitoring. The Dashboard provides a comprehensive view of the switch, enabling centralized management, advanced analytics, and troubleshooting capabilities.

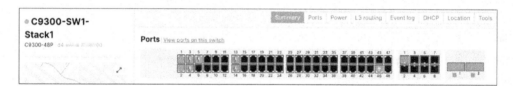

Figure 7-8   *Cloud-Managed Catalyst 9000 Series*

It is important to note that the availability and features of cloud monitoring and cloud management may vary depending on the Catalyst switch model and software version. We recommend consulting Cisco documentation or contacting Cisco support for detailed information on the cloud-based capabilities available for your Catalyst switches.

Designing the Access Layer

Properly planning and designing your Hybrid Campus deployment, including considering connectivity to network services, CoA integration, separate VLANs, QoS requirements, and downstream provisioning, will help ensure a secure, scalable, and robust enterprise network.

VLAN Deployment

When designing VLANs on Meraki MS switches, ensuring that all VLANs used by management and network services are correctly provisioned for and mapped at the appropriate access, distribution, and core switches is crucial. This involves determining the range of VLAN IDs, planning the VLAN interface IP addressing, and deciding on each VLAN's routing and gateway services. Here are a few considerations:

- **Allowed VLANs for trunk ports:** Plan VLAN and DHCP configurations per SSID and ensure that the corresponding trunk ports allow those VLANs.

- **Network services:** VLANs used by network services like RADIUS and DHCP must be routable to the access-level switches if you use Meraki wireless in a distributed environment.

- **Wireless roaming:** Consider client roaming requirements for relevant SSIDs to allow VLANs to facilitate proper roaming.

- **RADIUS integration:** Ensure that all VLANs utilized by external RADIUS services, like Identity Services Engine (ISE) that can perform Change of Authorization (CoA), are correctly mapped. This configuration allows client devices to switch between VLANs seamlessly.

- **Management VLAN:** Evaluate whether tagging RADIUS traffic and other specific traffic types in a separate VLAN other than the management VLAN is necessary. This can help isolate and prioritize traffic, ensuring efficient network operations and performance. Check out the Meraki Alternate Management Interface (AMI), shown in Figure 7-9, to separate management traffic from user or client traffic, providing enhanced security and isolation.

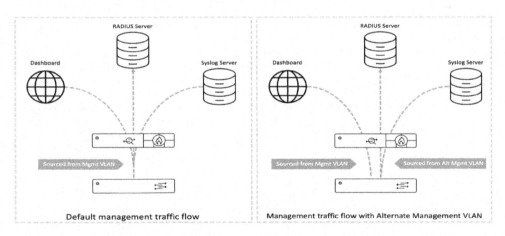

Figure 7-9   *Meraki Alternate Management Interface (AMI) Traffic Flow*

Using Native VLAN 1

In a hybrid Layer 2 access design with Meraki switches, there are two recommended approaches regarding the use of native VLAN 1:

- **Meraki hybrid Layer 2 access with native VLAN 1:** When operating in a hybrid switching environment, it's important to understand the default behavior and STP modes of various Cisco switching product lines. Consider a large network deployment that uses a mix of traditional Cisco Catalyst switches, MS390 switches, and cloud-native Meraki switches in the same network. In such a scenario, VLAN 1 is maintained as the native VLAN across the network. It assumes that the STP domain is extended from the access layer to the core layer. This configuration allows for flexibility in network segments, as VLANs can span across different stacks or closets. However, it is essential to note that the STP configuration and tuning become crucial, as Catalyst platforms may run different STP protocols than the Meraki MS390 switches. MST is the preferred STP mode in a hybrid Layer 2 deployment.

■ **All Meraki Layer 2 access without native VLAN 1:** This option eliminates VLAN 1 as the native VLAN and replaces it with another nontrivial VLAN assignment. Some customers prefer this configuration because it separates the native VLAN from the management VLAN. This option still allows VLAN flexibility and segmentation across different stacks or closets.

Planning QoS

Identify the specific Quality of Service (QoS) requirements for different SSIDs and applications in your network. Configure your switches to prioritize and allocate bandwidth appropriately for different traffic types, ensuring optimal performance and user experience. Meraki MS switches can be set up to adhere to an enterprise's QoS policies. MS switches possess six queues for traffic, each distinguished by a Class of Service (CoS) value. You can configure Differentiated Services Code Point (DSCP) to CoS mappings on the Dashboard, enabling traffic moving across the switch to adhere to your specified QoS settings. Options for QoS configurations include the following:

■ **Trusting incoming DSCP values:** The switch will respect the DSCP values set by the devices sending traffic through the switch, enabling differentiated traffic handling based on those values.

■ **Setting DSCP values per VLAN based on protocol and/or source/destination ports:** This gives you the ability to define your own DSCP values based on the type of traffic (protocol used) or where the traffic is coming from or going to (source/destination port numbers).

Pro Tip   The Meraki Dashboard allows you to configure QoS mappings on a per-VLAN basis, not a per-port basis. You are setting QoS policies for entire network segments (VLANs), not individual switch ports.

Fine-Tuning STP in a Hybrid Environment

When setting up Spanning Tree Protocol (STP) priorities, it is essential to follow certain best practices to ensure an efficient network topology:

■ **Choosing STP mode:** In a hybrid Meraki and Catalyst environment, it is recommended to use a single instance of Multiple Spanning Tree (MST) for simplified configuration and management, to maintain loop-free topologies, and to minimize disruptions.

- **Setting root priorities:** Assign the Root Bridge role, ideally to a central Catalyst switch or Meraki switch, by prioritizing it to the lowest value (0 or 4096). This helps control the STP topology by preventing newly added or misconfigured switches from significantly disrupting the STP topology of your network. To prevent IDF switches from becoming the root, set their priorities higher than the root switch. This ensures that the root switch maintains control over the STP topology. In a mixed environment (that is, PVST on Catalyst and RSTP on Meraki), it is critical that a PVST switch be the root of the spanning tree.

- **Root Guard:** Enable Root Guard on ports connecting to downstream switches that should not become the root. This protects against rogue root bridge election.

- **Loop Guard:** Enable Loop Guard on non-designated fiber ports in physically redundant topologies. This helps prevent unidirectional link failures and maintains loop-free network operation.

- **BPDU Guard:** Enable BPDU Guard on all end-user and server access ports. This protects against accidental or unauthorized connection of switches to access ports, which could disrupt the STP topology.

- **STP diameter:** It is recommended to keep the STP diameter (the maximum number of switches in a loop) under seven hops to ensure faster convergence and stable STP operation. Beyond seven hops, the convergence time and potential instability increase.

Tags to Optimize Deployment

Tags help identify switches for streamlined operations and automation. Tagging Meraki MS switches or cloud-managed Catalyst switches simplifies network management, organization, and policy enforcement. It enables easier firmware upgrades, configuration control, monitoring, reporting, and integration with other systems, as illustrated in Figure 7-10.

Name	Tags	Firmware version	Clients with usage ⓘ
SFO12-MS-2.2.18-Mint-VideoEdit-05	Mint-VideoEdit	MS 15.21.1	2
Closet 5.1- 2F Distribution	FloorDistribution	MS 15.21.1	778
Closet 5.1- 3F Distribution	FloorDistribution	MS 15.21.1	503
Closet 5.1- 4F Distribution	FloorDistribution	MS 15.21.1	904
Closet 5.1 - Interconnect 1	5thFloor MDF	MS 15.21.1	1277
Closet 4.1 - Servers	4thFloor 4.1	MS 15.21.1	16

Figure 7-10 *Tags Used to Classify and Group MS Switches in a Network*

MTU Recommendation

Ensure the Maximum Transmission Unit (MTU) is correctly configured on your Layer 2 IDF switches to match the MTU settings on your aggregation/backbone/Layer 3 switches. For example, if you use Meraki switches with an out-of-the-box MTU of 9000+, you may need to adjust it to 1500 or 15xx to match the MTU settings on your Cisco Catalyst or Nexus switches. However, using the default settings of 9578 MTU (jumbo frames) is recommended to improve network efficiency and performance, particularly for server-to-server and application traffic, by allowing more data to be transferred in each packet, thereby reducing the total number of packets, and therefore load, on the network and clients.

Connecting Trunk Ports

Both ends of the link must have matching configurations to ensure uninterrupted connectivity when linking a Meraki MS switch to a switch from a different vendor. Without this, the link may not function as intended due to mismatches in VLAN or native VLAN. Misconfigurations commonly occur in aspects such as switch port mode, trunk encapsulation type (*Dot1q*), native VLAN, and allowed VLAN configurations. Careful attention to these settings is key to preventing operational interruptions and ensuring efficient communication between switches.

Connecting MR Access Points

We recommend certain best practices for the optimal configuration of switch ports connected to Meraki access points when connecting Meraki access points. One such practice is using the SecurePort feature, which ensures a secure and automated connection between the MS switch port and the Meraki MR access point. Further details about this feature are provided in the upcoming "Securing Layer 2 Operations" section. Other recommendations include the following:

- Configure connected switch ports as trunk ports to allow the access points to pass traffic for multiple VLANs. At a minimum, include all VLANs used for transmitting SSIDs in the allowed VLAN list on the trunk port. Furthermore, since MR access points listen on all VLANs for rogue AP detection, it is recommended to forward all VLANs on access point trunks.

- Enable BPDU Guard on the switch ports connected to the access points. BPDU Guard helps protect against accidental or unauthorized connections of devices that could disrupt the network's spanning tree topology.

- Enable Storm Control on the switch ports to prevent excessive broadcast, multicast, or unknown unicast traffic from overwhelming the network. This helps maintain network stability and performance.

- Implement QoS settings on the switch ports to prioritize critical traffic generated by the access points. This ensures that important applications, such as voice or video, receive sufficient bandwidth and minimize latency or packet loss.

Layer 3 Best Practices

When planning your Layer 3 deployment, it's important to keep in mind several aspects of routing traffic like the use of OSPF or multicast and how that will impact your deployment needs and decisions. This section briefly covers some Layer 3–related best practices to keep in mind when planning to use Meraki switches as part of your Layer 3 traffic management.

OSPF Best Practices

Cisco Meraki Layer 3 MS switches support using the OSPF routing protocol to advertise subnets to neighboring OSPF-capable Layer 3 devices. OSPF may be desirable in more complex network topologies with a layered switch distribution, where static routes are not ideal. Here are a few recommendations for using OSPF on the Meraki MS platform:

- **Network type:** Meraki MS switches only support the OSPF broadcast network type. Ensure that all interfaces use broadcast mode for hello messages, facilitating proper neighbor discovery and communication.

- **Default timers:** It is advised to keep hello and dead timers at their default values (10 seconds and 40 seconds, respectively). If more aggressive timers are desired, thorough testing is crucial for network stability and proper convergence.

- **Backbone area:** All OSPF areas should be directly attached to the backbone area 0. Virtual links are not supported on Meraki MS switches, so design with area 0 as the central hub connecting all other areas.

- **Area types:** Configure OSPF areas as normal, stub, or NSSA based on network requirements. Consider stub or NSSA areas to reduce routing overhead and simplify OSPF configuration.

- **Priority in multi-area design:** In a multi-area OSPF design, it's crucial to consider several factors, including scalability, route table size, routed host count, MAC table size, and network topology. The default Meraki router priority is 1, but adjusting it can influence OSPF-designated routers and improve network convergence.

- **Equal-cost multipath (ECMP):** Meraki MS switches support up to 16 ECMPs per destination. Leverage this for load balancing and optimal network performance. Summarize routes when possible to minimize OSPF routing table size.

- **Route filters:** Use route filters to prevent asymmetric routing scenarios. By selectively filtering or controlling route advertisements, you can maintain consistent and predictable paths for traffic within your OSPF network.

- **Static route redistribution:** Meraki MS switches allow for selective redistribution of static routes into the OSPF domain. This provides greater control over which routes are shared within the OSPF network.

Multicast Best Practices

Configuring multicast routing on Meraki MS switches involves using the Protocol Independent Multicast Sparse Mode (PIM-SM) for efficient and scalable distribution of multicast traffic. IGMP snooping, which is enabled by default, can be enhanced with features like IGMP Querier for robust multicast infrastructure. However, if there are no Layer 2 multicast requirements, IGMP snooping should be disabled, as it is CPU dependent.

Pro Tip   For internal applications, it's recommended to use the 239.0.0.0/8 multicast address space.

Multicast traffic flow can be regulated through access control mechanisms such as IGMP filtering or access control lists (ACLs). It's also important to plan for a Rendezvous Point and consider blocking SSDP traffic when PIM routing is configured to prevent additional load. You can do so by blocking UDP traffic to destination 239.255.255.250/32 in the Switch> ACL page in the Dashboard.

In a multicast environment, it is common to set Storm Control to 1 percent to drop excessive packets if the limit is exceeded, but your environment may vary depending on what types of multicast applications you have deployed. These considerations ensure an optimized and efficient multicast configuration on Meraki MS switches.

Securing Layer 2 Operations

Securing Layer 2 operations involves implementing various security measures to protect the infrastructure, network access, and endpoints. Here are some key considerations for each aspect, which are described in more detail in the following subsections:

- **Infrastructure security:** Implement physical security measures to protect network devices.

- **Network access security:** Implement robust authentication mechanisms, such as IEEE 802.1X, to control access to the network.

- **Endpoint security:** Implement dynamic endpoint posture-based protection for wired and wireless networks.

- **Micro-segmentation (adaptive policy):** Explore how the future of network security is developing and changing traditional approaches.

Infrastructure Security

A well-designed and secure infrastructure is essential to a well-functioning network. Meraki offers some (often overlooked) security-related options to help protect the integrity of your infrastructure and the traffic passing through it. This section introduces several security features that you can enable to help ensure the secure operation of your network and reduce the chance of malicious actions impacting the network or its clients.

DHCP Snooping

The DHCP snooping feature available with MS switches is a network-wide setting that provides enhanced security for all switches or switch stacks within the network. It offers several features to protect against unauthorized or malicious DHCP servers. DHCP snooping will detect and block and/or alert when a new DHCP server is detected on the network. This helps prevent rogue DHCP servers from distributing IP addresses and potentially causing network disruptions. This feature can drop replies from unauthorized or malicious DHCP servers. This ensures that only authorized DHCP servers can provide IP configuration information to network devices. Unauthorized DHCP servers' responses are dropped and ignored, preventing potential security risks. DHCP snooping can also generate email alerts to notify network administrators when a rogue DHCP server is detected. This immediate notification allows prompt action to investigate and mitigate the threat.

The default configuration of MS switches allows all DHCP servers on the network, for easy installation in existing environments. To configure DHCP snooping to ensure that only trusted DHCP servers provide IP configuration to network devices, navigate to the Meraki Dashboard and go to **Switching > Routing and DHCP > DHCP Servers & ARP**. From this page, shown in Figure 7-11, you can set the Default DHCP Server Policy option to **Block DHCP Servers** and explicitly whitelist authorized DHCP servers in the Allowed DHCP Servers list or the Allowed DHCP Servers box.

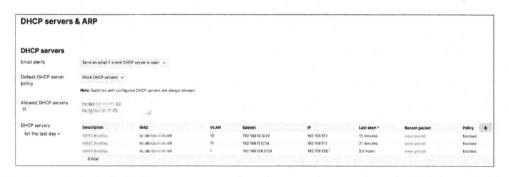

Figure 7-11 *Whitelisting Authorized DHCP Servers*

Storm Control

Storm Control on Meraki switches is a feature that helps prevent network downtime caused by abnormal events such as misconfigured or misbehaving network devices or end clients. As shown in Figure 7-12, Storm Control detects and manages three types of storms: broadcast, multicast, and unknown unicast. By setting thresholds for each traffic type, you can customize the behavior of the switch. The system will drop any traffic that exceeds the set threshold. This prevents the excessive traffic from impacting network performance.

Storm Control

Storm Control	Traffic types	% of available port bandwidth	
Storm control monitors the level of the defined traffic types over 1 second intervals. If traffic of the defined types exceeds the defined limit, excess packets will be dropped. The storm control rate defined is applied to each port based on the port's total available bandwidth.	Broadcast x	50 ⌄ %	✖
	Multicast x	20 ⌄ %	✖
	Unknown unicast x	10 ⌄ %	✖
	Add a storm control rule		

Figure 7-12 *Setting Storm Control Thresholds for Different Traffic Types*

For more information on Storm Control for MS, visit https://documentation.meraki.com and view the article "Storm Control for MS."

Dynamic ARP Inspection

To mitigate man-in-the-middle (MITM) attacks such as the scenario depicted in Figure 7-13, DHCP information gathered over time by Meraki switches in the network is used to create a mapping for *Host: IP: MAC* information per switch port. This mapping helps prevent malicious spoofing attacks. Dynamic ARP Inspection (DAI) assigns a trust state to each port on the switch. Trusted ports are exempt from DAI validation checks, allowing all ARP traffic. Untrusted ports undergo DAI validation checks, where the switch scrutinizes ARP requests and responses received on those ports.

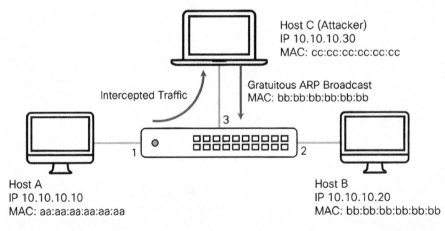

Figure 7-13 *Potential MITM Attack the Meraki DAI Feature Is Designed to Prevent*

To enable DAI in your network, you must define trusted and untrusted ports and enable ARP inspection. Designate ports as trusted if they are connected to trunks, are linked to access points (APs), or have static IP addresses. By default, all other ports are considered untrusted and will be treated as DHCP client ports. To enable DAI, navigate to the **Switching > DHCP Servers & ARP** section in your network settings and change the DAI Status field to Enabled to activate DAI functionality.

For more information on Dynamic ARP Inspection, visit https://documentation.meraki.com and view the article "Dynamic ARP Inspection."

SecurePort

Meraki MS SecurePort is a feature that provides secure provisioning of switch ports that have Meraki MR access points connected. As depicted in Figure 7-14, SecurePort automates configuring the switch port, establishing a secure connection, and allowing the access point to download its configuration from the Meraki cloud. By enabling SecurePort, the switch port is configured as a trunk port, with the native VLAN set to the management VLAN of the switch. This ensures the access point can connect securely and obtain a security certificate from the Meraki cloud. The access point is also authenticated via an onboard digital certificate before it is permitted to connect.

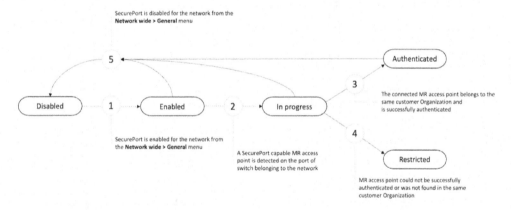

Figure 7-14 *SecurePort Authentication States*

SecurePort offers several advantages:

- It saves time by eliminating the need for manual per-port configuration on the switch.

- It enhances security by preventing the switch port from being used as a back door to access the network. For example, if someone removes an access point to plug in a laptop, the switch port will revert to its previous secure configuration, preventing unauthorized access.

■ It ensures that only access points that belong to the organization can connect, as any certificate mismatch will prevent unauthorized access.

For more information on SecurePort features, go to https://documentation.meraki.com and view the article "SecurePort."

Port Profiles

Meraki port profiles are designed to standardize and simplify port configurations on Meraki switches. You can create predefined port profiles based on specific functionalities or device types, such as printers or desktops. This feature empowers network administrators to apply consistent configurations to multiple ports effortlessly, streamlining the process. As shown in Figure 7-15, different port profiles can be created based on desired functionalities, ensuring ports with similar requirements share the same settings.

Profile name	Date created
Access_Point	March 27, 2023 03:03 PM
Printer	March 30, 2023 02:03 PM
Employee_Desk	March 30, 2023 02:03 PM
Public_Area	March 30, 2023 02:03 PM

Figure 7-15   *List of Several Example Port Profiles Shown in the Dashboard*

Creating a Meraki port profile is straightforward. Navigate to **Switching > Port Profiles** in the Dashboard and click **Add Profile**. In the dialog box that opens, define the profile, including VLAN configurations, PoE settings, and access control policies.

After you have defined port profiles, you can apply them efficiently to individual ports or groups of ports, facilitating quick and accurate deployment of desired configurations across the network.

Somewhat similar to port profiles is Meraki's Virtual Stacking feature, discussed later in the chapter, which helps you search for ports based on their characteristics or tags and make bulk changes (whereas port profiles allow you to define and assign a standardized configuration at scale).

VLAN Profile

VLAN profiles are designed to simplify VLAN management in large enterprise networks where VLAN numbers may vary across and within sites. This feature is especially beneficial when integrating with a RADIUS/ISE policy. Administrators can map VLAN names to site-specific VLAN numbers with VLAN profiles, as depicted in Figure 7-16. This allows consistent references to VLANs (like WORKSTATION in Figure 7-16) even if VLAN numbers differ across sites. This eases the configuration and management of VLAN assignments, particularly in multi-site scenarios.

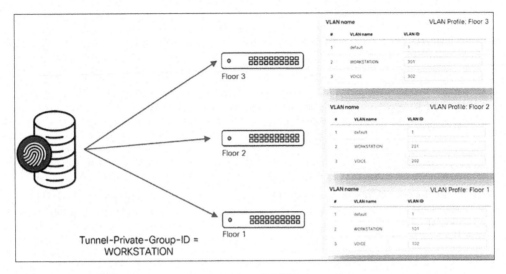

Figure 7-16 *Using VLAN Profile on MS with ISE Integration*

To set up VLAN profiles, go to the **Network-wide > VLAN Profile** page. There you can create VLAN profiles and define VLAN name mappings for each network. After you have configured VLAN profiles, you can assign them to specific ports or groups of ports. Enabling the Enable Port Profile option on ports ensures that authenticated users and devices are assigned to the correct VLAN based on the VLAN name specified in the ISE policy. This feature applies to both Meraki MR access points and MS switches, providing a comprehensive solution for efficient VLAN assignments throughout the network.

Network Security

This section emphasizes controlling network access to ensure that only authorized individuals or devices can connect. Techniques include implementing secure authentication protocols like 802.1X, utilizing VLAN segmentation to isolate traffic, and employing MAC address filtering. Adhering to the Zero Trust Network Access security policy, network access is granted only to devices that require it, and resource access is strictly based on need to know.

Sticky MAC

Sticky MAC is a security feature on switches that limits the number of MAC addresses a port can learn. It associates specific MAC addresses with a port, allowing only those devices to connect. Although Sticky MAC is helpful for basic security, like assigning a port for a printer, it is not foolproof, as MAC addresses can be spoofed. Therefore, it should not be the only security measure for protecting sensitive resources. Despite its limitations, Sticky MAC offers basic security without external authentication, is easy to set up, and can help prevent unauthorized access through specific ports.

Port Isolation

On Meraki MS switches, the port isolation feature lets you set specific ports as isolated, stopping communication between isolated ports but allowing communication with non-isolated ones. Enabling port isolation means devices on isolated access ports cannot communicate with each other but can still communicate with non-isolated ports, such as the uplink port. This is handy when you want to limit communication between devices on different access ports but still allow them to communicate with specific devices or resources on the network through non-isolated ports.

Port isolation adds an extra layer of security by preventing unauthorized access or potential threats from spreading across the network. By making an access port isolated and designating the uplink port as non-isolated, you can restrict a device on the isolated port from accessing other devices while still allowing communication with the specified non-isolated port.

802.1X Authentication

On MS switches, like many other switches, you can use 802.1X authentication to verify devices on both wired and wireless networks. This method usually involves an external RADIUS server, such as Cisco Identity Services Engine (ISE), for identity verification and authorization. Meraki MS switches offer four 802.1X host modes for flexibility:

- **Single-Host:** Allows one device per port after successful authentication (see Figure 7-17).

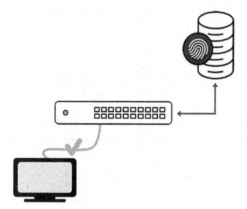

Figure 7-17   *Single-Host Authentication*

- **Multi-Domain:** Supports one authenticated device on each of two different VLANs, such as voice and data VLANs, on a single port (see Figure 7-18).

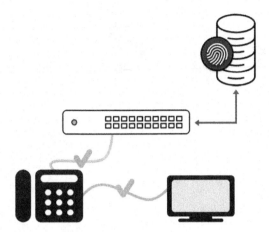

Figure 7-18   *Muti-Domain Authentication*

■ **Multi-Auth:** Permits multiple devices on a single data domain, often used when an unmanaged switch with multiple devices connects to a managed switch (see Figure 7-19).

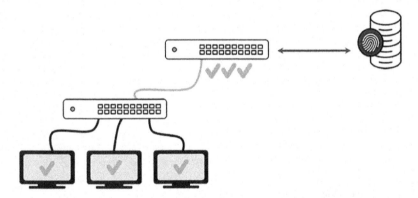

Figure 7-19   *Multi-Authentication*

■ **Multi-Host:** Authenticates only the first connected device; subsequent devices downstream are not authenticated (see Figure 7-20). This is used when the first device is trusted to authenticate on behalf of downstream devices. The multi-host mode may not provide the highest security, as only the first device is authenticated. It is commonly used when downstream devices are trusted, or downstream devices are authenticated by the connected network element.

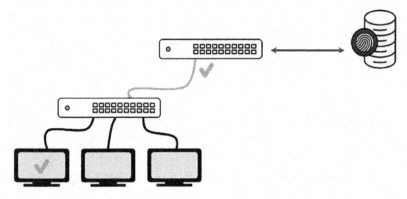

Figure 7-20   *Multi-Host Authentication and Switching*

802.1X Failed Auth VLAN

Cisco Meraki MS switches support a Failed Auth VLAN configuration (see Figure 7-21) to provide basic access to clients that fail 802.1X authentication. This feature assigns a specific VLAN to these clients, offering limited connectivity for scenarios like guest users or devices without valid corporate credentials.

Figure 7-21   *Defining a Failed Authentication VLAN in the Dashboard*

802.1X Critical Auth VLAN

MS switches support multiple RADIUS servers for redundancy. In cases where none of these servers are available, Meraki's Critical Auth VLAN feature (see Figure 7-22) allows you to define VLANs for data and voice traffic. This ensures continued network access and service availability during RADIUS server unavailability.

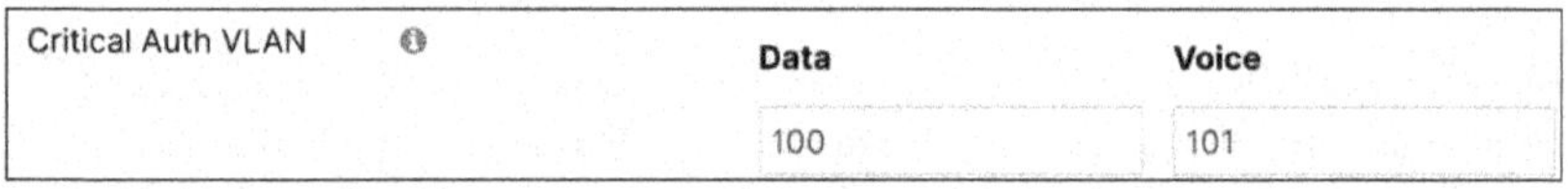

Critical Auth VLAN ⓘ	Data	Voice
	100	101

Figure 7-22   *Defining a Critical Authentication VLAN in the Dashboard*

When implementing 802.1X authentication on Meraki MS switches, choose the appropriate host and failure mode configurations based on network requirements and security. Also, ensure the external authentication server, such as Cisco ISE, is correctly configured to handle authentication requests and enforce access policies.

MAC Authentication Bypass

MAC Authentication Bypass (MAB) is commonly used for devices lacking built-in support for 802.1X authentication, such as printers, IP phones, or other legacy devices. By employing MAB, these devices can still be authenticated and granted network access based on their MAC address. When configuring MAB on a Cisco Meraki switch, the switch will transmit the client device's MAC address to the RADIUS server. The RADIUS server will verify if the MAC address is authorized and allow or deny access accordingly. If authorized, the client device will be granted network access.

It is important to note that while MAB offers a way to authenticate devices based on their MAC address, it is less secure than 802.1X authentication. MAC addresses can be easily spoofed, so additional security measures should accompany MAB to ensure proper network access control. Consider combining MAB with other security measures like VLAN segmentation, ACLs, and regular network traffic monitoring to enhance the security of devices authenticated through MAB.

Change of Authorization with ISE Integration

Integrating Meraki MS switches and Cisco ISE allows for dynamic security policy enforcement using 802.1X Change of Authorization (CoA). 802.1X CoA enables the RADIUS server, such as Cisco ISE, to change the authorization status of a session at any point during that session. This capability provides dynamic enforcement of security policies based on changes detected on the client or network. You can also leverage 802.1X CoA to perform real-time policy updates and enforcement. For example, suppose an endpoint device undergoes a change in compliance status or security posture, such as a malware detection or policy violation. In that case, Cisco ISE can send a CoA message to the Meraki MS switch to enforce a new access policy or restrict network access for that specific device.

By integrating ISE with Meraki switches, you can leverage the capability of ISE to communicate with LDAP (such as Active Directory) to retrieve user attributes and group membership information. You can then use this information to dynamically assign policies based on the user's role or group membership. For example, you can configure ISE to retrieve AD group information during authentication. Based on the user's AD group membership, ISE can assign different policies to the Meraki switch, which will then apply these policies to both wired and wireless connections. Using RADIUS attributes, you can define policies in ISE that align with different user roles or attributes. These policies can include varying levels of network access, security controls, bandwidth limitations, and more. This allows you to grant different privileges to user groups based on their AD group membership.

Additionally, you can utilize Group Policy Objects (GPOs) in your Windows AD environment to further enforce policy settings on both wired and wireless connections, as illustrated in Figure 7-23. You can use GPOs to configure specific security settings, software installations, and other restrictions or configurations based on user or device attributes.

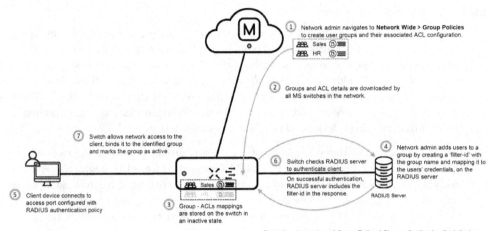

Figure 7-23 *Operational Overview of Group Policy to Enforce Policy Settings*

By combining the capabilities of ISE, Meraki switches, and group policy, you can achieve granular and dynamic policy enforcement based on user attributes, device posture, and network location, as illustrated in Figure 7-24. This enables you to provide differentiated access and privileges to different user groups, such as administrators, regular IT staff, students, and faculty, based on their organizational roles and responsibilities.

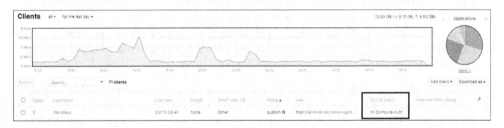

Figure 7-24 *ISE Integration and Associated 802.1X Policy Shown on Client Page*

Access policies contain the RADIUS host configuration information. You can configure one or more access policies by navigating to **Switch > Access Policies** in the Dashboard. You can then assign access policies directly to MS switch ports or via port profiles. When configuring integration with Cisco ISE, you must enable RADIUS CoA, as shown in Figure 7-25.

Use Cisco ISE to implement macro segmentation by assigning VLANs based on the department the user belongs to. This allows you to create separate network segments for different organizational departments or groups. Configuring the integration between Meraki and ISE is essential, ensuring that the policies and attributes align to enforce the desired access control and security measures across the network. This includes mapping the appropriate ISE policies to the corresponding Dashboard group policies for consistent and effective network access control.

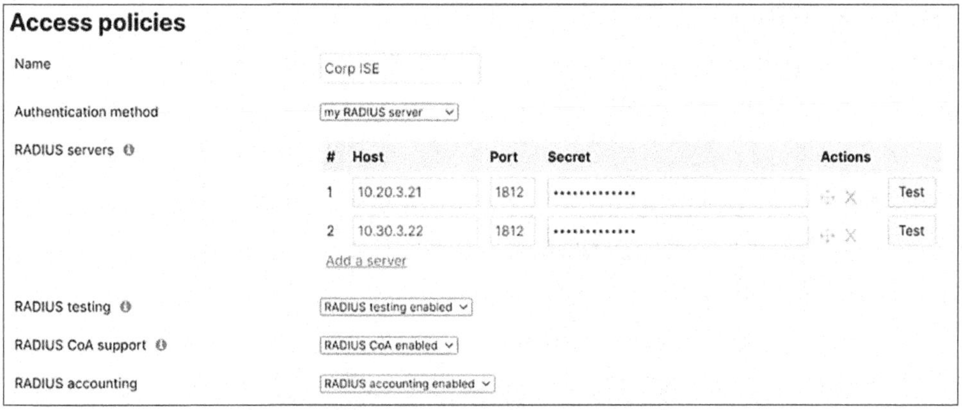

Access policies

Name	Corp ISE
Authentication method	my RADIUS server ⌄
RADIUS servers ⓘ	

#	Host	Port	Secret		Actions	
1	10.20.3.21	1812	••••••••••••	⊹ X	Test	
2	10.30.3.22	1812	••••••••••••	⊹ X	Test	

Add a server

RADIUS testing ⓘ	RADIUS testing enabled ⌄
RADIUS CoA support ⓘ	RADIUS CoA enabled ⌄
RADIUS accounting	RADIUS accounting enabled ⌄

Figure 7-25 *Enabling and Configuring RADIUS CoA in the Dashboard*

You can achieve micro-segmentation with ISE by mapping the Filter-ID with the Meraki Dashboard group policy. This allows you to assign additional Layer 3 rules automatically via the Dashboard group policy. Figures 7-26 and 7-27 show an example mapping for an ISE Filter-ID and corresponding Dashboard group policy.

Pro Tip Integrating ISE Filter-ID mapping with other products such as MR access points also allows features like additional Layer 7 and traffic shaping rules to be enforced via group policy.

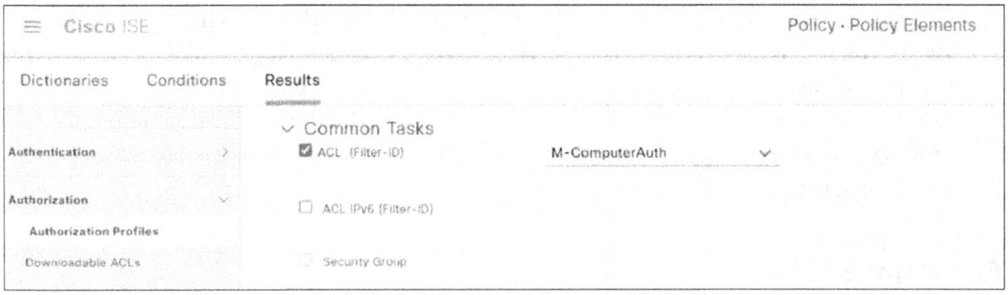

≡   Cisco ISE

Policy · Policy Elements

Dictionaries	Conditions	**Results**

∨ Common Tasks

☑ ACL (Filter-ID)   M-ComputerAuth   ⌄

Authentication   >

Authorization   ∨

☐ ACL IPv6 (Filter-ID)

Authorization Profiles

Downloadable ACLs

☐ Security Group

Figure 7-26 *Mapping an ISE Filter-ID to a Corresponding Meraki Group Policy*

For more information on MS Group Policy ACLs, visit https://documentation.meraki.com and view the article "Meraki MS Group Policy Access Control Lists."

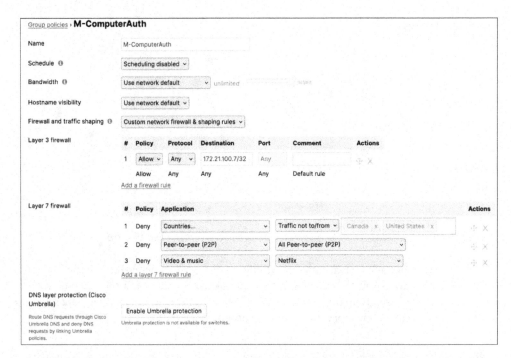

Figure 7-27   *Matching Meraki Group Policy for the Filter-ID in the ISE Authorization Profile*

Layer 3 capable MS switches also support 802.1X URL redirect, enabling the implementation of a walled garden approach for client authentication. URL redirect is enabled with Change of Authorization (CoA) on Meraki MS switches by default. This functionality allows you to redirect clients to a designated webpage for authentication before providing full network access. The walled garden feature lets you offer limited access to essential resources or permit access to specific websites without needing authentication. This proves valuable when clients require access to particular services or resources before completing the authentication process.

End Point Security

End device posture compliance, Mobile Device Management (MDM) integration, and supplicant provisioning are crucial in determining a dynamic security policy. Meraki group policy allows the creation and enforcement of network-wide policies across Meraki devices, providing a centralized method for applying rules and restrictions to client devices. These policies support dynamic assignment based on real-time conditions, such as time of day, location, or device posture.

Meraki's Systems Manager Sentry is a powerful tool and extension of the Dashboard that enables you to directly integrate Dashboard network policies, like Group Policy, with the monitoring power of Systems Manager on end devices. Sentry policies take standard Group Policies a step further by creating a link between Meraki group policies and dynamic tags generated in Systems Manager (Meraki's MDM solution) that can be used to further enhance the security of the end device. For example, if a device fails to meet certain criteria or compliance requirements, such as geo-fencing, Tor, or OS version, Meraki MDM can automatically assign a dynamic tag to it. This tag, when used in a Sentry policy, triggers specific policies within the Meraki group policy framework, allowing for dynamic policy enforcement, as illustrated in Figure 7-28.

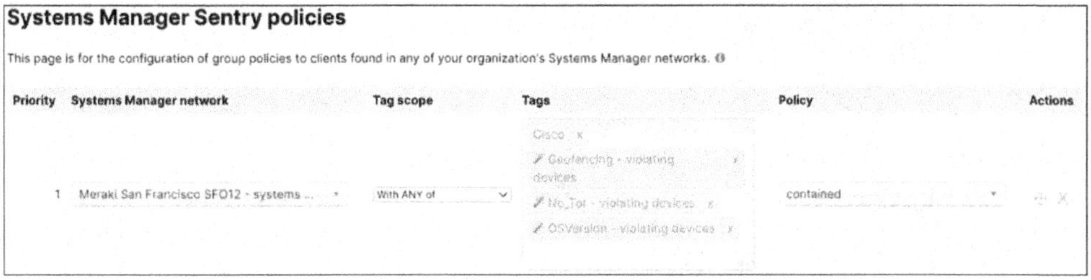

Figure 7-28 *Sentry Policy Mapping Between SM Tags and Group Policies in the Dashboard*

It is important to note that Sentry policies do not directly apply to MS switches. SM Sentry policies are enforced on Meraki MR access points and MX security appliances. This means that any device connecting to the network via an MR access point or passing traffic through an MX firewall can have Sentry policies applied.

Micro-Segmentation with MS (Adaptive Policy)

Adaptive Policy represents the evolution of traditional segmentation into a modern approach that eliminates the need for constantly mapping ACLs to IP addresses. Traditionally, network security has relied on IP-based access controls. However, as businesses increasingly establish their presence online, the importance of network security for maintaining business continuity has become more critical. Cisco Meraki offers a robust solution for securing network access through ACLs and group policies. However, these group policies can become challenging to scale as organizations evolve and expand.

Micro-segmentation with Meraki switches offers an organization-wide, intent-based policy that integrates seamlessly with the Dashboard in ISE 3.2 (see Figure 7-29). Micro-segmentation is achieved in Meraki using Security Group Tags (SGTs), a feature that is part of Cisco's TrustSec solution. This enables effective network segmentation and strengthens security by restricting lateral movement of threats within the network. By syncing natively with the Dashboard, Adaptive Policy ensures real-time visibility and control over the network policies, enhancing the overall network security management. Adaptive Policy functions through three key components: identity classification and propagation, security policy definition, and policy enforcement.

Group Tags

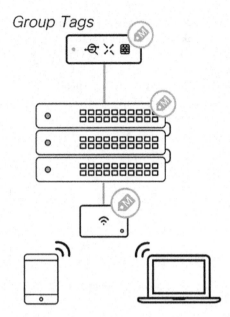

Figure 7-29   *SGT Tag Propagation Is Supported Across Multiple Meraki Platforms*

Identity Classification and Propagation

For Adaptive Policy using SGTs to function, you must first define the groups to be used. An Adaptive Policy group is a class of users or devices in an organization that require access to the same network services. Each SGT relies on a unique number (SGT value) associated with a specific group in an organization that can be defined when creating the group. Adaptive Policy utilizes organization-level policy groups (not to be confused with network-level group policies) defined in the Dashboard under the Organization> Policy Groups page to determine group membership. Here, policy groups can be created and defined based on multiple criteria.

Security Policy Definition

A security policy comprises a defined security SGT, a defined destination SGT, and the permissions for communication between them. Once you have defined the groups, you can define specific access restrictions based on group-to-group communication. For example, devices in the IoT group may have a defined policy that allows communication only to other IoT devices or related servers based on the selected groups within the security policy.

Policy Enforcement

Once traffic has left the source and entered the network, a matching SGT will be applied inline before the IP header based on the source, similar to an 802.1Q tag. From there, the traffic is intended to traverse the network while maintaining the applied SGT to the edge nearest the destination; at this point, the traffic is again inspected, and the destination SGT is determined. Then, the source SGT and destination SGT are compared to the defined security policies (see Figure 7-30) to determine whether the traffic should be forwarded to the destination client or dropped based on the applicable policy. This creates a highly scalable policy framework, as the network device only needs to evaluate the tags of the clients directly attached to it and not the IP prefixes.

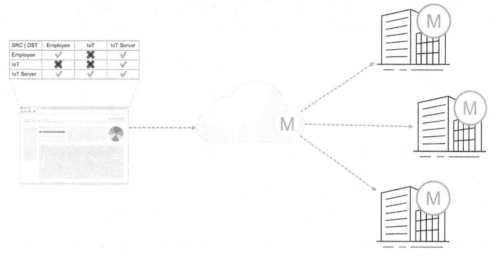

Figure 7-30   *Adaptive Policy Deployment Logic*

SGT Assignment Methods

In an Adaptive Policy network, after creating the Adaptive Policy tags, enabling Adaptive Policy, and classifying clients with relevant tags, the next step is policy enforcement. The critical feature of a tag-based network is that the policy is enforced at the destination network device. This setup makes the policy framework highly scalable, as the network device needs to consider only the tags of the clients directly connected to it, not the IP prefixes. However, this approach necessitates rigid requirements for micro-segmentation, including end-to-end support of the CMD encapsulation. Consider the different methods available for assigning SGTs:

- **Static port assignment:** Assign a fixed SGT to a specific port on the switch. This method is suitable for devices without a method of network authentication.

- **Static SSID assignment:** Assign a specific SGT to a single-use SSID, such as a guest network.

- **Dynamic via RADIUS:** Use RADIUS authentication and authorization for wired and wireless devices, supporting MAC Authentication Bypass (MAB), 802.1X, and Identity Pre-Shared Key (IPSK) with or without RADIUS integration.

- **IP prefix to SGT map:** Use this method to match traffic based on the IP subnet when no system is available to propagate SGT tags.

Caveats in Setting Up Adaptive Policy

For complete security and functionality, Adaptive Policy (SGT) must be supported by every device in the network. If an intermediate device does not support the CMD encapsulation used for SGT, it will drop SGT-tagged frames.

Pro Tip   Adaptive Policy definitions only apply in one direction. To block traffic entirely between two groups, you must manually define a block policy for both directions of traffic.

When considering MS SGT assignments, it is essential to keep the following considerations in mind:

- **Hardware requirements:**
  - **Switch and firewall:** Ensure that your Meraki switch and firewall model support SGT functionality. Check the datasheet or documentation for hardware compatibility.
  - **Catalyst in Meraki-managed mode:** If using a Cisco Catalyst switch in Meraki-managed mode, verify that the specific Catalyst model and software version support SGT assignments.
  - **Wireless:** If integrating SGT assignments with wireless devices, confirm that your wireless access points are compatible with SGT functionality.
  - **Compatibility with other Cisco technologies:** Consider how SGT assignments interact with your network's other Cisco technologies. Ensure compatibility with technologies such as Cisco ISE for authentication and authorization.
- **Software and licensing requirements:** The Adaptive Policy feature is part of the MS Advanced license, which provides additional security features beyond the standard Enterprise license. To use the Adaptive Policy feature, you need to have the appropriate licensing level that includes this feature. Refer to the official Cisco Meraki documentation to get accurate and up-to-date information about licensing requirements and feature availability.

For more detailed information regarding micro-segmentation on the Meraki platform, visit https://documentation.meraki.com and search for the keyword **Adaptive Policy or Micro-segmentation.**

Operating and Optimizing Meraki Switches

This section covers several tools and tricks available in the Dashboard to help you easily manage your switching deployment, regardless of the scope or scale of your deployment or the changes you are making.

Virtual Stacking

Meraki MS switches offer centralized management of switch ports through site-level virtual stack logic, enabling seamless search and configuration changes across thousands of switch ports in a network. Unlike traditional stacking methods, virtual stacking does not demand a physical connection, allowing switches to be located in different physical places and even consist of various switch models.

Consider the scenario of adding a new service VLAN that would require modifying the allowed-VLAN configuration across multiple trunk ports on multiple switches. In the Dashboard, you can open the virtual stacking page by navigating to **Switch> Switch Ports**. Once there, you can easily search for all trunk ports using the term **is:trunk**, as shown in Figure 7-31. You can then select a subset of these ports and make a bulk edit on the switch port.

You can also use combination filters to add more search criteria, such as **is:trunk VLAN:native 128** to search for all trunk ports configured with native VLAN 128, as shown in Figure 7-32.

Figure 7-31 *Using Virtual Stacking to Search for and Edit Multiple Trunk Ports in a Network*

Figure 7-32 *Using Combo Filters in Search Criteria*

Here are a few other useful search filters:

- **lldp:mr:** To search for switch ports connected to Meraki access points

- **lldp:mr56:** To search for switch ports connected to MR56 access points

- **is:uplink:** To search for uplink ports

- **vlan:"60"**: To search for switch ports on VLAN number 60

- **vlan:"native 60"**: To search for switch ports with native VLAN number 60

- **tag:"myfavport"**: To search for switch ports that match the given tag value

Note   These are only a few sample filters. For all available ports, search https://documentation.meraki.com with keywords **Searching ports.**

You can find more information on virtual stacking shortcuts at https://documentation.meraki.com by viewing the article "Switch Ports."

Firmware Upgrade Consideration on MS

We recommend allocating a minimum of 30 minutes for a firmware upgrade window on Meraki switches. The actual duration can vary depending on factors such as the time of day and the bandwidth of your Internet connection, which can affect the download speed of the firmware across all your switches.

During the firmware upgrade window, the switches will initiate the new firmware download. Once the download is complete, a 20-minute timer starts before the switches reboot and install the new firmware. Meraki recommends that, outside of an upgrade process, all switches within a network should run the same firmware version. This ensures consistency and compatibility across the network. In some cases, if necessary, the Meraki support team can pin a specific firmware version to a switch. This means the switch will not receive the standard firmware upgrades and will remain on the pinned version until further notice or a different pinning instruction is given.

By allowing sufficient time for the firmware upgrade window and ensuring that all switches within the network run the same firmware version, you can effectively manage firmware updates on your Meraki switches and maintain a stable and up-to-date network environment.

An important and useful feature to be aware of when working with switch firmware upgrades is the staged upgrade feature in Meraki switches, which allows administrators to divide a network of switches into smaller groups. Each group can then have its firmware upgraded at separate times. This approach provides more flexibility and control during the upgrade process.

When planning to upgrade upstream and downstream switches on the same day, it is extremely helpful to schedule a 30- to 60-minute interval between each stage. This time gap allows for the complete download and verification of the new firmware, ensuring it does not disrupt an ongoing upgrade in a downstream switch. Another common use case for staged upgrades is to upgrade a large network over an extended period of time, such as several days or even weeks. For example, initially the upgrade may be pushed to a single IDF closet each round, culminating with the MDF finally being upgraded after all IDF devices have successfully upgraded.

For more information on MS firmware upgrades, go to https://documentation.meraki.com and view the article "MS Firmware Upgrades."

Configuration Validations

To ensure a safe and stable configuration process, Meraki implements several specific mechanisms to ensure devices maintain a valid and functional configuration.

Config-Safe Mechanism

MS switches, like other Meraki devices, use a configuration fail-safe mechanism to ensure that the device is easily recoverable if a bad configuration is pushed that may impact device stability or connectivity. For MS devices, there are two important scenarios where this becomes relevant:

- **30-minute fail safe for new switch configuration:** When configuring a new switch, any changes made to the configuration are marked as safe only after the switch operates stably for 30 minutes. If the switch loses extended connectivity to the Dashboard or experiences other major connectivity issues within this period, the changes will automatically revert to the previous known safe configuration.

- **Two-hour safe marking after firmware upgrade:** After a firmware upgrade, any configuration changes made on the switch are marked as safe after two hours of stable operation. If extended dashboard connectivity to the switch is lost during this time, the device will power cycle and force a rollback to the last known good configuration.

Auto-Rollback on Bad Uplink

In the case of a bad uplink configuration on a Meraki switch, a Dashboard alert is displayed, like that shown in Figure 7-33. If the switch encounters a bad uplink configuration, it will try to obtain an IP address from an alternate VLAN. This allows the switch to establish a stable network connection and maintain connectivity.

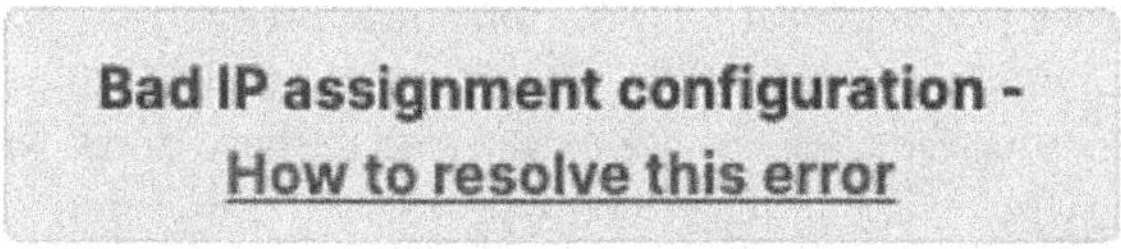

**Bad IP assignment configuration -
How to resolve this error**

Figure 7-33 *Dashboard Alert Resulting from a Bad Static Uplink Configuration*

If the switch does not achieve stable operation within two hours after the loss of connectivity, it will automatically revert to the previous safe configuration. This rollback ensures the switch returns to a known good state and minimizes potential extended disruptions.

After reverting to the safe configuration, the previous configuration that led to the bad uplink will be marked as bad. This helps identify and track problematic configurations for future troubleshooting or analysis.

> **Pro Tip**   Resiliency features like auto-rollback are built into Meraki switches, as well as other Meraki platforms, to help maintain network stability and mitigate the impact of bad uplink configurations.

MS PoE Budget

When PoE devices are connected to the ports of Meraki-managed PoE-capable switches, the ports on the switches are typically labeled with a lightning bolt symbol (see Figure 7-34). This symbol serves as an indicator that power is being supplied from the switch (called power sourcing equipment [PSE] in PoE terminology) to the connected, powered devices (PDs).

Figure 7-34   *Active PoE Ports as Shown on the Meraki Dashboard*

In a Meraki switch, the PoE power budget is determined based on the classification of the PoE devices connected to it. For switches other than the MS390 and Catalyst 9300-M, the power budget can exceed the available power on the switch, as the budget serves as an estimation of the overall power consumption that might occur. However, it is important to note that devices will continue to be powered until the total power consumption exceeds the available power. For the MS390 and Catalyst 9300-M, power will be supplied until the *budgeted power* reaches the PoE capacity of the switch. In either case, the switch will begin to prioritize power allocation if the total power requested surpasses the available power. When this happens, the lowest port numbers will take precedence, meaning power will first be supplied to the devices connected to these ports. As the power budget is exhausted, the switch will continue to provide power to lower port numbers while denying power to devices connected to higher port numbers.

PoE consumption on the switch can be monitored live from the Dashboard, including consumption, budgeting values, and port-specific information, by selecting a specific port and scrolling to the Status section, shown in Figure 7-35.

If your switches support power supply bonding or stacking, consider leveraging these features to increase PoE+ budgeting. Power supply bonding or stacking allows you to combine the power capacity of multiple power supplies or switches, providing additional power for PoE+ devices such as IP phones, wireless access points, and security cameras.

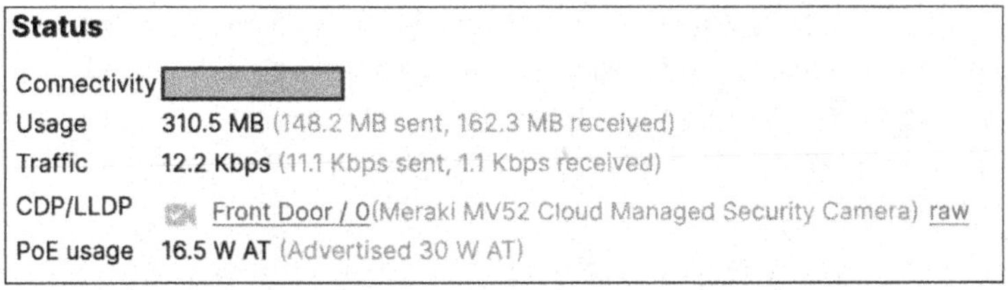

Status	
Connectivity	
Usage	**310.5 MB** (148.2 MB sent, 162.3 MB received)
Traffic	**12.2 Kbps** (11.1 Kbps sent, 1.1 Kbps received)
CDP/LLDP	Front Door / 0 (Meraki MV52 Cloud Managed Security Camera) raw
PoE usage	**16.5 W AT** (Advertised 30 W AT)

Figure 7-35 *Live PoE Consumption for a Switch Port*

MS Power Overview

In Meraki switches, the Power Overview section provides comprehensive information about the power usage and distribution within a switch or a stack of switches. As Figure 7-36 shows, the Power Overview section displays detailed information about the power utilization of each switch. It includes data such as the power budget and the maximum power available for devices connected to the switch. The actual power consumption by connected devices is also shown, allowing you to monitor and manage power usage.

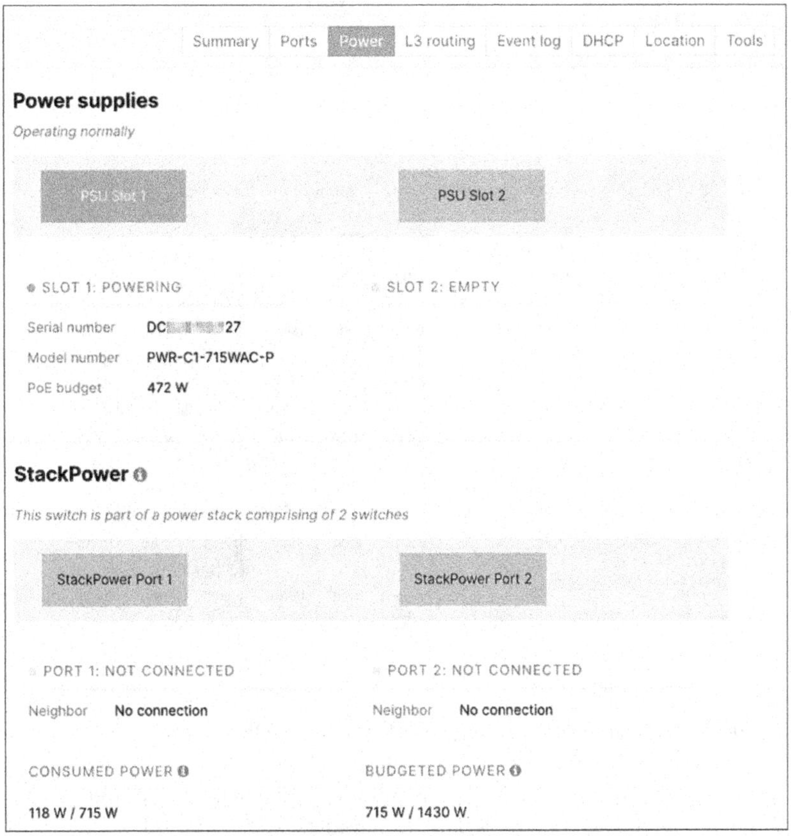

Summary   Ports   Power   L3 routing   Event log   DHCP   Location   Tools

Power supplies
Operating normally

PSU Slot 1   PSU Slot 2

● SLOT 1: POWERING   ○ SLOT 2: EMPTY

Serial number	**DC████████27**
Model number	**PWR-C1-715WAC-P**
PoE budget	**472 W**

StackPower ⓘ

This switch is part of a power stack comprising of 2 switches

StackPower Port 1   StackPower Port 2

○ PORT 1: NOT CONNECTED   ○ PORT 2: NOT CONNECTED

Neighbor	**No connection**		Neighbor	**No connection**

CONSUMED POWER ⓘ   BUDGETED POWER ⓘ

118 W / 715 W   715 W / 1430 W

Figure 7-36 *Power Overview and Stack Power Information in the Dashboard*

The StackPower feature (currently available on Meraki MS390 and Catalyst 9300-M) aggregates all the available power from each switch and manages it as a single shared power pool for the entire stack of up to four switches. This means that the power budget for the stack is effectively shared among all the switches, optimizing power distribution and utilization within the stack.

The Power Overview section provides insights into the actual power consumption of devices connected to the switches compared to the budgeted power. This allows you to monitor whether the power usage is within the allocated budget or exceeds the available power.

Sustainability Using MS

In Meraki MS switches, the Port Schedules feature, shown in Figure 7-37, allows you to automate the availability of a set of ports based on predefined schedules. This feature offers several use cases, such as defining access control for physical wired ports or saving power by turning off PoE clients during specific periods.

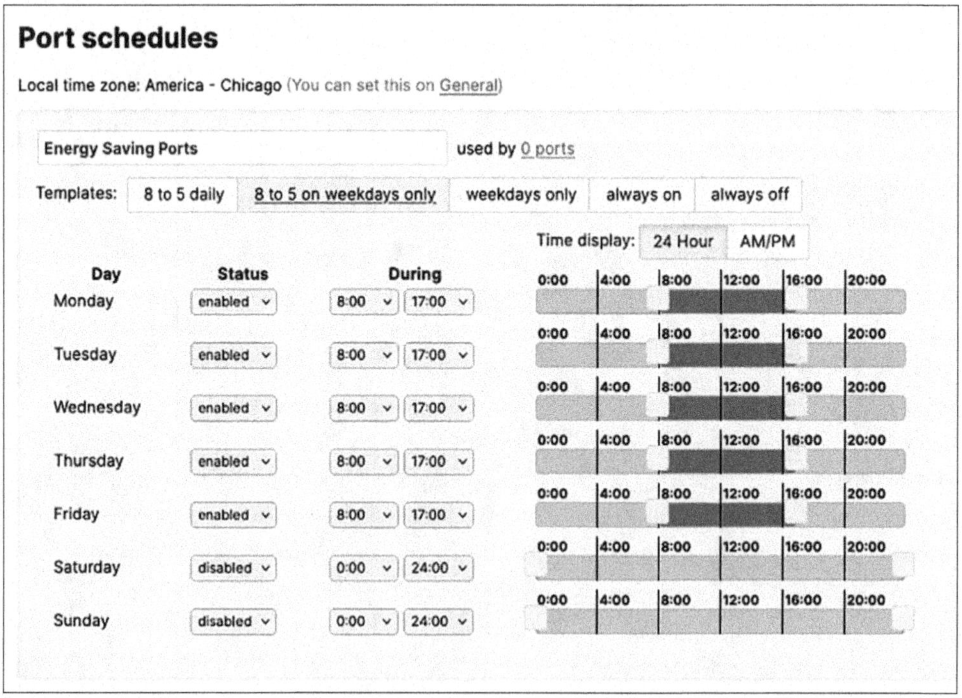

Figure 7-37 *Example of a Default Port Schedule Option on the Dashboard*

After you have created a port schedule, you can apply it to individual port configurations (see Figure 7-38) or as a virtual-stacking configuration update (see Figure 7-39).

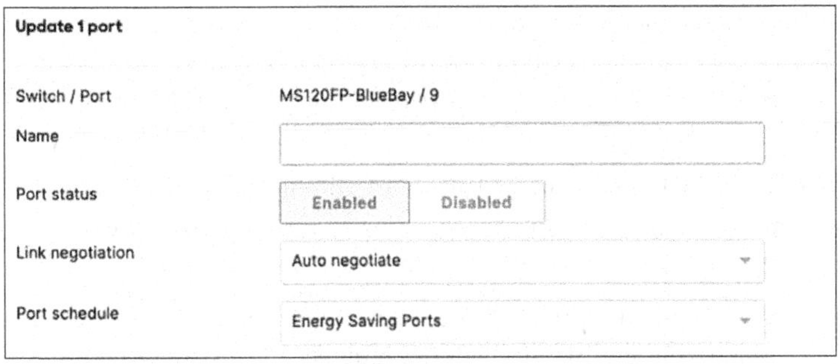

Figure 7-38 *Applying a Port Schedule to a Switch Port*

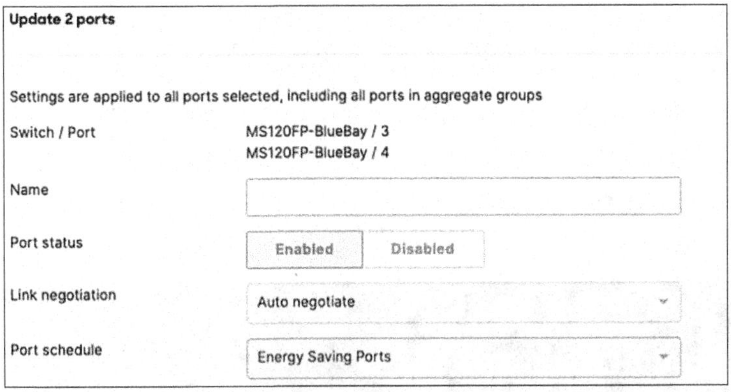

Figure 7-39 *Applying Port Schedule to Multiple Ports via Virtual Stacking in the Dashboard*

By utilizing the Port Schedules feature in Meraki MS switches, you can automate the availability and control of specific ports based on predefined schedules. This allows for greater flexibility, access control, and power savings in your network deployment.

Cloud-Monitored Catalyst

Cloud monitoring for Catalyst provides an integrated view of Catalyst 9200/9300/9500 series switches in the Meraki Dashboard, seamlessly integrated into a single-pane-of-glass experience. This provides centralized management and control of the Catalyst switch infrastructure, offering features like configuration management, monitoring, analytics, and troubleshooting. These switches will be automatically tagged with Monitor Only in the Dashboard to distinguish them from fully managed Meraki switches. While cloud monitoring solutions like the Dashboard can provide real-time information, statistics, and alerts for cloud-monitored Catalyst switches, these platforms are designed to provide read-only access for monitoring purposes and may not offer the same configuration capabilities as traditional management solutions.

You can see the IOS-XE version under the firmware details on a cloud-managed catalyst switch. The device also gets a Meraki serial number in addition to the original Catalyst serial number. The Meraki serial number will not be present outside the Dashboard or on the hardware.

For Meraki-managed Catalyst switches, you can launch a read-only terminal session directly through the Dashboard. Shown in Figure 7-40, this further simplifies the integration of Catalyst switches in a mixed Catalyst and Meraki environment.

Port-level traffic analytics are available with a DNA Essentials license for cloud-monitored Catalyst switches. Accessing client-level traffic analytics requires a DNA Advantage license, which provides advanced analytics and visibility into client-level traffic for Catalyst switches, allowing you to analyze the behavior, applications, and performance of individual clients on the network.

Figure 7-40   *Catalyst 9000 Terminal View on the Dashboard*

Troubleshooting Your Meraki Deployment

All Meraki MS switches offer a detailed suite of tools and features for comprehensive network analysis, troubleshooting, and control. This section briefly introduces some of the details and features available directly through the Dashboard to assist in troubleshooting and understanding your deployment.

Dashboard Reporting

For each device in a network, the Dashboard reports a number of details that can be useful when monitoring or troubleshooting a device. We start by reviewing some of the device reporting that can be useful for initial troubleshooting and scoping of an issue before looking at several Live Tools that are also available to further assist in troubleshooting.

- **Switch port details:** As shown in Figure 7-41, accessing the Summary tab of a switch provides a visual representation of all the switch's ports and their general status. Clicking a specific port provides a detailed status of that port. The connectivity graph displays a time bar graph of the connection state of each switch over the past 24 hours.

- **Switch serial numbers:** The Meraki platform displays unique serial numbers for all devices, including for both Meraki and Catalyst switches. This allows for easy identification and management of each switch within the network, regardless of whether it is a Meraki or Catalyst model.

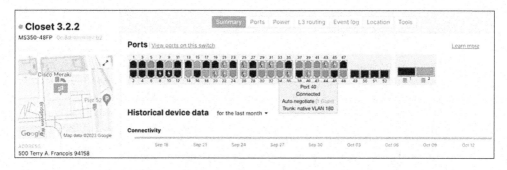

Figure 7-41 *Switch Port Details Displayed on the Dashboard*

- **Quick Launch to Topology:** This feature on the switch details page in the Dashboard lets you quickly jump to view any switch in the Network-wide > Topology page. This feature provides a streamlined way to view specific switches within the broader network topology.

- **Spanning Tree Protocol (STP) Info:** This section of the device details page (see Figure 7-42) provides crucial information about the STP status and operation for individual switches or a logical switch stack.

RSTP ROOT
CORE 1 (priority 0) via SFO12-MS-2.2.18-
Mint-VideoEdit-01 port 47 and SFO12-
MS-2.2.18-Mint-VideoEdit-01 port 48

Figure 7-42 *Detailed STP Information for a Switch Stack*

■ **Event Log:** Similar to other Meraki products, the Event Log feature on Meraki switches provides a detailed record of operational status and events for each switch. Shown in Figure 7-43, the Event Log offers valuable insights into the switch's historical activity, including changes, errors, and warnings. This feature is handy for troubleshooting, allowing network administrators to track events over time, and identify patterns that may indicate potential issues.

Time	Client	Event type	Details
Sep 16 11:48:13		Port RSTP role change	Port 24 disabled→designated
Sep 16 11:48:13		Port status change	port: 24, old: down, new: 1Gfdx
Sep 16 11:48:09		Port RSTP role change	Port 24 designated→disabled
Sep 16 11:48:09		Port status change	port: 24, old: 1Gfdx, new: down

Figure 7-43   *Example of Dashboard-Hosted Event Logs for the MS Platform*

■ **Wired client details:** This feature provides extensive information about each wired client connected to or passing traffic through a switch on the Client Details page (see Figure 7-44) for that client. This includes the client's MAC address, IP address, VLAN, and nearest switch port. A visual representation of each client's path through the network is also provided, alongside real-time troubleshooting data. Furthermore, detailed Application Visibility and Control (AVC) data for each wired client provides comprehensive network usage and performance insights.

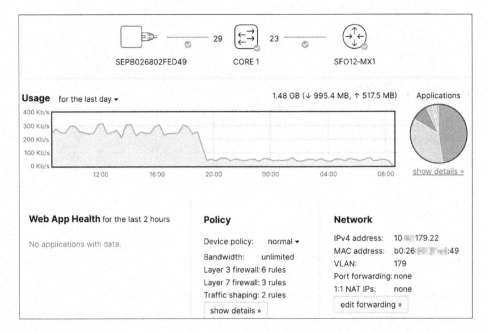

Figure 7-44   *Wired Client Details Page Shown in the Dashboard for a Client Connected Directly to an MS Switch*

■ **Automated root cause analysis:** This Dashboard-powered feature assists in identifying the underlying causes of network issues, such as VLAN mismatch CRC errors, among others. In the example of a VLAN mismatch, shown in Figure 7-45, the system provides suggested fixes, such as adding missing VLANs or modifying the native VLAN of one port. This feature greatly simplifies the troubleshooting process by automatically analyzing and highlighting potential issues from the Dashboard.

Figure 7-45 *RCA for a VLAN Mismatch on a Cloud-Managed Catalyst 9000 with a Suggested Fix*

Dashboard Live Tools

Live Tools are a set of features available on the Meraki Dashboard that allow network administrators to perform various real-time diagnostic and troubleshooting tasks directly from the Dashboard. These tools provide a convenient way to monitor and troubleshoot network issues without needing physical access to the switch or relying on command-line interfaces. The Live Tools features for Meraki switches are described in turn next.

Ping

By using the ping feature (see Figure 7-46) in the Dashboard for Meraki MS switches, you can easily test the reachability of various destinations or domains and check response times from the device management interface. This can help you to troubleshoot connectivity or DNS resolution issues within your network.

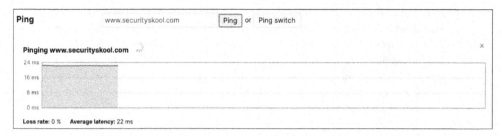

Figure 7-46   *Ping Test Live Tool in the Dashboard*

Pro Tip   Live Tools such as ping, packet capture, and MTR are available across multiple Meraki platforms.

Packet Capture

Meraki devices, including MS switches, offer a web-based packet capture tool through the Dashboard that allows administrators to capture and analyze network traffic passing through the switch. For MS switches, the packet capture tool supports capturing packets on multiple switch ports simultaneously and provides options to set capture filters and duration for focused and detailed analysis. Figure 7-47 shows the direct Packet Capture link from the client details page of a client, helping to facilitate quicker troubleshooting.

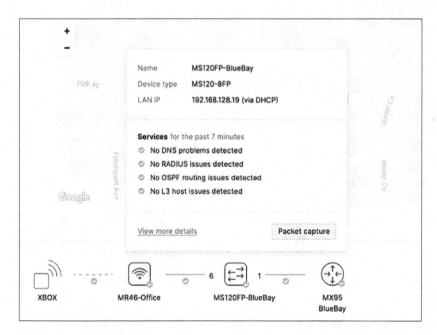

Figure 7-47   *Direct Link to Initiate a Dashboard Packet Capture for a Specific Wired Client*

When you execute packet capture from the details page of a specific wired client, the relevant traffic filters will be applied by default to capture traffic specifically for the related client. You can still manually add port- or protocol-level filters to refine the capture further.

Pro Tip   When capturing on the **Network-wide > Packet Capture** page, choose **View Output Below** to confirm your filters and data stream before switching to the **Download .pcap** option.

Note that this view also offers detailed information on upstream service interruptions for the selected client, including disruptions in services such as DNS, RADIUS, OSPF, and others. This feature allows network administrators to track and analyze service interruptions on a per-client basis, making it easier to identify and address issues that could impact network performance and reliability. This enhances the network's overall performance and ensures a seamless user experience.

MTR

The MTR (My Traceroute) test, shown in Figure 7-48, combines ICMP and traceroute functionalities to provide a more detailed reachability analysis. It performs a hop-by-hop analysis of reachability and can help identify potential causes for loss or delays to a destination from the switch's management IP. With the MTR test, you can specify the destination as an FQDN or an IP address. The MTR tool will then send ICMP packets to each hop along the path and provide detailed statistics on packet loss, latency, and other network performance metrics.

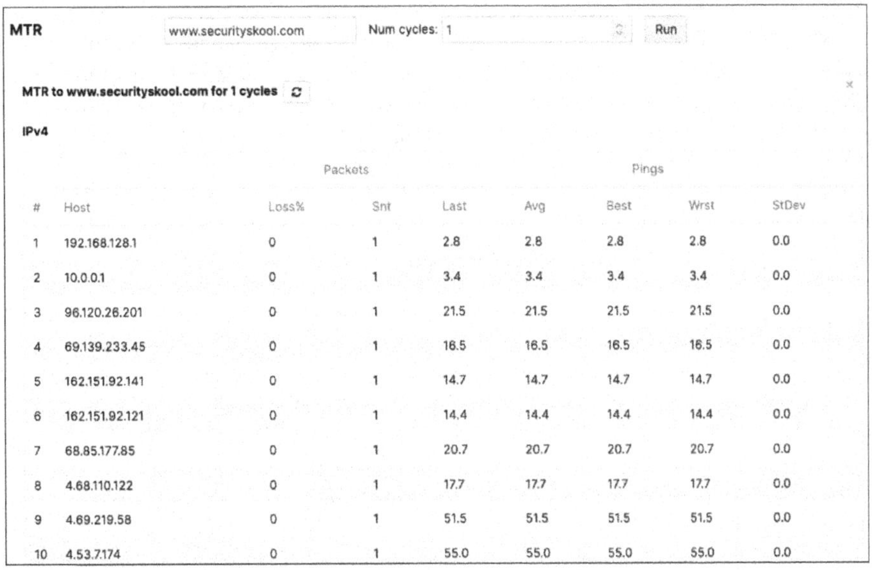

| | | | | **MTR** | www.securityskool.com | | | **Num cycles:** 1 | | | Run | |

MTR to www.securityskool.com for 1 cycles

IPv4

			Packets				Pings		
#	Host	Loss%	Snt	Last	Avg	Best	Wrst	StDev
1	192.168.128.1	0	1	2.8	2.8	2.8	2.8	0.0
2	10.0.0.1	0	1	3.4	3.4	3.4	3.4	0.0
3	96.120.26.201	0	1	21.5	21.5	21.5	21.5	0.0
4	69.139.233.45	0	1	16.5	16.5	16.5	16.5	0.0
5	162.151.92.141	0	1	14.7	14.7	14.7	14.7	0.0
6	162.151.92.121	0	1	14.4	14.4	14.4	14.4	0.0
7	68.85.177.85	0	1	20.7	20.7	20.7	20.7	0.0
8	4.68.110.122	0	1	17.7	17.7	17.7	17.7	0.0
9	4.69.219.58	0	1	51.5	51.5	51.5	51.5	0.0
10	4.53.7.174	0	1	55.0	55.0	55.0	55.0	0.0

Figure 7-48   *MTR Feature as Shown in the MS Live Tools*

MAC Forwarding Table

The MAC forwarding table (aka CAM table), shown in Figure 7-49, maps device MAC addresses to their corresponding switch port and VLAN. Note that the MAC forwarding table is dynamic and can change as devices connect or disconnect from the network. The Dashboard is able to provide a snapshot of the current state of the MAC forwarding table for a given switch at the time of viewing.

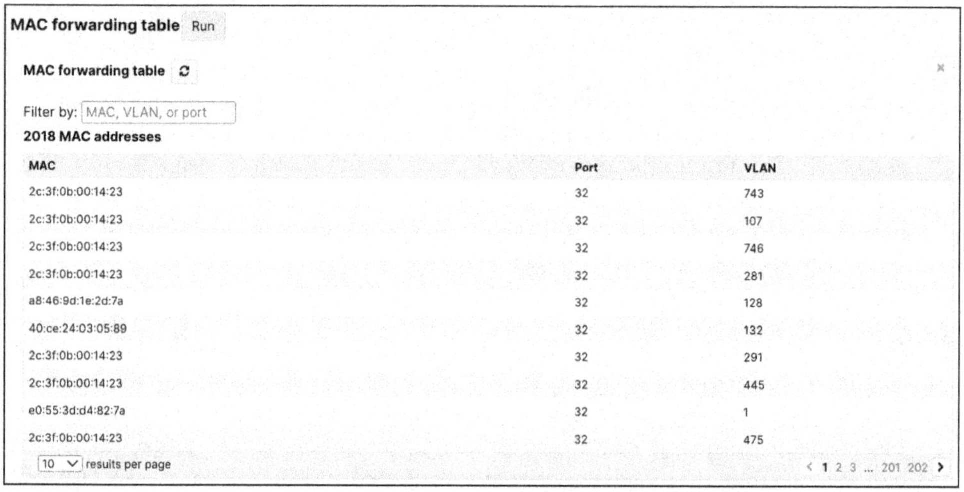

MAC forwarding table Run

MAC forwarding table ⟳   ✕

Filter by: [MAC, VLAN, or port]

2018 MAC addresses

MAC	Port	VLAN
2c:3f:0b:00:14:23	32	743
2c:3f:0b:00:14:23	32	107
2c:3f:0b:00:14:23	32	746
2c:3f:0b:00:14:23	32	281
a8:46:9d:1e:2d:7a	32	128
40:ce:24:03:05:89	32	132
2c:3f:0b:00:14:23	32	291
2c:3f:0b:00:14:23	32	445
e0:55:3d:d4:82:7a	32	1
2c:3f:0b:00:14:23	32	475

[10 ⌄] results per page   ‹ **1** 2 3 … 201 202 ›

Figure 7-49 *MAC Forwarding Table as Shown in the MS Live Tools*

Cable Testing

This tool, shown in Figure 7-50, allows you to test the connectivity and quality of Ethernet cables connected to a switch. It can help you identify cable faults or issues affecting network connectivity remotely without requiring a tech to be dispatched to disconnect the cable and manually test with a cable tester.

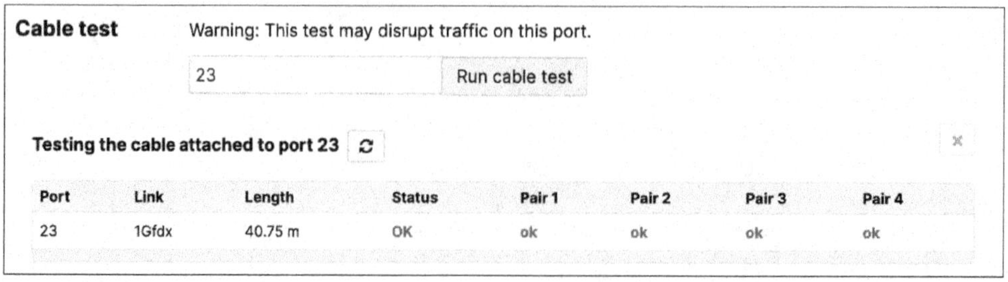

Cable test   Warning: This test may disrupt traffic on this port.

[23]   [Run cable test]

Testing the cable attached to port 23 ⟳   ✕

Port	Link	Length	Status	Pair 1	Pair 2	Pair 3	Pair 4
23	1Gfdx	40.75 m	OK	ok	ok	ok	ok

Figure 7-50 *Cable Test Feature Available in MS Live Tools*

Cycle Port

Shown in Figure 7-51, cycling a specific port on a switch via the Cycle Port tool can be helpful in scenarios where you want to reset the connection on that port or troubleshoot connectivity issues. It can help clear potential issues related to the port configuration or the connected device.

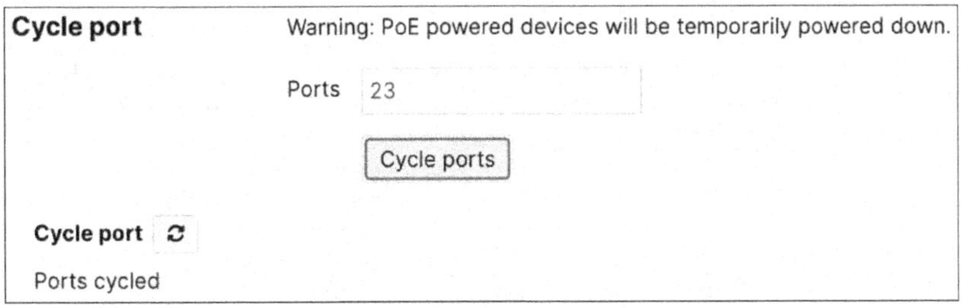

Cycle port	Warning: PoE powered devices will be temporarily powered down.
	Ports 23
	Cycle ports
Cycle port ↻	
Ports cycled	

Figure 7-51 *Cycle Port Tool for MS Switches in the Dashboard*

> **Pro Tip** Cycling a port will temporarily disrupt the connectivity of any device connected to that port. Inform affected device users beforehand and schedule the port cycle during a maintenance window if necessary. This will also cycle power to connected PoE devices.

Wake-on-LAN

The Meraki Wake-on-LAN tool, shown in Figure 7-52, allows administrators to remotely wake up client machines that have been configured with Wake-on-LAN enabled. This can be useful for remotely powering on devices for maintenance, updates, or other purposes without requiring physical access to the machines.

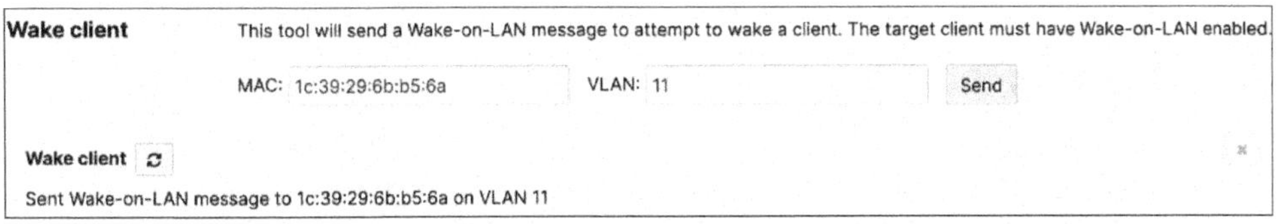

Wake client	This tool will send a Wake-on-LAN message to attempt to wake a client. The target client must have Wake-on-LAN enabled.		
	MAC: 1c:39:29:6b:b5:6a	VLAN: 11	Send
Wake client ↻			✕
Sent Wake-on-LAN message to 1c:39:29:6b:b5:6a on VLAN 11			

Figure 7-52 *Wake-on-LAN Feature in the Dashboard*

You can find more information on using the MS Live Tools at https://documentation.meraki.com by viewing the article "Using the MS Live Tools."

Summary

The Meraki platform offers numerous advantages that make it an ideal choice for managing network operations. It significantly simplifies IT operations through built-in automation, reducing manual tasks and increasing efficiency. This enhanced visibility into the full stack of Cisco products allows for comprehensive network monitoring and management. Meraki also significantly reduces the total cost of ownership (TCO) by eliminating the need for on-premises management hardware and dedicated data lakes. Instead, the management platform and data storage are securely offloaded to Cisco's networking cloud. This cloud-based approach simplifies network management, reduces hardware costs, and eliminates the need for dedicated IT resources to maintain and manage infrastructure.

The Meraki platform comes with sustainability tools that aid in achieving eco-friendly IT practices. Significant operational expense (OPEX) savings can be realized through remote management capabilities that reduce the need for onsite interventions.

Meraki MS switches also support zero-touch deployment, further simplifying the setup process and reducing deployment time. The efficient root cause analysis feature helps swiftly identify and address network issues, thus minimizing downtime.

Integration with Cisco technologies such as ISE enables uniform policy enforcement across the network, enhancing security and compliance. In summary, the Meraki MS platform offers a comprehensive, efficient, and user-friendly solution for network management, making it a preferred choice for many organizations.

The Meraki Dashboard offers a unified interface, or a single pane of glass, not only for the Meraki MS product line but also for the broader Cisco Catalyst platform. This gives administrators a comprehensive view of their network infrastructure from one central point. This dramatically simplifies network management and control, allowing for easy monitoring, configuration, and troubleshooting across both Meraki and Cisco Catalyst devices. The unified approach enhances efficiency and provides a more streamlined and cohesive network management experience.

Additional Reading

Meraki Campus LAN; Planning, Design Guidelines and Best Practices: https://documentation.meraki.com/MS/Meraki_Campus_LAN%3B_Planning%2C_Design_Guidelines_and_Best_Practices

Hybrid Campus LAN Design Guide (CVD): https://documentation.meraki.com/MS/Deployment_Guides/Hybrid_Campus_LAN_Design_Guide_(CVD)

Storm Control for MS: https://documentation.meraki.com/MS/Other_Topics/Storm_Control_for_MS

Switch Ports: https://documentation.meraki.com/MS/Port_and_VLAN_Configuration/Switch_Ports

Dynamic ARP Inspection: https://documentation.meraki.com/MS/Other_Topics/Dynamic_ARP_Inspection

Using the MS Live Tools: https://documentation.meraki.com/MS/Monitoring_and_Reporting/Using_the_MS_Live_Tools

MS Firmware Upgrades: https://documentation.meraki.com/MS/Firmware/MS_Firmware_Upgrades

Meraki MS Group Policy Access Control Lists: https://documentation.meraki.com/MS/Access_Control/Meraki_MS_Group_Policy_Access_Control_Lists

Adaptive Policy/Micro-segmentation: https://documentation.meraki.com/General_Administration/Cross-Platform_Content/Adaptive_Policy/Adaptive_Policy_Overview

Chapter 8

Meraki Wireless Best Practices and Design

The wireless portion of Meraki's portfolio is the oldest and most established hardware platform, dating back to Meraki's inception as a company in 2008. Since that time, Meraki's wireless offerings have expanded greatly to provide more-focused hardware options to best serve the varied needs and deployments of its customers. From its newest hardware that offers indoor/outdoor Wi-Fi 6 and Wi-Fi 6E connectivity to its more specialized products like the MR36H access point, which offers an integrated four-port Power over Ethernet (PoE) switch to provide both wired and wireless connectivity for spaces like dorm rooms, the Meraki MR series of devices offers hardware to suit nearly any need in any deployment.

All Meraki MR access points fully integrate with the Meraki Dashboard platform and are designed to take advantage of the features and capabilities available through the Dashboard. This includes but is not limited to advanced client monitoring and alerting, RF monitoring, and IoT connectivity for devices like MT sensors. This chapter discusses the various Dashboard features available for the MR series of devices and a number of tips for designing and fine-tuning your wireless deployments.

Additionally, the Meraki and Catalyst wireless teams have combined to bring new functionality to Cisco's CW916x series of access points through the advent of dual-persona wireless. This allows traditional Cisco hardware to operate in a mode that brings Meraki Dashboard integration and functionality to pure Cisco hardware, further enabling hybrid environments of traditional Cisco hardware mixed with Cisco Meraki hardware and allowing the power of the Dashboard to be utilized with existing deployments.

This chapter focuses on a number of different aspects of designing, configuring, and optimizing a Meraki wireless deployment, with special attention paid to working with large-scale networks such as large campuses. These large deployments typically require much more planning than is required for smaller deployments, but many of the principles discussed in this chapter apply to both large and small deployments.

Note This chapter is not intended to serve as a comprehensive setup guide for MR access points or the related features discussed here. It is intended to provide a basic overview of many of the most popular features and options that are available in the platform while emphasizing several general recommendations and best practices that often are overlooked or underutilized in many customer deployments. You can find in-depth setup and step-by-step configuration guides for the MR product line at https://documentation.meraki.com by clicking the **MR – Wireless LAN** link on the main page.

Scoping and Scaling the Dashboard

As discussed in Chapter 2, "Building the Dashboard," and Chapter 3, "The Meraki Admin Experience," a network in the Meraki Dashboard is a logical construct that does not necessarily have to represent the actual physically deployed network. Depending on the scale of the deployment, a single network could contain devices from a single floor, from a single building, or from an entire campus. For large-scale deployments, it is common to separate Dashboard networks using some sort of physical boundary, such as per building or per area, to break up the deployment and management into more approachable groups.

A large Meraki wireless deployment, such as for a university campus or corporate head-quarters, may include thousands of Meraki devices. Although the Dashboard UI does not restrict the number of Meraki devices used in the same deployment, we recommend limiting the size of any individual Dashboard network to under ~800 Meraki devices to help reduce the impact of large-scale network-wide updates and configuration changes.

Similarly, for extremely large deployments that include more than ~25,000 devices, multiple organizations may be needed, at which point you can begin to take advantage of several of the features introduced in Chapter 2, such as the Global Overview page.

Pro Tip Be aware when combining networks that the ~800 device recommendation applies to both the original standalone networks and the final combined network.

Additionally, breaking up a large deployment across multiple Dashboard networks can be useful when configuring monitoring and alerting for each network, such as the SNMP and syslog alerting discussed in Chapter 2, because network-wide alerts can be quickly configured for each network that encompass only the subset of devices within that network, reducing the amount of custom alerts and tagging that would need to be done to accomplish the same level of granularity if all the devices in the entire deployment were contained within a single network.

When working with any deployment, it is important to appropriately scope administrator privileges and access. This is increasingly important as the size and scope of your deployments expand and more administrators are required to monitor and manage the deployment. Administrator privileges and scoping are discussed in detail in Chapter 2, including using tags for precision permissions scoping, using role-based access control such as Guest Ambassadors for user management, and implementing other related best practices that become increasingly important as the scope and scale of a deployment increase.

Physical WLAN Design

When designing the physical side of your wireless deployment, there are several Meraki best practices and recommendations that you should keep in mind. We present the most important of these aspects in the following subsections, along with our recommendations as they relate to that feature or consideration.

Pro Tip   Whenever possible, a professional site survey should be performed both before and after deployment to best determine physical AP placement and RF configurations such as appropriate transmit (TX) values and bitrates for your specific deployment.

Location-Aware Wireless Network

Cisco Meraki APs monitor and record the wireless signal strength and Bluetooth Low Energy (BLE) responses of nearby clients to track the client device location relative to the APs. Uploading a custom floorplan to the Dashboard and placing the APs appropriately, as shown in the example in Figure 8-1, can greatly aid in locating potentially troublesome areas of the deployment based on recorded client issues and locations.

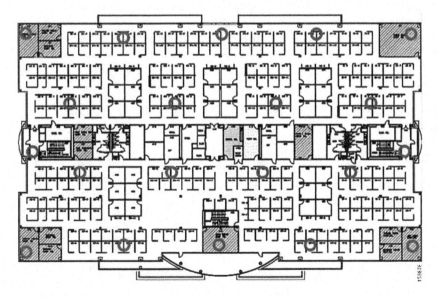

Figure 8-1   *Example Office Floor Plan with AP Locations Marked*

Pro Tip   A minimum of four APs is recommended to most accurately triangulate the client position relative to the APs.

You can find more detailed information regarding location planning, client location analytics, and floor plans at https://documentation.meraki.com in the following documents:

- Location Deployment Guidelines
- Location Analytics
- Using a Floor Plan or Custom Map in Dashboard

Note   The "Additional Reading" section at the end of this chapter provides the full URL for every article that is cross-referenced in this chapter. Alternatively, you can search for the article title at https://documentation.meraki.com to locate it.

Wi-Fi 6E and Dual 5-GHz Mode

With the new Meraki and Cisco Wi-Fi 6E–capable models of AP, in addition to the new dual-persona Wi-Fi mentioned previously, a new feature known as dual 5-GHz mode is also available. This feature enables you to configure the access points in a way that repurposes the 6-GHz radio to allow for dual 5-GHz client-serving radios to function simultaneously, at the expense of giving up the 6-GHz functionality.

At the time of writing, many devices are not yet capable of utilizing the 6-GHz band, so this mode offers an excellent way to upgrade and future-proof a new deployment while still also providing excellent service to existing clients and still allowing the option to quickly implement a 6-GHz client network at any time in the future. Figure 8-2 shows the Flex radio selection screen for several APs capable of but not configured for dual 5-GHz mode.

Figure 8-2   *Flex Radio Selection Options in the Dashboard Showing Both Flex Radios Configured for 6 GHz*

6-GHz RF Propagation

When working with Meraki 6 GHz, it's important to know that the 6-GHz antenna coverage patterns for Meraki devices are nearly identical to the 5-GHz patterns, with the caveat that 6 GHz typically requires +3dB of TX power to match the propagation of 5 GHz. Figure 8-3 shows a visualization of the 5-GHz and 6-GHz coverage patterns, overlapped for comparison.

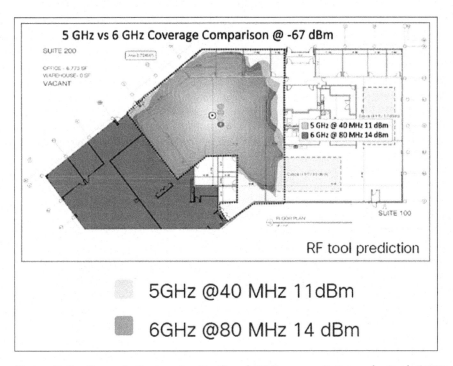

Figure 8-3 *Example Comparing Predicted RF Coverage Patterns for Both 5 GHz and 6 GHz*

AP Mounting Recommendations

We have several general recommendations for mounting Meraki APs. However, keep in mind that your deployment is unique, and you should always approach it as such by getting a professional site survey performed to help determine the required number and location of APs for your unique deployment. Aspects such as expected client density, expected traffic types, and analytics requirements should all be considered and discussed prior to your deployment to ensure the hardware and configurations chosen will meet the needs of your deployment.

To ensure the greatest level of flexibility across deployments, the following different types of external antennas are available, depending on the selected model of AP, each with its own characteristics and intended use cases:

- **Omni-directional antenna:** Best for deployments that require 360-degree coverage around the AP or wireless mesh networks

- **Sector antenna:** Provides a targeted coverage area; best for building mounted APs, mesh bridges, or other deployments where targeted coverage is ideal

- **Patch antenna:** Provides a large, semi-targeted coverage area; ideal for large spaces like fields or warehouses

- **Stadium patch antenna:** Designed for high-density deployments with large numbers of APs and clients such as event centers or stadiums

When mounting in an indoor space such as a classroom, the maximum height of the AP should be no more than 15 to 18 feet for APs using integrated/internal antennas, to allow for proper signal propagation across the space.

When mounting outdoor APs, or indoor APs in a space with a high ceiling such as a lecture hall or auditorium, we recommend using models of APs that support the addition of external antennas to better serve the space. Your Meraki sales representative can help you determine the best model(s) of AP to use based on your specific deployment and requirements.

Pro Tip   When using external antennas with indoor APs, the APs will auto-detect the connected antenna type. However, outdoor models of AP using external antennas need to have the antenna type configured from the drop-down menu on the AP details page, as shown in Figure 8-4.

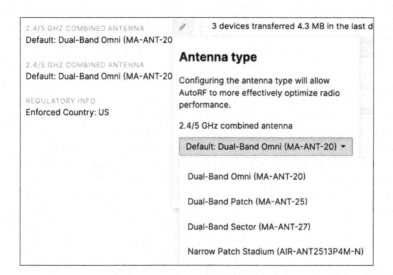

Figure 8-4   *Antenna Selection Drop-Down Menu for an Access Point in the Dashboard*

AP Adjacency and Overlap

In the early days of Wi-Fi, it was common to design for maximum coverage and minimum density, where the least possible number of access points were deployed to ensure that a client could see and connect to the wireless network. Since most client devices were still connected to Ethernet, Wi-Fi was not as mission critical as it is today. As Wi-Fi technology evolved and mobile devices became much more prevalent, a greater importance was placed on Wi-Fi. More networks are moving to a wireless-first or even a wireless-only model, where most if not all clients are wireless and only access points, printers, phones, and other non-user devices are connected to switches. Modern wireless networks need to be designed to handle the density and performance requirements of modern users.

AP adjacency and overlap is best determined with a site survey. Identifying some key requirements beforehand can help establish the measurements that need to be considered during the survey. Client capabilities, for example, play a large part in design. A common design is to tune the transmit (TX) power of the access points to the least capable client device. If the TX power is set too high, client devices may experience issues with connectivity, roaming, and performance. Reducing the TX power means the access points need to be closer to each other to maintain good adjacency. This is important for seamless roaming, where client devices that need to move through the space maintain a consistent, good experience as they move about.

Noise and signal-to-noise ratio (SNR) are important factors, as well. Use a spectrum analyzer to determine the noise floor, which is the amount of "noise," or background interference, that can be heard by wireless devices. Once you determine the noise floor, you can determine AP adjacency by analyzing the APs after they've been placed on the map in the survey tool. For example, if neighboring APs receive signal from each other at −65 dBm and the noise floor is −95 dBm, then the effective SNR is 30 dB, which is really good for applications like voice and video, as well as roaming, as clients will have a higher SNR.

SNR has a direct impact on a client device's performance. A higher SNR value means that the client has a better signal, which translates to higher data rates and better throughput. Conversely, a lower SNR means that the client has moved away from the access point and has lower data rates and less throughput. By ensuring good AP adjacency, as the client moves away from the AP, it gets closer to the neighboring AP and can easily roam to it.

Pro Tip   Meraki APs list all nearby neighboring APs from the same Dashboard network that they can see, as well as the incoming signal strength of those APs.

Configuring Meraki Wireless

When configuring a Meraki wireless deployment, there are two primary areas of configuration required: the SSID configurations, which determine the security and authentication settings for each SSID, and the RF configurations, which determine the radio broadcast settings for each AP in the network such as band selection (2.4 GHz vs. 5 GHz vs. 6 GHz), TX power, and bitrate requirements.

To configure the initial SSID settings, such as SSID name, security/authentication requirements, and IP assignment methods, navigate to the **Wireless > SSIDs** page or **Wireless > Access Control** page. To configure the hardware radio settings for each AP, such as band selection, channel availability, max TX power, and more, navigate to the **Wireless > Radio Settings** page.

Every wireless deployment has unique requirements and a variety of deployment scenarios that should be accounted for when creating and optimizing the configurations for the deployment. Differences between individual APs, such as the physical location and surrounding RF environment, can require special considerations or configurations to ensure that each AP is able to provide a high level of connectivity and performance for any connected clients. For example, an AP serving a less populated outdoor area would have very different configuration requirements when compared to an AP serving a high-density auditorium or a small classroom. Unlike the SSID configurations, these RF configurations typically require more in-depth planning and an understanding of the deployment and the APs involved.

While the Dashboard does provide the option to individually configure the RF settings of each AP, such as band, TX power, minimum bitrate, channel width, and more, configuring these settings for every individual AP becomes troublesome and tedious for deployments with more than just a small handful of APs. Fortunately, Meraki has designed the Dashboard to support the use of RF profiles, which can help to simplify the RF configurations required for a deployment by creating and applying unique profiles to selected APs, removing the need for every AP to be manually configured with the appropriate RF configurations. Figure 8-5 shows the selection of default RF profiles available on the Dashboard.

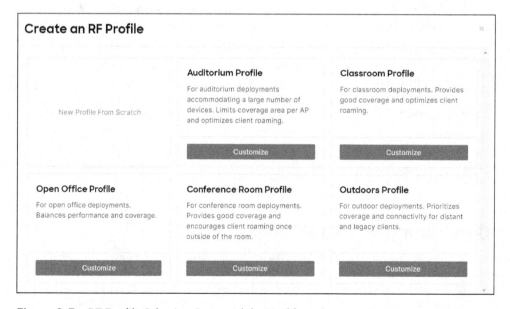

Figure 8-5 *RF Profile Selection Screen of the Dashboard*

This feature enables you to create unique profiles for different purposes, such as an Outdoor profile designed for coverage of large outdoor areas, an Auditorium profile designed for high-density coverage in a large indoor space, and a Classroom profile for high-density coverage of a much smaller space. By fine-tuning these example profiles, you can save a lot of time and effort when deploying APs in each role by simply applying the custom profile to one or more APs through the Dashboard and allowing them to use the profile-defined configurations. After applying the profile settings, you can further tune and adjust individual AP configurations as needed for the best performance in your unique environment by going to the **Wireless > Radio Settings** page in the Dashboard.

Note As with all best practices presented in this book, the recommendations in this chapter are generalized and may not be the best choice for your specific deployment, depending on the requirements and environment unique to your deployment. When making recommendations, we will explain why the recommendation is being made and what types of environmental or other factors may play into making that recommendation the right or wrong choice for your specific deployment needs.

You can locate RF profiles in the Dashboard from within a given network by navigating to **Wireless > Radio Settings > RF Profiles**. By default, there are two profiles available, a default Indoor profile and a default Outdoor profile. You can use these profiles in their default configurations, modify them directly to best suit the needs of your deployment, or clone them to use as a baseline for a new custom profile. Additionally, you can create new profiles either from scratch or from one of several predefined template profiles, depending on the needs of your deployment.

Pro Tip When you're working with the default profiles, you can always revert any changes to the default configuration by clicking the **Restore Meraki Defaults** button at the bottom of the page for that profile, as highlighted in Figure 8-6.

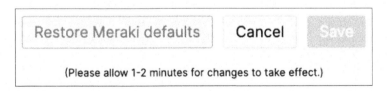

Figure 8-6 *Restore Meraki Defaults Button Displayed on One of the Default RF Profiles*

RF Profile Best Practices and Recommendations

When you are initially configuring a Meraki wireless deployment, there are a number of options available to configure for both the SSID and RF configurations. If you choose to use RF profiles, you'll find that Meraki has worked to ensure that profiles can be modified and configured in a way that best serves nearly any deployment requirements. This section looks at several of the different options available in an RF profile and how you can use them to fine-tune the RF behavior of devices in that network. When applicable, we make additional recommendations for initial configuration values to help provide you with a starting point when configuring a new deployment.

A simple yet often overlooked method to help ensure consistency and reduce the amount of manual effort required when deploying a new network or site is to create and maintain one or more networks or templates with the optimal starting RF profiles and SSIDs already configured. These can be used when creating new sites to eliminate the need to manually configure new SSIDs and RF profiles for each new site, either by creating the new site as a clone of the existing network or by attaching the new network as a child network to the existing configuration template so that it inherits the existing RF profiles and SSID configurations.

For example, by designing deployments to have a consistent starting configuration of SSIDs, PSK/Enterprise Security settings, and RF profiles across sites, you can use configuration templates and cloning of existing networks to significantly speed up the creation and configuration of new sites in the Dashboard. Additionally, using a configuration template still enables you to configure local overrides for devices in each network, as discussed in Chapter 4, "Automating the Dashboard." This makes initial configuration and deployment of a site quick and easy while still allowing the fine-tuning necessary to get the most out of each unique deployment.

Pro Tip   Whenever possible, a professional site survey should be performed both before and after deployment to best determine AP placement and RF configurations such as appropriate TX values and bitrates for your specific deployment.

Band Selection: Per SSID Versus All SSIDs

As Figure 8-7 shows, when you are configuring the band selection in an RF profile, you can choose to have the band selection settings apply to all SSIDs broadcast by an AP under that profile or to have a separate broadcast band configuration for each SSID. This type of flexibility enables you to, for example, configure and use a single RF profile to broadcast a legacy or IoT SSID on the 2.4-GHz band only, while simultaneously broadcasting a different, client-serving SSID on both the 5-GHz and 6-GHz bands.

This type of flexible configuration is also available for other settings such as minimum allowed bitrate and band steering, the latter of which works with SSIDs being broadcast across multiple bands (2.4, 5, or even 6 GHz) to steer clients to the highest supported frequency band when possible, while still allowing the 2.4-GHz band (and/or 5-GHz band if utilizing a 6-GHz–capable AP) to be used if the client is unable to create or maintain a connection on the 5-GHz (or 6-GHz) band. Depending on the needs of your deployment, you can configure all these options in the RF profile to either apply to all SSIDs broadcast by an AP or apply only to select SSIDs on a per-SSID basis.

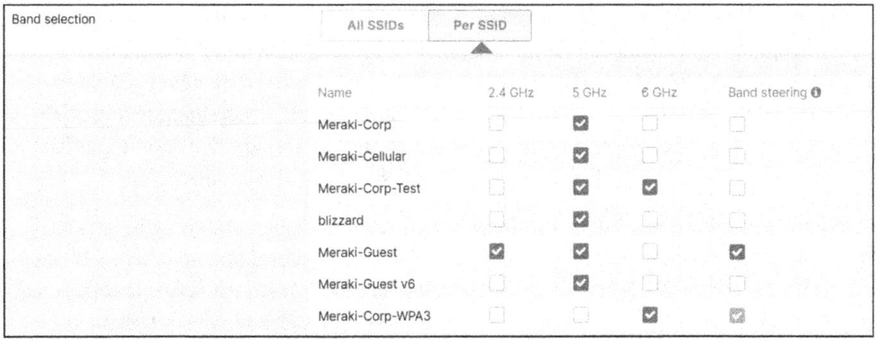

Band selection	All SSIDs	Per SSID			
Name	2.4 GHz	5 GHz	6 GHz	Band steering ❶	
Meraki-Corp	☐	☑	☐	☐	
Meraki-Cellular	☐	☑	☐	☐	
Meraki-Corp-Test	☐	☑	☑	☐	
blizzard	☐	☑	☐	☐	
Meraki-Guest	☑	☑	☐	☑	
Meraki-Guest v6	☐	☑	☐	☐	
Meraki-Corp-WPA3	☐	☐	☑	☑	

Figure 8-7 *Per-SSID Band Selection Settings in an RF Profile of an Example Meraki Network*

Client Balancing

Client balancing is a feature that can be enabled in the RF profile to help intelligently distribute clients across multiple nearby access points to avoid overloading a single AP. Client balancing functions in two ways: active client balancing and passive client balancing. Both methods work by recording observed client RSSI and 802.11 capabilities at each AP as well as AP load metrics, then exchanging those details between APs directly over the LAN. This allows each AP to build and maintain a database of clients and their respective RSSI and wireless capabilities, which is used to make decisions and determine which clients should be balanced and between which APs.

Passive client balancing is simpler and used with clients that do not support 802.11v. This method of balancing is only able to balance clients between APs at the time of association and relies on the client to select a different AP when being balanced. When a client is being passively balanced, the client will attempt to associate to an initial access point, and the AP will reject the association with Code 17, indicating the AP is busy and the client should attempt to associate with a different device. If the client continually attempts to associate to the same AP, effectively ignoring the client-balancing attempts, then the client will be allowed to associate after the second rejected attempt. This ensures that clients that are for any reason unable to associate to a different AP are still able to access the network regardless of the client-balancing configuration.

Active client balancing is used with clients that support 802.11v. It actively redirects and balances clients between nearby APs at any time, either during association or post-association, through the use of BSS-TM frames that include a list of suitable nearby APs for the client to connect to. When a client first attempts to associate with an AP, the AP will record the client details, such as RSSI and 802.11v support. That data is then exchanged with other APs on the LAN, just like in passive client balancing, to build a database of clients, their capabilities and connection details, and additional metrics such as AP load. Just like passive client balancing, if a client repeatedly ignores the attempt to actively balance it, it will be allowed to remain on the current connection and is marked in the internal database as Persistent so that no further attempt to steer it will occur for the remainder of the current association.

The primary difference between passive and active client balancing is that passive balancing is only able to balance clients during association and is unable to provide a list of potential alternate APs to the client when balancing. Active balancing is able to balance clients at any time through the use of BSS-TM frames, which include a list of nearby APs for the client to reassociate to, providing much more guidance and control during the balancing process when compared to passive client balancing.

One common concern when looking at implementing client balancing on a network is how that can affect roaming of clients between APs while maintaining an active real-time stream such as a VoIP call. When client balancing is enabled, for both active and passive, clients are allowed to fast-roam between APs and reassociate at will without client balancing interfering with that process, specifically to help reduce the potential interruption to any real-time traffic during a roam.

Minimum Bitrate

Because Wi-Fi is a shared medium, the minimum bitrate is an important aspect of the configuration to take into account. As a result of this shared medium, devices on a given SSID/AP will only be able to communicate at the highest bitrate supported by all connected devices. Therefore, if the minimum bitrate for an SSID is configured too low and allows connections either from legacy devices incapable of transmitting at higher bitrates or from modern devices with too poor signal to communicate at higher bitrates, all clients connected to that same AP/SSID will be slowed to match the rate of the slowest client. It is for that reason that Meraki recommends raising the minimum bitrate to force devices to use a value that maintains a speedy network and encourages proper roaming. The specific values that should be used will always be deployment specific, but we do have some general recommendations for non-legacy SSIDs to provide a starting point for your deployment.

Minimum bitrate settings can also have a direct impact on the client roaming experience. If configured too low, a client may not roam to a more optimal AP until the signal quality from the initial AP deteriorates to potentially unusable levels. Increasing the minimum bitrate can force clients to roam to a more optimal AP sooner, resulting in a higher quality experience for the client.

A higher minimum bitrate will require a better quality signal between the client and AP, resulting in the client roaming away from the original AP and to a more optimal AP sooner. Configuring a higher minimum bitrate is recommended, especially in a high-density environment. However, keep in mind that configuring too high of a minimum bitrate may cause clients to disassociate from an SSID too early, or to transition between frequency bands unintentionally.

Pro Tip   If the minimum bitrate for an SSID is configured higher than the minimum bitrate supported by a client or achievable between a client and a given AP with current signal conditions, the client will be unable to associate.

When you're configuring the minimum bitrate, there are two options available in each RF profile: configure the minimum bitrate on a per-band basis, which will set the configuration for all SSIDs being broadcast on each band (2.4 GHz vs. 5 GHz vs. 6 GHz) respectively, or configure the minimum bitrate on a per-SSID basis, which enables you to configure each SSID with a custom minimum bitrate independent of other SSIDs or band settings.

There are a few important aspects to keep in mind when tuning the minimum bitrate configurations for your deployment:

- Legacy bitrates
- Client capabilities

As mentioned previously, unless intentionally configuring an SSID to be used for legacy devices, we recommend increasing the minimum bitrate to prevent unwanted connections to a given SSID.

For 2.4 GHz, we recommend setting the minimum bitrate to 12 or higher, as shown in Figure 8-8, unless it is expected to serve older 802.11b clients that are not OFDM capable. When working with clients like that, we recommend having a dedicated 2.4-GHz SSID for legacy clients, to reduce their impact.

Figure 8-8   *Minimum Bitrate Slider Set to 12 to Prevent Legacy Clients from Connecting*

For 5 GHz, we recommend setting the minimum bitrate between 12 and 24. We also recommend keeping this value below 36 unless working with an extremely high-density environment, such as a stadium, in which case clients should always be connecting to the closest AP.

One other important aspect to review and keep in mind when configuring minimum bitrates is the capabilities of clients that will actually be connecting to and using the network in question. It's important to understand and know the limitations of your least capable and most important clients to help fine-tune the wireless profile based on the actual devices that will be on the network and the type of expected network usage.

The Meraki Dashboard records and presents client capabilities, such as supported 802.11 standards and capabilities, for clients that have connected to the network previously. To access these details, navigate to the **Network-wide > Clients** page and add the **Capable Wi-Fi Standards** column, as shown in Figure 8-9. For more details about individual clients, select the individual client from the **Network-wide > Clients** page and click **Details** to view the client details, as shown in Figure 8-10.

Policy ▾ Forget | Search... ▾ | **32 client devices** | Add client ▾ | Download as ▾

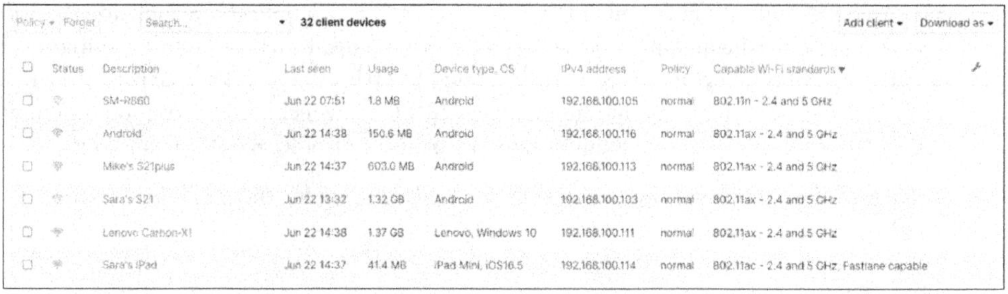

Status	Description	Last seen	Usage	Device type, OS	IPv4 address	Policy	Capable Wi-Fi standards ▾
	SM-R860	Jun 22 07:51	1.8 MB	Android	192.168.100.105	normal	802.11n - 2.4 and 5 GHz
	Android	Jun 22 14:38	150.6 MB	Android	192.168.100.116	normal	802.11ax - 2.4 and 5 GHz
	Mike's S21plus	Jun 22 14:37	603.0 MB	Android	192.168.100.113	normal	802.11ax - 2.4 and 5 GHz
	Sara's S21	Jun 22 13:32	1.32 GB	Android	192.168.100.103	normal	802.11ax - 2.4 and 5 GHz
	Lenovo Carbon-X1	Jun 22 14:38	1.37 GB	Lenovo, Windows 10	192.168.100.111	normal	802.11ax - 2.4 and 5 GHz
	Sara's iPad	Jun 22 14:37	41.4 MB	iPad Mini, iOS16.5	192.168.100.114	normal	802.11ac - 2.4 and 5 GHz, Fastlane capable

Figure 8-9 *Client Capabilities for Recent Clients of an Example Network as Shown on the Network-wide > Clients Page*

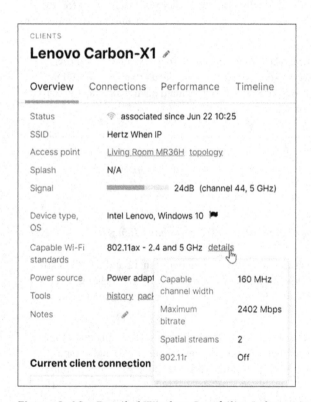

Figure 8-10 *Detailed Wireless Capability Information for a Client as Shown on the Client Details Page*

> **Pro Tip** You can also observe supported bitrates and other client capabilities for specific clients by taking a wireless packet capture (**Network-wide > Packet Capture**) from an AP the client is attempting to associate to, then investigating the 802.11 association requests sent by the client. That packet will report the client capabilities, including the current supported bitrate values for the client in question.

Channel Planning Best Practices

Proper channel planning and assignment is one of the most crucial aspects of a functional wireless deployment. This encompasses planning configurations such as the channel width and available channels/channel selection within each band for devices to broadcast on for the 2.4-GHz, 5-GHz, and 6-GHz bands.

To try and mitigate as much wireless interference as possible, it's necessary to ensure that each AP is broadcasting on a frequency and at a power that allows clients to communicate with the AP without producing interference for other nearby APs or clients. In many deployments, this is accomplished by manually configuring the TX power and 802.11 channels for each band on each AP to ensure that nearby APs are not using overlapping channels, or broadcasting at a power that will cause interference with other potentially nearby APs on the same channel if in a high-density deployment.

With the power of the Meraki Dashboard, you can simplify the planning and configuration even further by utilizing the Meraki Auto RF feature set. Before we explain that, however, we will briefly address some of the common configuration areas and provide a few general recommendations to follow when deploying a wireless network, as a refresher.

Frequency Bands

When you're working with legacy clients that do not support newer 802.11 standards, we recommend limiting those clients to connecting to a dedicated legacy device's SSID and the 2.4-GHz band, allowing newer and more capable devices to better utilize the 5-GHz band or even 6-GHz band.

When you're working with SSIDs that are broadcasting across multiple frequency bands, such as both the 2.4- and 5-GHz bands, we recommend enabling band steering to try and steer clients toward connecting on the highest supported band when possible while still allowing devices to fall back to an alternate band if necessary.

If you're configuring an SSID for the 6-GHz band, be aware that only clients that are capable of WPA3 and 6 GHz will be able to connect without also enabling the 5-GHz band.

Pro Tip   Enable the **Capable Wi-Fi Standards** column on the **Network-wide > Clients** page to check the wireless capability of previously connected clients.

Channel Width

The default value (and Meraki-recommended value) for channel width across spectrum bands is 20 MHz, which supports the largest selection of available channels to prevent channel overlap and provides the greatest flexibility for planning your deployment.

If your deployment is in a low-density environment, a wider channel width will allow for greater throughput for connected clients at the cost of fewer channels available per band to use for channel planning while preventing overlap, as well as potentially increased RF interference for each channel as a result of the wider channel width. For example, a channel width of 20 MHz allows for 28 non-overlapping 5-GHz channels, while a channel width of 80 MHz allows for only 7 non-overlapping channels and is more likely to see potential interference on any given channel due to the large frequency width of each channel.

Channel Selection: DFS Channels

In an effort to help provide additional airspace to prevent interference and channel overlap, the 5-GHz band includes several channels known as Dynamic Frequency Selection (DFS) channels. The specific frequencies used for these channels vary by country, but generally the frequencies are those reserved and prioritized for other use cases, such as military, weather, and aviation radar, as well as satellite communications.

Because these frequencies are generally reserved for non-802.11 use, there are several restrictions in place when being used for an 802.11 implementation. Primarily, these channels are available for use on the condition that the primary use of these frequencies (radar, etc.) is not impaired. As a result, when in use by an AP to broadcast an SSID, the AP must be constantly monitoring for non-802.11 use of that frequency and, if detected, must immediately stop broadcasting on that frequency and move to any other available frequency. As a result, any connected clients would be forced to roam immediately anytime a DFS event is detected, which can cause a noticeable interruption in client service.

Because of the nature of DFS channels, their feasibility for use is dependent on the specific deployment in question and the airspace surrounding that location. For example, a site in rural Kansas may be able to use multiple DFS channels without issue, but a site located next to a military base or airport would likely be unable to use DFS channels with any amount of consistency due to the likelihood of interfering transmissions taking priority in the surrounding airspace.

Fortunately, Meraki makes it easy to determine if DFS channels are feasible for each deployment by actively reporting in the Network-wide > Event Log whenever a DFS event is detected by an AP in the network, as shown in Figure 8-11. This, combined with properly configured network alerts, makes it easy to determine if the use of DFS channels is causing an impact on your deployment.

Event log for access points ▾

Access point: Any		Client: Any		Before: 12/31/2023		12:00		(PST)

Event type include: DFS event detected x		Event type ignore: None

Search   Reset filters

Download as ▾   « newer   older »

Time (PST) ▾	Access point	SSID	Client	Category	Event type	Details
Dec 29 15:55:50	SFO12-5-AP09			DFS	DFS event detected	band: 5, channel: 118, radio: 1
Dec 25 11:02:36	SFO12-5-AP32			DFS	DFS event detected	band: 5, channel: 60, radio: 1
Dec 25 00:08:42	SFO12-5-AP20			DFS	DFS event detected	band: 5, channel: 124, radio: 1

No more matching events found between Dec 24 12:00 and Dec 31 12:00.

3 total

Figure 8-11   *Network-wide > Event Log Filtered to Show Only Recent DFS Events*

For deployments that should exclude the use of DFS channels, you can disable them by navigating to **Wireless > Radio Settings > Edit Profile > Change Channels Used by AutoChannel > Deselect DFS Channels** and deselecting the DFS channels in each RF profile. Figure 8-12 shows the 5-GHz channel selection list with several DFS channels enabled.

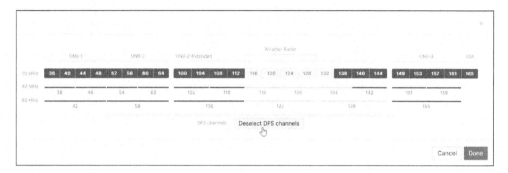

Figure 8-12 *5-GHz Channel Availability Configuration with Non-Weather Radar DFS Channels Enabled*

Meraki Auto RF

As mentioned previously, through the use of the Meraki cloud, you can greatly simplify the configuration of general channel planning and power management required across a wireless deployment. Although you can manually specify TX power levels and broadcast channels for individual APs, the Meraki way of quickly and easily bringing up a deployment is to define the basic RF parameters in each RF profile and then let Meraki Auto RF begin working to automatically adjust the channel planning and TX power configurations for each AP based on the surrounding environment. Auto RF automatically adjusts the TX channel and power level of APs in a network over time to tune the network automatically for excellent operation and performance based entirely around the specific deployment within that network.

Auto RF makes these decisions based on RF data gathered by the dedicated scanning radios placed in each AP and exchanged between the APs and the Meraki cloud. This data is then aggregated and analyzed in the cloud to determine a network performance score and automatically tune the channel assignment and transmit power for each access point in the network to achieve an optimal configuration across the deployment.

Auto RF is designed to work within the boundaries defined in each RF profile to individually configure the broadcast power and channel assignment for every AP in the network based on reported RF data from the individual APs and aggregated data from APs across the network. This enables Auto RF to ensure that both the individual AP and the network as a whole are operating in an optimal configuration with regard to channel planning and cell overlap.

Pro Tip   To allow Auto RF to work at its highest potential, we recommend separating APs in different physical locations, or deployments, into separate Dashboard networks to allow Auto RF to use more accurate data and make more accurate decisions within each network for each location.

Recently, Meraki has worked directly with Cisco to develop an enhanced version of the existing Auto RF feature that incorporates and utilizes the power of Cisco's AI-enhanced Radio Resource Management (RRM) to make Auto RF more effective than ever before. This new AI-enhanced Auto RF brings with it several new features in addition to improving the existing and proven Auto RF technology to make it more powerful and accurate. Figure 8-13 shows the new AI-enhanced Auto RF view in the Dashboard.

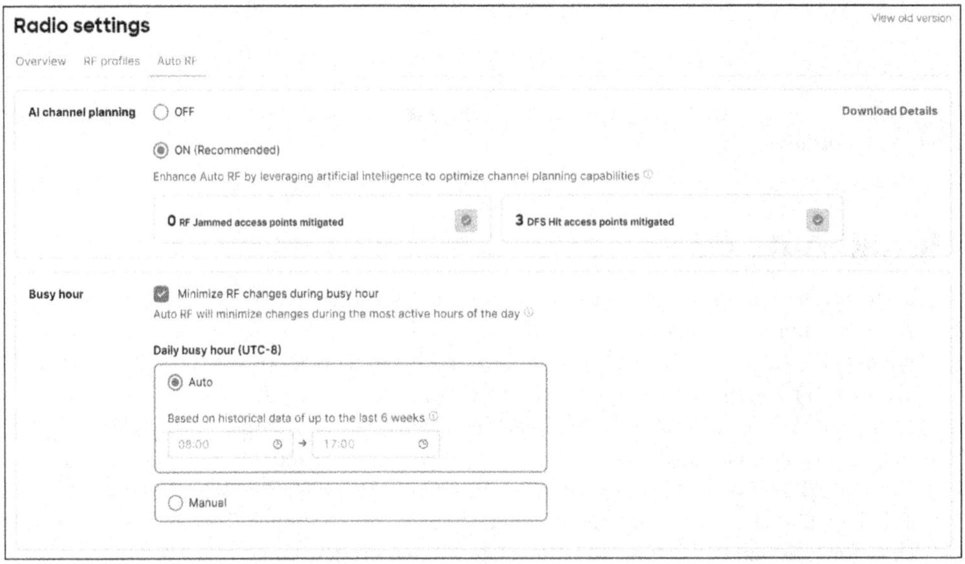

Figure 8-13   *AI Channel Planning Section of the Auto RF Page on the Dashboard*

For more detailed information on the exact operation of Meraki Auto RF, visit https://documentation.meraki.com and consult the article "Meraki Auto RF: Wi-Fi Channel and Power Management."

One of these new features is automatic busy hour detection, where Auto RF will observe and automatically identify the busiest times of day for each network and intentionally avoid making RF changes during those times to reduce the impact of any automated changes on the client experience. This helps to ensure that the changes made by Auto RF cause as little disruption as possible while still allowing for the network to be adjusted and tuned over time.

Another improvement brought with the new AI-enhanced Auto RF is additional logic when dealing with disruptive behaviors like forced channel changes from DFS events or jammed channels. This new logic supports monitoring of events over a longer timeframe to make more-informed long-term decisions, which enables sites impacted by these types of events to better avoid their disruptive nature by better understanding which channels are typically impacted and automatically avoiding them, all without requiring manual intervention to remove those channels from the available channel list.

Pro Tip   You can also download a CSV file, shown in Figure 8-14, listing all the decisions used for AI channel planning in a network, including AP details, channels impacted, and event timestamps.

AP Name	AP Mac	AP Serial	Issue	Band	Channel	AI Channel Planning Mitigation	Start Time	End Time
SFO12-4-AP28	2c:3f:0b:f2:be:8f	Q3AB-SXS4-S97X	Frequent DFS Hit	5 GHz	52	Channel Monitored	2023-05-12T22:24:29Z	2023-06-11T22:24:29Z
SFO12-5-AP08	2c:3f:0b:f2:bf:28	Q3AB-BG3K-GR34	Frequent DFS Hit	5 GHz	52	Channel Monitored	2023-05-06T00:24:13Z	2023-06-05T00:24:13Z
SFO12-4-AP34	2c:3f:0b:f2:bf:a0	Q3AB-UXAL-35DB	Frequent DFS Hit	5 GHz	52	Channel Avoided	2023-05-22T04:24:50Z	2023-05-23T04:24:50Z
SFO12-4-AP24	2c:3f:0b:f2:ba:27	Q3AB-9VB9-Z5DN	Frequent DFS Hit	5 GHz	52	Channel Avoided	2023-05-22T22:24:52Z	2023-05-23T22:24:52Z

Figure 8-14   *Example CSV Logging Recent Configuration Changes as Part of AI Channel Planning*

Other Design Considerations for Meraki Wireless

Starting with this section, the rest of the chapter focuses even more on large campus design. As noted previously, many of the aspects that are required for designing and deploying a large campus network can be scaled down and applied as needed to smaller deployments based on your deployments needs. By discussing these at scale, we can address the most complex implementations of these concepts, which you can then take and apply as needed based on your unique deployment.

Why Distributed Networks?

One key aspect to keep in mind when designing and deploying Meraki wireless is that Meraki uses a distributed data plane approach instead of a centralized, controller-based approach. Although the Meraki cloud is used as a controller for the management of Meraki devices, with most configurations, client traffic is passed from the AP the client is connected to directly on to the LAN, instead of being forwarded across the LAN to a central controller and then forwarded back to the destination. With Meraki, any configured traffic filtering or policing is performed directly at the AP or at the local firewall instead of on a remote controller.

Meraki's distributed data plane approach offers the following advantages compared to a more traditional centralized, controller-based deployment:

- **No reliance on a central controller to process all client traffic:** This allows for improved throughput and general performance across the network by reducing latency and path complexity. This is key for taking full advantage of improvements offered by Wi-Fi 6 and Wi-Fi 6E and beyond.

- **Much smaller failure domains for APs:** Instead of hundreds or thousands of APs being down due to a controller failure, only directly impacted APs are down with Meraki.

- **Lower costs to implement high availability:** HA can be implemented without the need to scale out redundant controllers.

Meraki also preserves flexibility by allowing distributed SSIDs to be broadcast while at the same time allowing other SSIDs from the same AP to be backhauled to an MX concentrator. This ability can be used for SSIDs that require additional, centralized control, such as guest or IoT SSIDs.

Authentication and Encryption

When designing your deployment, it's important to consider the types of clients that will be connecting to the network and how. For most networks, especially large deployments, multiple SSIDs are needed based on differing use cases and security requirements of the clients connecting to the network. Because of this, it's important to make sure you select the right type of encryption and authentication methods for each SSID based on the intended use case.

Pro Tip   All SSID-level authentication and encryption settings are configured from the Wireless > Access Control page in the Dashboard.

For example, you would not want to use a fully open SSID for internal communication that could contain sensitive data, and likewise it would likely be overkill to require 802.1X authentication for a basic guest SSID. Like all planning decisions, your ideal configuration will be specific to your deployment and intended uses. The following list provides some of the most frequently used authentication and encryption methods:

- Open authentication

- MAC-based authentication (printers)

- Pre-Shared Key

  - PSK

  - IPSK with or without RADIUS

- Opportunistic Wireless Encryption (OWE)

- WPA2/3 with 802.1X

Pro Tip   Every MR access point can act as a network access server (NAS) to connect to your AAA server for 802.1X authentication.

You can find more details about the configuration and operation of these authentication and encryption methods and other supported options at https://documentation.meraki.com by searching for the related technology or feature name.

VLAN Considerations

Because Meraki access points do not use a centralized controller, client traffic is passed directly from the AP to the wired LAN. Therefore, when you're working with Meraki APs, you should keep in mind the following points regarding VLAN configurations on each SSID and the upstream switchports:

- Each SSID should be tagged with a VLAN that is configured and switchable/routable throughout the local network.

- Switchports leading to APs should be configured as 802.1Q trunk ports (with Portfast enabled) that allow all tagged VLANs in use for each SSID.

- The native VLAN for untagged wireless client traffic is also the management VLAN of the access point. If the AP management VLAN is untagged, then the wireless client traffic will be as well. If the management VLAN is configured with a VLAN tag, then any untagged client traffic forwarded by the AP will be tagged with the same VLAN tag when leaving the AP.

- As a result of this and Meraki's 802.1X implementation, the management VLAN for each access point is also the defined NAS subnet that will be used by default for RADIUS communication.

Pro Tip   MR access points support an alternate management interface (AMI) that can be optionally configured if you wish to decouple Meraki cloud communication from internal, authentication-related traffic.

When you're working with large deployments, especially those that may be distributed across physical locations or being consolidated between existing deployments, the named VLAN (aka VLAN profiles) feature can be especially helpful to reduce the amount of effort required to maintain a consistent configuration. This feature works with 802.1X or MAB authentication by providing a dynamic, RADIUS-based assignment of VLANs to devices/users/endpoints based on an alphanumeric name instead of a raw VLAN number.

This feature, which also works with MS switches, reduces the required configuration on the RADIUS server and onsite by allowing sites with different-numbered VLANs to be able to use the same RADIUS access policy, despite the end VLAN number not matching between sites. For example, if there are two sites and site 1 has the guest VLAN configured as VLAN 10 and site 2 has the guest VLAN configured as VLAN 50, the VLAN profiles feature allows for a "Guest" VLAN to be defined in the Dashboard and used for the RADIUS authentication and policy application, which is then automatically translated to the appropriate numerical VLAN ID for each specific site based on the VLAN profile configuration assigned to the client.

You can find more detailed information on the configuration and operation of VLAN profiles both on the Meraki Dashboard and with regard to the RADIUS server at https://documentation.meraki.com by searching for **VLAN Profiles**. Chapter 7, "Meraki Switching Design and Configuration," also briefly covers VLAN profiles.

AP Tag Use Cases

Chapter 2 briefly discussed how tags in the Dashboard can be used to scope network and device configurations. One of the examples provided showed how to use device tags to scope an SSID to be broadcast only by specific APs. This section briefly covers several additional ways device tags can be used with Meraki access points to add configuration possibilities as well as improve reporting and general usability in the Dashboard.

Pro Tip   As a reminder, you can configure device tags for APs at scale from the **Wireless > Access Points** page.

You can use device tags with Meraki access points for the following purposes:

- **SSID availability:** As noted in Chapter 2, you can configure SSIDs from the **Wireless > SSID Availability** page to broadcast only on APs that have had a designated tag applied to the AP.

- **RF profile assignment:** You can quickly and easily filter access points to apply an RF profile to groups of devices based on applied device tags. By tagging devices based on use cases or locations, as shown in Figure 8-15, you can quickly filter and apply the appropriate RF profile from the **Wireless > Radio Settings Overview** page with just a few clicks.

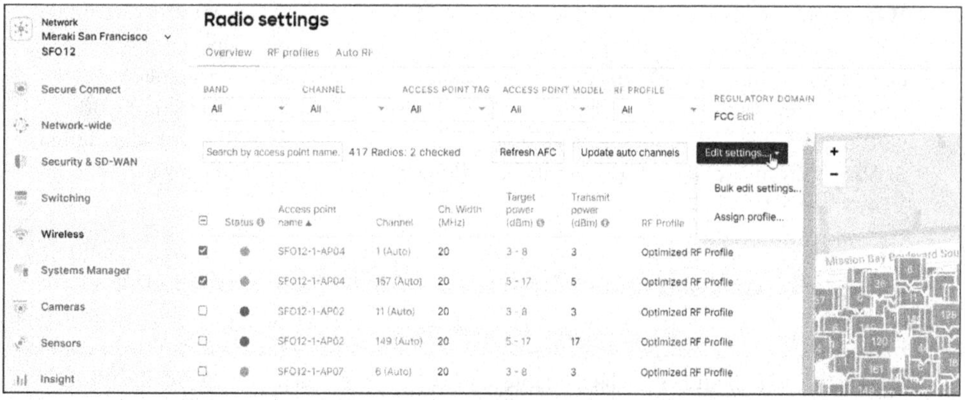

Figure 8-15   *Wireless > Radio Settings Page Showing the Option to Bulk Assign an RF Profile or Edit Settings*

■ **Advanced Dashboard reporting:** As shown in Figure 8-16, by tagging devices in logical groupings, you can create more advanced and granular reporting by utilizing the applied device tags across multiple different reporting tools in the Dashboard to retrieve data for only specific subgroups of APs in a network based on the selected device tags when creating the report.

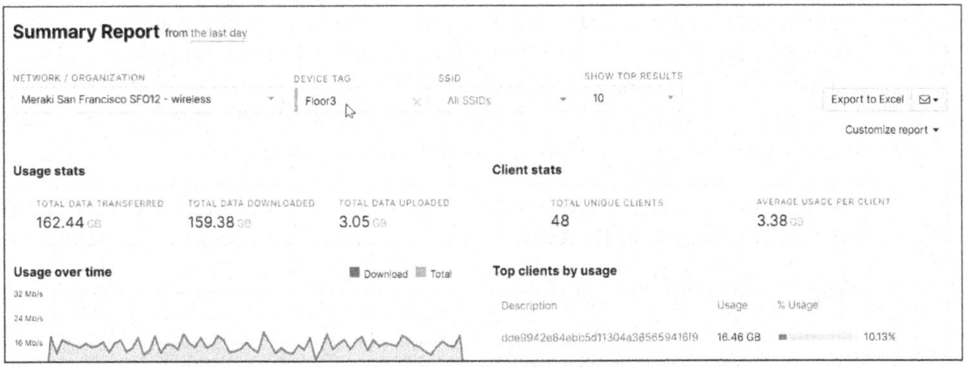

Figure 8-16 *Example Summary Report Demonstrating How the Report Can Be Filtered Based on Device Tag*

■ **SSID VLAN configurations:** From the **Wireless > Access Control** page, you can also use applied device tags to configure multiple VLAN IDs for a single SSID to allow a single SSID configuration to be deployed in multiple areas that may require Layer 2 segmentation between them. An example of this type of configuration is shown in Figure 8-17.

Figure 8-17 *Example SSID Configuration That Utilizes Different VLAN Tags for Client Traffic Based on an Assigned Device Tag*

Setting Up Enterprise-Grade Meraki Wireless

This section approaches planning a large campus deployment from the ground up to explore how the topics discussed so far in this chapter can be applied in a real-world example scenario.

Defining Roaming

The first step to building and deploying a Meraki wireless network is to define your roaming domains. But before defining your roaming domains, you need to understand what types of roaming exist and how they can impact your roaming domain plans.

First, you have to understand that a *roam* is any client connection where the client reassociates from the currently connected AP to a new AP and remains connected to the same SSID without being required to complete a full association and authentication. When clients move to a connection outside of the current roaming domain, even with the same SSID, they are required to perform a full reauthentication. With that in mind, there are a few more specific types of roaming that you should be aware of:

■ **Seamless roaming:** This is a roam where the client is able to maintain a stateful connection with a consistent IP and security policy applied both before and after the roam. A good example of this type of roaming is a basic Layer 2 roam between two different APs within the same VLAN with the same SSID/PSK. This allows clients to roam while maintaining any active/open sessions, albeit with the possibility for a slight interruption during the roaming process itself for any real-time traffic.

Note that if the client roaming requires crossing a Layer 3 boundary, the client will require a new IP assignment, which will result in a break in connectivity for any existing sessions and will no longer be considered seamless roaming, even if connecting to the same SSID.

■ **Fast and secure roaming:** This is a more advanced type of seamless roaming with the primary goal of keeping the entire roaming process as short and secure as possible, ideally with an interruption of less than 10 ms. This is important any time clients may be roaming between APs while actively requiring real-time connectivity, such as while making a VoIP or video call. This type of roaming requires a slightly more advanced configuration, such as enabling 802.11r or Opportunistic Key Caching (OKC).

■ **Distributed Layer 3 roaming:** This type of roaming allows devices to effectively perform a seamless roam between APs that cross Layer 3 boundaries without the use of a dedicated concentrator. This allows clients to roam across Layer 3 boundaries while also maintaining a consistent IP and security policy. This can be extremely useful for large deployments where, for whatever reason, it may not be feasible to place all APs in the same VLAN or Layer 2 domain but clients still require seamless roaming between APs, such as between floors in a large building.

In short, distributed Layer 3 roaming functions by designating the first AP to which a client connects as an "anchor" AP. Then, when the client roams to a new AP that does not have access to the original Layer 2 domain, a tunnel is automatically built between the new "host" AP and the last anchor AP to allow the client traffic to be forwarded from the host AP to the anchor AP and allow the client to maintain connectivity with the original Layer 2 domain and provide a seamless roaming experience to the client, despite the new host AP not having direct access to the original client VLAN/Layer 2 domain.

Defining Domains

Properly planning a wireless deployment requires properly understanding and defining the different domains for a network so they can each be properly scoped and planned. This section covers roaming domains, Layer 2 domains, and Layer 3 domains to help you better understand how to define and scope each domain to ensure optimal performance and manageability.

Roaming Domains

Now that you know the different types of client roaming that can happen within a roaming domain, you can begin looking to define the actual roaming domains for your deployment.

One of the most important aspects to know when defining roaming domains for an enterprise wireless network is the expected roaming requirements for clients using the network. By understanding where seamless or fast roaming is and is not required, you can properly designate roaming domains around the deployment and begin optimizing the user experience even before any hardware is deployed.

A roaming domain is determined by the need for clients to have uninterrupted RF coverage across a geographical area. As noted previously, a roaming domain is characterized by an area where clients are able to connect to the same SSID across multiple access points without requiring a complete reauthentication.

Pro Tip   The Meraki Dashboard exists as a hard boundary for client roaming. When roaming between access points in different Dashboard networks, clients are forced to perform a full authentication regardless of any existing connections or other configurations.

Roaming domains can be scaled to appropriately fit the needs of a deployment and can be based on physical, geographic, or other boundaries, such as different buildings or even floors within each building, depending on your expected deployment size and use case for wireless clients.

In the hypothetical large campus deployment depicted in Figure 8-18, roaming domains are designated based on building boundaries and outdoor areas around campus. For example, clients are unlikely to require seamless roaming as they move between different buildings around campus, or between different dorms, while they likely would want to seamlessly roam while moving from one room to another within the same building.

Figure 8-18   *Example Campus Broken Down into Multiple Wireless Roaming Domains*

This approach allows administrators to designate each building location as a unique roaming domain, while also designating large outdoor areas like a student courtyard or sports fields as separate roaming domains, allowing students to retain seamless connectivity in the areas they are most likely to require it while moving between APs. Since most students are not actively relying on important low-latency streams while walking around campus, the campus can be broken up into separate roaming domains to help ensure the best experience where it matters most.

Pro Tip   In a more traditional Catalyst environment, this type of network/roaming boundary may be mapped to a site tag instead.

Layer 2 Domains

When you're planning for large-scale networks that will likely have large roaming domains, it's equally important to properly consider the Layer 2 segmentation and design that goes alongside the roaming domain. Within each roaming domain, you want to ensure there is appropriate L2 connectivity throughout the domain to enable clients to seamlessly roam without issue. While the specifics of this will depend heavily on your unique deployment, the following are some general policies to keep in mind when planning your L2 design:

■ Consider the MAC table limits on aggregation and core switches based on the number of clients per network and number of APs per VLAN. For example, a switch with a MAC table size of 16,000 can have around 400 APs per VLAN, assuming an average of 40 clients per AP (16000 / 40 = 400).

- For switchports connecting to APs:

  - Configure ports as 802.1q trunks with SSID VLANs allowed.

  - Configure Spanning Tree Portfast Trunk (when using non-Meraki switches).

  - Configure BPDU Guard and/or Root Guard.

  - Prune VLANs appropriately from trunk ports whenever a roaming domain may span multiple switches.

Pro Tip   To easily configure and plan roaming domains, we recommend all roaming domains exist as a 1:1 mapping to a single local VLAN for each domain.

Layer 3 Domains

To properly define your roaming domains, you also have to consider your Layer 3 domains and boundaries. A proper Layer 3 boundary will map to an L3 interface, likely on a distribution switch, and allow for connectivity across multiple Layer 2 domains. A single Layer 3 domain does not necessarily have to map directly to a single roaming domain, but doing so makes managing your domains much easier. Keep in mind that your Layer 3 domains will also partially define your roaming domains unless you are specifically implementing Layer 3 roaming.

Pro Tip   When planning L3 domains for dual-stack clients, remember that each end host will consume more resources from the upstream infrastructure to support IPv4 (e.g., ARP entries) and IPv6 (e.g., NDP entries). Be sure to take this into consideration when implementing dual-stack connectivity in your deployments.

Defining DHCP Scope

When designing the DHCP scope for your roaming domains, there are a few things that you should keep in mind, such as the expected client density of the domain. For example, if the domain is expected to be relatively small, such as a library or other single location, a smaller subnet could be used, while a more heavily utilized or higher density area such as a stadium would require a much larger subnet for the roaming domain.

Additionally, the length of the DHCP leases for each domain are equally important and depend on the expected use cases, just like the overall DHCP scope. For example, in a roaming domain that covers a campus dorm, you could consider using a longer DHCP lease time, like 8 to 12 hours or more, as the unique device count is less likely to fluctuate drastically and devices are likely to stick around longer in such an area. In an area such as a cafeteria, where large numbers of unique devices may connect during peak times but remain in the area only for a short period of time, you could consider using a short lease time, like 1 to 2 hours, to allow for a smaller DHCP scope to be used and still adequately serve clients throughout the day.

> **Pro Tip**   Setting DHCP lease times to a very low value may seem like a solution that will work in any location, but this can cause unnecessary load on the DHCP server if many clients are requesting DHCP renewals more frequently than necessary.

Security Features and Wireless Security Best Practices

Aside from selecting the right authentication and encryption protocols for each of your SSIDs, as briefly touched on in the "Authentication and Encryption" section earlier in this chapter, there are several additional security features that you should consider.

Air Marshal

Air Marshal is Meraki's approach to helping identify and even prevent potentially malicious activity within the airspace surrounding your wireless deployment. Air Marshal uses a dedicated scanning radio within every Meraki access point to continuously scan and monitor the nearby airspace for potentially malicious activity such as spoofed SSIDs, rogue SSIDs, malicious broadcasts, or containment attacks, as well as packet floods from client devices. While not all of these may be intentionally malicious, each has the ability to disrupt the operation of an otherwise well-functioning wireless network and can be particularly difficult to troubleshoot in a more traditional environment, potentially requiring additional hardware to be deployed for scanning or monitoring of the nearby airspace.

With Meraki's Air Marshal feature set, your access points are constantly scanning and monitoring the surrounding airspace, ready to alert or even take action against a potentially malicious behavior. In addition to simply monitoring the nearby airspace for disruptive activity, Air Marshal can also be configured to automatically act to help reduce the impact of events such as a spoofed SSID.

In the event of a spoofed SSID, Air Marshal can be configured to automatically begin containing clients attempting to connect to that spoofed SSID by impersonating the spoofed or rogue AP BSSID and forcing clients connecting to the potentially malicious SSID to deauthenticate. This can completely prevent clients from successfully connecting to the potential threat, therefore preventing a potentially malicious SSID from compromising the clients on the network.

For more details about the functionality and operation of Air Marshal, visit https://documentation.meraki.com and search using keywords **Air Marshal**.

> **Pro Tip**   Be careful when setting containment policies in Air Marshal. It's possible to contain legitimate networks unintentionally, so use containment only as an option of last resort.

Traffic Segregation and Access Control

An important part of properly securing a network is to appropriately segregate traffic and provision access control across devices on the network. There are a number of ways to approach this, from simple VLANs with an appropriate authentication type, as discussed previously, to enabling more advanced security features such as Meraki's Adaptive Policy feature set or one of the other features introduced here.

Alternate Management Interface (AMI)

Alternate Management Interfaces can be used to segregate internal management traffic like syslog and RADIUS from the Dashboard-bound cloud management traffic. This enables you to apply separate security policies based on the management interface of the device the traffic was sourced from, allowing the internal management traffic to remain on a locked-down, internal subnet while separating the cloud management traffic and allowing that traffic to be easily routed out to the public Internet without potentially compromising the internal management traffic between the devices and servers.

Per-SSID Group Policy

One of the simplest ways to apply security policies to wireless clients through the Dashboard is to use a per-SSID group policy. This allows any predefined group policy to be automatically applied to any client that connects to a given SSID. This can be used to quickly and easily enforce specific configurations, such as Layer 7 firewall rules, or to enforce more custom configurations, such as per-client bandwidth limits only during peak usage times while allowing unlimited bandwidth after-hours. An additional advantage of this feature is that the group policy only applies to clients connected to the configured SSID, so a client can be automatically assigned a policy for SSID 1, while being assigned a different or no policy on SSID 2. Additionally, these automatic policy applications can always be overridden, allowing a default policy to be applied, then modified or removed for certain clients on only specific SSIDs if needed.

Mandatory DHCP and Dynamic ARP Inspection

For additional security on wireless SSIDs, we recommend enabling both mandatory DHCP and Dynamic ARP Inspection (DAI). Mandatory DHCP requires clients to complete a DHCP exchange when connecting to the network, preventing clients from passing traffic if they do not complete it. This prevents clients from connecting using a static IP or attempting to bypass IP-based restrictions.

> **Pro Tip**   Enabling mandatory DHCP will impact the ability of clients to seamlessly roam, as they will be required to complete a DHCP exchange when connecting to their new AP.

Similarly, Dynamic ARP Inspection can work in conjunction with mandatory DHCP to prevent ARP spoofing or MITM attacks. By comparing ARP exchanges to clients with snooped DHCP exchanges, Meraki devices are able to validate the ARP responses of each device compared to their DHCP entries. If there is a mismatch in this comparison, then the suspect traffic will be dropped, helping to prevent ARP spoofing or other MITM-type attacks.

mDNS Support

Network segregation can impact client discovery relating to network services such as printers, SAMBA filesharing, Apple AirPlay, and more. Fortunately, Meraki offers a simple way to quickly and easily configure multicast DNS (mDNS) forwarding for certain services between specified VLANs to allow these exchanges. By simply enabling the feature referred to as "Bonjour forwarding" from the **Wireless > Access Control** page for the appropriate SSID and selecting the appropriate destination VLAN to forward traffic to for each service, clients connecting to that SSID will be able to utilize mDNS exchanges to enable local network discovery of services outside the local client VLAN.

> **Pro Tip**   Many of these security features can also be configured on MX and/or MS devices as well.

Adaptive Policy, Cisco SGT, and Microsegmentation

Meraki's Adaptive Policy feature works with the use of Security Group Tags (SGTs) from the Cisco TrustSec architecture to provide IP-agnostic security policy applications for connected clients. Through the use of inline tagging within the IP header of a packet, SGTs can be applied to identify the specific security group that traffic belongs to, and by extension the appropriate traffic policy that should be applied based on that tag.

By defining security policies, which consist of a defined source group, destination group, and permissions/rules to govern communication between those groups, you can easily segregate and implement traffic policies based around the devices involved and the specific traffic types, instead of defining policies based on IP or port boundaries. As long as all devices along the traffic path between the source and destination support SGT tagging, this can greatly reduce the burden of configuring security policies and ACLs across the network at scale.

The operation and configuration of Adaptive Policy is covered in great detail at https:// documentation.meraki.com; search using keywords **Adaptive Policy**. Chapters 5 and 7 also cover Adaptive Policy in more depth.

A major emerging use case for Adaptive Policy or Cisco SGT is in the realm of IoT. Because IoT devices are quite often some of the least trusted devices on a network, you can use Adaptive Policy to easily define a security policy to only allow IoT devices to reach their necessary endpoints, whether that be other local IoT devices or out to the Internet, and then apply that policy across multiple sites and subnets without manually configuring individual rules or policies on every network device that traffic may traverse.

RADSec

As part of Meraki's secure approach to networking, it has also introduced support for RADSec to ensure secure communication between Meraki APs and your RADIUS server through the use of certificate-based TLS authentication and encryption. RADSec ensures not only that data between the AP and your clients will be secure, but also that any communications between the AP and your internal network will remain equally secure to ensure full security for data across the network.

For details on how to configure RADSec for Meraki access points and its operation, search at https://documentation.meraki.com using the keyword **RADSec**.

SecurePort

SecurePort enables you to easily automate the configuration of individual Meraki switch ports to which a Meraki access point will be directly connected to ensure that each port has the appropriate configuration for the AP to be connected, which enables you to avoid any manual, port-level configurations. This works by allowing a SecureConnect-enabled Meraki switch to automatically detect when a Meraki AP is connected to a port, at which time the switch automatically reconfigures the port to allow a restricted level of connectivity for the AP to connect out to the Meraki cloud and fetch a security certificate.

The AP then performs an 802.1X authentication with the switch to confirm whether the AP belongs to the same Dashboard network as the switch and, if so, to move forward with configuring the port to allow full communication for the AP and any connected devices.

This greatly simplifies the per-port configuration required when deploying new APs, as this feature allows an AP to be connected to any available switch port and automatically gain the necessary levels of access to come online and, following a successful authentication, allows the AP to begin serving clients as intended without requiring any manual port level configurations.

Operating the Network

The remainder of this chapter briefly covers several of the most useful features for monitoring and troubleshooting in a Meraki wireless deployment after the initial design and deployment phase is complete.

> **Note**   For more details on all of the following features, including implementation, configuration, and operational information, visit https://documentation.meraki.com and search using keywords **Meraki Health**.

Site-Level Wi-Fi Overview

After planning and deploying your network, it's critical to continually monitor the operation and performance of your network to ensure that your initial design has made the transition to reality well and that the network is functioning as intended. The Meraki Dashboard provides a number of useful tools and pages to help you understand the operation of your network at a high level, without requiring you to drill down to individual clients. There are many tools, views, and data points available within many of these pages.

This section covers only some of the more impactful Wi-Fi features, but you can find more details about everything discussed in this section, as well as additional features and data points not covered, at https://documentation.meraki.com by searching using keywords **Wireless Health**.

The first tool to discuss is the Location Heatmap, which you can access by navigating to the **Wireless > Location Heatmap** page in the Dashboard. When APs are properly placed in a floor plan on the Dashboard, this view, demonstrated in Figure 8-19, shows location analytics for clients across the network in relation to the APs for both Wi-Fi and Bluetooth Low Energy (BLE) clients. This can help you to identify where clients are physically located most often when using the network, making it easy to quickly tell at a glance where the client hotspots are, whether those line up with the expectations from your planning phase, and whether you may need to consider making coverage adjustments based on client load and activity.

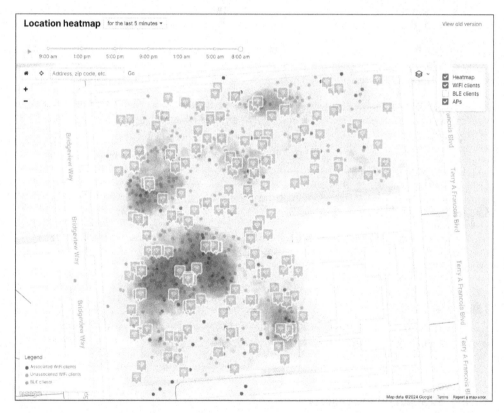

Figure 8-19   *Wireless Location Heatmap of the Cisco Meraki Campus in San Francisco*

Pro Tip   When configuring floor plans, make sure the plan is scaled appropriately to the AP layout in the Dashboard. Additionally, we recommend creating per-floor floorplans to allow for the best visibility of client locations across the deployment.

Wireless Health and Overview

Possibly the most helpful single page when looking at overall wireless performance of a network is the aptly named Wireless Overview page, shown in Figure 8-20. This page, which you can access from the **Wireless > Overview** link in the Dashboard, provides a summary of several of the most impactful connection-related metrics for a wireless network and can help you to easily identify any major issues within the network.

Figure 8-20 *Example of the Wireless Overview for a Well-Functioning Network*

This page has the following three major sections, which more clearly break down issues into distinct aspects of the wireless user experience. The following list also provides the key performance indicators (KPIs) relating to each section, also shown in Figure 8-20.

- Connection Health
  - Failed Clients
  - Time to Connect
  - Roaming
- Performance Health
  - Latency
  - Packet Loss
  - Signal Quality (SNR)
- Network Service Health
  - RADIUS Success
  - DHCP Success
  - DNS Success

For each of these KPIs, you can get more details either by clicking the KPI itself, which will expand a data graph related to that KPI, such as shown in Figure 8-21 for the Failed Clients KPI, or by clicking the **Health** tab at the top of the Wireless Overview page to see more detailed reports.

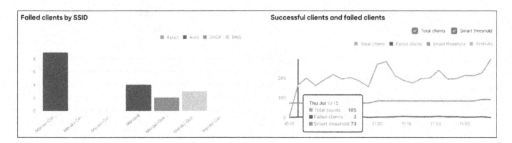

Figure 8-21   *Example of Additional Client Connection Data Presented in the Wireless Overview and Health Pages*

The data presented here can also be filtered further to only display data relating to a specific SSID or time period.

Again, you can find more information regarding the features available through Meraki Health, including several features that are not directly covered in this chapter, at https://documentation.meraki.com by searching using keywords **Meraki Health.**

Anomaly Detection (Smart Thresholds)

Chapter 2 discusses configuring standard network-level alerts, which enables you to set varying alert types to be generated based on specific behavior, such as devices going offline for a specified period of time. For some alerts, like clients failing to connect or experiencing certain service failures such as DHCP or DNS, you can configure custom alert thresholds to fine-tune the alert generation based on specific parameters and thresholds for each alert type. However, there is also another option that again takes advantage of Meraki's cloud-managed platform to both simplify the configuration of these alerts and thresholds and improve the accuracy of these alerts based on the specific deployment and common behaviors observed in that deployment. This feature set is a part of the larger Meraki Health solution, specifically referred to as Smart Thresholds.

When you configure an alert and enable the use of Smart Thresholds, the Dashboard will begin to analyze the network and client behavior observed over the last 6 weeks of operation, using an advanced machine learning model, to determine an appropriate baseline of behavior for the given network. With this information, the Dashboard is able to create a custom baseline metric for each of the four major aspects of onboarding wireless clients for the chosen network (association, authentication, DHCP, and DNS), which helps to improve the accuracy of alerts when anomalous behavior occurs for clients in the network.

Enabling and using Smart Thresholds not only improves the accuracy of alerts based on the typical behavior of a network, it also reduces the effort that would be otherwise required to manually tune the alert thresholds for each network, which allows for a quicker and simpler deployment.

These abilities, combined with additional contextual detail included with the alert (which is also made possible by the use of machine learning algorithms and full-stack cloud reporting), provide much greater insight into the specific behaviors that generated the alert as well as insight and suggestions for troubleshooting the root cause. This can help to greatly reduce the mean time to resolution (MTTR) of issues and to further simplify the general day-to-day operation of your Meraki networks in a way that other vendors can't offer.

Pro Tip   Smart Thresholds for supported alerts can be enabled after enabling the alert from the **Network-wide> Alerts** page on the Dashboard, shown in Figure 8-22.

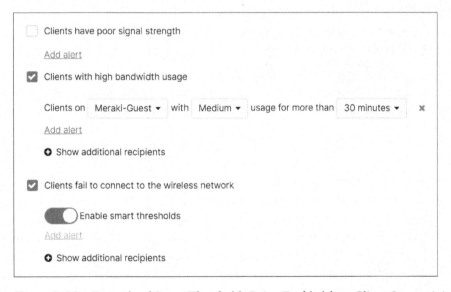

Figure 8-22   *Example of Smart Thresholds Being Enabled for a Client Connectivity Alert*

With Smart Thresholds enabled, you can more easily look for anomalous behavior and quickly track it down when combined with the additional visibility provided via the Meraki Health solution.

Navigate to the **Wireless > Health** page on the Dashboard to review the overall status of the wireless network, as shown in Figure 8-23. Looking at this example network, you can see that there are a large number of clients failing to connect to the wireless network, with the major failure points being part of the authentication and DHCP process.

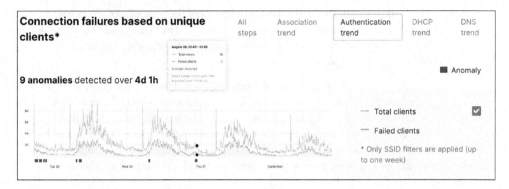

Figure 8-23   *Wireless > Health Page Showing Recent Connection Failure Details and Anomalies*

Thanks to the implementation of Smart Thresholds, you can be confident that the 59 failed clients reported are representative of anomalous behavior and specifically require additional attention.

From the Connection Log tab on the same page, you can quickly review and filter wireless connection logs from the Event Log, such as shown in Figure 8-24. By filtering to the specific window of time the anomaly was reported and then filtering by failure step, you can quickly review all the failed connections during that time across the network and more easily identify if these issues are scoped to a specific access point, physical location, or network service.

Figure 8-24   *Wireless Connection Log Filtered to Show Only Recent DHCP Failures*

Additionally, the Timeline view can provide some additional information about recent client connections and can be similarly filtered based on client, access point, connection step, and more. For failed connections, the Timeline view can also help to provide some additional detail regarding the failure and likely cause or resolution based on the observed behaviors, such as client signal strength (see Figure 8-25) or a network service issue (see Figure 8-26).

Figure 8-25 *Example of the Timeline View for Recent Wireless Connections*

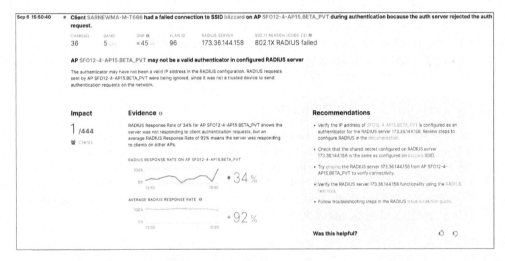

Figure 8-26 *Example of an RCA for a Recent Wireless Connectivity Failure Shown in the Timeline View*

Server RCA

The availability and performance of network servers and services such as DHCP, DNS, RADIUS, and more play a crucial role in the wireless client experience. Another important part of Meraki's Wireless Health feature set is the Server Root Cause Analysis (RCA) feature. This feature is designed to take the data and events reported back to the Dashboard by Meraki APs and provide a likely RCA for observed failures, along with several suggestions for further troubleshooting and resolving the behavior.

Meraki has tailored the Server RCA feature to show the scope of impact, supporting evidence, and recommended troubleshooting steps for a variety of service failures, including multiple RADIUS failure modes as well as DHCP- and DNS-related failure that can directly impact the wireless client experience. Figure 8-27 shows another example of a DHCP server RCA similar to the RADIUS RCA in Figure 8-26.

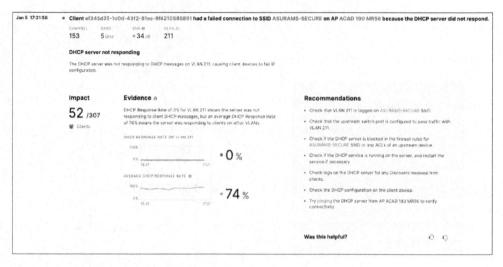

Figure 8-27 *Another Server RCA, This Time for a DHCP Failure*

Device Monitoring and Reporting

In addition to network-wide features such as Server RCA and Smart Thresholds, the Meraki cloud also enables device-level analysis at both the access point and client device levels. In addition to the typical historical data like connection logging and general performance logging for connected clients, Meraki's latest development in this area is intended to assist in troubleshooting potential roaming issues for clients roaming between access points within the network.

Roaming Analytics

The Roaming Analytics feature takes the reported logging data from devices in the network and further analyzes it to provide direct insight into the roaming performance of clients in the network. This includes identifying bad or suboptimal roams, such as when a roam takes an extended period of time (>250 ms) or results in the client roaming to a new AP with a notably lower client RSSI, and identifying unintended roaming behavior such as ping-pong roaming, where a client repeatedly roams between multiple APs in short succession.

Figure 8-28 shows an example of the Roaming Analytics report, specifically highlighting a bad roam that was reported as the result of a client roaming to a new AP with significantly lower client RSSI.

Client Overview

In addition to the data presented in the Wireless Health pages for a network, you can also review client-specific details on the **Network-wide > Clients** page. By default, only basic client details are provided on this page, but you can easily add new columns via the wrench/settings icon at the top right of the clients list. As shown in Figure 8-29, columns like Onboarding, which reports the percentage of successful connections out of total connection attempts for the chosen timeframe, and Performance, which provides a percentage value of the time the client has an SNR of 21dB or more for the selected time range, can be very useful for quickly identifying individual problem clients or verifying user claims at a glance.

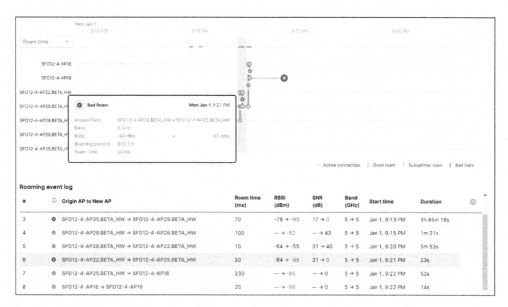

Figure 8-28 *Example Roaming Analytics Report Highlighting a Recent Bad Roam from a Client*

Figure 8-29 *Client Overview Page, Highlighting the Additional Info Columns That Can Be Enabled*

Pro Tip   The Network-wide > Clients list can be filtered further based on timeframe, policy application, and even client location such as MR clients vs. MX clients to help provide additional visibility.

Client Details

When selecting a specific client to investigate further, the Client Details page of that client will provide a wealth of information regarding the client, its capabilities, and both current and historical connection data for the client. An example client is shown in Figure 8-30, where you can see the access point the client was most recently connected, the network path that client traffic takes to exit the local network, and a wireless health report for just this client for recent connections.

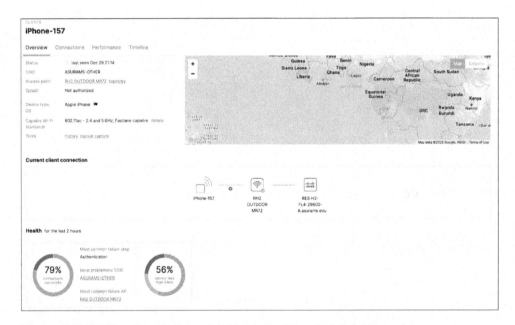

Figure 8-30   *Client Details Page of an Example Client in a Lab Network*

In addition to the Overview tab, the Client Details page also contains tabs for Connection, Performance, and Roaming data that report in the same way as the network-wide reports in the general Wireless Health page, but for the selected client only.

Client Timeline

The final tab available on the Client Details page is the Timeline tab. Shown in Figure 8-31, this tab provides a historical timeline of all wireless connection events for the client, up to the last 30 days, that can be further filtered based on criteria like SSID, access point, band, connection step, and connections status. These events report data such as the type of event, like a connection, disconnect, or roam, as well as event-specific data such as the client SNR at that time, and potential failure reasons for failed connections to assist in troubleshooting failures.

Pro Tip   By partnering with multiple device vendors, Meraki can report more than 80 different detailed failure reasons for precise and quick troubleshooting of client failures.

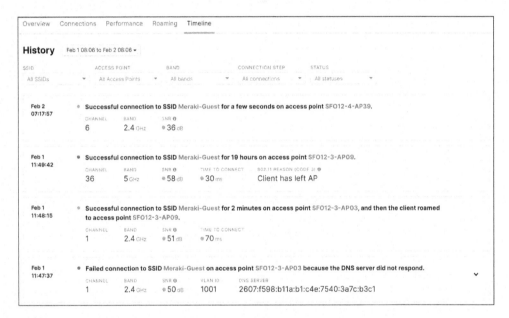

Figure 8-31   *Unfiltered Client Timeline View of an Example Wireless Client Showing Recent Connections*

Access Point Timeline

Similar to the Timeline tab on the Client Details page, each Meraki access point also has a Timeline tab, as shown in Figure 8-32. Its focus is the timeline of events involving the selected access point (instead of a specific client.) The access point Timeline view can be filtered in much the same way as the client Timeline view to allow for troubleshooting from the AP perspective as well.

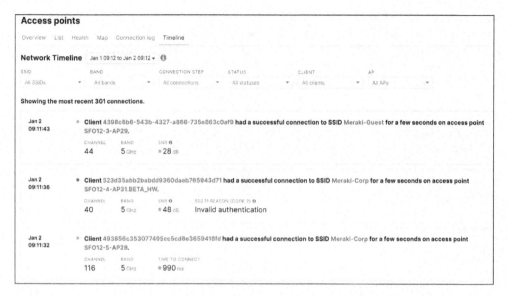

Figure 8-32 *Unfiltered Timeline View from an Access Point Perspective*

Summary

This chapter covered how the Dashboard network configuration can impact the design and deployment of your physical WLAN as well as how to appropriately scale the Dashboard to work best based on the size of your deployments.

This chapter also covered some of the more important aspects to keep in mind when designing your physical WLAN deployment, such as defining roaming domains and some Meraki-specific recommendations and considerations. In addition to the physical deployment and scoping of the Dashboard, this chapter covered a number of recommendations and best practices for configuring RF profiles, channel planning using Meraki Auto RF, and some of the Meraki-specific features available on the Dashboard to assist in monitoring and troubleshooting various aspects of the network.

Next, Chapter 9 discusses the deployment and operation of Meraki's IoT and MV camera solutions and how they can help improve the monitoring of your environment.

Additional Reading

Location Deployment Guidelines: https://documentation.meraki.com/MR/Monitoring_and_Reporting/Location_Deployment_Guidelines

Location Analytics: https://documentation.meraki.com/MR/Monitoring_and_Reporting/Location_Analytics

Using a Floor Plan or Custom Map in Dashboard: https://documentation.meraki.com/ General_Administration/Monitoring_and_Reporting/Using_a_Floor_Plan_or_Custom_ Map_in_Dashboard

RF Profiles: https://documentation.meraki.com/MR/Radio_Settings/RF_Profiles

Channel Planning Overview: https://documentation.meraki.com/MR/Radio_Settings/ Channel_Planning_Overview

Meraki Auto RF: Wi-Fi Channel and Power Management: https:// documentation.meraki.com/MR/Monitoring_and_Reporting/Location_Analytics/ Meraki_Auto_RF%3A__Wi-Fi_Channel_and_Power_Management

Roaming Technologies: https://documentation.meraki.com/MR/Wi-Fi_Basics_and_Best_ Practices/Roaming_Technologies

Seamless Roaming with MR Access Points: https://documentation.meraki.com/MR/ Wi-Fi_Basics_and_Best_Practices/Seamless_Roaming_with_MR_Access_Points

Client Roaming Analytics: https://documentation.meraki.com/MR/ Client_Roaming_Analytics

Meraki Health Overview: https://documentation.meraki.com/General_Administration/ Cross-Platform_Content/Meraki_Health_Overview

Meraki Health – MR Access Point Details: https://documentation.meraki.com/ General_Administration/Cross-Platform_Content/Meraki_Health_Overview/ Meraki_Health_-_MR_Access_Point_Details

Meraki Health Alerts – Smart Thresholds: https://documentation.meraki.com/General_ Administration/Cross-Platform_Content/Meraki_Health_Alerts_-_Smart_Thresholds

Chapter 9

MV Security and MT (IoT) Design

The Cisco Meraki MV line of surveillance cameras represents a significant leap forward in security camera technology, emphasizing ease of use, advanced intelligence analytics, and powerful integrations while offering a secure and robust solution. Usability features like Motion Search, Motion Recap, and Motion Heatmap help to enhance user engagement with the system.

This chapter first explores the MV camera solution along with some recommended use cases. Then, it touches on the MT line of IoT devices and how they can be integrated with the MV camera solution to further enhance the security and surveillance capabilities of your deployments.

Redefining Surveillance: The Meraki Difference

Meraki's camera solution utilizes a unique architecture designed to provide simple and easy deployment while also offering robust functionality and secure operation of both the camera hardware and software. By utilizing the power of Meraki's cloud architecture and machine learning based processing built-in to every camera, Meraki's MV cameras can also provide powerful video analytics within an easy-to-use security solution that can be deployed in nearly any use case.

Meraki Camera Architecture

The architecture of the Cisco Meraki MV camera solution is designed to minimize both physical infrastructure and software dependencies. Users can bypass the hassle of specific software requirements or browser plug-ins, streamlining their day-to-day experience. One of the defining features is the cloud-augmented edge storage, which removes the need for traditional network video recorders (NVRs).

MV Video Architecture

Unlike traditional surveillance systems that require separate hardware for video processing and storage, Meraki MV cameras have integrated processing power and storage. Each camera has high-speed, high-endurance solid-state storage integrated directly into the device, which utilizes secure encryption, ensuring the confidentiality and security of captured footage. This means the video footage is processed and stored directly on the camera itself, reducing the bandwidth and storage requirements on the network. This helps to ensure available network resources are not constantly utilized for transferring recorded footage to remote storage, compared to a traditional NVR-based deployment.

The operational interfaces of the MV camera solution are designed to offer unparalleled ease and versatility. Whether it's viewing live video or historical video, users can access video footage locally or remotely through multiple platforms, including the Meraki Dashboard, Vision Portal, Meraki Display app for Apple devices, and the dedicated mobile app for iOS and Android.

Whether the camera connectivity is wired or wireless, or the stream is local or remote, the MV camera architecture ensures robust security through automatic end-to-end video encryption. Figure 9-1 illustrates the general MV video access architecture.

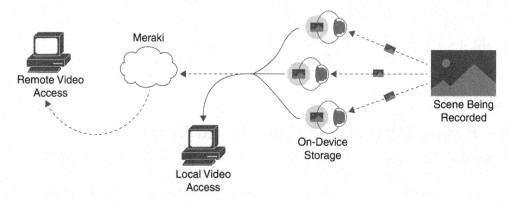

Figure 9-1   *Meraki Camera Video Access Architecture*

This easily scalable architecture offered by Meraki's MV cameras can comfortably support systems ranging from a single camera to setups of over 10,000 cameras. By leveraging the unified cloud-based solutions provided by Meraki MV cameras, you can ensure a consistent and seamless experience when accessing and managing camera feeds regardless of your location or your camera's location. Beyond just accessing recorded video, it's important to be confident that the retrieved video is both secure from unwanted access and unaltered. To achieve this confidence, Meraki has implemented many different security mechanisms to protect access to secure video and data as well as ensure the integrity of any stored or retrieved footage.

Ensuring Security

When you're planning your deployment, you need to consider the "who," "what," and "when" aspects of accessing sensitive data such as recorded video and audio. We strongly recommend implementing role-based access control (RBAC) to meet any regulatory and compliance requirements. This method of access control utilizes precise user access controls, empowering administrators to define and oversee access to specific system components based on specific needs. We will discuss some different ways to implement RBAC later in this chapter.

All MV cameras are preconfigured with encryption mechanisms for data at rest and data in motion, eliminating the need for manual configuration. At the core, a secure boot mechanism is coupled with signed firmware and encrypted storage to guarantee the integrity and authenticity of the software and video stored on the MV camera.

For meticulous activity tracking, a video access log available through the Meraki Dashboard also records all user interactions related to video footage, providing a transparent audit trail whenever needed.

Built-in Analytics

The Meraki MV camera system stands at the forefront of surveillance technology thanks to its advanced edge-processing capabilities. This industry-leading onboard processing facilitates high-definition video capture and paves the way for intricate machine learn-ing–based analytics. One of the standout features enabled by this computational strength is the system's ability to perform object and person detection, which is expertly powered by this integrated machine learning technology.

Beyond recognizing objects, the Meraki MV camera solution is able to further refine its reporting with the use of intelligent motion indexing. This feature, paired with a dedicated video and motion event search engine, allows users to swiftly navigate through long hours of footage to pinpoint specific motion events, making it a paragon of efficiency and precision in surveillance. For instance, you can use people and/or vehicle detection to assist in narrowing down motion search results to locate a specific incident. Meraki's MV cameras also have the ability to detect sirens or other audible alerts through the use of advanced sound detection analytics that can help identify specific audio patterns or events when audio recording is enabled. This again reduces reliance on external tools and analysis by performing video analysis directly on the camera, further reducing network complexity and enabling a more advanced deployment with fewer devices.

These built-in analytics tools, such as motion heat maps, object detection, audio analytics, and people and vehicle counting, make it easy to provide deeper insights into surveillance footage. This is especially valuable for businesses seeking active surveillance capabilities. We will discuss each of these functionalities and their practical use cases later in this chapter.

Designing with Purpose: Building an Effective Surveillance System

When you're starting to design your MV camera solution, the following are key phases and steps that you should take to help ensure an easy deployment and full coverage of your most important resources:

1. **Stakeholder input:** Engage with stakeholders who will be using or affected by the surveillance system to understand the key business priorities and intended outcomes. This includes business leaders, security personnel, facility managers, employees, and other stakeholders. Their insights will provide a unique perspective on areas that might have been overlooked and offer a more holistic view of security needs that may alter your approach depending on the business needs.

   For example, Meraki has multiple camera monitoring systems that are designed to cater to the different requirements of various teams, e.g., the Dashboard view for the IT team who may need to manage devices as well as access footage, the Meraki Vision Portal for the facilities team who only needs to be able to view select camera streams, the Meraki Display app to view video walls on a large or public standalone display, and the Meraki mobile app for easy remote access.

   This phase assists in identifying key business priorities such as physical security and operational analytics. If your intended use case goes beyond the analytics offered by the Meraki Dashboard, you can explore the option of engaging Meraki Marketplace partners to access additional solutions.

> **Pro Tip**   Check Meraki Marketplace at https://apps.meraki.io for MV integration partners and the unique use cases that can be solved using the Meraki ecosystem.

2. **Building analysis:** Every building or facility has unique challenges and potential security vulnerabilities. Recognizing these vulnerabilities and addressing them requires a thorough understanding of the requirements and identifying potential areas of security concern. These can range from main entrance points, parking lots, and storage areas to more specific areas like server rooms and other restricted zones.

   Designing a surveillance system entails more than just determining camera placement; it also involves selecting the appropriate camera feature set, such as indoor versus outdoor, wide angle versus narrow angle, and so on, to guarantee efficient monitoring of critical areas. This phase should provide an initial rough estimation of the total number of cameras needed and their required basic feature sets.

3. **Conducting a site survey:** A site survey goes beyond just understanding the building on paper. It involves physically inspecting the site to understand the lighting conditions at different times of the day, potential obstructions, and wiring and camera installation logistics. This step is crucial as it gives insights into the practical challenges faced during the installation and operational phases. Using this information

and existing floor plans, the best camera mounting locations can be determined for full coverage. This phase, alongside the building analysis, helps to determine more specific camera requirements, such as required IP ratings, infrared (IR) night vision, and IR range, and estimate appropriate mounting heights and required accessories for proper installation and optimal operation.

4. **Exploring constraints:** Consider limitations affecting the camera system's seamless integration. Detailed planning is needed for any network changes, taking into account how the data flow may shift and any new bandwidth requirements. Planning for Power over Ethernet (PoE) budgeting is also essential to ensure cameras operate optimally. This phase helps identify any potential technical and implementation challenges, providing a more accurate budget estimate.

For example, by default Meraki MV cameras use the built-in high-speed solid-state storage. However, if your deployment requires extended video storage for up to a year, you may need to consider the additional cost and bandwidth requirement to utilize a feature such as MV Cloud Archive or consider adding a local NVR endpoint to supplement the onboard camera storage.

Planning Camera Mounting Options and Accessories

Every MV camera includes standard mounting hardware, suitable for direct attachment to flat surfaces such as walls or ceilings, which also plays a role in cooling the camera by providing a direct conduction path from the cooling gel contained within the camera, to the camera body, to the mounting surface, helping to draw away excess heat. For example, while the indoor MV22 model comes with an adapter plate for 4-inch junction boxes, the outdoor MV72 features an additional conduit adapter to safeguard electrical wiring. There are multiple optional mounting accessories like arms or brackets available to ensure a proper mounting solution for any deployment. Accessories like these might be needed when direct mounting isn't feasible, when the optimal field of view (FoV) isn't achieved with direct mounting, or to shield the camera lens from water droplets or other weather, ensuring unobstructed surveillance.

Administrators planning their new deployment need to identify areas that require specialized accessories such as a mounting arm or a bracket based on the mounting location and angle of view. These areas include mounting on a wall, ceiling, pole, junction box, T-rail ceiling grid, and so forth.

We recommend reviewing the available mounting options, depending on the specific needs of your deployment:

- Wall mount
- Pole mount
- Corner mount
- Ceiling mount
- L bracket mount

You can find details on mounting options and accessories at https://documentation.meraki.com by searching using the keywords **MV Mounting Options and Guidelines**.

Pro Tip   Identifying all installation dependencies and the appropriate camera mounting accessories early on will help to create an accurate bill of materials (BOM) for your deployment.

Technology Considerations

When considering the Meraki MV camera system, it is vital to evaluate the specific needs of the environment and the quality of coverage required. Different environments and scenarios demand different camera types. Whether it's the flexibility of a varifocal lens, the broad coverage of a wide field of view, the clarity provided by high-resolution cameras, or another specific advantage of a particular camera type, each decision plays a critical role in ensuring optimal surveillance outcomes. For instance, in indoor areas where it is essential for the cameras to blend with the decor, you could choose dome cameras for their discreet appearance and use indoors.

When planning your deployment, you must consider the organizational priorities for video coverage and quality requirements when considering the technology requirements. These include lens type, field of view, and maximum resolution.

Lens Types

Multiple lens type options are available across the different MV models to best suit the varied deployment needs of customers. These options are listed here along with a brief description that highlights the capabilities of each type of lens:

- **Fixed lens:** These lenses are ideal for situations where the area of interest does not change. They provide a consistent FoV, making them suitable for environments where the monitoring needs are well-defined and constant.

- **Varifocal lens:** Varifocal lenses allow the user to adjust the camera's FoV. They are beneficial in dynamic environments or when specific areas need closer monitoring at particular times.

- **Fisheye:** Fisheye cameras are specially designed to provide wide-angle panoramic views, making them ideal for comprehensive monitoring of expansive areas. Meraki's implementation of the fisheye lens includes the ability to see and record a 360 FoV and perform digital pan/tilt/zoom.

Field of View

The FoV defines the total area a camera can capture at any given moment. A wider FoV is crucial for monitoring large areas, such as lobbies or parking lots. However, this might reduce the detail on distant objects. Conversely, a narrower FoV, or a telephoto zoom option, might provide more detail over a smaller area. Make sure to choose the appropriate camera based on the coverage area's size and the level of detail required. Varifocal lenses are oftentimes able to provide more versatility through the use of optical zoom, maintaining high image quality and facilitating more precise post-installation framing.

Resolution

Resolution determines the clarity and detail of the video footage. Higher resolution cameras capture finer details, essential for identifying faces or license plates. However, remember that higher resolutions also demand more storage and bandwidth. The Meraki MV camera system offers multiple resolution options across camera models; selecting the right one should balance the quality required and the associated infrastructural demands.

Other Deployment Needs

For locations that require enhanced durability, we recommend ensuring cameras have both IK10 (vandal-resistance) and IP67 (waterproof) ratings. Always be sure to verify the camera's operating temperature range when deploying in outdoor conditions or other adverse locations.

For low-light or nighttime recording, ensure the chosen camera model camera provides IR illumination and assess the effective range compared to your deployment needs. For outdoor and dimly lit areas, consider external IR illumination solutions.

To better learn what camera models may be best for your use cases and deployment, engage the Cisco Meraki sales team, who can assist you in obtaining a trial to ensure your deployment is utilizing the most appropriate hardware.

Cisco Meraki MV52: An Example of MV Camera Offerings

As an example hardware analysis, this section looks at one model of Cisco Meraki MV camera, the MV52, and reviews its capabilities. Figure 9-2 shows the MV52 as it would be mounted.

Figure 9-2   *MV52 Ultra-Long-Range Telephoto Camera*

The MV52 offers an ultra-long-range telephoto feature with a varifocal lens, capable of up to 3× optical zoom. It has enhanced night vision capabilities with IR illumination reaching up to 50 m (164 ft). It is also able to capture detailed images with its 8.4MP sensor at up to 4K resolution on 1 TB of internal storage.

The MV52 is well-suited for demanding outdoor settings, benefiting from an IK10+ and IP67 rating, external audio recording, and DC power supply integration. Additionally, due to their extended shape, bullet cameras like the MV52 offer a more extended range when compared to a traditional dome camera and are generally regarded as easy to mount and adjust, making them further well-suited for outdoor environments.

Choosing the Right Storage

Determining the type and amount of storage necessary to support your deployment is crucial to ensuring relevant footage is available to be retrieved and reviewed when needed. Meraki offers several different options for video storage with MV cameras, outlined here:

■ **Built-in storage:** The Meraki Dashboard offers dynamic estimates on video retention based on current camera configurations, any available historical video data, and available built-in storage. MV series models ending with X typically offer higher storage and resolution. For instance, the MV63 offers 4MP resolution and 256 GB of solid-state storage, while the MV63X provides 4K/8MP resolution and 1 TB of storage.

For more details on video retention expectations, search http://documentation.meraki.com with the keywords **Video Retention.**

■ **Cloud Archive:** Meraki's MV Cloud Archive exemplifies the next generation of surveillance solutions. MV Cloud Archive is ideal for situations requiring longer video footage retention due to legal or regulatory needs. Once a Cloud Archive license is activated, cameras will upload and store footage in the Meraki cloud, offering 7, 30, 90, 180, or 365 days of uninterrupted recording. Cloud Archive is supported on all MV models with the appropriate additional licensing.

■ **Export camera feed (RTSP):** With Meraki cameras, you can also utilize the Real-Time Streaming Protocol (RTSP) for external storage, applications, and integrations. External RTSP is useful for administrators who want to leverage third-party software that utilizes RTSP streams to provide additional analytics or integrate Meraki cameras into existing legacy camera deployments.

Planning for Power Requirements

Ensuring that the camera system operates efficiently and without interruption means understanding and planning the power requirements. Here is a breakdown of the key considerations:

■ **Upstream PoE consideration:** Before deploying the cameras, verify the PoE capabilities of your existing equipment. Check if the upstream ports are PoE-enabled and able to supply the appropriate PoE power standard. Equally crucial is assessing whether there is a sufficient PoE budget to accommodate the added load from the security cameras.

- **Understanding power consumption:** The outdoor models of Meraki MV cameras have built-in heaters that activate in colder environments to maintain consistent camera functionality. This heater can result in potentially unexpected increased power consumption if not planned for ahead of time. Therefore, it's important to always consider the maximum power consumption for each camera model and match it against the PoE capabilities of the upstream equipment.

- **PoE injectors:** In instances where a switch is not PoE-capable or PoE is otherwise insufficient, you will need an intermediary solution. In such cases, adding a PoE injector can provide the necessary power to the camera. This is especially handy for switches that do not inherently support PoE. When integrating PoE injectors, ensure they meet the power requirements for the specific camera models.

By properly assessing and planning for these power needs ahead of time, you will ensure an easier installation and dependable performance from your MV camera system.

Planning Camera Connectivity: Wired and Wireless

As mentioned previously, Meraki MV cameras support both wired and wireless connectivity to ensure easy setup and robust connectivity for your surveillance network. When planning for the connectivity of your cameras, there are several considerations you should keep in mind.

Pro Tip   A comprehensive QoS network policy should be in place throughout the network. MV cameras automatically tag for QoS, simplifying configuration for upstream network devices, which need only trust the tag.

General Network Considerations

Establishing proper Layer 3/VLAN boundaries has long been a staple in network security, enabling administrators to segregate traffic to help safeguard devices and data. It is highly advisable to create a dedicated VLAN solely for security cameras. This allows for the use of access control lists to configure fine-grained control over direct device access. It also helps to facilitate VLAN-based Quality of Service (QoS) implementations across the entire campus or building network.

Pro Tip   The recommended QoS marking for surveillance camera video is DSCP 40 (CS5 – Broadcast Video).

Considerations for Wired Connections

Meraki MV cameras commonly use a wired PoE connection for both data and power. With a PoE connection, the camera can receive power and pass data through a single Ethernet cable, simplifying the installation and reducing the need for additional power outlets. If the upstream port, such as a switch or router, is not PoE capable, a PoE injector can be used. Using a direct wired connection provides a stable and simple MV installation option.

Pro Tip   When using a wired connection, ensure that the upstream port is configured as an access port for the appropriate VLAN.

Considerations for Wireless Connections

Wireless connectivity eliminates the need for running Ethernet cables, which can simplify and expedite the installation process. This additional flexibility allows for easier placement of cameras in locations where wired connections are challenging or not feasible. Starting with the Gen2 series introduced in 2018, MV cameras are equipped with an integrated wireless chip, enabling them to function as wireless clients. To begin a wireless deployment, first connect the cameras via a wired LAN connection to allow them to check in and obtain the necessary wireless configurations from the Dashboard. Once this step is complete, position the cameras within the range of an access point while ensuring a stable power supply.

For cameras intended to connect wirelessly, make sure to configure both primary and secondary wireless profiles to ensure the cameras are able to maintain consistent connectivity. Figure 9-3 shows an example wireless profile configuration for an MV camera.

Figure 9-3   *Wireless Settings on MV*

To set up a wireless profile for a camera, navigate to **Cameras > Camera Profiles** in the Dashboard. In the wireless profile settings, select both a Primary and Secondary SSID. If necessary, you can also specify a Backup SSID.

Pro Tip   When initially staging a camera for wireless operation, be sure to maintain a stable connection to the Dashboard for at least 30 minutes after applying the wireless profile. This step helps guarantee stable configuration and operation before full installation.

For those upgrading from traditional analog cameras to a wireless Meraki camera deployment, the Cisco MV Low Voltage Power Adapter (LVPA) can be employed. This accessory transforms existing low voltage (12/24 V) power supplies into PoE power. In this new arrangement, video data is wirelessly conveyed from the camera to the computer for viewing. The double power cables previously used by the analog camera can be rerouted to connect to the LVPA and provide suitable power for the wireless Meraki camera. The analog camera's coaxial data cable then becomes redundant and can remain embedded in the wall, simplifying the replacement process for the new deployment.

Building an Optimized Camera System

To improve operational efficiency and scalability of any Meraki solution, it's highly recommended to utilize tags for each product. These tags can be used to classify various parameters such as use cases, ownership, location, and other details that are crucial for monitoring and managing the devices. This practice significantly improves the organization and administration of the IoT system.

Defining Camera Names and Tags

By default, Meraki cameras use their MAC address as a device name/identifier. While this is useful for initially identifying a device, a 12-character code can be inconvenient for everyday use, especially in larger setups. This is where device naming and tagging can come in handy. To make things clearer, it's best to give each camera a descriptive and logical name to make it easy to quickly identify in a list. For example, a device named "Second Floor Stairway Camera" will be returned when searching for any of the relevant keywords such as "Stairway" or "Second Floor."

Device tags enable you to group similar cameras together and easily locate them within the Dashboard. With device tags, you can easily sort or locate a set of cameras and even apply certain configurations, administrative privileges, or restrictions. The configuration of device tags and their potential uses were discussed in Chapter 2, "Building the Dashboard."

Pro Tip A single camera can have multiple tags, giving you flexibility in organizing and managing your camera system.

Defining Camera Administrators

Managing security and access is crucial, especially for sensitive systems like surveillance cameras. The Meraki Dashboard has two primary methods to create Camera-only admins: manually define camera administrator roles on the Dashboard and SAML integration. This allows for flexibility in defining access to sensitive data like recorded audio and video.

When combined with device tags, this can be used to build a powerful, yet flexible and easy to use, Role Based Access Control system to ensure each administrator only has access to the required data within your Organization. This also makes meeting any regulatory or compliance standards relating to video access quick and easy to both configure and enforce.

You can find additional details on restricting access to cameras by searching https://documentation.meraki.com using the keywords **Camera Access**.

Dashboard-Defined Camera-only Administrators

Administrator roles defined on the Dashboard can be used to control access to the Dashboard itself, the Meraki Vision Portal, Meraki Display app, and Meraki mobile app. For more general information on creating and defining Dashboard administrators, refer to Chapter 2. This section focuses on how to define Camera-only administrator roles.

To create Camera-only roles, navigate to the **Network-wide > Administration** page. In the Camera-only Admins section, you can define granular camera access for each administrator. You can explicitly define the scope of access for each administrator by selecting individual cameras or by using device tags. For example, Figure 9-4 shows the permissions for two camera admins. The first admin listed can view live camera footage or export historical footage from all cameras with the Front_Lawn or Garage device tags. The other admin has permission to view and export any footage from all cameras in the network.

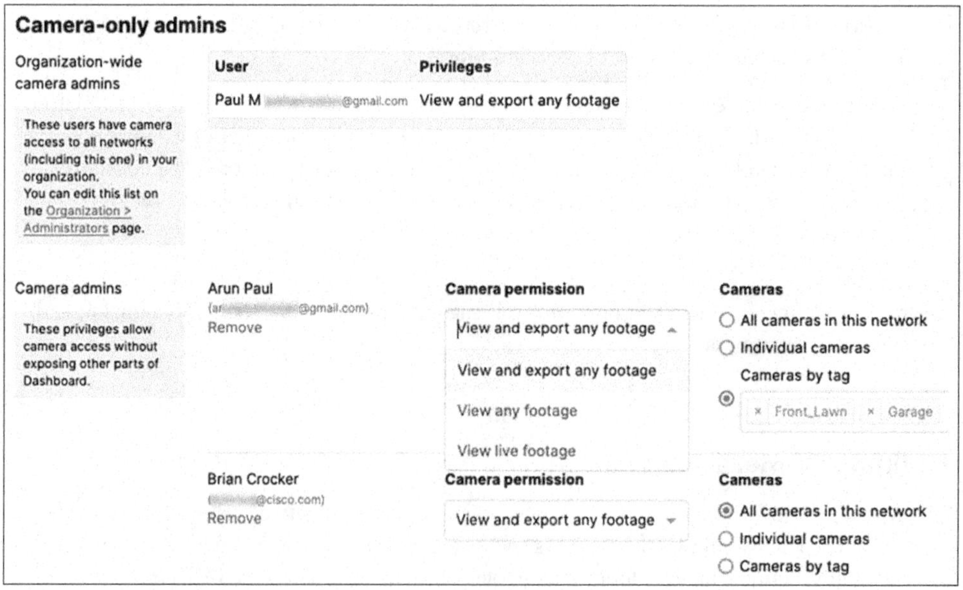

Figure 9-4 *Defining Dashboard Camera Admin Role*

Role-Based Camera Permissions for SAML/SSO

An alternative to manually defining camera administrators and permissions on a per-user basis is to utilize role-based SAML authentication with the Dashboard. By utilizing SAML authentication, organizations can achieve centralized user management, strengthen security with single sign-on (SSO), and simplify access control for their camera infrastructure. After enabling and configuring SAML authentication with the Dashboard, like discussed in Chapter 2, you can configure SAML Camera-only admin roles on the **Organization > Camera Roles** page. Figure 9-5 shows the Camera Role Management page with several roles already defined.

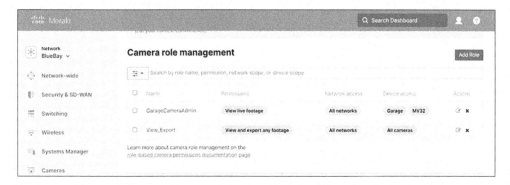

Figure 9-5   *Defined SAML Camera Admin Privileges on the Dashboard*

For details on configuring role-based camera permissions for SAML, search https://documentation.meraki.com using keywords **Camera Permissions**.

Pro Tip   If there are conflicting Network/Organization Admin roles and Camera-only roles defined, the Dashboard will match the SAML login with a Network/Organization Admin role first. For best practice, a Network/Organization Admin role should be passed first and Camera-only role(s) after.

Accessing Footage: Meraki MV Camera Views

As previously mentioned, Meraki offers four distinct ways to access MV cameras:

- Meraki Dashboard
- Meraki Vision Portal
- Meraki Display app
- Meraki mobile app

These options provide unparalleled flexibility to use the best tool based on the viewer's role and the intended use cases. The Meraki Vision Portal offers additional features not found in the Dashboard, such as cross-network video walls and Event search, which refines video searches by linking people and/or vehicle detection.

Meraki Dashboard

The Meraki Dashboard serves as a comprehensive tool tailored primarily for administrators who handle a spectrum of Meraki products. Envisioned with a strong IT orientation, the Dashboard is fundamentally geared toward configuration and management tasks, providing an integrated platform to effectively manage multiple sites. Figure 9-6 shows an overview of deployed cameras as viewed in the Dashboard.

Cameras	⊙ Last month ∨						View on Meraki Vision
1 Offline ⚙	0 Alerting ✷	32 Online ⚙	3 Dormant ⚙				

Status	Name	MAC address	Connectivity	Schedule	Firmware version	Cloud Archive	
⊘	Bike Room - Central Racks (Fisheye)	08:....68	No Connectivity (Aug 24 10:43-10:44)	Always on	MV 5.3	Disabled	
⊘	Bike Room Exterior Entrance - Narrow	0c:....e0		Always on	MV 5.3	Disabled	
⊘	5th Floor Coffee Bar - Seating SE	0c:....2c		Always on	MV 5.3	Disabled	
⊘	Bike Room - Exterior Entrance (internal angle)	0c:....21		Always on	MV 5.3	Disabled	
⊘	4th Floor - Stairwell	0c:....d4		Always on	MV 5.3	Disabled	
⊘	Bike Room - Entrance Rack	0c:....dd		Always on	MV 5.3	Disabled	
⊘	IDF 1.1 - Door Entrance	0c:....97		Always on	MV 5.3	Enabled	

Figure 9-6   *Example Cameras List in the Meraki Dashboard*

The Dashboard provides a single interface to seamlessly access both local and remote cameras. For each stream being viewed, an icon on the lower-left corner of the stream indicates whether the footage is streamed from a local camera or remote camera. A green check mark, as shown in Figure 9-7, denotes local/direct access, such as over a LAN or site-to-site VPN connection.

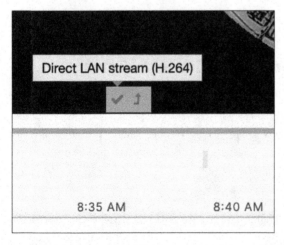

Figure 9-7   *Indicator Reporting a Direct Local Video Access Stream on the Dashboard*

The Dashboard also allows you to access and view remote sites through the same portal interface. A cloud icon displayed at the lower left of the stream signifies cloud proxy streaming, as illustrated in Figure 9-8.

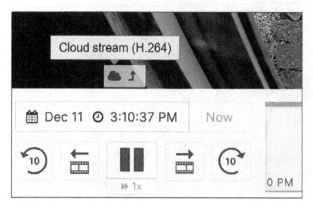

Figure 9-8 *Indicator Reporting a High Bitrate Cloud Proxy Stream from a Remote Site*

The Dashboard automatically transmits encrypted video through a cloud proxy if the client lacks a direct IP route to the camera's private IP address. To ensure the security of any remote streams, Cisco Meraki devices only trust certificates from the Cisco Certificate Authority (CA), so they will not establish any connections if an unknown certificate is injected into the chain.

Through this method, Meraki can detect if SSL inspection occurs upstream, such as in the case of a potential man-in-the-middle attack. This adds an additional layer of protection for customer data.

Meraki Vision Portal

The Meraki Vision Portal is a camera-focused, lightweight portal designed for core physical security tasks. It's ideal for those who desire all Dashboard streaming features in a camera-focused interface. Figure 9-9 shows an example view of the Meraki Vision Portal.

There are two ways to access the Vision Portal. From the Dashboard, you can navigate directly to **Cameras > Meraki Vision Portal** to access the Vision Portal. Alternatively, you can access it directly by visiting https://vision.meraki.com and logging in.

Assuming floorplans have been previously configured and devices placed appropriately via the Dashboard, the Vision Portal enables users to visualize their cameras' current field of view and nearby cameras on an interactive map, allowing for easy navigation between different camera feeds, as illustrated in Figure 9-10.

Figure 9-9   *Meraki Vision Portal Layout*

Figure 9-10   *Relative Camera Positions on a Floorplan as Shown from the Meraki Vision Portal*

The Vision Portal also provides full Event Search functionality, including the ability to filter results based on people or vehicle detection, making it easier to find and track individuals or vehicles in an event search. Figure 9-11 shows part of the Event Search in the Meraki Vision Portal.

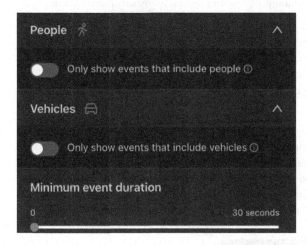

Figure 9-11 *Event Search Option in Meraki Vision Portal*

Meraki Display App

Video wall systems are essential for a complete video surveillance setup. They are helpful for onsite and remote security monitoring, providing a way to oversee multiple locations simultaneously. The Meraki Display app, an Apple TV application downloadable from the Apple App store, allows simultaneous live streaming of up to 16 cameras on a single screen for video wall monitoring.

By leveraging the Meraki platform and Apple TV hardware, Meraki Display provides a high-quality, customizable, 24/7 viewing experience that can be easily configured through the Dashboard. It seamlessly handles both remote/cloud and local streams, ensuring maximum visibility.

It is important to note that Meraki Display exclusively supports MV cameras and requires a software license for full access to its features and capabilities.

Meraki Mobile App

Meraki also offers a free mobile app for iOS and Android that allows users to monitor and manage all Meraki devices, including MV cameras, from their mobile devices. This mobile app provides a convenient and user-friendly interface for accessing and controlling Meraki devices on the go.

For camera users, the mobile app is particularly useful during installation and fine-tuning. The live view feature on the app enables users to view the camera's feed in real time, allowing for easier adjustments and optimization during the installation process. This can help to ensure optimal camera placement and image quality during the install phase, reducing or even eliminating the amount of fine-tuning and adjustment needed after mounting.

Additionally, the mobile app offers the ability to quickly scan and claim multiple devices. This feature simplifies the process of adding and configuring multiple Meraki devices, including MV cameras, to your network. By scanning each device's barcode, the app can efficiently claim and add the devices to your Meraki Dashboard for centralized management.

The Meraki mobile app seamlessly transforms sophisticated security tools into an accessible mobile format. This means that users can securely access video feeds straight from their mobile devices, including the intricate layouts of video walls. However, the app does not stop at mere viewing. It empowers its users with robust event investigation and search tools, ensuring that security breaches or anomalies do not go unnoticed or unaddressed. Figure 9-12 shows an example of several camera views from within the mobile app.

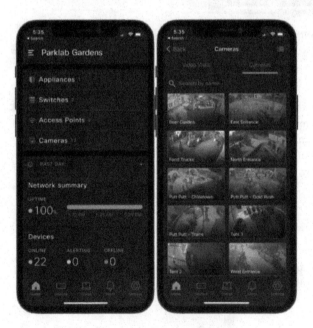

Figure 9-12   *Meraki Mobile App*

With the mobile app, users can do all of the following:

- **Navigate between cameras:** This option is accessible only when at least one Meraki MV camera is linked to the Dashboard.

- **Use the video player:** The player facilitates zooming, playback speed adjustments, full-screen mode, and a swift return to live streaming. It also indicates the streaming mode, either local/direct or remote/cloud.

- **Access the timeline:** This feature visually represents motion events positioned below the player. Motion Recap images or stacks further highlight periods with notable activity.

- **Search for Events:** A dedicated event search function lets users filter through footage based on parameters like region, detection type, and time.

- **Monitor multiple cameras with video wall:** This requires initial configuration via the Vision Portal or the Dashboard. Users can view streams simultaneously; deeper analysis is just a click away on any stream.

- **Onboard devices:** Admins can easily add more camera devices by scanning barcodes or entering serial numbers.

- **Configure video settings:** Depending on the camera model, users can tweak focus, zoom, and HDR settings, and more.

- **Access troubleshooting tools:** The app houses a suite of tools, like DNS Lookup and Traceroute, for diagnosing network issues. MV cameras further benefit from remote LED activation and reboot options.

- **Export and share:** Authorized administrators can extract video snippets and effortlessly share them with others, promoting collaboration.

Configuring and Optimizing MV Cameras

The following sections explain how to best configure Meraki MV cameras and optimize them for a better surveillance experience using the Meraki Dashboard.

Listing Camera Details

From the **Cameras > Cameras** page on the Dashboard, you can view a full list of all MV cameras currently added to the selected Dashboard network. From this page you can select the desired fields to display essential information like recent connectivity, alerts, connected SSID information, and more, based on your requirements.

Like other device pages in the Dashboard, these options are available by clicking the selection gear, as shown in Figure 9-13. A properly configured landing page that provides the right information on product configuration and critical alerts at a glance helps improve operational efficiency.

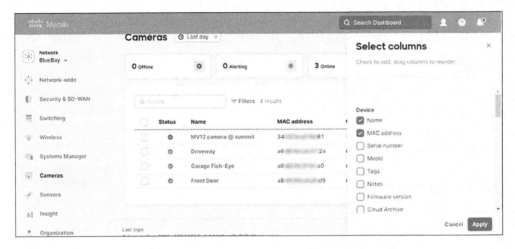

Figure 9-13   *Listing Relevant Information on the Camera Landing Page*

Configuring Camera Profiles

You can use camera profiles to establish one or more standardized video quality and recording/retention configurations that you can then apply to multiple cameras. This method facilitates a standard set of configurations for multiple cameras, streamlining the overall configuration process and saving time, particularly in large-scale deployments. The settings discussed in this section can also be configured on a per-camera basis, but the focus here is on the use of profiles for configuration.

To create a camera profile, navigate to **Cameras > Camera Profiles > Create New Profile**, then create your new profile.

A good example use case and recommendation for camera profiles is to establish a distinct camera profile for cameras with Cloud Archive enabled, due to potential quality and retention settings that might not be accessible for those specific cameras.

Furthermore, we recommend categorizing and grouping cameras and their configurations to optimize management and functionality. One practical approach might be to group them according to their make or specific functionality, to allow for quicker and more consistent configurations across devices through the use of a configuration profile. Figure 9-14 shows an example configuration profile.

There are multiple configuration options available within each profile. The following list briefly touches on some of the most impactful options, all of which are displayed in Figure 9-14:

- **Recording schedule:** When you define recording schedules, you can use this drop-down menu to select between different defined schedules.

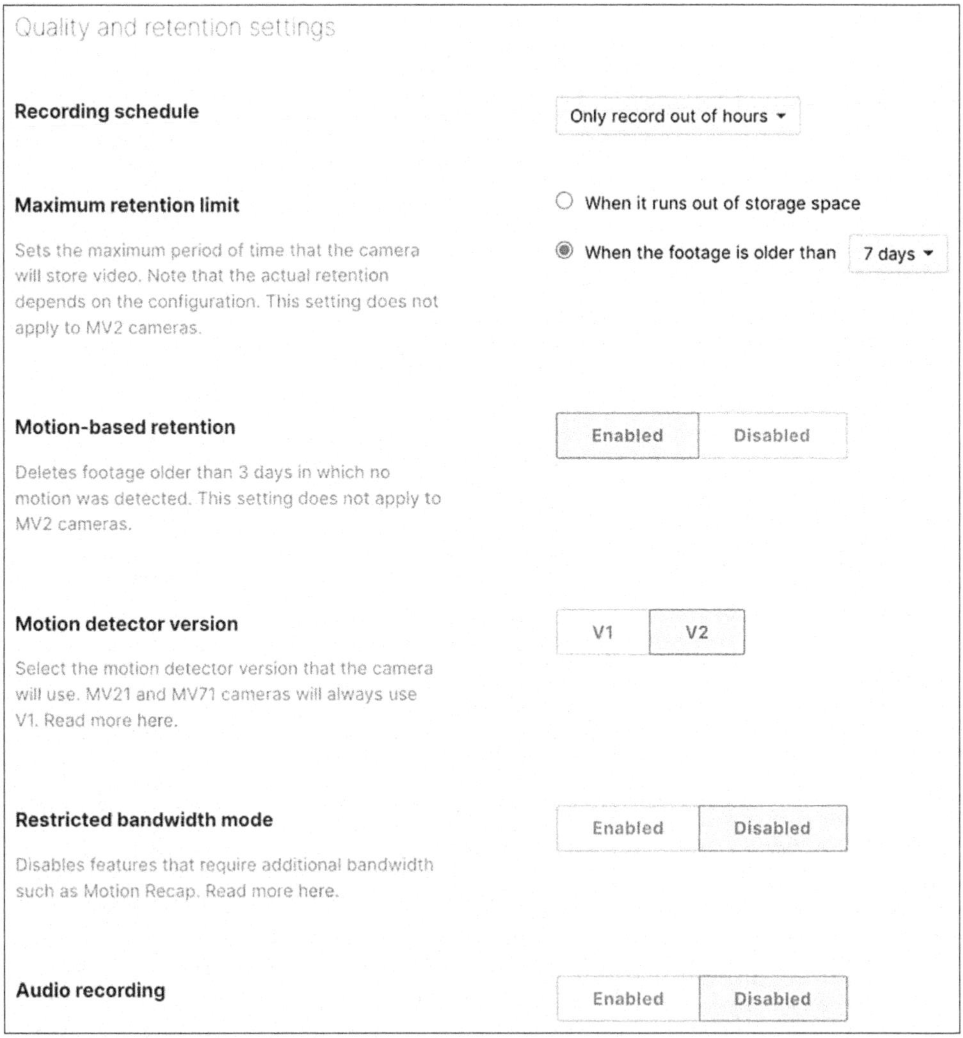

Quality and retention settings

Recording schedule

Only record out of hours ▾

Maximum retention limit

○ When it runs out of storage space

◉ When the footage is older than   7 days ▾

Sets the maximum period of time that the camera will store video. Note that the actual retention depends on the configuration. This setting does not apply to MV2 cameras.

Motion-based retention

Enabled | Disabled

Deletes footage older than 3 days in which no motion was detected. This setting does not apply to MV2 cameras.

Motion detector version

V1 | V2

Select the motion detector version that the camera will use. MV21 and MV71 cameras will always use V1. Read more here.

Restricted bandwidth mode

Enabled | Disabled

Disables features that require additional bandwidth such as Motion Recap. Read more here.

Audio recording

Enabled | Disabled

Figure 9-14 *Example Camera Profile Settings*

■ **Maximum retention limit:** This feature controls which footage gets overwritten when the camera reaches its local storage limits. To determine the actual retention period for each camera model, scroll down to the bottom of the Camera profile, where you will find a table summarizing the camera model, storage, configured video quality, and the resulting average retention time in days.

Note that the retention time listed will be updated whenever any relevant camera configurations are modified. You can define specific video quality settings for each camera model in your network, and the Dashboard will calculate the average retention days based on the current settings, as illustrated in Figure 9-15.

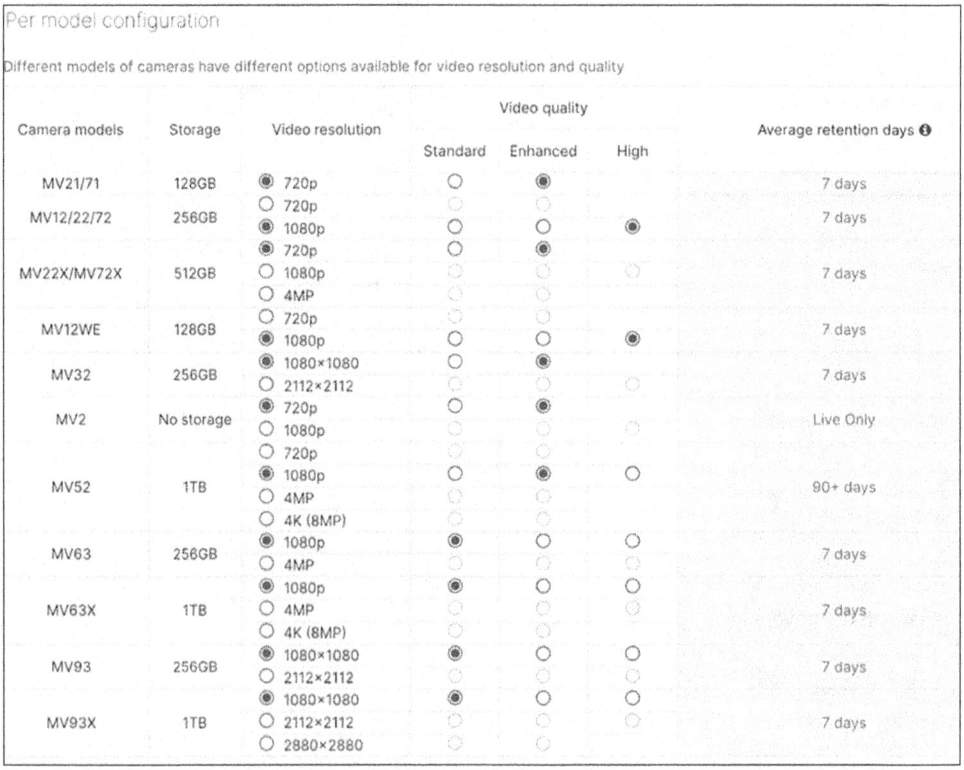

Per model configuration

Different models of cameras have different options available for video resolution and quality

Camera models	Storage	Video resolution	Video quality			Average retention days ❶
			Standard	Enhanced	High	
MV21/71	128GB	● 720p	○	●		7 days
MV12/22/72	256GB	○ 720p				7 days
		● 1080p	○	○	●	
MV22X/MV72X	512GB	● 720p	○	●		7 days
		○ 1080p				
		○ 4MP				
MV12WE	128GB	○ 720p				7 days
		● 1080p	○	○	●	
MV32	256GB	● 1080×1080	○	●		7 days
		○ 2112×2112				
MV2	No storage	● 720p	○	●		Live Only
		○ 1080p				
MV52	1TB	○ 720p				90+ days
		● 1080p	○	●	○	
		○ 4MP				
		○ 4K (8MP)				
MV63	256GB	● 1080p	●	○	○	7 days
		○ 4MP				
MV63X	1TB	● 1080p	●	○	○	7 days
		○ 4MP				
		○ 4K (8MP)				
MV93	256GB	● 1080×1080	●	○	○	7 days
		○ 2112×2112				
MV93X	1TB	● 1080×1080	●	○	○	7 days
		○ 2112×2112				
		○ 2880×2880				

Figure 9-15 *Example Average Retention Time per Camera Model, Based on the Current Profile Configurations*

- **Motion-based retention:** You can enable this feature to considerably extend local storage retention. Meraki's motion-based retention system ensures continuous recording 24/7, later trimming the footage based on indexed motion events once the local storage has reached capacity to leave only footage with recorded motion events. This method is advantageous over traditional motion-based recording, where only footage with recorded motion events is saved to storage, as it guarantees no crucial events are missed.

With this setting, your camera will always keep a continuous record of the last 72 hours. Beyond this timeframe, only motion-containing footage is retained. The unique method of motion-based retention is possible because of the unique way MVs handle motion—analyzing video on the camera itself and indexing it in the cloud.

For more details on expected retention, and motion-based retention specifically, visit https://documentation.meraki.com and search using the keywords **Video Retention**.

- **Restricted bandwidth mode:** Restricted bandwidth mode is designed for deployment scenarios where there is a need to limit bandwidth usage. Enabling this mode will disable bandwidth-intensive features such as Motion Recap. It's important to note that when the Motion Recap feature is enabled, there may be occasional bandwidth spikes of ~200 Kbps.

- **Audio recording:** Audio recording can be enabled on supported MV models. However, it's important to note that specific jurisdictions may regulate or even prohibit audio recording. It is the responsibility of the camera operator to ensure compliance with all relevant laws and regulations.

Assigning Camera Profiles

After defining a camera profile, you can assign configuration profiles through the Cameras list page by selecting the cameras and choosing **Assign > Quality & Retention Profile**, as shown in Figure 9-16, or you can assign configuration profiles for each camera individually in the camera settings.

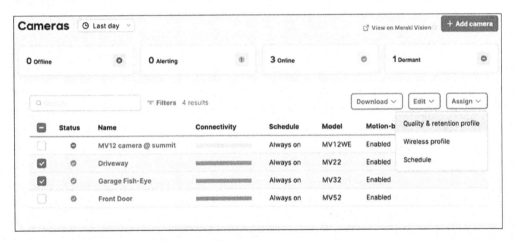

Figure 9-16 *Assigning Profile to Multiple Cameras*

Manual Camera Configurations

While camera profiles offer a quick and easy way to establish a base configuration across multiple cameras, you may still need to fine-tune specific individual camera configurations. For example, you might need to set a privacy window or low light recording (infrared) settings for individual cameras. To assign per-camera configurations, select a camera from the Cameras list, click the **Settings** tab, click the **Quality and Retention** subtab, and then click **Manual Configuration**, as shown in Figure 9-17.

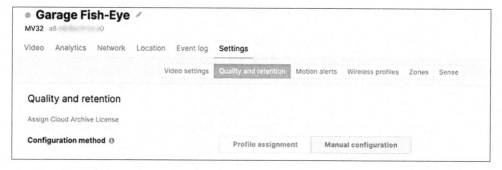

Figure 9-17 *Specifying a Manual Configuration Override on Camera*

From within the Quality and Retention tab you can scroll to the bottom of the page to discover the estimated retention time based on the current configuration and any historical video data as shown in Figure 9-18.

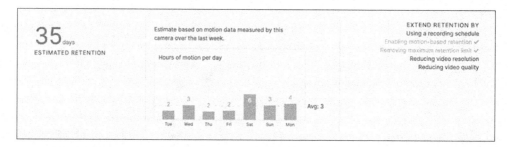

Figure 9-18 *Calculating Estimated Retention for an Individual Camera*

Pro Tip The estimated retention time will update automatically when you adjust any related camera configurations.

Recording in Low Light

Meraki's MV camera solution introduced a standout low light recording feature. Through the use of built-in IR illumination, these cameras can capture high-quality footage even under suboptimal lighting conditions, ensuring crucial details remain visible and clear, regardless of the time of day or the ambient light available. Whether monitoring after-hours activities in office spaces or securing dimly lit parking lots, the Meraki MV camera's low light capability offers a reliable surveillance solution, guaranteeing that no event goes unnoticed.

To set recording in low light, navigate to the **Settings** tab and then the **Low Light Mode** subtab, as shown in Figure 9-19.

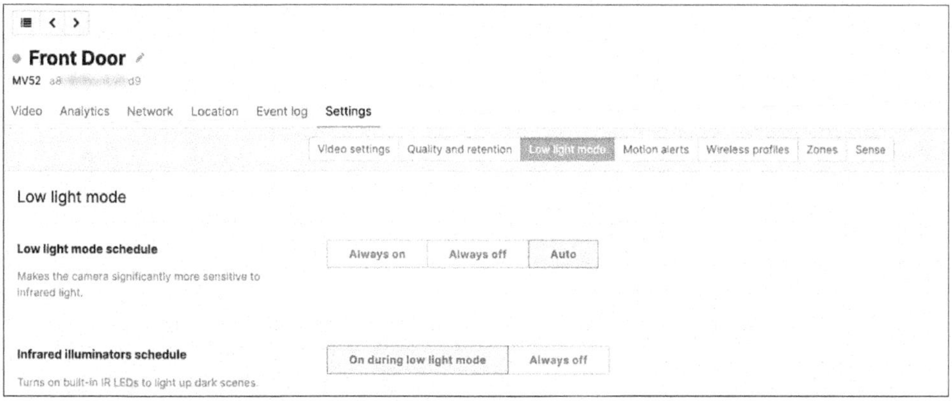

Figure 9-19 *Configuring Low Light Mode Options*

By default, MV cameras switch to night mode automatically and turn on the built-in infrared illumination. You can disable this feature manually for situations where it is not needed or where the built-in infrared illumination may cause unwanted glare or visibility concerns.

Additionally, disabling the IR illumination can be useful in situations where the presence of the camera needs to be discreet or hidden. Criminals or intruders may use the visibility of IR illumination to detect the presence of cameras, especially when using devices with the ability to directly see infrared light, such as some smartphones. By disabling the IR illumination, the camera operates in a more covert manner, making it harder for potential perpetrators to identify and avoid detection.

There is also the option to enable Run Dark Mode to turn off all LEDs on the camera. You can access this option under **Network-wide > General**, as shown in Figure 9-20.

Figure 9-20 *Running MV Cameras in Dark Mode*

Camera Motion Alerts

Like other devices, Cisco Meraki MV cameras offer the ability to configure email alerts for certain events. The most popular alert type is for detected motion. Motion alerts send email notifications when any motion is detected throughout the entire frame or within a designated region. Enabling motion alerts ensures users are promptly notified of any movement the camera detects. This feature is handy for areas that require strict motion tracking and enables efficient monitoring, particularly during specific schedules or after hours.

To configure email recipients, first navigate to the **Network-wide > Alerts** page, as shown in Figure 9-21. From here, you can directly configure alert recipients and other alert settings for all devices in the network.

Alerts Settings

Default recipients

All network admins   x   iot-admin@xyz.com   x   +

Figure 9-21   *Setting Default Alert Recipients*

A behavior to be aware of is that the default alert recipients configured under Network-wide Alert Settings will receive all alerts not only from the MV cameras but also from alerts generated by other Meraki products in the same Dashboard network. You can configure custom recipients for various alert types if those users should get motion alerts only and no other Meraki alerts.

> **Pro Tip**   All network alerts will be sourced from the same email address. To ensure that alerts are not being lost to a spam filter, add **alerts-noreply@meraki.com** as a trusted email source.

Fine-Tuning Camera Alerts

You can set custom alert recipients for users who should exclusively receive certain types of alerts such as motion alerts without other Meraki notifications. As shown in Figure 9-22, you can accomplish this by checking the **Custom Recipients for Motion Alerts** check box and entering the intended recipient's email address.

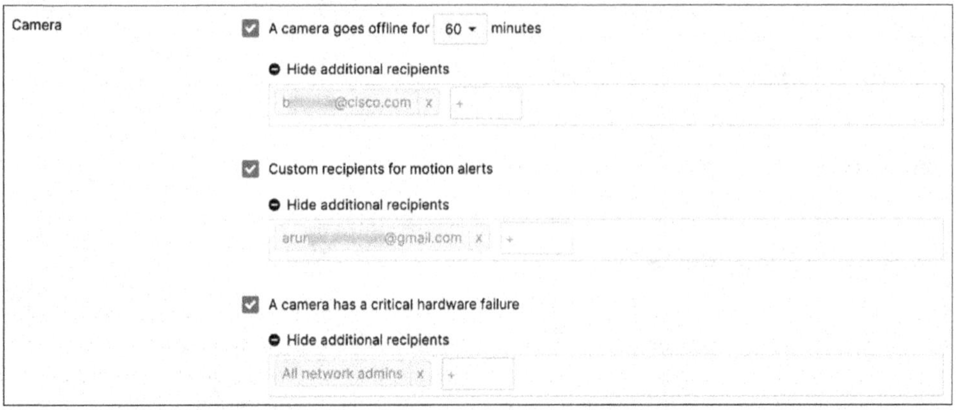

Camera

☑ A camera goes offline for 60 ▾ minutes

⊖ Hide additional recipients

b▒▒▒▒@cisco.com   x   +

☑ Custom recipients for motion alerts

⊖ Hide additional recipients

arun▒▒▒▒@gmail.com   x   +

☑ A camera has a critical hardware failure

⊖ Hide additional recipients

All network admins   x   +

Figure 9-22   *Enabling Custom Recipients for Motion Alerts*

Pro Tip   Consider using aliases or group mailers instead of multiple individual emails for critical notifications.

To ensure you receive pertinent alerts while minimizing unnecessary notifications, consider fine-tuning the settings available on the Motion Alerts tab, which include the following:

■ **When should this camera send alerts?:** Click the **Scheduled** button and configure specific periods during which alerts should be active. This is particularly useful for defining specific hours for alerts. Figure 9-23 shows an Alerting Schedule example.

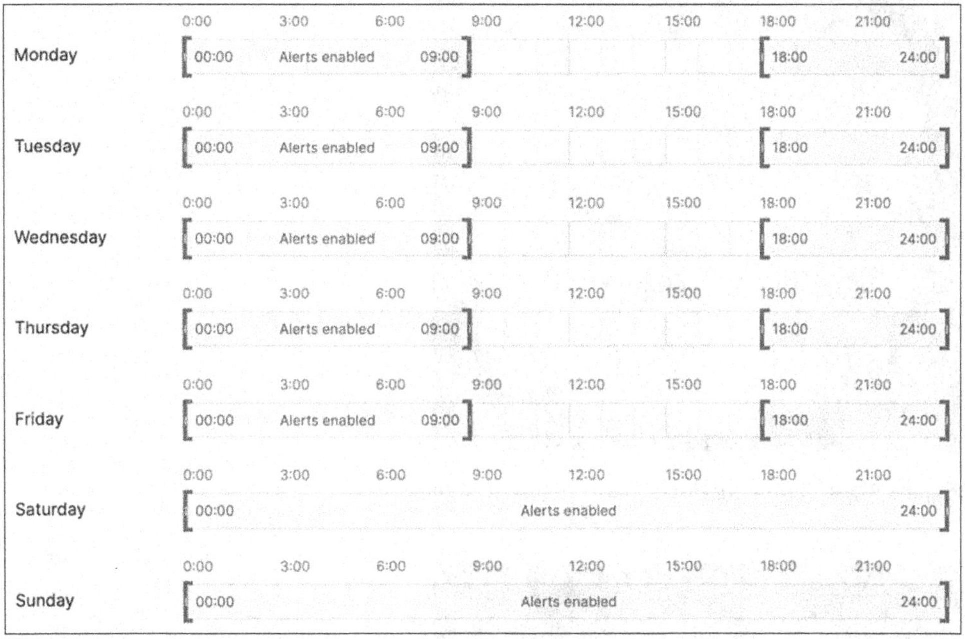

Figure 9-23   *Example Alerting Schedule*

■ **Minimum event duration for trigger:** Adjust this setting to filter out shorter motion events and reduce false-positive alerts.

■ **Motion sensitivity for trigger:** Define the portion of the field of view that should trigger an alert. For instance, a slightly higher than default sensitivity will notify you of people but not necessarily small birds or insects.

■ **Motion Recap image within alert:** This feature is explained later in this chapter and is not available when Restricted bandwidth mode is enabled.

■ **Alert only on people detection:** Activate this option to receive alerts exclusively when people are detected. This ensures that you receive notifications only when people are spotted.

■ **Defining Areas of Interest:** You can configure areas of interest on individual cameras to restrict the monitored region within the FoV. You can use this with motion-based retention to define specific areas within the FoV that should be monitored for motion and have the video retained. You can configure areas of interest by navigating to **Camera > Motion Alerts** and clicking the **Enabled** option for Areas of Interest. Figure 9-24 shows an example of configuring an area of interest. You can also adjust the vertices to achieve a more precise shape for the area of interest, as shown in Figure 9-25, to highlight a door or window within view of a fish-eye camera.

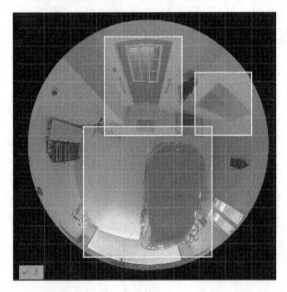

Figure 9-24   *Drawing Basic Shape for Area of Interest*

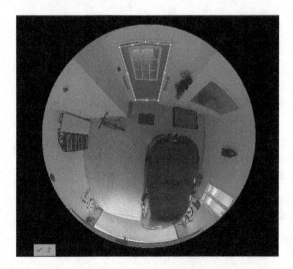

Figure 9-25   *Advanced Areas of Interest Focusing on the Main Entrance Doors*

Pro Tip   By default, motion alerts are disabled. Ensure you enable and configure them per your requirements.

You can find more comprehensive details on other customization options at https:// documentation.meraki.com by searching using keywords **Designing Camera Solutions**.

Configuring Privacy Windows

You might need to deploy cameras in areas where there are restrictions on video recording, such as a viewable monitor screen or other restricted area. To help simplify deployment in these situations and maintain security and compliance, you can configure privacy windows for each camera, which work to block specific areas of a camera's view from being recorded. Similar to creating areas of interest, go to the **Camera Settings > Privacy Window** section for a given camera and create a polygon within the current camera view. Once a privacy window is applied, any video within that designated area won't be recorded and will remain blacked out in both the live stream and in any recorded footage.

Setting Up RTSP Integration

Real Time Streaming Protocol (RTSP) is supported on Meraki's second- and third-generation cameras, which can stream up to two simultaneous streams per camera.

To configure RTSP integration:

Step 1.   Navigate to **Cameras > Cameras** and select a camera from the list.

Step 2.   Select **Settings > Video Settings**.

Step 3.   For the External RTSP option, click **Enabled** and use the provided stream link to access the camera (see Figure 9-26).

External RTSP

Enables an external RTSP interface for third party analytics. | Enabled | Disabled | RTSP stream link: rtsp://192.168.128.18:9000/live

Figure 9-26   *Enabling External RTSP*

Configuring Video Walls

Video walls enable security personnel to monitor multiple camera feeds simultaneously from a central location. They facilitate investigations by providing a real-time view of events across various cameras. Video walls can be organized based on camera mounting locations or tailored to meet specific monitoring needs. Utilizing the Meraki Vision Portal, you can even create a video wall that comprises cameras selected from more than one network. Additionally, you can incorporate multiple views from individual fish-eye cameras into the same video wall, as demonstrated in Figure 9-27.

Figure 9-27 *Video Wall Made of Multiple Views from a Single Fish-Eye Camera*

From any video wall, you can also perform Motion Searches and Share or export video, just like when viewing an individual camera. Auto-rotation can also be configured to cycle through different video wall views to allow for even greater flexibility. The Dashboard will display an estimated bandwidth requirement for the current setup when creating or editing a video wall based on the number of cameras and views selected, as demonstrated in Figure 9-28. After creating a video wall view you can access the video wall through the Dashboard, Meraki Vision Portal, Meraki mobile app, and the Meraki Display app.

Figure 9-28 *Viewing Estimated Bandwidth Requirement for an Example Video Wall*

Operating Meraki MV Cameras

Now that you are familiar with the initial configuration and deployment of the cameras, this section discusses some of the more day-to-day operations of working with Meraki MV cameras and the Meraki Dashboard.

Navigating the Video Timeline

When reviewing live or historical video, the video timeline is displayed below the current stream. From this timeline you can easily review recorded footage and search for detected motion events.

As demonstrated in Figure 9-29, the green bar at the top of the timeline corresponds to the availability of video recording. If a Cloud Archive license is applied to the camera, there will be an additional blue bar to denote that video is also available via the Cloud Archive.

Figure 9-29 *Viewing Local and Cloud Archive Timeline*

You can navigate forward and backward on the timeline by

- Clicking and dragging the timeline bar
- Using a touchpad to scroll forward and backward while hovering over the timeline
- Clicking the left or right arrows that appear when hovering at either end of the timeline

You can expand or limit the time range displayed on the timeline bar by using the + and − buttons to the right of the timeline. Clicking anywhere on the timeline bar will navigate to that timestamp and display any recorded video from that time.

You can find more information on best practices for viewing video on MV cameras, including how to use digital zoom, use keyboard shortcuts, and jump between timestamps, at https://documentation.meraki.com by searching using keywords **Viewing Video**.

Built-in Analytics

With built-in edge processing and powerful analytics, the Meraki camera can help comprehend motion patterns and pinpoint hotspots within your field of view over time.

To view per-camera analytics, check the **Camera > Analytics** page. Figure 9-30 demonstrates a sample Motion Heatmap analytics.

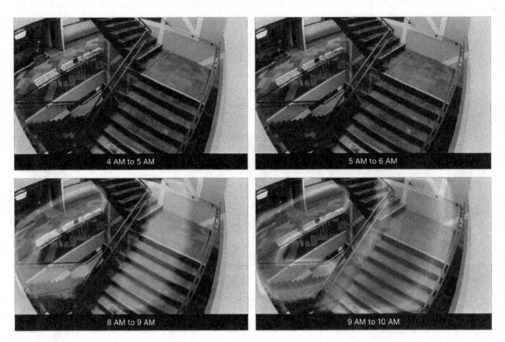

Figure 9-30   *Motion Heatmap Analytics from the Meraki SF Office*

The included analytics features are also able to detect and track people (see Figure 9-31) and vehicles (see Figure 9-32) for each camera.

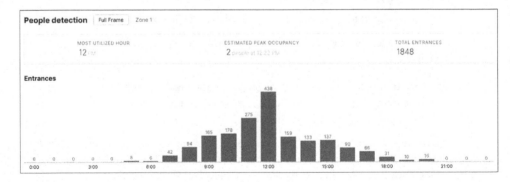

Figure 9-31   *People Detection Analytics*

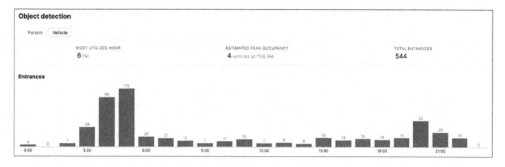

Figure 9-32 *Vehicle Detection Analytics*

Audio Detection

When audio recording is enabled on supported models, the audio detection feature allows MV cameras (second generation onward) to detect distinct noises like fire alarms and emergency sirens, providing situational awareness for potential emergency events. To enable this feature, you will need an additional MV Sense license applied to the camera in question.

To configure audio detection, navigate to the **Camera> Sense** page. To activate the feature, click the **Enabled** button for both the Sense API and Audio Detection features, as demonstrated in Figure 9-33.

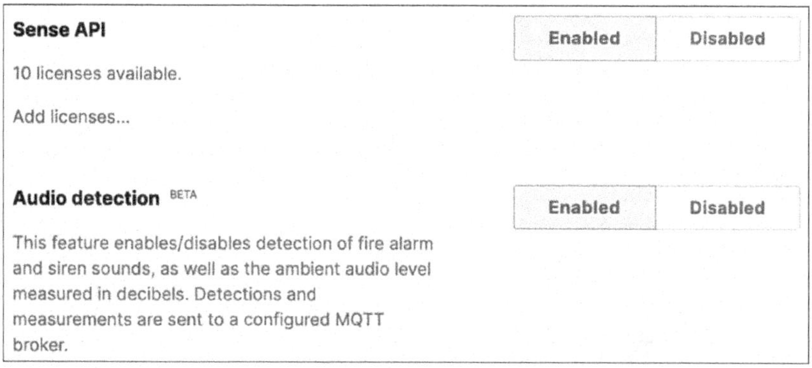

Sense API

Enabled   Disabled

10 licenses available.

Add licenses...

Audio detection BETA

Enabled   Disabled

This feature enables/disables detection of fire alarm and siren sounds, as well as the ambient audio level measured in decibels. Detections and measurements are sent to a configured MQTT broker.

Figure 9-33 *Enabling Audio Detection Features*

Motion Search and Motion Recap

As mentioned previously, Meraki MV cameras are equipped with an advanced Motion Search feature that enables users to quickly identify movement within recorded footage. This feature eliminates the need to manually review hours of video, saving time and enhancing efficiency in incident response.

By using the Motion Search feature, users can specify a specific timeframe and area of interest and the camera will analyze the recorded footage to identify any motion within that timeframe and area. This allows for swift identification of relevant events without the need to review every minute of recorded video.

The latest third-generation MV cameras from Meraki, equipped with improved motion detection capabilities, can be harnessed to execute specialized searches for people and vehicles. This function is especially beneficial in camera search situations where it's crucial to accurately identify events based on the presence of people or vehicles.

To begin a search, we usually start with a time and date input to jump to the rough timeframe we want to search within. Through the power of the cloud Dashboard, we can use natural language to define the timeline for the search. For example, we can search for "yesterday noon" instead of keying in a numerical date and time, as demonstrated in Figure 9-34.

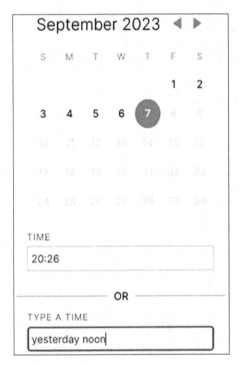

Figure 9-34 *Using Natural Language–Based Search to Quickly Navigate the Timeline*

Then, we can define a region of interest within the video feed by highlighting a grid selection and setting a specific period of time within the timeline to initiate a search. The camera will then analyze the footage based on the provided parameters to identify motion events and return any matching results. Figure 9-35 shows an example of defining a region of interest and a timeframe for a refined event search.

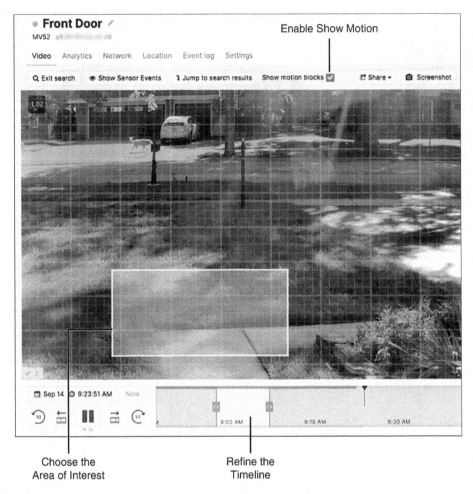

Figure 9-35 *Defining Region of Interest for a Refined Event Search*

While reviewing recorded video, users can activate the Show Motion Blocks option to access the Motion Recap feature, providing a visual summary of motion events directly from within the timeline view. This feature facilitates a swift comprehension of any recorded motion activity without watching the entire clip.

Motion Recap arranges multiple thumbnails to ensure users are shown all relevant activity for that event. When selecting a Motion Recap image or thumbnail, users are directed to the start of that specific motion event in the video playback, as shown in Figure 9-36.

Users can further narrow down the search results based on event duration from 0 to 35 seconds, to filter out short or unimportant motion events. Additionally, there is an option to show only results triggered by detected people for a more focused search, as demonstrated in Figure 9-37.

Figure 9-36 *Hovering over a Detected Motion Event Provides a Motion Recap and Event Preview*

Figure 9-37 *Filtering Event Using Sensitivity, Duration, and People Detection*

Motion Recap is able to significantly expedite the video review and investigation process by presenting a condensed overview of motion events.

You can find details on Meraki Motion Search and Motion Recap at https://documentation.meraki.com by searching for keywords **Motion Search and Motion Recap.**

Sharing Video

As a camera administrator, you can internally share a video stream with other admin users. You can select the **Share > Share Link Internally** feature (see Figure 9-38) from either a specific camera view or a video wall view. The shared link will contain a time-stamp and match the camera admin privileges that originally shared the link to allow any user with the link to open and view the relevant video.

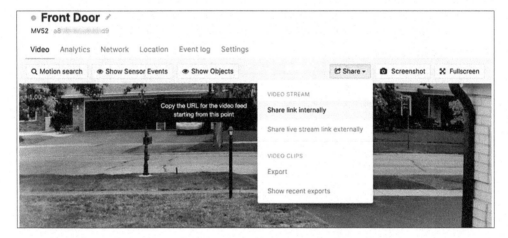

Figure 9-38 *Accessing the Video Sharing Menu from a Live Stream*

In situations where you need to share camera access externally with individuals who are not part of your Meraki Dashboard admin group, we recommend providing access to camera footage through access-controlled links rather than sending the footage as a file attachment. You can use the **Share > Share Live Stream Link Externally** option (see Figure 9-39) option to provide a camera link in these cases. Recommended best practice is to always include a description in the field provided to explain the reason for sharing the feed externally, to assist in any future security audits or reviews.

The sharing method offers the capability to generate access-controlled links that allow external users to view camera footage securely. By sharing that link, you can grant temporary or limited access to specific camera feeds, allowing external individuals to view the footage without having direct access to your Dashboard or administrative privileges.

Share live stream link externally   ✕

Add new recipient

EMAIL	NAME	DESCRIPTION	
▓▓@cisco.com	Philip	Sending Morning View	Share stream

Existing stream shares

☐	Email	Name	Description	Expires in
☐	B▓▓@cisco.com	Brian	Sharing incident	23 hrs 59 mins

Figure 9-39 *Reviewing the Video Sharing Settings*

These access-controlled links ensure that the shared footage remains secure and is not downloaded or stored by the external user. Instead, they can only view the live or recorded footage through the provided link, and the access can be revoked or expired as needed.

This approach provides a more secure and controlled method for sharing camera footage externally, ensuring that sensitive video data is not exposed to unauthorized individuals and maintaining better control over who can access the footage. These shard links typically have a default 24-hour access period, but that can be modified, extended, or revoked/deleted as needed, as shown in Figure 9-40.

Existing stream shares

① share selected				Extend for 1 hour	Delete

☑	Email	Name	Description	Expires in
☑	B▓▓@cisco.com	Brian	Sharing incident	23 hrs 58 mins

Figure 9-40 *Modifying Existing External Video Shares*

Exporting Video

There might be situations where you must preserve specific video clips or multiple clips from various cameras to assist in an investigation. Using the Export Video option prevents crucial clips from being overwritten based on the camera's retention settings. This feature allows you to select the start and end times for your video clip and export it. The Meraki cloud ecosystem will store the exported footage for 1 year. The exported clips can range from a minimum of 5 seconds to a maximum of 12 hours. If there are concerns about potential bandwidth usage during the export from the camera(s) to the Meraki cloud, you can also schedule your exports for a more convenient time.

Navigate to the **Camera > Exports** page to gain visibility into all the exports from within the current network. From this page, you can also combine exports and provide a single playable file for an entire incident, like the example shown in Figure 9-41.

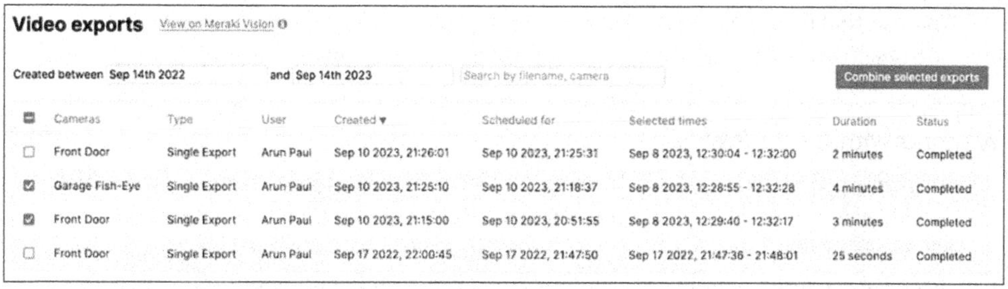

Figure 9-41 *Combining Multiple Video Exports*

From the Dashboard, you can export from either a video wall or the camera status page of any given online camera.

Pro Tip   Exported video can be downloaded as an .mp4 file or shared as a URL that is valid for seven days.

You can also check the status of any recent exports by navigating to **Share > Show Recent Exports** for each camera, as depicted in Figure 9-42. From here you can click individual entries to copy the video link, delete the export, or calculate the checksum, as depicted in Figure 9-43. You can use the checksum to confirm the integrity of any exported video when necessary.

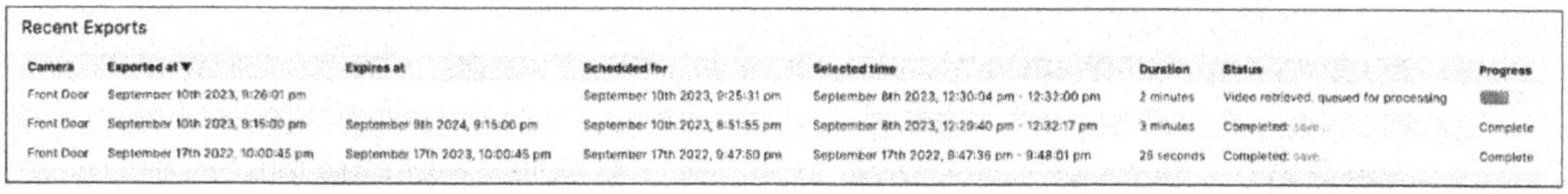

Figure 9-42 *Reviewing Export Status*

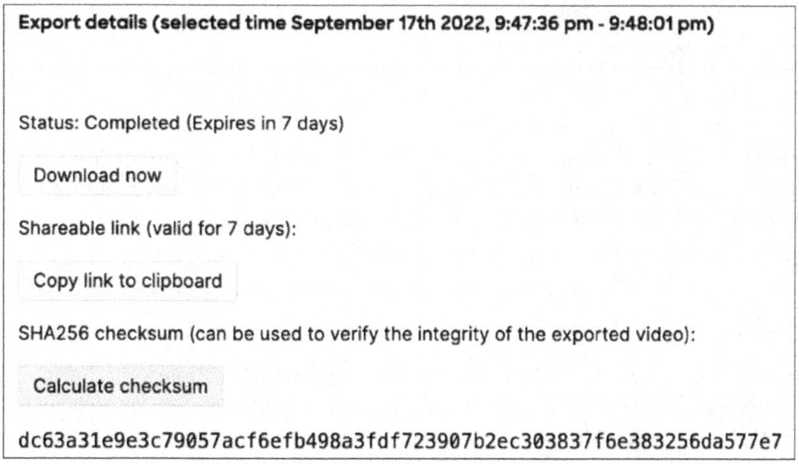

Figure 9-43 *Checking the Checksum of a Video Export*

You can find more information on the Exports page and combining exports at https://documentation.meraki.com by searching using keywords **Video Export**.

Working with Cloud Archive

As mentioned previously, in addition to the onboard storage available on every camera, Meraki also offers a Cloud Archive option with the purchase of an additional license that allows video to be automatically backed up to a secure, offsite cloud storage location for extended retention. This feature provides the additional retention options offered by a traditional surveillance system while reducing the need for additional onsite infrastructure and hardware. Selecting Meraki Cloud Archive for your video storage needs brings numerous advantages:

- **Scalability:** Meraki Cloud Archive offers scalable storage options, allowing you to effortlessly expand capacity as your requirements grow.

- **Simplified management:** With Meraki Cloud Archive, video storage and management seamlessly integrate into the Dashboard.

- **Redundancy and reliability:** Storing video footage in the cloud eliminates the risk of data loss due to local hardware failures or accidents.

- **Cost-effectiveness:** Meraki Cloud Archive eliminates the need for on-premises storage infrastructure, reducing upfront capital expenditure and ongoing maintenance costs. You can choose from different storage plans based on your retention requirements, optimizing costs according to your specific needs.

- **Security and compliance:** Meraki's cloud infrastructure provides robust security measures to protect your video footage, including encryption and access controls. This ensures compliance with data protection regulations and safeguards sensitive information.

When using Cloud Archive, both the camera and the cloud maintain copies of the video, and the on-camera recording remains unchanged. Videos stored in the cloud are consistently in the form of continuous 24/7 footage.

In terms of video retrieval, the Dashboard gives priority to video stored locally on the related camera, unless the camera is unreachable from the cloud or the requested video's timestamp exceeds the available local storage. Even if the camera temporarily loses connection to the cloud, it will still record footage as long as it has power, although the footage will not be backed up to the cloud until the camera regains WAN/cloud connectivity.

Accessing Video Event Logs

The video access log contains the record of all video access–related actions for all cameras within a network and external stream users. To access the video access logs, navigate to **Cameras > Video Access > Video Access Log** on the Dashboard (see Figure 9-44).

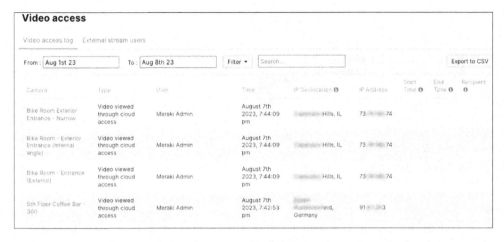

Figure 9-44 *Reviewing the Video Access Log*

Click the **External Stream Users** tab (see Figure 9-45) to view a list of all users who have shared live stream links and the expiration status of those links.

Video access

Video access log   External stream users

Email	Name	Description	Expiration	Cameras
ilovecoffee@mv.com	Coffee Lover	To know how long the coffee bar line is	February 15th 2020, 3:29:55 pm	5th Floor Coffee Bar - Seating SE
ge...@meraki.com	Meraki MV Product Team	To monitor office entrance on 10/29	October 30th 2020, 9:54:19 am	2nd Floor - Balcony 1
ge...@meraki.com	Fun Camera Viewer	Check out this view	October 30th 2020, 9:56:44 am	Fun Camera - Uber Bldg

Figure 9-45 *Reviewing Access Logs for External Stream Shares*

For more information on sharing video clips or a video stream from both the video wall or the camera status page, search https://documentation.meraki.com using the keywords **Sharing Video.**

Meraki MV Sense

As previously discussed, Meraki cameras have built-in capabilities to detect people, vehicles, and motion. With the MV Sense feature, you can utilize Custom Computer Vision (Custom CV) to deploy and execute custom machine learning (ML) models directly on MV cameras, enabling them to learn and perform custom object detection.

One of the foundational capabilities of MV Sense is its ability to use *artifacts*, which are essentially ML models. These models can be uploaded directly to the MV camera via the Dashboard. Once provisioned, the camera becomes a source of intelligent data. Figure 9-46 illustrates the high-level architecture of Meraki MV Sense.

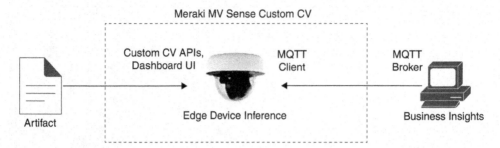

Figure 9-46 *MV Sense Architecture*

MV Sense utilizes several aspects of the MV camera system to perform these functions:

- **Edge processing:** MV Sense harnesses the raw computational power of the MV camera's onboard processors. Instead of sending data to a central server for analysis, the camera analyzes the data at the source. This edge processing ensures faster response times, reduced network congestion, and more efficient operation.

- **MQTT for telemetry:** Using MQTT, a lightweight messaging protocol, MV Sense ensures that data transmission between the camera and other systems is efficient and rapid. This is particularly useful in IoT environments where real-time data exchange is crucial.

- **Versatile ML models:** When equipped with MV Sense, the MV camera can understand and interpret multiple ML models simultaneously. This means it can concurrently detect people, vehicles, motion, and more, adapting its insights according to the specific ML model in use. This multifaceted detection capability opens up many applications, from monitoring foot traffic in retail environments to optimizing parking solutions in urban settings.

Enabling the MV Sense feature set further enhances security and becomes a valuable tool for businesses seeking insights into their operational environments. It directly showcases the vast potential of integrating advanced machine-learning capabilities into surveillance systems.

Troubleshooting Meraki MV Cameras

Meraki MV cameras are designed to be simple to deploy. However, in the event that you encounter unforeseen issues, there are some special steps that you should take into consideration when approaching troubleshooting related to MV cameras.

Enabling Firewall Ports for Meraki Cloud

All Meraki devices utilize specific TCP and UDP ports to communicate with the Meraki cloud for management, logging, and other critical functions. When deploying Meraki devices in a network, ensuring that the correct TCP and UDP ports are open is essential.

You can review the subnets, ports, and protocols that MV cameras use for cloud communication by going to the **Help > Firewall Info** page on the Dashboard.

Providing Camera Access to Meraki Support

By default, Cisco Meraki support technicians do not have access to view video or listen to audio. However, you have the option to grant temporary access if you require assistance with tasks like adjusting focus, configuring zoom settings, or resolving video and audio quality concerns. This temporary access will automatically expire based on a predefined time limit or can be revoked manually at your discretion. To provide temporary permission for Cisco Meraki support agents to view camera footage, you can access this feature in the Dashboard by going to **Help > Get Help.**

Strengthening Security: Implementing Meraki IoT with MV

Now that you are aware of the potential applications and recommendations for an MV deployment, in this section you'll take a look at Meraki's MT line of IoT sensors and see how you can use them to provide a more productive workspace and how you can implement them alongside the MV series of cameras to further enhance the general monitoring and surveillance capabilities for nearly any environment.

Building Smarter Spaces with Meraki MT Sensors

The integration of Meraki IoT sensors allows for the digitization of information used to manage physical infrastructures. This digitization process involves capturing and analyzing data from various IoT sensors deployed in the infrastructure, such as environmental sensors, occupancy sensors, or security sensors. This provides real-time insights into the status, performance, and security of physical infrastructures. By leveraging Meraki IoT sensors and digitizing the data they provide, organizations can make data-driven decisions, proactively identify issues or anomalies, and ensure compliance with relevant regulations and standards. This integration ultimately contributes to improved safety, enhanced security, and meeting business compliance requirements.

For example, environmental sensors can monitor factors like temperature, humidity, and air quality, allowing businesses to ensure optimal conditions in their facilities and comply with regulatory standards. Furthermore, security sensors, such as door sensors or motion detectors, can enhance physical security by monitoring access points and detecting unauthorized entry attempts. This helps improve safety measures and ensures compliance with security protocols.

Designing Smart Spaces with Meraki MT Sensors

Meraki MT sensors provide the necessary visibility and insight to meet the demand for efficient, adaptive, and user-focused spaces by intelligently transforming various environments. Meraki MT sensors help to redefine spaces, making them safer, smarter, and highly efficient. The following are some examples:

- **Office spaces:** Offices have transformed into ecosystems designed to amplify productivity and creativity. MT sensors contribute by regulating environmental comfort, advocating for sustainability, optimizing resource utilization, and streamlining processes.

- **Commercial/public spaces:** Commercial spaces like malls and stores benefit from MT sensors by maintaining an ideal ambiance, utilizing data insights for enhanced user experiences, automating operations for flexibility, and overseeing storage conditions to mitigate losses.

- **Restricted spaces:** Restricted areas such as data centers can effectively rely on MT sensors to regulate access, use analytics for efficiency, instantly alert for environmental inconsistencies, and prioritize energy, HVAC operation, and resource conservation.

Ensuring Sustainability

The modern business is not just about profits—it is also about responsibility. Organizations are increasingly under pressure to operate under more sustainable models. With real-time environmental monitoring, Meraki MT sensors enable businesses to conserve resources efficiently, economically, and ecologically.

Cisco Meraki MT sensors facilitate adherence to guidelines set by leading industry bodies such as the American Society of Heating, Refrigerating and Air-Conditioning Engineers (ASHRAE). Organizations can effectively reduce energy consumption by ensuring compliance with these standards, furthering their commitment to environmental responsibility.

As part of Meraki's sustainability goals, the Meraki MT environmental sensor line is able to provide more than just raw environmental data. Using the power of the Dashboard, you're able to further analyze and review that data to gain additional insights about the environment and help make better decisions in how that environment is managed. Tools such as the psychrometric chart are able to use MT sensor data to provide a more insightful view of how the current environmental conditions could be altered to provide a more comfortable environment while also improving the efficiency of environmental control systems like HVAC.

You can access the comprehensive psychrometric chart by navigating to the **Sensors > Psychrometric Chart** page. The psychrometric chart, shown in Figure 9-47, offers a visual representation of multiple environmental factors, enabling users to grasp the connections between temperature, humidity, and other variables to better understand how that impacts their environment and how they can adjust their environment to better serve the intended use case. This visual aid is extremely valuable for analyzing and designing or controlling HVAC systems more efficiently. In simplest terms, the psychrometric chart helps you understand what combinations of temperature and humidity are considered comfortable.

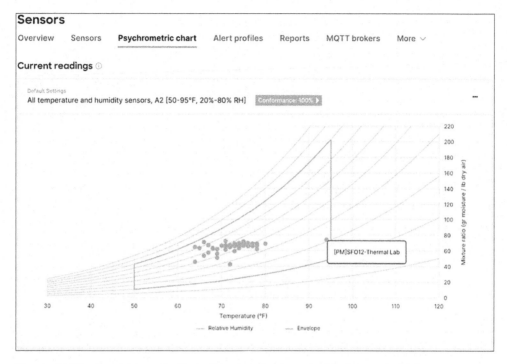

Figure 9-47 *Psychrometric Chart Showing the Current Reading and Conformance for Temperature and Humidity Sensors at a Given Location*

Organizations can utilize Meraki's psychrometric chart, based on leading industry best practices, to achieve substantial sustainability results. After implementing Meraki's MT environmental sensors and reviewing psychrometric chart data, many customers have reported energy consumption reductions ranging from 20 to 50 percent, resulting in lowered operational costs and reduced carbon footprints.

For comprehensive insights into the alignment of Meraki MT sensors with sustainability goals, refer to the Cisco Meraki whitepaper "Six Ways for IT Leaders to Reduce Their Carbon Footprint," available at https://meraki.cisco.com/about/sustainability/.

Understanding MT Security Architecture

With the increasing complexity of business operations and the ever-present cyber threats, safeguarding every network layer is paramount. Unlike the numerous sensors and third-party IoT gateways that have become vectors of security compromises, Meraki MT sensors are designed with security at their core, ensuring that all data points, transmissions, and integrations are protected against potential breaches. This includes using the Cisco-proprietary tamper-resistant TAm chip and secure BLE and data encryption mechanisms. This section briefly covers some of the design steps to take to ensure that Meraki MT sensors are able to provide consistently secure and reliable operation.

- **JTAG interface removal:** Meraki has eliminated any direct physical connections to the sensor's board or multipoint control unit (MCU) through end-to-end manufacturing process control. This step alone almost dramatically reduces the threat of malicious firmware sideloads. Even if an attacker were to somehow establish a physical connection, the MCU's no-read protection would protect the contents of the internal memory, bolstering the sensor's physical integrity.

- **Image signing:** Every MT software image undergoes a unique signing process involving hashing and encryption with Cisco's private key. This ensures the authenticity and integrity of any executed software. Meraki MT devices are effortlessly kept up to date through a unified Firmware Management portal on the Meraki Dashboard, with firmware management and patches handled by the Cisco Product Security Incident Response Team (PSIRT).

- **Trust Anchor module (TAm):** MT sensors are also equipped to ensure secure encryption and authentication through Cisco Trust Anchor technology. The TAm chip is embedded in Cisco products and is resistant to tampering. It offers a range of security and cryptographic services, including random number generation (RNG), secure storage, and key management. TAm's capacity to provide unique device identity and other cryptographic services is pivotal in enhancing device security.

- **Device Identity:** Every sensor is equipped with a Secure Unique Device Identifier, a certificate that establishes an immutable identity. This simplifies processes such as configuration, security, and management. These credentials are based on Elliptic Curve Diffie-Hellman (ECDH) and are securely stored in the TAm chip, making cloning futile.

- **Secure IoT gateway:** Meraki minimizes the potential threat surface by utilizing existing MV camera and MR access point product lines as secure IoT gateways for the MT series of sensors, as illustrated in Figure 9-48. The MT sensors perform a certificate-based handshake between themselves and the selected IoT gateway device to ensure security for every data transmission.

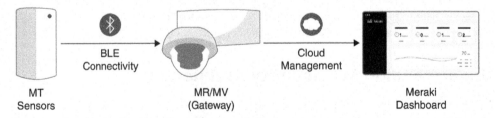

Figure 9-48   *Secure IoT Architecture with MR/MV as a Gateway*

The explicit use of Bluetooth Low Energy (BLE) for communication in Meraki sensors also aids to simplify deployment. By avoiding the IP stack, these sensors reduce the complications often linked to network segmentation in other IoT systems.

This not only streamlines deployment but also lowers the risk of network-based threats. The system provides gateway redundancy, security, and ease of IoT operations.

■ **Device authentication and encryption:** The Meraki Dashboard, integral to the Meraki MT sensors, functions as the verification authority. It ensures that only authenticated sensors can establish a connection to the gateway. Upon successful authentication, a shared Long Term Key (LTK) is generated for data encryption, as illustrated in Figure 9-49. This LTK ensures that data remains encrypted during transit, preserving its confidentiality.

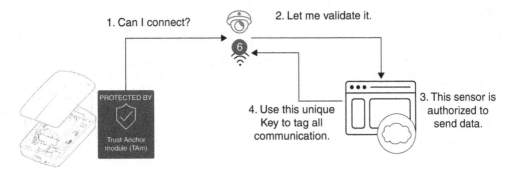

1. Can I connect?   2. Let me validate it.

PROTECTED BY

Trust Anchor module (TAm)

4. Use this unique Key to tag all communication.

3. This sensor is authorized to send data.

Figure 9-49 *MT Sensor Authentication Flow*

Protecting Business Assets Using MT Sensors

Meraki offers a varied line of MT sensor devices, capable of monitoring and alerting for numerous different physical or environmental conditions. By appropriately utilizing different sensors in critical areas, you can further enhance the security and monitoring abilities of a given deployment, going beyond just visual monitoring. The ability to tie certain MT sensor alerts to automatic MV camera snapshots through the Meraki Dashboard allows for unparalleled monitoring capabilities.

Environmental

Business-critical equipment often operates in environments with specific temperature and airflow requirements. Cisco Meraki MT sensors offer a real-time monitoring solution, identifying potential hot spots or airflow inconsistencies that might compromise the efficiency or lifespan of this equipment. By mitigating these types of risks, businesses are able to better protect their investments and contribute to longer product life cycles.

The Meraki Dashboard can provide real-time alerts for your critical infrastructure and assets. There are many instances where MT sensors have saved DC equipment and operations by providing critical environmental alerts after an unexpected equipment failure, allowing action to be taken before reaching a critical threshold. Figure 9-50 shows a real-life example of MT reporting during an HVAC failure in a data center.

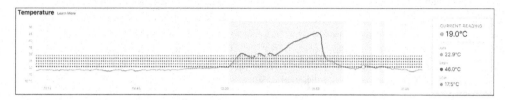

Figure 9-50   *Real-Life Example of Meraki Sensors Detecting HVAC Failure*

To know more about how the sensor saved the data center, search https:// community.meraki.com with the phrase **sensor saved the datacentre** (note the British spelling of datacentre).

Physical

In addition to environmental monitoring, the MT sensor line of devices also offers physical sensors that can be employed to further monitor access to secure areas and device power usage, and can even be tied in with an MV camera deployment to generate visual snapshots of an area when a physical alert is triggered, such as whenever a door to a secure location is opened, or whenever the Smart Button is pressed. This integration, referred to as Sensor Sight, provides an additional level of monitoring and security by automatically tying together physical events with camera snapshots, providing a visual record alongside the physical event, for every event.

Exploring MT Sensors

Your specific goals will guide the choice of sensors for your deployment. Whether you're transforming conventional spaces into intelligent hubs, enhancing safety and security, or optimizing operational efficiency, Cisco Meraki provides an MT device that offers a precise solution for each purpose. In this section we provide a basic overview of the different sensor types currently available; if you want to learn more about the different sensor types and how they might best be utilized in your specific deployment, please reach out to the Meraki sales organization, who can provide additional information based on your deployment needs.

Figure 9-51 provides a visual overview of some of the different Meraki MT sensor types and their capabilities.

The Meraki MT Sensor Lineup - Single Sensor

Temperature & Humidity

MT10
Temp range from 0°C to 55°C (32°F to 131°F)
Humidity range from 0-95% RH (±2.5% accuracy)
3 year warranty and up to 5 years battery life

Cold Temperature

MT11
Temp range from -40°C to 55°C (-40°F - 131°F)
Bare Metal or Glycol Temp Probe Sold
Separately
3 year warranty and up to 5 years battery life

Water Leak Detection

MT12
Detects as little as 3 mL of liquid
8' water leak detection cable Sold Separately
3 year warranty and up to 5 years battery life

Open/Close sensor

MT20
Magnetic field sensor
3 year warranty and up to 5 years battery life

Smart Button sensor

MT30
Webhook/API call manual trigger button
3 year warranty and up to 5 years battery life

Smart Power Controller

MT40
Inline power control and monitor
Range of 100-120VAC @ 12A max and 200-
240VAC @ 10A max (±1% accuracy)
3 year warranty *Power Cables Sold Separately*:
MA-PWR-C14-C15-1
MA-PWR-CORD-XX (Country specific)

The Meraki MT Sensor Lineup - Multi Sensor

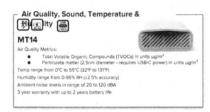

Air Quality, Sound, Temperature &

MT14
Air Quality Metrics:
- Total Volatile Organic Compounds (TVOCs) in units µg/m³
- Particulate matter (2.5nm diameter - requires USB-C power) in units µg/m³
Temp range from 0°C to 55°C (32°F to 131°F)
Humidity range from 0-95% RH (±2.5% accuracy)
Ambient noise levels in range of 20 to 120 dBA
3 year warranty with up to 2 years battery life

Air Quality, Sound, Temp & Humidity

MT15
Air Quality Metrics:
- CO2 in ppm
- Total Volatile Organic Compounds (TVOCs) in units µg/m³
- Particulate matter (2.5nm diameter) in units µg/m³
Temp range from 0°C to 55°C (32°F to 131°F)
Humidity range from 0-95% RH (±2.5% accuracy)
Ambient noise levels in range of 20 to 120 dBA
3 year warranty and is powered via USB-C or 802.3af Poe (power only)

Figure 9-51   *Meraki MT Sensor Lineup*

Physical Infrastructure Monitoring

Physical infrastructure monitoring can take on many forms depending on the specific deployment and needs of that deployment. Because of this, Meraki currently offers several different MT sensor options that can be used to monitor various aspects of physical infrastructure. From leak detection to door sensors and smart power monitoring, employing a variety of MT devices in your deployment can help provide unparalleled monitoring and security, all accessible directly through the Meraki Dashboard.

MT12—Water/Leak Sensor

The MT12 water sensor is equipped with water sensing probes that can quickly detect the presence of water or heavy moisture. It can be placed in areas prone to leaks or where standing water or heavy condensation may be cause for immediate concern, such as server rooms, basements, or areas with water supply lines. Figure 9-52 shows recent water detection events from an example MT12.

Figure 9-52 *MT12 Water Detection Alerts as Shown on the Dashboard*

This sensor is equipped with multiple leak detection options to cater to varied deployment needs:

- An 8-foot water leak detection cable, with an option to attach a second cable to double its length. The entire length of this cable can detect water.

- A spot leak detection cable.

MT20—Door Sensor

The MT20 door monitoring sensor is designed to detect and report the status of doors in real time. It can detect whether a door is open or closed, providing visibility on physical security and helping to ensure security and compliance. Figure 9-53 shows an example of the basic door open/close reporting offered by the door sensor.

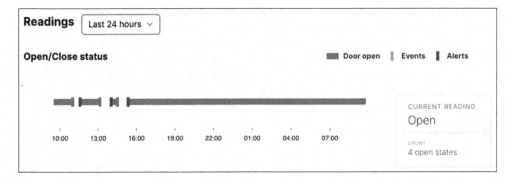

Figure 9-53 *MT20 Door Open and Close Alerts*

By linking an MT door sensor with an associated MV camera pointing at or near that same door, you can provide even further visibility and enhanced security by automatically triggering the MV to record a snapshot of the view at the time the sensor alert is triggered. These alerts are automatically stored on the Dashboard and can also be sent as part of configured email alerts to allow for even more robust event reporting. More details on configuring Sensor Sight are provided in the "Configuring and Monitoring Alerts" section later in this chapter.

MT40—Smart Power Controller

The MT40 smart power controller is able to both monitor and remotely control power for connected devices. These sensors are equipped with features designed specifically to provide remote insights into power conditions, equipment status, and consumption, helping reduce downtime and extend equipment lifespan.

Features of the smart power controller include an inline power monitor for measuring energy usage, benchmarking, and anomaly detection, alongside the capability to

- Remotely control power to connected devices, reducing the need for manual intervention or site visits to simply power cycle a device.

- Lock/unlock features to regulate remote power control.

- Provide flexible alerts via various channels like email, SMS, and mobile push notifications.

- Automate functions through the use of the Dashboard API for custom development and integrations.

Figure 9-54 shows an example power report from a smart power controller, highlighting power consumption, stability, and power condition.

Environmental Monitoring

Outside of the physical environment, monitoring factors such as temperature, humidity, and air quality is important to ensure a comfortable and productive workplace for both equipment and people. That's why Meraki's IoT line of sensors also includes a variety of environmental monitoring sensors, designed to provide additional insight into our everyday work environments so we can better understand and control major systems like HVAC within a deployment.

MT11—Cold Storage Sensor

The MT11 cold storage sensor is designed explicitly for cold temperature operations, with a temperature probe for monitoring refrigerated environments to safeguard perishable goods in cold storage, such as refrigerators and freezers.

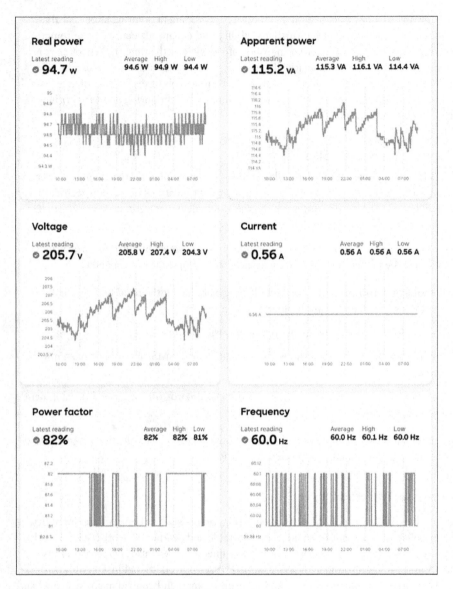

Figure 9-54   *MT40 Power Controller Alerts*

The MT11 can be fitted with either a bare metal probe or a glycol-encased probe (both shown in Figure 9-55) to best suit the needs of your deployment. The glycol-encased probe acts as a buffered sensor, smoothing out smaller, temporary temperature fluctuations to provide a more accurate representation of the actual temperature within refrigerated environments, especially for perishable goods. The bare-metal temperature probe is more responsive to changes, capable of more quickly identifying smaller or more abrupt temperature variations within refrigerators, freezers, and other cold storage environments.

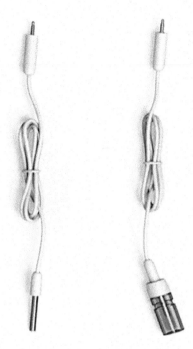

Figure 9-55   *Two Different Types of Cold Storage Sensor Probe Accessories*

Temperature, Humidity, and Air Quality Sensors

Whether monitoring a server closet or an office floor, the air temperature, humidity, and air quality of that location are important variables to be aware of. As highlighted in the "Building Smarter Spaces with Meraki MT Sensors" section earlier in this chapter, active environmental monitoring can provide alerts about critical system failures such as HVAC and allow action to be taken before resulting in network or server outages or even equipment damage.

Additionally, this type of monitoring can provide insights to more environmentally conscious deployments by directly monitoring the effect of changes to HVAC systems and planning, allowing for more accurate planning and scheduling based on the actual cooling and ventilation needs of various locations and systems within the deployment.

Meraki offers several different environmental monitoring options within the MT line of IoT devices. From the standard temperature and humidity monitoring offered by the MT10, shown in Figure 9-56, to the more advanced MT14 and MT15, which offer temperature and humidity monitoring in addition to more advanced air quality and environmental monitoring, including air particulate levels, CO_2 levels, ambient noise, and more, as shown in Figure 9-57.

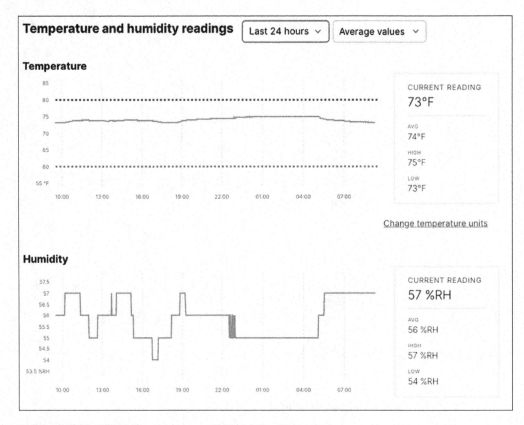

Figure 9-56   *MT10 Temperature and Humidity Reporting*

By adding this additional level of advanced environmental monitoring, you can ensure that your deployment is providing optimal working conditions for both your equipment and personnel, making for a more comfortable and productive working environment across the board. Like other Meraki products, all MT environmental sensors are capable of alerting based on defined conditions and thresholds as well as additional reporting and interaction through the use of the Dashboard API.

Pro Tip   When deploying an environmental MT sensor, it's recommended to ensure adequate airflow to any vents on the device to ensure proper monitoring and reporting.

You can find more information on MT qualitative rating metric at https://documentation.meraki.com by searching using the keywords **Air Quality**.

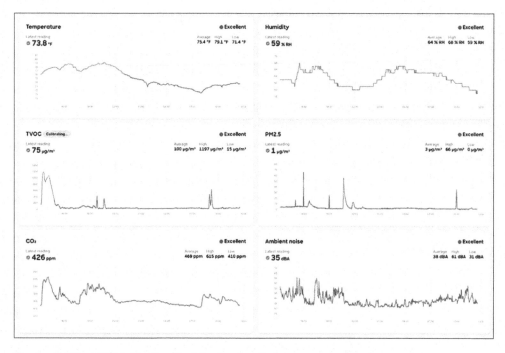

Figure 9-57 *MT15 Air Quality Monitoring Report*

MT30—Smart Automation Button

The MT30 Smart Automation Button is designed to integrate with other devices and solutions through the Meraki Dashboard and provides a simple and intuitive way to trigger actions or automate workflows with a single button press. It connects wirelessly to the Dashboard using the same IoT gateway methodology as Meraki's other IoT solutions, allowing for easy deployment, configuration, and management of the button and any associated integrations.

Smart Button Automation

The Meraki platform offers several built-in automation options within the Dashboard and also allows for custom automation to be configured through the integration of webhooks to external resources. For detailed information on automation with Meraki, including specific examples involving the MT30 Smart Automation Button, refer to Chapter 4, "Automating the Dashboard."

Here are a few brief example actions that can be triggered through the Smart Automation Button:

- Capture a time-stamped snapshot from a specific MV camera.

- Enable/disable an SSID from being broadcast for MR access points.

- Toggle the state (enabled/disabled) of an MS switch port.

- Send a push, SMS, or email with a custom message.

- Trigger Webhook alerts to external endpoints for cross-platform logging or automation.

You can easily configure these actions in the Dashboard by navigating to the **Sensor > Automations** section, as shown in Figure 9-58.

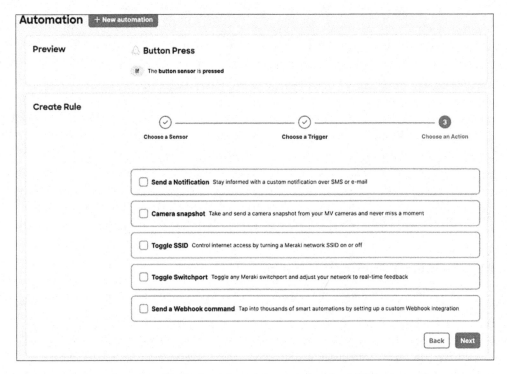

Figure 9-58   *Built in Meraki Platform-Based Automation for MT30*

Deploying Meraki MT Sensors

Meraki MT sensors encapsulate the essence of user-friendly design, offering a straightforward plug-and-play experience. Integrating them into a network with either an MV or MR device functioning as the gateway instantly makes the MT device operational.

Basic Configuration and Setup

Upon adding the MT sensors to a compatible network, they immediately begin operation, requiring minimal user intervention. As previously discussed, the Meraki MT sensors use

MV cameras or MR access points as secure IoT gateways. Therefore, before deploying MT sensors, ensure you have an online and operational IoT gateway device (MR or MV) in the network where you intend to deploy the sensors. Because of the dedicated BLE communication used between the MT device and IoT gateway, determining the optimal mounting locations based on the sensor and the specific use case is also essential.

Understanding Meraki IoT Gateways

An MT sensor can be associated with and track only one IoT gateway at a time. While the sensor may be able to detect multiple gateways within its range, it will only connect and communicate with one gateway. This single gateway will then relay the sensor's data to the Meraki cloud. For a stable and high-quality connection, it's best to design your setup so that each gateway supports no more than 32 unique sensors.

You review connected gateways, signal strength, and more on the **Sensors > Sensors** page, as shown in Figure 9-59.

	Status	Name	Model	Alert profiles	Latest reading	Conformance	RSSI		Battery	Related MV	
	⊘	MT20 Door @Summit	MT20				-		-		
	⊘	Family Room Air Quality	MT14	Clear air	95 IAQ	Conforming	-81 dBm Garage Fish-Eye		100%	Garage Fish-Eye	
	⊘	Air Quality Guest Bedroom	MT14		94 IAQ	Conforming	-67 dBm MR46-Office		100%	Garage Fish-Eye	
	⊘	Master Bed Air Quality	MT14	Clear air	97 IAQ	Conforming	-63 dBm MR46-Office		78%	Front Door	
	⊘	MT30 Button @Office	MT30				-56 dBm MR46-Office		83%	Garage Fish-Eye	
	⊘	MT12 Water @Summit	MT12		All clear		-54 dBm MR56-Foyer		95%	Garage Fish-Eye	

Figure 9-59   *Reviewing Gateway Signal Strength and Other Device Details for a Group of MT Sensors*

To get comprehensive details on supported MV and MR models and their minimum firmware requirements, refer to the "MT Frequently Asked Questions" document on https://documentation.meraki.com.

Accounting for Distance to Sensors

Meraki MT sensors harness the power of Bluetooth Low Energy (BLE) 4.2 for their communication needs. Because this technology operates within the 2.402- to 2.480-GHz range, its functional range is influenced by the same principles governing 2.4-GHz Wi-Fi. It's important to take this into account when planning your deployment, for both client wireless needs and MT sensor requirements.

Power Considerations

Meraki MT sensors can operate on either battery or via DC power supply/PoE, depending on the model and intended use cases. Sensor operations and communications are optimized to conserve battery life, which involves adjusting the sampling rate and wake-up/connection intervals based on the type of MT sensor and the configured alert profile.

Configuration Considerations

Beyond configuring alert profiles, MT sensors are designed to operate without any additional configuration requirements. It is important to note that MV devices do not support network templates for template-based configurations. Therefore, it is advisable to prioritize MR devices as MT gateways in template-bound networks to ensure optimal compatibility and efficiency. When deploying MT sensors for the first time, working from a new configuration template is recommended if possible. If you are working with existing configuration templates that do not include the MT sensor product section, you must add the MT template to the existing template within the organization.

You can find more information about working with network configuration templates, including how to create and modify existing templates for MT sensors and other devices, in Chapter 4 or by searching https://documentation.meraki.com for keyword **template**.

Configuring and Monitoring Alerts

Meraki MT sensors are designed to provide robust and user-friendly alert mechanisms to notify users when threshold breaches occur through the use of alert profiles. Like camera profiles for MV, alert profiles allow a single alert configuration to be applied across multiple sensors, simplifying configuration and deployment.

To create an alert profile, navigate to **Sensor > Alert Profiles** in the Dashboard. From this page you can create multiple alert profiles, each of which you can align with specific sensors or a group of sensors. Within each profile you can define an alerting schedule and specify conditions or thresholds for alert parameters, as well as define the recipients of email, SMS, and Webhook alerts from sensors.

Setting Alert Types

Within an alert profile, you can establish specific alert thresholds for each sensor reading. By creating multiple alert profiles based on your specific business needs, you can fine-tune your IoT setup to only provide relevant and critical alerts based on the alert type and device location. Figure 9-60 illustrates an example configuration for several environmental alert thresholds available in alert profiles.

Reviewing Generated Alerts

The MT Overview on the Dashboard, accessible by navigating to the **Sensors > Overview** page and shown in Figure 9-61, provides a single, easy to read interface that summarizes all recent alerts triggered by MT sensors. These alerts are based on the thresholds set in assigned alert profiles, improving the accuracy of alerts and helping to reduce incident resolution time.

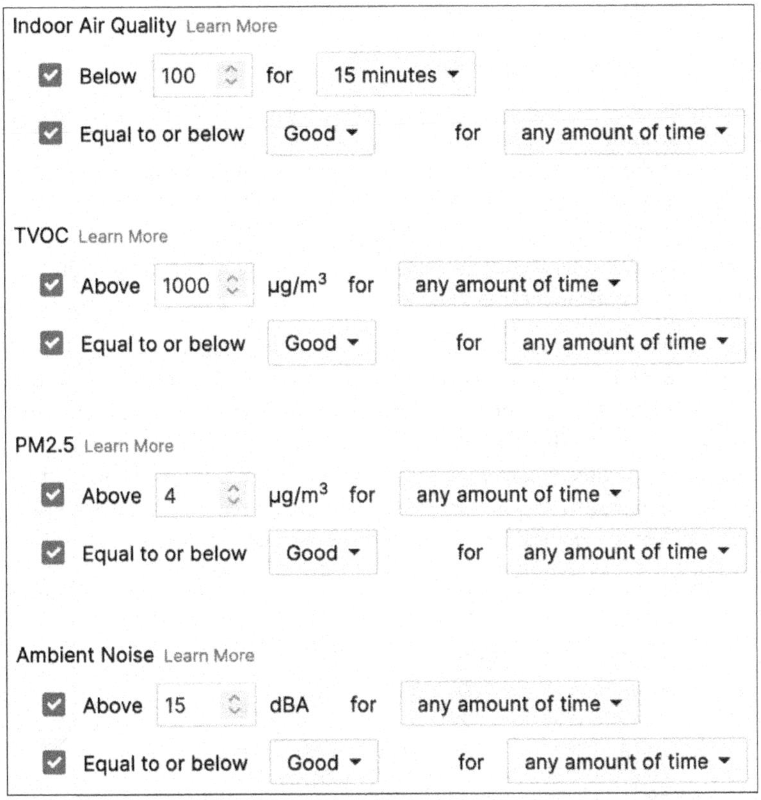

Indoor Air Quality Learn More

☑ Below 100 ⌄ for 15 minutes ▾

☑ Equal to or below Good ▾ for any amount of time ▾

TVOC Learn More

☑ Above 1000 ⌄ µg/m³ for any amount of time ▾

☑ Equal to or below Good ▾ for any amount of time ▾

PM2.5 Learn More

☑ Above 4 ⌄ µg/m³ for any amount of time ▾

☑ Equal to or below Good ▾ for any amount of time ▾

Ambient Noise Learn More

☑ Above 15 ⌄ dBA for any amount of time ▾

☑ Equal to or below Good ▾ for any amount of time ▾

Figure 9-60 *Environmental Alerts Thresholds Set in Alert Profile*

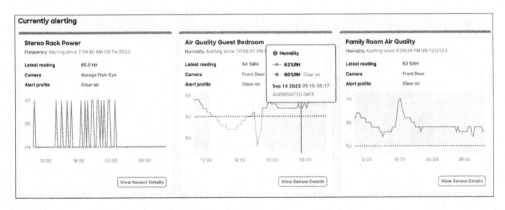

Figure 9-61 *Currently Alerting Sensors View*

Sensor Sight

In addition to the regular alerting options available for all Meraki devices, MT sensors have the ability to integrate automatic MV snapshots alongside the MT alert. This integration provides a timestamped visual snapshot from a specified MV camera at the time the alert was generated from the MT sensor. By configuring this integration with your most important MT sensor alerts, like door open or close events (MT20 door sensor) or power change events (MT40 smart power controller), you can obtain significantly more detail and information for each alert, providing an unprecedented level of context and additional information for your most critical events.

To configure Sensor Sight, first ensure that both the relevant MV camera and MT sensor are available in the same Dashboard network, and then from the related MT sensor details page, select the **Link a Camera** option on the **Summary** tab. You can then select from any available MV camera in the same network to link with the chosen sensor. Once linked, a live stream from the linked camera is shown on the status page of the related sensor, and any alerts generated by the sensor will automatically generate a timestamped MV snapshot alongside the alert. Figure 9-62 shows the live stream view of an MT sensor with Sensor Sight integration configured.

Pro Tip While each sensor can only be linked to one camera, each camera can have multiple sensors linked to it.

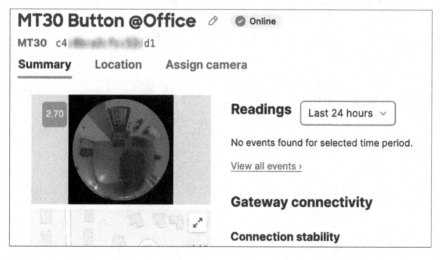

Figure 9-62 *Sensor Sight Integration with an MT30 Smart Button*

IoT Operational Best Practices

As in every design, it's crucial to ensure optimal configuration that aligns with your business requirements and incorporates system resilience. This section briefly summarizes and reiterates some operational best practices for MT to kickstart your IoT implementation journey and ensure a smooth, easy deployment:

- **Sensor type and location:** Ensure you're selecting the most appropriate sensor type and location for your needs. If you're monitoring temperature inside a cold-storage freezer, the MT11 cold-storage sensor combined with an MT20 door sensor will offer better performance as compared to an MT15 air quality sensor. Likewise, if you're monitoring air quality in an office, an MT15 placed in the middle of a wall at eye level will provide more useful readings than the same sensor placed in the top corner of a room near the AC vent.

- **Sensor/gateway design:** Prioritize redundant gateways for all sensors and ensure adequate signal conditions between sensors and gateways. Ensure that each sensor has multiple usable gateways and that each gateway has no more than 32 sensors relying on it.

- **Gateway addressing strategy:** Utilize DHCP addressing for gateways to allow for self-recovery to maintain consistent connectivity and reduce gateway downtime. By ensuring each sensor has multiple available gateways, even if one gateway becomes unusable, the sensor is able to maintain operation and connectivity through any other available gateways.

- **Sensor Sight integration:** is a transformative integration that synergizes the potential of Meraki MV cameras and MT sensors to provide unprecedented visibility into IoT alerts and operations.

- **Tuning the sampling rate:** MT sensors primarily stay in sleep mode to provide optimal battery usage (for battery-powered models). They periodically wake up to send data to the nearest IoT gateway, which then forwards it to the Meraki cloud for long-term storage and review. The frequency of sampling rates is contingent on the specific sensor type and directly impacts the expected battery life and connection intervals. Some MT sensor models allow sampling rates to be configured beyond the default values to provide more accurate data depending on your deployment needs.

For more insights into the sampling rate and connections per device type, see the "MT Frequently Asked Questions" document on https://documentation.meraki.com.

Troubleshooting Meraki MT Sensors

This section discusses a few recommended initial steps for troubleshooting your MT sensors. For detailed information on troubleshooting MT sensors, visit https://documentation.meraki.com and search with keywords **MT Troubleshooting**.

Monitoring Sensor Status

To monitor general sensor status, navigate to the **Sensors > Overview** page. Here, you will find a summary reflecting the operational health and status of each sensor, as illustrated in Figure 9-63.

Figure 9-63   *MT Sensor Overview*

Viewing Sensor Event Logs

To review all event logs generated by sensors, navigate to **Network-wide > Event Log** and choose **For Sensors** from the Event Type drop-down list. Figure 9-64 illustrates an event log for all sensors on a specified date. This includes events related to gateway connectivity between sensors and gateways.

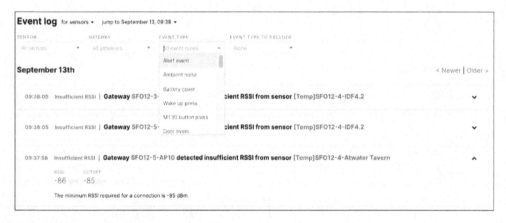

Figure 9-64   *Reviewing MT Sensor Event Logs*

Monitoring BLE Signal Strength

To quickly and easily review the reported BLE signal strength between sensors and their chosen gateways (MV or MR), navigate to the **Sensors > Sensors** page on the Dashboard, then activate the **RSSI** column from the gear/settings menu on the right, which shows the current BLE signal strength from the best available IoT gateway for each sensor.

To check all available IoT gateways for a sensor, select the sensor and review the Signal Strength section under the Device Details tab, which lists all available gateways and the respective signal strength for the chosen sensor. A value of −85 dBm or better is recommended for operational signal, as shown in Figure 9-65.

Signal strength

Gateway	RSSI	Last reported	Last connected
MR56-Foyer	⚠ -80 dBm	a few seconds ago	6 minutes ago
MR57-Stairs	⚠ -83 dBm	2 minutes ago	--
MR46-Office	⚠ -83 dBm	a few seconds ago	--
Garage Fish-Eye	🛈 -91 dBm	a few seconds ago	--
Driveway	🛈 -93 dBm	a few seconds ago	--

Figure 9-65 *Reported Signal Strength for All Available IoT Gateways from a Single MT Sensor*

Summary

As we've demonstrated, both the MV line of security cameras and the MT line of IoT devices are each individually able to provide numerous benefits when it comes to monitoring and surveillance of a deployment. When combined through the Meraki Dashboard, they offer an unparalleled monitoring and surveillance experience, allowing for a level of reporting not possible before without significant effort using a more traditional system. When combined with the full power of the Dashboard and Cisco Meraki's other networking solutions, you have the ability to provide unprecedented levels of network monitoring and security with a simpler, more easily managed interface that is designed to meet the requirements of nearly any deployment.

In this book we've only briefly touched on some of the many potential applications of the different solutions offered by Cisco Meraki. From the Dashboard itself to MX security appliances, MS switches, MR access points, and MV/MT solutions, you can find more detailed information about all of Meraki's solutions and products by searching Meraki's online documentation database at https://documentation.meraki.com or by reaching out to the Meraki sales organization.

Additional Reading

MV Camera References

MV Mounting Options and Guidelines: https://documentation.meraki.com/MV/Physical_Installation/MV_Mounting_Options_and_Guidelines

Video Retention: https://documentation.meraki.com/MV/Initial_Configuration/Video_Retention

Designing Meraki MV Smart Camera Solutions: https://documentation.meraki.com/ Architectures_and_Best_Practices/Cisco_Meraki_Best_Practice_Design/Best_Practice_ Design_-_MV_Cameras/Designing_Meraki_MV_Smart_Camera_Solutions

Viewing Video: https://documentation.meraki.com/MV/Viewing_Video/

Restricting Access to Cameras: https://documentation.meraki.com/MV/Advanced_ Configuration/Restricting_Access_to_Cameras

Sharing Video: https://documentation.meraki.com/MV/Processing_Video/Sharing_Video

Event Search on Vision Portal (BETA): https://documentation.meraki.com/MV/Viewing_ Video/Event_Search_on_Vision_Portal_(BETA)

Cisco Trustworthy Technologies Data Sheet: https://www.cisco.com/c/dam/en_us/about/ doing_business/trust-center/docs/trustworthy-technologies-datasheet.pdf

MT Sensor References

MT Sensors Security Architecture: https://documentation.meraki.com/MT/MT_General_ Articles/MT_Security_Architecture

Common Sensor (MT) Event Log Messages: https://documentation.meraki.com/MT/ MT_General_Articles/Common_Sensor_(MT)_Event_Log_Messages

MT Frequently Asked Questions: https://documentation.meraki.com/MT/MT_General_ Articles/MT_Frequently_Asked_Questions

MT Template Best Practices: https://documentation.meraki.com/MT/MT_Installation_ Guides/MT_Template_Best_Practices

Air Quality Metrics Explained: https://documentation.meraki.com/MT/MT_General_ Articles/Air_Quality_Metrics_Explained

MT Troubleshooting Guide: https://documentation.meraki.com/MT/MT_Installation_ Guides/MT_Troubleshooting_Guide

Sensor Saved the Datacentre – Again!: https://community.meraki.com/t5/Sensors/ Sensor-saved-the-datacentre-again/td-p/198385

Appendix A

Cisco Meraki Licensing

All Cisco Meraki devices require an associated license be applied within the same Meraki Dashboard organization to allow for proper operation of the device and access through the Dashboard. Currently, Meraki offers several different licensing models to best fit your deployment and fiscal planning requirements. Each of these models is applied on a per-organization basis, allowing different Dashboard organizations to operate under different licensing models as needed. This appendix briefly covers the different licensing models and their general operation, along with some aspects of each to keep in mind when deciding which licensing model best fits your needs.

This appendix does not go into detail about every license type for every product. The goal is to provide a general overview of the different licensing models and a basic understanding of device licensing within each. When applicable, any special licensing requirements are noted in their related sections in the full text. Complete details about each license type and the features available with that license are also available by either searching https://documentation.meraki.com for the related license type/model, such as MR Advanced License or Co-termination, or by reaching out to either the Meraki sales team or your local Meraki reseller.

Enterprise Licensing Versus Advanced Licensing

While the licensing model may differ, the actual licenses purchased and applied to organizations or devices are consistent across models. All Meraki products have a base tier of licensing (commonly referred to as an Enterprise license) that provides full access to the Meraki Dashboard and allows access to the majority of features and configurations available through the Dashboard. However, some features may require additional tiers of licensing to be configured.

An excellent example of this is the intrusion detection and prevention system (IDS/IPS) available for MX security appliances, or Umbrella integration with MR access points, both of which require an Advanced license applied to the related device to be configured.

The current per-product license types are as follows:

- **MG/MV/SM:** Enterprise
- **MS:** Enterprise and Advanced
- **MR:** Enterprise, Upgrade, and Advanced
- **MX:** Enterprise, Advanced Security, and SD-WAN+
- **MI:** X-Small, Medium, Large, and X-Large

Pro Tip   Some device series require model-specific licenses in addition to the license type, such as an MX75 requiring a license specifically for an MX75. However, other devices, such as an MR or MG, are model agnostic, allowing a single device license to apply to any device within that series, such as either an MR33 or an MR45.

External Licensing for Integrations

Some integrations, such as ThousandEyes or Cisco Umbrella integration, also require additional licensing for the integrated service in addition to the required Cisco Meraki licensing. For example, with both ThousandEyes and Umbrella integrations, each requires a valid Dashboard license of the correct type on the Meraki side in addition to a valid license for the integration product (e.g., ThousandEyes/Umbrella) to allow proper functionality of the integration.

Dashboard Licensing Models

Licensing is handled on a per-organization basis, with each organization able to utilize one of several different licensing models. Each licensing model offers different advantages to managing licenses for devices and networks within the organization, allowing you to select a licensing model that best matches the business and planning needs for each Dashboard organization. This section provides a brief overview and summary of each licensing model while highlighting some of the unique features of each.

Co-termination Licensing (Classic)

Co-termination (Co-term) is the original licensing model used by the Meraki Dashboard. For anyone who has worked with Meraki in the past, you are likely somewhat familiar with the Co-termination model. In this model, all licenses are applied at the organization level and are agnostic to any specific device, with validation only checking against the total licensed device count compared to deployed devices. Essentially, this model works under the premise of a total number of licenses for active devices deployed anywhere within the organization and does not keep track of or care about the specific devices deployed as long as the device models and counts are within the limits of available licensing for the organization.

Pro Tip   MX pairs configured in a high availability (HA) pair only require a single MX license for the HA pairing.

This allows for an organization to have, for example, licensing for three MS120-8 switches, ten MR access points, and two MX75 devices. As long as the numbers and models of deployed devices are within the current license limit counts for the organization, the organization will be marked as Valid. If, for example, one of the MS120-8 switches is replaced for an MS120-24 switch, the organization will fall out of compliance unless an associated MS120-24 license is also applied. However, because the licenses are not specifically tied to any one device with Co-term, the specific MS120-8 switches can be moved between organizations without needing to move an associated license as long as the device counts remain within limits.

Although the Co-termination model seems pretty straightforward, there is some complexity involved when determining exactly when licensing expires and how to properly renew/extend any existing licensing, or when dealing with certain advanced licensing types. There are two potential caveats to be aware of when working with an organization using Co-term licensing: the actual license Co-termination dates and applying advanced licensing.

Implied by the name, the Co-termination licensing model uses a weighted algorithm to tie all applied licenses together to achieve a single Co-termination date for all active licenses in the organization. This means that regardless of when the device or license was added relative to the rest of the devices and licenses in the organization, all licenses will expire on the same date and time.

This can cause confusion and difficulty in planning for a full license renewal, as any time a new license is added to the organization, it will affect the Co-term date for the entire organization based on the weight of the new license. Depending on the new license and the current licensing state of the organization, this can either extend or reduce the time remaining until the Co-term date. For example, if an organization is initially deployed with 5-year licenses for all devices, then 1 year later a number of new access points are added with all 1-year licenses, the Co-term date for the organization will likely be shortened to account for the difference between the weight of the remaining 4 years on the original licensing and the weight of the new 1-year licensing, bringing the total Co-term to somewhere between 2 to 4 years, depending on the specific number of devices and licenses present.

The preceding scenario happens because the Dashboard is aware that the new 1-year licenses will expire long before the remaining 4 years from the original licenses, so to maintain a single Co-termination date for all licensing, some of the license time from the remaining 4 years of original licensing is used to extend the new 1-year licensing based on the license weights, resulting in a Co-termination date for all device licenses somewhere between the original Co-term date and the date of expiration for the newly applied licensing.

This adjustment happens every time a new license is added to the organization, so it's clear how this can potentially cause confusion or difficulty in planning for when a full license renewal of all devices in the organization is required, especially for large customers who are frequently adding new devices and licenses as their deployments grow.

A final caveat to be aware of when using the Co-termination model is that if an organization is out of licensing compliance for any reason for over 30 days, then the entire organization will go into a restricted access mode until the licensing is back in compliance. Whether this is achieved by removing deployed devices from a Dashboard network to move under the current license limit or by adding additional licenses to either renew/extend the Co-term date or increase the current license limit, this situation will directly impact the ability to manage devices across the organization until it is resolved.

Pro Tip Practice good Dashboard hygiene. If a device is not in use, remove it from a network. This way, it does not burn a license.

Per-Device Licensing

Unlike the Co-termination model, Per-Device Licensing (PDL) requires licenses be directly assigned and tied to specific devices within the organization and tracks the license expiration for each license independently. This model provides a more traditional and consistent experience when planning for license renewals, as the license expiration dates for each license are unchanged once activated.

As part of this fundamental change to the licensing model with PDL, several caveats with Co-term licensing can be avoided. One of the most noticeable is the impact caused by expired licenses or otherwise unlicensed devices. Because PDL directly associates every license with a specific piece of hardware, when a device is no longer licensed appropriately, it can now be acted upon individually instead of directly impacting the entire organization like in the Co-termination model.

Like Co-term, PDL also allows for limited movement of licenses and devices between different organizations while maintaining the license application. This can help to greatly simplify moving devices between organizations, as it allows for the associated device licensing to be moved alongside the device itself without direct assistance from Meraki support.

Pro Tip It is possible to convert a Co-termination organization to the Per-Device Licensing model, but this is a one-way conversion and cannot be undone. We recommend consulting with your Meraki representative if you have a Co-term organization and would like to consider migrating to using PDL.

Meraki Subscription Licensing

The most recent addition to Meraki's available licensing models is Meraki Subscription Licensing. Designed to provide a more simplified and flexible licensing model, Meraki Subscription Licensing can be purchased in more flexible terms, allowing for customer-determined license lengths and start/end dates for their subscriptions. This allows for more flexibility when planning for growth and future license renewal.

Additionally, Meraki Subscription Licensing has simplified the SKU requirements for device licensing. Instead of requiring model-specific licensing for devices like MX security appliances or MS switches, models are now grouped into product classes, with each class of license applying to multiple product models within that family. For example, instead of requiring three different model-specific licenses for an MX75, MX84, and MX85, with Meraki Subscription Licensing you would only require three MX Medium licenses, as the MX Medium license covers all three device models within a single SKU. Along with this change, the Advanced Security license tier has been collapsed with the standard Enterprise licensing, to bring full Advanced Security functionality to the base tier of licensing, MX Essentials. Additional advanced features are available through the use of MX Advantage licensing.

Pro Tip   In addition to bringing Advanced Security features to the base level of licensing, this change aligns Meraki's licensing terminology with the rest of Cisco, making it easier to keep track of your licensing requirements across platforms.

A final notable change offered by the Meraki Subscription Licensing model is the ability to deploy multiple license types across different networks within the same organization. Because Meraki Subscription Licensing is tracked on a per-network/device level instead of at the organization/device level like PDL, or purely at the organizational level like Co-term, customers are able to deploy Advanced Licensing to only specific networks or devices as needed, instead of having to pre-plan for their entire organization or split devices across multiple organizations. This makes it easy to deploy a combination of MX Essentials and Advantage licensed devices within the same organization, allowing for much simpler management and configuration than with previous licensing models.

Summary

This appendix provided only a brief introduction to the different licensing models and actions available when using the Meraki Dashboard. As previously mentioned, you can find more detailed information about everything discussed in this appendix by searching Meraki's documentation at https://documentation.meraki.com or by reaching out to either a Meraki sales representative or partner who can provide additional insight and details regarding licensing models and pricing.

Additional Reading

Meraki Licensing FAQs: https://documentation.meraki.com/General_Administration/Licensing/Meraki_Licensing_FAQs

Meraki Co-termination Licensing Overview: https://documentation.meraki.com/General_Administration/Licensing/Meraki_Co-termination_Licensing_Overview

Meraki Per-Device Licensing Overview: https://documentation.meraki.com/General_Administration/Licensing/Meraki_Per-Device_Licensing_Overview

Meraki Subscription Licensing Overview: https://documentation.meraki.com/General_Administration/Licensing/Meraki_Subscription_Licensing_Overview

The Science Behind Licensing Co-termination: https://documentation.meraki.com/General_Administration/Licensing/Meraki_Co-termination_Licensing_Overview/The_Science_behind_Licensing_Co-termination

How to Convert an Org from Co-term to Per Device Licensing: https://documentation.meraki.com/General_Administration/Licensing/How_to_convert_a_Co-term_Licensing_organization_to_Per_Device_Licensing_organization

Index

Numbers

A

Register your product at **ciscopress.com/register**
to unlock additional benefits:

- Save 35%* on your next purchase with an exclusive discount code

- Find companion files, errata, and product updates if available

- Sign up to receive special offers on new editions and related titles

Get more when you shop at **ciscopress.com**:

- Everyday discounts on books, eBooks, video courses, and more

- Free U.S. shipping on all orders

- Multi-format eBooks to read on your preferred device

- Print and eBook Best Value Packs

Cisco Press